Published by Wider Vision Publishing, Australia
Manufactured in the United States of America

ISBN: 978-0-9808653-0-1

Lyrics from the following music are used with the kind permission of the respective copyright holders:-

"The Sunscreen Song" by Baz Luhrmann
words by Mary Schmich © 1997 Chicago Tribune
"Route 66" by The Rolling Stones
written by Bobby Troup © 2002 Troup-London Music
"Human Touch" by Bruce Springsteen
written by Bruce Springsteen © 1992 Bruce Springsteen
"The Gambler" by Kenny Rogers
written by Donald Schlitz © 1978 Sony/ATV
"Nature Is The Law" by Richard Ashcroft
written by Richard Ashcroft © 2002 EMI
"A Better Man" by Thunder
written by Luke Morley © 1992 EMI
"Nowhere Man" by The Beatles
written by John Lennon/Paul McCartney © 1965 Sony/ATV

Also used, writer unknown:-

"On Top Of Old Smokey" – traditional
© unknown

The following poems are also printed:-

"The Road Not Taken" by Robert Frost (1874–1963)
from 'Mountain Interval' © 1916, 1921 Henry Holt, New York
"If…" by Rudyard Kipling (1865–1936)
from 'Rewards and Fairies' 1909

A LIFE SOLD

or

What ever happened to that guy

who sold his whole life…

…on eBay?

by

Ian Usher

Dedicated to my father,
Foster Usher,
whose influence continues
to colour my life
all these years later.

The Road Not Taken

by

Robert Frost

Two roads diverged in a yellow wood,
And sorry I could not travel both
And be one traveler, long I stood
And looked down one as far as I could
To where it bent in the undergrowth;

Then took the other, as just as fair
And having perhaps the better claim,
Because it was grassy and wanted wear;
Though as for that, the passing there
Had worn them really about the same,

And both that morning equally lay
In leaves no step had trodden black
Oh, I kept the first for another day!
Yet knowing how way leads on to way,
I doubted if I should ever come back.

I shall be telling this with a sigh
Somewhere ages and ages hence:
Two roads diverged in a wood, and I -
I took the one less traveled by,
And that has made all the difference.

Contents

Prologue

View From A Bridge

I stood quietly on the bridge above the dark empty freeway, looking down at the smooth tarmac below. In the distance behind me I could hear the engine of a large truck as it approached at speed. I looked around and saw the lights heading my way, and thought grimly to myself, "This is it. This one is yours."

I would have to get the timing just right. If I jumped too early I would land on the freeway below, probably breaking both legs. That would hurt, but only for a short time, until the truck hit. Wait a minute though! What if I jumped early enough for the truck driver to see me, giving him time to react? What if he somehow managed to miss me? All I would have achieved would be a collection of broken bones, and more misery to pile on top of what I already knew was coming.

I would need to delay my jump as long as possible. Perfect timing would mean I'd hit the ground at the instant the truck reached the impact point, bringing the instant relief of endless darkness. But what if I delayed just a little too long? The truck was heading south, and I was on the south side of the bridge, facing south too. The truck would be out of sight as it passed under the bridge below me. Timing my jump was going to be tricky, as for a second or two I would not know exactly where the thundering juggernaut was. If I jumped too late I had visions of landing on the cab roof, and then bouncing along the top of the container, before falling off the back end into the road. There was a good chance I might survive that, and lay broken on the road, again to face pain and misery.

I should have planned this a little better. But how? If I stood on the north side of the bridge, facing the on-coming truck, the driver might possibly spot me climbing onto the parapet, preparing to jump. Would he be able to avoid me? Probably not, but I wasn't sure.

Maybe I should be down at the side of the freeway, hidden in the bushes. I could just run out at the appropriate moment, without having to consider the pain of broken bones from a poorly timed jump.

What about the driver? How would he cope with the aftermath of such an event? I don't imagine it would be easy to come to terms with something like that, even if one is completely blameless.

Good grief, if I was going to be such a coward about the whole thing, I should perhaps resort to the much less painful bottle of paracetamol tablets washed down with a bottle of whiskey. Ah, but I wouldn't want to wake up in hospital having my stomach pumped.

All of this, and more, flashed through my mind in the few short seconds as the truck closed the distance between us. The moment of truth approached.

I watched the truck pass below me and didn't make a move. The real truth was that I knew I was never going to go through with anything like this. My mind was simply whirling quickly through a theoretical set of scenarios that might provide an easy escape route from what was to come.

With a heavy heart I turned my cycle around, and began pedalling back up the cycle track alongside the freeway. I knew there were some long dark months ahead, despite the approach of another hot bright Australian summer.

PART 1

ALife4Sale

Chapter 1

A New Start

Two years later, in November 2007 I looked back at the challenges with which life had recently presented me, and decided it was time to make some changes. I needed a new start and I had a plan. I was going to sell my life!

The previous two years had taken my soon-to-be-sold life in a new direction, one which had completely taken me by surprise. I had never imagined working in the job I was now doing, and the life I was now living was so far removed from my expectations of two years earlier.

At that time, towards the end of 2005, life had been progressing nicely, according to a semi-structured plan. In November that year my wife and I celebrated our fifth wedding anniversary, inviting all our friends to a big party in the lovely house we had built together in the outer suburbs of Perth in beautiful, sun-kissed Western Australia.

But only days later my life was knocked violently off-course, when I discovered that my wife had met someone else, and told me that she no longer loved me.

After a traumatic few months we had separated. During those dark, lonely, early days I thought a lot about the incredibly happy past I had shared with Laura. I struggled to understand how it could have all gone so horribly wrong, without ever spotting, until it was much too late, a single sign that anything was amiss.

I suppose my journey through life up to this point hadn't quite been the usual progression that most people follow, from school to college, to an entry level job in a chosen field, and then onward up the career ladder.

I did go to college eventually, but only after taking a year off between leaving school and finally settling down to further my education. I had managed to secure a place at Liverpool Polytechnic, where I would be learning how to teach outdoor activities. However, keen to see some of the world first, I deferred entry for a year. During that year I worked in a factory to save some money, and then travelled with one of my school buddies. We went to live on a kibbutz in Israel, where I worked in all sorts of jobs, as a foreign volunteer sharing the life of the community. Afterwards we travelled through Egypt, and then to Greece, where we bought a very cheap car, and drove back home via several European countries.

A short, but well-paid second summer in the local sign-making factory paid off my debts before college. I thoroughly enjoyed my years in Liverpool, but never wanted to work as a teacher in a school, my experiences in teaching practice convincing me of that. Eventually I settled in a job working for British Rail for a couple of years. I worked in their residential outdoor activities facility in the north-east of England, teaching their youth trainees skills such as communication, co-operation, teamwork, and leadership.

But a couple of years later boredom started to creep in and I decided to make a change. Inspired by a couple of friends who seemed to be making a very good living dealing in second-hand cars, I left British Rail, and moved into the small terraced house I had just bought.

Over the following years I managed to do fairly well, making a living doing the odd bit of freelance outdoor training work, dealing in cars and motorcycles, and trying my hand at several other ideas and businesses that looked like they might turn an easy profit.

In those years I managed to make a fairly decent living, but I could see that I was never going to become rich unless one of the many businesses I tried became a runaway success. As a means of self-motivation I started to make a list of things I would like to do, places I would like to see, and possessions I would like to own when lack of money was no longer an obstacle.

It was while on holiday in Kenya that I stumbled upon the sport that was to shape the next few years of my life. This new direction would eventually lead to meeting my wife, and ultimately moving half way around the world.

In partnership with my life-long friend and motor trading buddy, Bruce, I set up and then ran “Scarborough Jet Skiing” for five fantastic summer seasons. We hired out jet skis to holidaymakers at the beach, and sold new and second-hand skis. We also sold accessories, did some servicing and repair work, and sold a range of beach toys too. The north-east coast of England doesn’t have a very long summer, so when the weather was good we worked all the hours we could, seven days a week. That didn’t stop us enjoying life to the full, and in 1993, during the second summer on the beach, the most fantastic person I have ever met walked up to our caravan, and into my life.

Laura and I maintained a long-distance relationship for a couple of years, seeing each other as often as we could, and eventually she came to live with me for the summer season of 1996. The next year she finished college and moved over from Manchester to live with me permanently.

During the off-seasons, when it was too cold to run the jet skis, and later, after we sold the jet ski business at the end of the 1996 summer season, Bruce and I had tried a few other businesses. These had included cycle hire, wedding cars, and magazine publishing. None of them had offered the same success or fun of the beach.

I worked for the local council at the outdoor swimming pool for the 1998 summer season, the job being relatively easy to get because of both my background in outdoor activities, and my recent experience of dealing with the public in a watersports business. This ultimately led on to a fulltime job at the indoor swimming pool.

During this time Laura and I took our first trip to Australia, where her mother had been born and raised. Laura had dual nationality. Having been born in England she was registered as British, but was also registered as Australian due to her mother's nationality. She had a grandmother, aunties and uncles, and several cousins in Australia that she had never met. We spent six glorious weeks in the Southern Hemisphere summer as England's chilly winter held its grip back at home.

The following year we took our second trip, and were with friends in Sydney for New Years Eve 1999, which was enormous fun. Having thoroughly enjoyed both of our extended visits, we decided that we would perhaps like to go and live there.

Back in England we considered our options. We had often told each other that we both expected to be together for the rest of our lives, and the subject of marriage came up easily. We wanted to be together, we wanted to move to Australia, and we decided that after seven years together, we wanted to be married.

The big day was early in November 2000, and we couldn't have asked for better weather. It was a beautiful cold, crisp, blue-sky autumn day. The wedding ceremony at the registry office was simple, and afterwards Bruce took us up to Oliver's Mount in his van – we hadn't bothered with the expense of fancy wedding cars, saving our money for our future move to Australia. Lunch was in a Chinese restaurant, followed by an afternoon pub crawl down through the town centre to the seafront.

After dark at the beach we had everyone meet and bring along fireworks, enjoying a wonderful, but completely disorganised display. One of Laura's friends had brought along her new boyfriend, who was in the army. He had already thoroughly enjoyed the afternoon pub crawl, and provided great entertainment crawling around on the sand trying drunkenly to light more fireworks as others exploded in wild colours around him. It looked like a battle scene from some sort of psychedelic war movie as he belly-crawled from one firework to the next, and it was amazing that he didn't have to be whisked away to the casualty ward.

The reception took place in a town centre social club, and we had booked an Irish cèilidh band to play, which meant everyone could join in for some well organised Irish-style barn-dancing.

It was such a wonderful day, and I couldn't have been happier, knowing that I was now married to the person that I wanted to spend the rest of my life with.

A year later, after several more jobs, including working as manager of a mobile phone shop, a collector for a finance company, and a labourer on a building site, we sold pretty-much everything we owned. We said goodbye to all our friends and family, and moved halfway around the world to make a fresh start together.

We soon settled into our new life, and absolutely loved Perth, warm and sunny, on the beautiful Indian Ocean on the west coast of Australia.

We lived in a wonderful shared-accommodation house almost on the beach for our first year there, and then rented our own smaller unit in nearby Scarborough, namesake of the English coastal town where we had shared much of the previous seven years.

Australia offered a good life, and although my first foray into business there, renting deckchairs on the beach at Scarborough was doomed to failure, we both found great jobs, and lived a nice, easy-going life together.

Another eighteen months later, after much research, we took the plunge and bought our first piece of land, and built our first Australian home. The house, finished just less than three years after our arrival in the country, was like a dream come true. It was bigger and nicer than anything we could have ever have afforded back in England, and we worked hard together to create a fantastic home and garden. We had a few parties there, always enjoyed by our growing group of friends, and the pool table in the huge living room was always a central attraction.

Our longer term plan had always been to make this house the first stepping stone on our journey to planned financial freedom. Our goal was to end up in a home completely mortgage-free, our target time being within a period of five years. With completed homes often being worth around 25% more than the combined land and build price, the house had already gone up in value. We had also chosen the land well, and houses in our suburb had increased in value even further.

Our next step had been to look for another block of land to repeat the process. Our plan was to build our next house there, to move into that as soon as it completed, and to sell the first house at the same time.

In our next chosen suburb, land was selling well, and we had to queue overnight, sleeping in our cars in order to secure the block of land upon which we had set our hearts. It was in this queue that we met Andy, another expat Brit now enjoying the sunny Perth lifestyle, also trying to benefit from the on-going property boom.

Little did I suspect that this chance meeting would be the catalyst that would irrevocably alter my relationship with my wife and send my semi-planned life careering off the rails less than a year later.

I had my suspicions that something was going on, but could never have imagined the full devastating reality of discovering that Laura had fallen for someone else. That night, when life blindsided me, I cycled away from our home, and without ever planning to, had found myself on the bridge over the freeway. For the first time in my life I fully understood the awful decision and devastating action some people choose when life's terrible surprises come calling. I chose to cycle home and face the future.

Laura claimed it was all a huge mistake and said I was the one she wanted to be with. We decided that we would try to forget what had happened, and move on with our lives. No one else knew our situation, or needed to, I suggested. Laura assured me that all contact with Andy had been severed.

For a while we had tried to get our life together back on course. But a couple of difficult months later it was apparent that all was not well between us. When I discovered that Laura had seen Andy again, I confronted her about it, and she told me she thought that perhaps she no longer loved me.

I was heart-broken, and the following terrible weeks were filled with endless arguments, recriminations and blame. Laura still didn't seem to know what she wanted to do, but after more talks and a painful visit to a marriage guidance counsellor, her wavering indecision ended. It was clear that we had no future together. I was utterly devastated. In that one horrible moment I realised that my whole future had finally been stripped from me, and I faced a bleak, unknown darkness ahead.

Our current work and financial situations meant that the most practical decision was that I should move out. We decided to sell the house immediately, split the money, and go our separate ways.

Somehow we managed to do this without recourse to lawyers, and although on paper it all sounds very civilised and easy, there were weeks of arguments, tears, regrets, and sorrow. I hated every minute of it, and although I had fought with everything I had to try to save our marriage, I knew I had now lost her. I had to accept her final decision and move on.

During those miserable first weeks after our separation, as well as wondering where it had all gone wrong, I also did a lot of thinking about what I wanted to do next. I made some decisions of my own. I had been working at the same shop for the past three years, acting as a rug salesman, and eventually as assistant manager, at the family-owned business. At the age of 42 it was officially the longest job I had ever had – I tend to get bored pretty easily working in one place, and like to challenge myself to take on new roles and learn new skills.

One of the main decisions I took involved my immediate future. If one huge part of my life in Perth had changed completely, then I could not simply continue in the same job, and live a shadowy half-hearted version of my previous life. It was time to leave my job, and do something completely new!

I also needed to earn quite a lot more than I was currently earning, as when we had separated, Laura and I had decided that we would sell the house we had been sharing. We agreed that I would take over ownership of the new block of land we had bought the year before. I would make all payments on it, in addition to all payments for the house-build that was due to commence there very soon.

After talking to a few friends, I decided to follow the path that many others in Western Australia chose when they needed to earn more money, and enter the mining industry. I had no relevant experience at all, but didn't really see this as a big hurdle. I started taking truck driving lessons in order to get the driving license that I would need to drive the monster trucks used in the mines.

I soon had the license I required, and handed my notice in at the rug shop, having started to apply for dump truck driving jobs. The way a lot of mining works in Western Australia is on what is called a "fly-in fly-out" basis. This means that you live in Perth, but fly in to a remote mine site to work, and then fly back out for your time off. This most common work pattern is a “2 on, 1 off” roster, meaning that you fly in and work for two weeks, usually 7 day shifts and 7 night shifts, then fly home for a week off.

As the end of my time at the shop drew closer I had not yet found a job. It appeared that companies were reluctant to take on new people, often referred to as “greenies”, for a fly-in fly-out position. Many of the agencies which I approached explained that companies generally did not take greenies as they were unsure of how newcomers would handle the work conditions. They did not want the expense of training someone new, only to find that the trainee hated the job, and left shortly afterwards. Employers wanted people with previous experience.

Following a couple of weeks of fruitless unemployment, I took a friend’s advice, and packed my car with the few belongings I had that were not stored away. At the time I was staying in a borrowed apartment near the beach, the completion of my new house was still about six months away, and I had no other ties. After a few farewell drinks in the local pub with some friends, I packed the last of my meagre belongings into the car, and hit the road early the next morning, heading east out of Perth

Kalgoorlie lies about six hours drive away from Perth, in the middle of the desert, and exists mainly because of the huge open pit goldmine there. I drove into town on 4th July 2006 knowing nobody, with nowhere to stay, and no promise of a job at all.

However, things went very well for me there and within 48 hours I had a small but comfortable room, and a job driving a machine called a slag hauler, working in the local nickel smelter. The job also involved driving a nice Mercedes tipper truck with a decent auto gearbox, and an older tipper truck with a very cranky manual gearbox that took a lot of practice to use smoothly. I had to learn a lot of new skills very quickly.

It took me a while to get used to working strange new rosters and hours, and having to cope with night shift work too. During this time I kept pestering the Human Resources guy at the Superpit recruitment office to get me the job that I really wanted – trainee dump truckie in the huge open pit gold mine right at the edge of town.

I would often go to the lookout and gaze down into the pit, watching the huge trucks go around and around. One day soon, I thought, I hope to be driving one of them. Less than five weeks later, I was offered a trainee position as a driver there, handed my notice in at the nickel smelter, and went to start my new career!

The trucks are absolutely enormous and the training was very challenging, but I loved it. At times it was very frustrating, and I made plenty of mistakes, as did many of the other greenies there. But because this was one of the only places in the country that took on trainees, there were quite a few of us to share the mistakes around. Many of us had drifted into town from elsewhere to learn to drive these monster trucks, and I found myself working with a great group of people, all going through the same challenging learning curve.

After the first three months or so I found that the work was now much easier. The twelve-hour shifts did not seem so long, and night shift did not seem so bad. Handling the truck was pretty-much second nature too, and now many of us found that we could drive around, listen to the two-way radio, the FM radio, pour a cup of coffee and eat an apple all at the same time – well, almost!

Every second week, at the end of our block of dayshifts the whole crew would all go to the pub after work. A few of us who had started around the same time together would laugh about how difficult it had all seemed at first, and share stories of some of the dumb things we had done, and still did occasionally.

It was a simple life, filled with hard work, but also filled with a lot of laughter and a huge amount of fun. I met some great people there, some of whom I know wiil be friends for the rest of my life.

For me it was also a very important part of my healing process. Living out in Kalgoorlie, with a totally new group of people, meant that nobody knew my past, so it was never mentioned. Long days sat in a truck with just my own thoughts meant that I had time to start to come to terms with the huge, unexpected upheaval in my life.

I spent a total of five months working in the Superpit, and absolutely loved it, but by the end I was ready to go back to Perth. I missed being by the ocean too much, and I missed my friends back in Perth too. I had a final date for completion of my house, and I had enough experience to get a fly-in fly-out job. This would pay more money, and in my personal circumstances, would suit me much better, I thought.

Just before Christmas 2006, a little over a year after my awful marital discovery, I moved back to Perth, and into the newly completed house that Laura and I had designed together. We had planned to live there together for a year or so as the next step on our journey towards financial freedom. Now, as I moved the furniture that we had shared in our previous home into place, I felt utterly alone.

For the past five months I really hadn't needed to confront too directly the huge loss, but now being surrounded by all of the reminders from my past, I had to face head-on the gaping hole that Laura's departure had left in my life.

I hated it! I didn't like being in the house alone. I missed my friends in Kalgoorlie, and the easy camaraderie we had shared as a group. I felt trapped in this new place, a reminder of everything that had once been, of all that I had hoped and believed was to come, and I hated it. I couldn't simply sell up and move on. To avoid Capital Gains Tax, Australian law stipulates that a house has to be your main home for a period of twelve months before you can sell. This had always been our original idea. We had planned to live in this place for a year while we bought the next piece of land, and built the next step of our dream.

I didn't feel like I had much choice, and had to accept that I would have to stick it out for a year. I had already landed a mining job that would mean I was only at home for one week out of three, the other two weeks being up on site in the desert far to the north. I would manage somehow.

Over the next few weeks I made the place my own, turning it into quite a nice bachelor pad with the addition of a large-screen home theatre system and an outdoor hot tub. I bought myself a motorbike, something I had always loved when I had lived in England, but had never had in the five years I had been in Australia. Slowly the house started to feel a bit more like home, although still filled with reminders of a past that was now long-gone.

I started dating again, and met Mel, who was originally French, but had lived in Perth for the past fourteen years. She was in much the same position as I was, although she was officially divorced and had two girls. I was only separated and had no kids to tie me down. We got on pretty well, and started an easy-going relationship about fourteen months after my separation from Laura.

Around the time I met Mel I started my new job, and flew up for my first shift at the end of January 2007. I had landed a great contract, working a 13/8 roster, made up of 6 day shifts, 7 night shifts, and then 8 days off. My flights up and back would earn me frequent flyer points, all food was provided on site, and the pay was significantly better than Kalgoorlie. At the mine site accommodation village there was a canteen, a bar, internet room, a large swimming pool, gym, squash courts and a few other sports facilities. I had really landed on my feet, and soon settled in to the new job.

Since everything was provided for two weeks out of three, and I was being well paid for the long shifts I was working, over the following months I managed to make a fairly significant reduction in my mortgage.

It wasn't all easy sailing though. The work could be hot and boring, and the 12 hour shifts could really drag sometimes, particularly the nights, when it could be a real battle just to keep your eyes open. I missed the easy friendship of the group I had worked with in Kalgoorlie. I made plenty of new friends at Telfer, but because everyone had different lives, and lived in different places in a bigger city, somehow it was not the same as the close-knit little community I had enjoyed in Kal.

One advantage (or disadvantage, depending on how you looked at it) was that you got plenty of thinking time as you drove endlessly up and down in the huge open pit. I really found that I quite liked it, often happy to turn the radio off for long stretches at a time, and think my own thoughts. I always carried a notebook and pen to write any ideas down, or work out finances for some new business plan.

As the year progressed, life continued in a fairly uncomplicated fashion. I would fly off to work and be away for two weeks at a time, and then return for a week. I became happier in my house as I made it more like my own personal bachelor pad, and I enjoyed spending time with Mel and her two girls.

However, as the end of the year approached, I started to think about selling the house. Prices were high, and it was looking increasingly like the market may have reached a high point. I didn't feel like the time was right to buy another piece of land, as it all seemed to be very much over-valued. And to be honest, without Laura, my heart really was no longer in the long-term plan we had shared.

So there I was, in late 2007, sat in a dump truck in a gold mine in the far north of Western Australia, having spent a large part of the previous ten months driving around the same hole in the ground. I had been in my new house for almost a year, and could now sell it without financial penalty. I started to think about my future, and what I might like to do next.

I really didn't want to stay working in the mine during the approaching southern summer, as temperatures would be extreme in the desert. I had worked long and hard, had paid a good chunk off my mortgage. I fancied a bit of a break, and perhaps some travel and adventure.

I made the decision to sell the house. Although a lot happier living there now, the house and its contents still provided a strong, and sometimes saddening reminder of a previous life, and although I felt that I was adjusting well, I wanted to complete the moving-on process, and this required getting rid of the house. It also made great financial sense, as I had paid quite a bit off the mortgage, and the house value had shot up quite dramatically over the year since completion. I would therefore be able to release a good nest egg of cash. One idea I had was perhaps to buy a big motorhome, and travel the country a bit. Perhaps I would work in a mine for six months of the year, over the winter, and then travel for six months each summer. Financially this would be quite viable once the house sold.

What would I do with the furniture, I wondered? Perhaps I could sell it all with the house, offering a fully furnished package. But I also had a car, and a motorbike, and I was considering buying a jet ski for the coming summer too. What would I do with all of them? Maybe I could include them as part of one big lifestyle package?

It hit me suddenly! I remembered an idea my old friend Bruce had had many years before. He must have had a particularly bad day at work, and came stomping into the pub, saying, "That's it, I'm going to get rid of the lot! The business, the car, the house, everything! I am going to sell my life!" He explained that the idea had just come to him. He would advertise the whole package in the Sunday newspapers, as he reckoned that despite the occasional bad day, he had a pretty enviable lifestyle.

However, when he checked the price of a full page advert in a national Sunday newspaper (this was long before the days of the internet) he was a bit disheartened, and he let his idea fall by the wayside.

Now, fifteen or more years later, as I drove my truck down the main pit ramp, the idea solidified into a plan. "That's what I am going to do! Sell my life! I'll include the job too, and will include an introduction to some friends. That's brilliant! How and where will I sell it? Auction it on eBay, of course!"

When I returned to Perth for my next week off I ran the idea past three good friends, whose opinions I valued. I was surprised and encouraged by the results. Two of them thought it was a fantastic idea, one going as far as saying that she could imagine doing the same thing right now herself, as it was exactly how she felt. The third opinion was exactly the opposite, wondering in disbelief how anyone could possibly consider leaving behind everything they had worked so hard to build up.

I thought that if the idea could produce such strong opposing opinions, then there would be the chance to get some publicity for the project, which I knew I would need for the idea to be a success. If I had got three indifferent responses I would have probably abandoned the idea there and then.

I didn't take any immediate action, but let the idea stew a bit, and back at work jotted down ideas and thoughts as I drove up and down the ramps. The idea seemed to be one that just would not go away though.

In December I handed my notice in at work, and flew home after my last shift on Christmas Eve. I had decided to take at least a couple of months off, and between Christmas and New Year I went shopping for a small campervan. I trawled the backpacker hostel adverts boards, and soon found what I wanted. A Swedish traveller was selling the Toyota Hiace camper that had taken her and her friend around Australia for the past six months, and I bought myself a bargain.

I spent the months of January and February on an extended trip across Australia from west to east, on the way calling in to visit old friends in Kalgoorlie, and skydiving at as many different dropzones as I could find on the way. Over the past five years skydiving had become my sport of choice, and I tried to jump as often as I could.

On the journey across the huge open spaces of the country that I had come to call home, I thought a lot more about the "life for sale" idea. I met up with Mel and her kids and we travelled together for a few days, discussing the idea in much detail. Mel embraced the idea with enthusiasm, encouraging me to consider it more seriously.

I finally made the decision that I was going to go ahead. It would be fun, I thought, and might just raise a bit more than selling the house and contents separately, if I managed to get enough publicity.

Mel offered to help me create the website, and between us we mapped out a rough design. I bought and registered the website "ALife4Sale.com". During a week-long stay with friends in Melbourne I started to write some of the content for the site, while Mel, back in Perth, started putting a website together, inserting my content as I wrote it.

I needed a date to provide a framework and timescale, and decided to aim for a seven day auction period finishing at the end of June, which is the end of the financial year in Australia. It was a pretty arbitrary choice, and when I looked at a calendar and saw that the 30th of June was a Monday, I decided that it might be better to end the auction on Sunday 29th. This meant the start date for the auction would be the 22nd.

I had decided to have a 100 day countdown from the launch of the website to the start of the auction. This was for two reasons. Firstly I thought that it may take a couple of months to build up a bit of publicity for what I was about to do, and secondly I was looking for a serious buyer, and I wanted to give someone time to sort out their finances, and perhaps even visas if they were from further afield than Australia.

I thought a lot about who might be a potential purchaser of the package I was putting together, and imagined several possible scenarios. Perhaps a Perth based property investor might be interested in the package as a buy-to-let, already furnished and ready for a tenant. When we bought the land we had chosen well, as the house was in a pleasant location, with a nice westerly outlook over a natural bushland reserve, but was also an easy five minute walk to a train station on the newly completed southern railway line.

Perhaps someone from the other side of Australia might be interested in buying a ready-to-move-into lifestyle, particularly if they were coming over to join in the huge West Australian resources boom that was still pushing up house prices, and offering fantastic wages in the mines.

Maybe someone emigrating from abroad might be tempted in the same way by a ready-made lifestyle. Perth has an ever-expanding population, as more and more people realise what a wonderful place it is to live.

Over the next few days, while I had good access to an internet connection at my friends' house in Melbourne, the website really started to take shape, and I started to get very excited about the whole idea. As a practical way of selling everything at once it was brilliant, I thought. It would be a great experience and a lot of fun too.

We came up with the skeleton of the website over the course of five or six days, and I thought it looked pretty good. I continued my journey to Sydney in the campervan, where I did may last bit of skydiving for the journey. I sold the campervan, and flew back to Perth. I was now fully committed to the idea of selling my life, and was keen to get on with it.

We had about two weeks to complete the website, and worked pretty much flat-out to make it as good as we possibly could. We took many pictures of the inside and outside of the house, and all its contents. We took pictures of the car, and the motorbike, the hot-tub and the home entertainment system.

There was a lot of cleaning and tidying involved, and many times as we took pictures, there was a pile of junk just outside the frame, which was shuffled from room to room as we progressed.

On the website itself we included a guestbook and a voting page, where people could make comments or become involved by expressing their opinion on the whole idea. We also built in a bulletin board page where there could be some back and forth discussion on the matter too.

I still was unsure whether we were building something that nobody would ever see, or whether I might be successful in creating some publicity for the forthcoming auction.

I made the decision that if I was going to do this, I was going to do it properly, and leave absolutely everything behind. On the website, I stated that when I was paid by the new buyer, I would walk out of the house with just one set of clothes, and my wallet and passport, nothing else at all.

I knew that I had to get as much publicity as possible for the auction, and spoke to my friend Simon, who lives in London, and works as a freelance reporter. I asked him what he thought the best approach would be to let people know what I was up to. He suggested that he could write a press release aimed at the UK newspapers, focusing on the fact that I was an expat Brit now living in Australia. If it makes it to a UK national newspaper, he explained, it would probably be picked up all around the world. "You may even get to do something on local radio," he suggested, and I thought publicity like that would be fantastic.

Many years before, I had written a book about how my wife and I had met. It was hand-written, and had only ever been intended for an audience of one. It told the story of how back in 1989, Bruce and I had started racing motorcycle road race sidecars together, and how we had eventually set up the jet ski hire business. There had been some very funny moments, and some great achievements.

I wrote about how one day in 1993, the person who was to become my wife walked up to our caravan on the beach, and stepped into my life. I described how we started our relationship, and some of the struggles and challenges we had faced.

I had thoroughly enjoyed the process of telling our unusual tale, even though the book would only ever have one reader. I had re-read it when it was complete, and thought it told the story very well, expressing how I felt about this wonderful person that had come into my life.

The next weekend that Laura and I were together, we drove up to Oliver's Mount, where we would stand together several years later on the day we married, and I handed the book to her, incredibly proud of what I had created. I truly believed we would happily spend the rest of our days together. Laura suggested that perhaps one day we might show the book to our grandchildren.

Eventually, of course, seven years after we met, we had married, and made the decision to start a new life together in Australia.

Five years later, as the relationship crumbled before my eyes, during one teary discussion about what had changed, I pointed out the book, and asked, "But what about that? What about all that we had to go through, all that we had to fight for to be together? That book says everything that I can't find the right words to say right now. What about all that?"

The devastating answer I had received was, "That doesn't mean anything now."

Therefore, as I put the website together, I thought I might publish the book online too. I knew people might want to know some of the background that could bring someone to the point where they decide to sell their whole life on the internet. I thought the story showed how much I felt I had lost, and would perhaps provide some context, so that people might understand. I also thought, somewhat bitterly, why not publish it? After all, it meant nothing to anyone else now!

The book was included as part of the webpage, as an introduction to the rest of my story. I hoped to write this during the build-up to the auction, telling the continuing saga of my adventures. It would cover our move to Australia, the life we created there together, the devastating break-up, and my change of direction that eventually led to the auction.

One of the last pieces of the whole package that I had struggled to find an answer for was how to include my job. I could not think of any reason why a mining company would want to be involved, and the logistics of trying to organise that would have been far too complicated. Eventually I hit on the perfect solution. I went back to the rug shop where I had worked for three years. It was a small family business run by husband and wife, Jenny and Dennis, who had been incredibly supportive and helpful as my marriage had collapsed.

Jenny loved the idea, and as they had a staff member leaving, there would be a position that I could fill on a temporary basis, a job which could eventually be offered to the new owner of my life. I knew the shop might benefit from some publicity if I ever got this off the ground, but Jenny just wanted to be a part of it because she thought it was a fun idea.

Finally, I spoke to a few of my friends too, explaining what I was about to do. I wondered if they would be happy to be included as part of the package. I explained that I was not proposing to sell them, but was simply offering an introduction to the new owner of my life to some wonderful people that were an important part of my life. Quite a few friends were very happy to support me, and thought it would be fun to be part of such an unusual idea.

With everything in place, and the website almost complete, it was final decision time. Was I really going to do this? Did I really want to get rid of everything?

It was now over two years since Laura had finally decided that she was going to leave me, and although my life had improved, particularly since meeting Mel, it was obvious that all was still not well, otherwise this might not seem like such a good idea.

Two years later, nothing had done much to diminish how much I missed my wife. I had moved 600 kilometres out into the desert and had started a new career. I had moved into a brand new house. I had lived a completely new lifestyle working in the hot dusty mines of the outback. And of course, I also had a new girlfriend. But none of this had really changed anything for me. I still ached for my friend, my partner, my lover, my everything – my wife.

Every day, small things would remind me of the past that was now long gone, but still ever-present. The tiles on the shower wall that Laura had chosen, the rug on the living room floor that she had designed herself, the sweater hanging in the wardrobe that she had bought for me on my birthday, the same day I had done my first skydive. The plates in the kitchen that we had rescued from the back garden of the house that we had first moved into in Perth, and that we had washed and cleaned together. The small metal puzzles on the kitchen counter that we had bought on our first trip back to England, two years after migrating to Perth.

We had moved from England at the start of 2002 with almost nothing but a rucsac of clothes each, and so everything in the house that I now lived in alone had been bought in the wonderful four years we had shared together in Australia.

Everything about the house, and everything in the house reminded me of Laura. I decided that if I was going to get rid of the place and move on, I would be just as well getting rid of absolutely everything else too, and making a completely fresh start.

After all, it was only "stuff", I reasoned. The logical and optimistic parts of me thought that the idea might generate some interest, and hopefully sell as a complete package, perhaps for a pretty decent price too! If this happened I would be completely free to travel for a while, and if ever I needed "stuff" again, I would always be able to re-buy new "stuff".

Travelling now seemed like a good idea, I had decided. I hoped this might be the final step in my long process of coming to terms with the gaping hole in my life that Laura's departure still left.

Chapter 2

A Life Online

"That's it!" said Mel. "ALife4Sale is now online. Good luck!"

The 14th of March had arrived quickly, and the website was almost complete. There was a long list of minor adjustments, and some additions that would need to be made, but we were ready to go! Mel had uploaded the pages to the online website server, and I wondered just what we might have set in motion.

Simon had written his article back in London, and that day offered it to a couple of the UK national dailies. He phoned and told me that he had had some interest from both The Sun and The Telegraph, but nothing definite yet. There was a rejection from The Daily Mail, and he was just about to offer it to my old local newspaper, The Northern Echo.

The next day only The Northern Echo had run with the story, printing a huge full-page article on page three of the paper. It was complete with pictures and information from the website, which had just gone live online the day before. They had also run the full article online on their website.

I was pretty excited, but also a little disappointed that I had not made it into The Sun, which has one of the largest readerships of any English language newspaper. Now that would have been publicity, I thought, but at least I had made a successful start.

I had no idea of what was about to come!

Not long after the article appeared in The Echo, Simon phoned to say that he was getting a lot of interest from some of the national papers now, and asked if it was okay for him to give them my phone number. Of course it was!

The phone rang again soon, and I found myself talking to a reporter from The Independent. I was quite excited, and pleased to tell the story of how this had all come about. The interview was very positive and encouraging.

A short time after I hung up, the phone rang again, and a reporter from The Sun asked me roughly the same set of questions. This was all going much better than I had hoped for, and if these two ran articles, the coverage would be fantastic.

On the Monday morning UK-time, which was mid-afternoon in Perth, Simon rang again. He was delighted to tell me that there were articles in both The Telegraph and The Daily Mail, although neither of these had rung me. The Independent and The Sun had also run their pieces after speaking to me over the weekend, so I had made at least four of the UK national dailies. This couldn't possibly get any better, I thought!

I had had a few other calls from UK newspapers, and "WHO?" magazine in Australia had also called. Despite this I was not quite prepared for the next call, which came from the producer of Australian breakfast TV show “Sunrise”. They wanted me to come in the next morning and appear live on the show at around 8am. The time difference between Sydney and Perth meant that I would have to be at the studio at around 5:30am!! I cancelled the idea of going out to celebrate St Patrick’s Day that evening!

I set off for the studio just before 5am, and was met by a cameraman and shown into the building. I was very surprised by how empty and quiet the whole place was. There was only myself and the cameraman in the studio. A sound guy fitted me with an earpiece and microphone and then disappeared back into a little control room. Other than the security guard who had let me in there was nobody else around.

I sat in the chair at the desk, with a photo-backdrop of the Perth skyline behind me, looked nervously at the huge camera pointing at me and listened to the show itself live in my earpiece. I have to admit I was pretty tense, but excited too. I took another sip of the glass of water at my side. Finally, in my earpiece, I heard a producer from the Sydney end of the connection ask if I could hear everything okay. “You’re on live in 30 seconds.”

I tried to relax, but couldn’t supress the nerves, and all of a sudden I was live on air, chatting to Mel and Kochie, the household-name presenters. I felt that I did pretty well, didn’t stutter and stammer at all, and wasn’t given any tricky questions. It was all over in a couple of minutes.

I was out of the studio before 6:30am, and went to visit Mel, as she lived close by. I was pretty high with excitement – I had just been on live TV on the east coast, and it would show here in Perth in about an hour. We watched the TV as I came on at 8am, and congratulated each other on a job well done. We had certainly created some publicity about the auction now!

My next port of call was at the rug shop on my way home. Jenny was very excited, but Dennis had a few well-chosen words of advice! “You looked very serious! It looked like you had a broomstick up your backside! Relax and have fun.” I thought about this, and thought that yes, it is just meant to be fun, and if I ever got the chance again, I would try to enjoy the moment much more.

By the time I got home the message bank on my home phone was full and could accept no new messages. I had turned my mobile on after I left Mel’s, and it had started ringing almost immediately. There was also a message to tell me the mobile phone message bank was full.

At home I turned my computer on and pressed “Send/Receive” on my email software. It took a while for the “receive” to complete, and when it did, over 1,000 messages had flooded in. As these downloaded, both my phones had started ringing again.

I tried to wade through as many of the emails as I could, but it was an almost impossible task. As soon as I hung one phone up the other would ring. Often both would be ringing together, and in the end I disconnected the home phone and just answered the mobile whenever it rang.

I soon got the chance to give my TV interview technique another try. I was invited to appear on a different Australian breakfast TV show the next morning, followed that afternoon by a live link-up with a UK breakfast TV show. I really tried to relax during both of these, and later my friend Karen told me that I had looked so confident and natural. I was really starting to enjoy all of this, but was panicking a little about all the unanswered emails and phone messages.

The next days were absolutely crazy. It was just non-stop. There were constant phone calls, interviews, photographers taking pictures for newspapers, and many radio show appearances. I was also trying to deal with the never-ending flood of emails. Calls started to come in from America and other parts of the world, and I appeared on US breakfast TV show "Good Morning America".

I was absolutely worn out. I was often up before 5am to dash to a TV studio for an appearance, and then still doing interviews with US radio stations at 11pm. On many occasions people would call to schedule a radio interview time, but I explained that I could not really promise that my phone wouldn't be engaged, as it was ringing constantly. In many cases I was then asked if I could go live on air right there and then, and within 30 seconds I was in the middle of another interview.

One morning I woke up and thought, "Oh no, I've even started dreaming about doing interviews in the middle of the night!" But I paused for a moment, thinking, "Wait a minute! That feels a little more real than any dream."

I looked at my mobile phone, and found I had forgotten to turn it off before going to bed. I checked the call register, and discovered that I had received a twelve minute call at 3:30am. I had no idea who I had spoken too, or what I had said, but had a vague feeling that I had done okay. I just laughed – I had wanted some adventure and excitement, and I was getting more than I could have possibly imagined! I was going to try to enjoy every aspect of this experience.

But not everything was positive. The Daily Mail in the UK ran a huge double-page spread about the book I had written. They had obviously got a copy from the website, and had gone through it with a fine-toothed comb. They had cherry-picked certain sections, choosing incidents and events from the story to sensationalise. Taken out of context, the parts the article focussed on made the book sound like a terrible warts-and-all exposé. The huge spread had featured a photo of Laura, and I had no idea where they had got it from. It was a picture I had never seen before.

I discovered later that they had turned up on my mother's doorstep back in England, and had hounded Laura's parents too. Laura called me, outraged firstly that I had told our story, secondly about the newspapers hounding her parents, but mainly about the fact that her photo was in the paper. "How did they get my photo? Could they have hacked into my computer? Or did you hack into my computer, steal it and give it to them?"

What?!! I tried to explain that this particular paper had never even spoken to me, that I had released the book simply as background, and still stood by it as a wonderful love story. None of this was being done to get back at her in any way. That had never been my intention at all. In regard to the photo, I had no idea how it had appeared in the newspaper, or where they had got it from, but tried to convince her it was certainly none of my doing. "I don't believe you, I don't know what you're capable of any more!" she said, and hung up.

I thought long and hard about my motivations for publishing the book. I had to admit that if I was completely honest, there was a somewhat cynical, financial element to my decision. I had thought I might be able to make some extra money from the book. But in my heart I also knew my intention had never been to cause anyone any hurt. It was obvious that I could not simply state that I planned to sell my whole life without providing some sort of background. The book would provide such detail, explaining how I felt about Laura, and give some insight into how losing her had affected me. I still stood by what I had written as a wonderful story of love triumphing over adversity.

I took the book down from the website, refunded everybody who had bought a copy, and cancelled all access to the material, which was password protected. I wrote an apology to any and all concerned, and published it online. I had been pretty naïve, I realised, about how it might be interpreted, but we all make mistakes and misjudgements at times, and this was one I was going to have to live with. I had done my best to put it right.

I was really surprised about the overall level of interest there was in me, and my reasons for taking this action. Most people seemed to perceive my decision to sell everything to be an extreme response to my situation. I really had imagined most of the interest would be about the lifestyle package that I was offering, not the motivations behind the package. Naïve again, perhaps?

In those early days I was also contacted by several documentary makers, all based in the UK. They all sounded very professional, and a few of them said they would send me discs of some of the TV documentaries that they had produced. It all sounded very exciting.

When I told Dennis at the rug store, he suggested I should talk to a friend of his who was a Perth-based documentary producer.

It was just before Easter weekend, and I arranged to meet up with Celia, whose company had quite an impressive resume of programs that they had produced. We got on pretty well, and she suggested that they were in a much better position to document what was happening, as they were right here in Perth, and could be with me much more than someone from the UK. She also suggested that they would like to start as soon as possible, as some amazing things were happening right now, and they would like to film over the long weekend. An overseas team would miss a lot of the initial early chaos.

I was in two minds about how it would be to have a documentary made about what I was doing. I took a bit of time to think about it, whenever I managed to get a few brief minutes of thinking time between calls and interviews. I quite liked the idea of being the focus of an unusual tale, I must admit, but I also wondered about the downside of always having someone there with a camera in my face.

I spoke again with Celia, and she put my mind at ease, convincing me that they certainly wouldn't be there all day every day. Eventually we came to a tentative agreement that we would start filming over the long weekend, with no formal agreement as to where that may lead. This was something that we would be able to firm up over the following days.

I felt pretty comfortable with the arrangement, and met Britt, who would work as the main cameraperson and interviewer for the documentary. She would also occasionally use another camera team to record material if we went out and about.

Over the weekend Britt was at the house quite a lot of the time, and filmed much of what was going on. She would film me while I did interviews on the phone, and I found that it didn't take too long to forget, at times, that she was even there. Often, at the end of an interview, I would look up to see her filming me from along the corridor, and would be slightly surprised.

We did a lot of face-to-face interview-type of questions whenever the phone wasn't ringing. Britt would ask me a question, but wanted me to resond with the question included in the reply, so that the answers were fully self-contained statements. I found this a bit tricky to remember at first, as all the other interviews simply needed a response to the question. Eventually, with a bit of prompting every now and then from Britt, I managed to get the hang of it.

I really enjoyed the process, and Britt was very easy to get on with. It was quite different from the many radio and newspaper interviews I was still doing, where I found that I was often asked the same, or at least a very similar set of about five questions. I soon heard myself sounding a bit like a parrot, giving the same set of answers to the now familiar questions. I had found ways of expressing these answers that felt natural and comfortable to me, and tended to stick to these, trying some variations every now and then.

After a few days I told Britt I was about to do another telephone interview, and wondered if she wanted to film it? No, she said, as I would probably be saying pretty much the same stuff she had filmed me saying in most of the other interview she had seen me do.

I continued to enjoy Britt's face-to-face interviews, as she asked some fantastic questions, and really got me thinking about a lot of stuff that I hadn't given much consideration to recently. She managed to delve subtly into my past, emotions, motivations, relationships, future plans, and much more. It was quite a fascinating process to go through, and I tried to be fully open about everything. I did wonder in the back of my mind how it all might look when finally edited.

Over the Easter weekend, and during the weeks following, there were also developments in a new and very exciting direction. I had received a few emails from Hollywood production companies and independent producers interested in my story. I had responded to them and given them a contact number, but never really expected to hear any more from them.

My first inkling that there may be some serious interest in the possibility of my story being used as a movie script was a call from a guy in the US called Andrew Panay. I had a long chat with him, and he told me that he was one of the producers of the movie "Wedding Crashers". Oh dear, I am not really a big Owen Wilson fan, but after our chat I did take a look at the movie, and quite enjoyed it. Andrew told me that he was in contact with Walt Disney Pictures, and the President himself there was very interested in the idea as a movie script.

I tried to retain a healthily protective scepticism about the whole thing, but over the next few days I received several other calls form both major studios and independent producers.

One of the more surreal conversations I had went as follows:

Movie Producer (very casually): "We see this project as a Tom Hanks-type of rom-com!"

Me (a quick, tongue-in-cheek response): "Tom Hanks? No, no! I rather saw George Clooney playing me!"

Movie Producer (not picking up on any of the humour in my voice): "Yes, we could possibly make that happen!"

Me (almost speechless with surprise!): "Riiiiiight….."

One of the best contacts I made during those first few weeks was with a guy who specialised in publicity for unusual internet projects. I received an email from Evan, and wrote back when I got the chance. We kept in touch, and eventually, when things calmed down a bit, I gave him a call to see what help he might be able to offer. He told me of his work with Kyle McDonald, who had created an unusual internet project. He had started with one red paperclip, and had swapped it for something else. He swapped the new item again and repeated the process over and over until he eventually ended up with a house. Kyle had just signed a movie and book deal, arranged through Evan, and another of his contacts, a movie agent called Brandon.

Evan, Brandon and I had a conference call one evening, at the point when there were quite a few emails and calls coming in from movie producers and studios. I had realised that if I was at all interested in following up with any of these potential offers, I really needed an agent who knew what he was talking about.

Again, I had spoken to Dennis at the rug shop, and he had suggested I should perhaps speak to an Australian-based representative, and gave me a couple of ideas of people who might be suitable. I eventually got to talk to one of these guys, and was quite unimpressed. He seemed completely confused by what I was doing, and had nothing to suggest other than perhaps selling the story to an Australian women's magazine. I told him about the movie studio contacts and the interest from documentary makers. He said he would think about it over the weekend and get back to me. I never heard from him again, and didn't bother calling him back.

I had a couple of further discussions with Brandon and Evan, and was starting to feel a bit pressured by the documentary makers with whom I was currently working. They were keen to make a formal agreement about the material they were filming. They were obviously inputting a lot of time and effort, and were keen to know that they had an end result to work towards.

I had put them in touch with a UK-based production company that had been interested in my story as an episode of an ongoing documentary series. An agreement had been made between a producer at the BBC and the Australian team about filming the episode for them.

I was quite excited and flattered. I mean, how often is it that the BBC wants you to be the central character of a forty minute documentary? But a problem was becoming apparent. I had spoken to Brandon about the documentary, and he had told me that there may well be a potential conflict between a movie being scripted, and a documentary being filmed.

I considered both possibilities at some length, and spoke to several friends about my dilemma. I was really enjoying the documentary process, and now felt pretty confident that the people making it would do a great job, and would present the story in a truthful and honest fashion. A movie would be quite a different matter, and, I imagined, would end up being far-removed from any of the reality of the story.

But there was one key difference, and a lot of my friends had asked me the same question. "How much would you get paid for each option?" Although my original intentions had been to sell my house and belongings in order to move along to the next phase of my life, there was of course a desire to sell my house for the best price I could get. And if I could maximise that through other options too, then that would give me the best possible start for the next part of my life.

I asked the documentary makers about any possible payment, and actually felt a bit bad about doing so. I mean, what a great opportunity it all was, and what fun too. I was informed that documentaries were never paid for, as it may have an impact on the impartiality of the final outcome. I understood, I told them, but in the back of my mind I thought it did seem slightly unfair. As several friends had also pointed out, everybody else involved would be getting paid – the camera people, the documentary company, the producers and the TV company.

I eventually appointed Brandon as my official representative with regard to any possible movie deal, and felt relieved that he could look after that whole side of the crazy situation. Any emails or contacts that came in about movie deals were forwarded straight to him. I was pretty confident that he would do a good job, as he worked on a percentage basis, and It was in his interests to do the best he could for me.

In the meantime I had worked out another deal with Evan, with regard to publicity for the auction. The publicity campaign that I had initially imagined had been achieved many times over in the first week after the launch of the website, but of course, additional publicity would not do any harm. Evan usually worked on a monthly fee basis, but I explained that I could not afford this, and would really have no idea how effective his work had been, as I had generated such a huge amount of publicity myself

Eventually we worked out percentage-based deal, which would pay Evan on a sliding scale, dependent upon the final price that the auction raised. I was quite happy with this arrangement, as anything that Evan got paid would be out of extra money that I raised over and above my initial hopes and expectations. Evan was very positive about how the auction would go, estimating a low figure of $600,000, but suggesting that $1million could be a realistic possibility. My original target had been $450,000.

Brandon worked with all of the movie contacts I forwarded to him. He informed me that the original contact from Andrew Panay and Disney was looking like the most realistic possibility, but there would definitely be an issue with a documentary being made. I discussed this with the documentary people, and they argued pretty strongly that there was no reason why both could not be made, and would possibly even be beneficial to each other.

I went back to Brandon to argue their case, as I was still keen to make the documentary. He discussed it further with Disney, but eventually came back with the same answer. Disney would not permit a documentary to be made if they were to enter into a movie deal.

I felt caught in the middle of all this, and was feeling a little under pressure. Eventually I decided to take myself out of the equation altogether, and put the documentary people in direct contact with Brandon. A day or two later the documentary people decided that without a formal agreement at this stage they could no longer go on spending money in a speculative fashion, as it appeared unlikely they would end up with a finished program. I understood, of course, but felt that I had now burned my bridges, and hoped that something concrete would eventually come out of the extended negotiations with Disney.

During all of this, the craziness of the on-going media attention continued. I had returned to the rug shop to work, but would spend a lot of time answering my phone, and dealing with one interview request or another. On a couple of occasions camera teams from Australian or international news shows would come to the shop to do an interview, and Jenny, who loved all the publicity, made a couple of TV show appearances too.

I received an email from a producer at the Jay Leno Show in America, and was quite stunned. Now that really would be big time publicity! Unfortunately nothing ever eventuated from that, but a trip to the US would have been great.

I was also contacted by a producer at The Tyra Banks Show. I had never heard of Tyra Banks, and did a little internet research. I was somewhat worried by the content of her shows. It certainly seemed to be targeted firmly at the trashy, sensationalist end of the market! When I next spoke to the producer I raised my concerns, but he informed me that the show was a one-off, featuring people who had decided to make radical change in their life.

I made it very clear that I had never discussed publicly the details of the break-up of my marriage, and would not be prepared to do so on the show. I pointed out that I had only ever stated in any interview that I had made a discovery one evening that had blindsided me, and that our marriage had ended shortly afterwards. With this proviso agreed upon, it looked like I might be heading to New York very soon.

Unfortunately, the producer had left things until the very last minute, and although I was prepared to go on short notice, flights were very expensive. The show's budget would not stretch to that expense and another trip to America fell through.

I was continuing to write a daily blog about what was going on in the 100 days countdown to the start of the auction. Finding the time to do so was a bit of a challenge sometimes, but I knew it was worth it as it would serve as a great diary of these strange and interesting days.

Often I would write about what was going on, but I was always aware that part of the reason for the blog was as a sales pitch for the "product" that I was offering. Often my blogs were therefore about great days out in Perth, the wonderful weather, and the laid-back beach lifestyle.

I continued to receive huge amounts of email from individuals who wished me well, or offered support and encouragement. Probably about 95% of the incoming mail was positive, but there was certainly quite a bit that was very negative too. Some people suggested that I was an attention-seeking idiot. Why couldn't I just deal with my problems quietly like any normal person would, without having to tell the whole world about it? I think many people missed the point that I was not doing this for sympathy, merely in order to sell up and move on. I had simply told the story about how I had reached this point as background, to explain how I had arrived at my decision.

The bulletin boards on the website were proving to be equally interesting. Again, a huge part of it was positive, encouraging and supportive, but there was a small and very vocal minority that were very negative too.

I had one particularly enthusiastic detractor who accused me of being a hoax and a fraud, suggesting that the auction would never happen, and that I was conning the world's media. For what purpose, I wondered, in response? Other people wanted to know the ins and outs of my finances, my personal relationships, and other private details. My reluctance to divulge absolutely every private detail about myself was taken to be some sort of proof that there was some big fraudulent scheme developing here.

I quite enjoyed the negative comments and criticisms, as it gave me a chance to respond to issues that many others must be wondering about too, and an opportunity to show people that all was exactly as I presented it on the website and in the press. But as I was to discover, there really is no convincing some people!! I didn't worry about it too much.

Although I tried to avoid it as much as I could, it was impossible to avoid my private life being dragged into the press. One unusual and somewhat surprising story appeared in the local Perth newspaper. I thought that the Australian press had a bit more integrity than much of the UK's gutter tabloid press, but the article was a bit of a disappointment.

Mel and I had been in a relationship for about a year by this point. We had met over a year after my separation, and enjoyed a pretty easy-going relationship. I was often asked if I had a current partner, and never really answered directly. Firstly, Mel did not want to have any part of the publicity, and secondly, I believed that any current relationship was nothing at all to do with the sale.

However, one local reporter did not see things that way, and went and did some digging, quizzing colleagues at my skydive club. The article that was written was not very positive, and suggested that the "heartbroken" man selling his life on eBay was perhaps not all that heartbroken after all, as he was in a happy relationship. What was not pointed out was that this was now two years after my separation.

On the bulletin boards, my favourite critics picked this up as proof that all was not right here, and that if I was lying about this, what else might I be lying about? I decided to address the issue head-on, and linked directly to the article myself, pointing out that a couple of years had passed since my marriage had ended. I asked how long I was supposed to wait until I began looking for a new partner, and some new happiness in my life. Also, after some discussion with Mel, I pointed out that our relationship had not quite been the blissful union that the news article had suggested, and that we had in fact now separated. Mel had eventually lost patience with my lack of commitment to the relationship, and had decided to move on. I really didn't like having to make such personal matters public, but had to be somewhat realistic, and accept that this was part of the down-side of all the publicity.

After a few weeks the publicity died off a little, and things started to return to some semblance of normality. A couple of friends from the east coast of Australia had moved over to Perth to start new careers in the mining industry, and they stayed with me for a few weeks. Another friend from the UK came and stayed for a while too, as he visited several companies with a view to getting a job in Australia, and moving over with his family to live here. It was nice to have some visitors that were also making some huge changes in their own lives, who understood my position and actions, and offered plenty of encouragement and support.

In the calmer days after the initial craziness died away, Mel and I made up and got back together again. We had discussed our relationship, and what being together again might mean. I had been at pains to point out that I really didn't want anything too serious or involved, and hoped to keep things very much on a casual, friendly basis. Mel seemed happy to agree to such an arrangement, and a little sense of normality returned to life as things settled back into some sort of routine, and I resumed my duties at the rug shop.

I was still doing occasional interviews, answering the same set of questions that I had been asked hundreds of times before. In most interviews the series of questions was very predictable, and my answers had become pretty automatic. This generally is what I would be asked:-

"Can you tell us what you are doing?"

"Why have you decided to do that?"

"How much do you think it will all sell for?"

"What will you do afterwards?"

"What do friends and family think about it?"

Sometimes there would be other questions included, such as why my wife and I had separated, or what she thought of the whole idea. Another favourite was about how I could sell my friends. I was always very keen to explain that I had never, ever said that I was selling friends. I was simply offering, as part of the package, an introduction to a wonderful circle of people who would be prepared to offer a warm welcome to a newcomer.

I must have been getting a bit too comfortable doing these interviews, as I really enjoyed it when something a little different happened. I really enjoyed the breakfast radio show type of interview, where there would be a panel of two or three presenters, and laughs were their main aim. They were much more challenging, and a lot more fun. You really could have anything thrown at you, and had to be pretty quick on your feet with a snappy answer.

It was the fourth question on the list that always gave me the most difficulty. I had been asked so many times in interviews and on the ALife4Sale website forum what I thought I might do once I sold my life. I didn't really have an answer, even for myself. My usual glib response was that I would be able to do anything I liked!

But in the back of my mind, I wondered what it was that I really would like to do. One day I was chatting on the phone to Evan, the US-based internet publicity guy. He suggested that after the auction, when I came out to LA, we would go skydiving together, and he would show me what his city had to offer.

"Great," I had said, "but I guess that depends on how the finances look, and where I am working at the time."

"Work?" said Evan. "No, no, no! You don't understand! This is your chance to never have to work again!"

"Well, I like your thinking Evan," I replied, "but I haven't got a clue what you're talking about! How would I do that?"

"Well, you have to come up with a follow-up project. Something that is internet-based, is quirky and interesting, that follows on logically from what you are doing now, and most importantly – and this is where your money comes from – has a book deal in it!"

"Righto. Sounds good. So what is that then?" I asked.

"I have no idea, that's up to you, buddy!" Evan had laughed.

"Hmm, okay, I'll get to work on it."

This advice sat in the back of my mind for the next month or so. People continued to ask in interviews what I planned to do next, or where I intended to go, and I always answered that I still didn't really know. All I knew was that I wanted to do some travelling.

One day on the "ALife4Sale" website, a forum contributor called Tess had asked if I had any sort of a "life-list", or set of goals. I did have an old list somewhere that I had written out a few years earlier.

Not long after I had searched unsuccessfully for my old list, Mel and I spent an evening together at her house, and were well into our second bottle of wine. I could still remember many of the goals from my original list. I told her with enthusiasm about many of the things that I had always wanted to do or see. I estimated that out of the list of 100 things I wanted to achieve in my life, in five years since I had written them down, I had only ticked off perhaps six of the goals. That obviously wasn't going to work. If I maintained the same rate of achievement, I was going to die one day with the larger part of my list still incomplete.

In one sudden flash of wine-fuelled inspiration, an idea came to me. As soon as I sold my life, I would set off to achieve all of the things on my list. I would re-write a list of 100 goals, and give myself a time limit. And there it was, almost fully formed, the idea for my next two years – 100 goals in 100 weeks.

As soon as the idea flashed across my somewhat inebriated mind, I thought, "That's it!!" It perfectly filled Evan's criteria, and it would be incredibly exciting to do too. I knew immediately that this is what I would be doing next. My future was looking very exciting indeed.

However, in my excitement, I didn't notice Mel's crest-fallen look, and when I look back on this occasion, I can only imagine the hurt I must have caused.

Mel, as always, supported and encouraged me. She threw herself into designing another new website, cataloguing the goals, designing search options, setting up blog, photo and video pages, and much more.

As I added text to each of the goals, and background to the reasons behind my choices, I became increasingly excited and focused on making this all become a reality.

For almost as long as I can remember, I have always had goals, even when I never fully grasped the importance of doing so.

When I was very young, I can remember watching a documentary about Ernest Hemingway, a writer born in 1899. He lived a full life, settling in different locations for several years at a time to write, and then moving on. Inspired by his visits to Spain, in 1926 he wrote his first novel, "The Sun Also Rises". When the documentary covered this part of his life, it showed quite a lot of footage of the Running of the Bulls in Pamplona. I can clearly remember sitting and watching those people running wildly through the streets with bulls thundering around among them, and thinking to myself, "I'm going to do that one day!"

When I told my parents they smiled and wished me luck. They were always supportive of anything my brother or I wanted to do, but I don't know if they believed I would ever do it.

As I started to gather my list of 100 goals, including things I have always wanted to do, and places I have always wanted to see, I thought of that day, probably over 30 years earlier. Of course, on the list I started to make, running with the bulls at Pamplona went right at the top!

There were many other things that I had often said I wanted to do, but had never managed to find the time to get around to doing. It was time to put that right. Once everything sold I would have little to tie me down, and hopefully plenty of cash from the sale. My list of goals started to grow.

Chapter 3

The Auction

My idea was to break the news of my goal-achieving new plans just as the auction finished, with publicity at its highest. I would hopefully kick-start my new adventure in fine style.

As the end of June approached, the press interest began to increase again. By the time the auction started, I had stopped working at the rug shop again in order to ensure that all went smoothly with the sale, and to complete work on the 100goals100weeks.com website.

However, the start of the auction didn't quite go according to plan. I had been contacted by eBay, who had seen some of the publicity about the auction, and had allocated me my own personal eBay rep. Matthew was there to help me with any issues that may come up, and his first requirement was that the sale be listed under "Real Estate", as the house was the major asset included in the whole "life" package.

This meant that the eBay auction could only offer an introduction between buyer and seller, as house sales were covered by many different laws in each state. Ultimately any final bid would not be binding on either the buyer or the seller. This sounded great to me, as eBay could therefore not charge an end-of-sale commission, and the total cost to make the listing online would be a mere $49.95.

I asked how we could deal with the potential problem of fake bids, and Matthew suggested that we set up the sale as a "Registered Bidders Only" auction. Anybody wanting to bid would have to answer whatever questions I cared to ask, and I could choose who would be allowed to bid. This would enable me to weed out people who looked like they may not have made any sort of arrangements to have finances in place, or considered whether they would need any sort of visa to come to Australia. Anyone from abroad would, as a minimum, have to at least be familiar with the requirements of the Foreign Investment Review Board.

Out of the hundreds of potential bidders, I imagine I rejected about a third, mainly because many of these had made no sort of plans should they be the winning bidder. I thought I had every eventuality covered.

On the morning that the auction began, many friends came round, and there were a few bottles of wine, and even one of champagne too. There was a wonderful celebratory atmosphere, and at noon Mel and I set the auction in motion! Matthew had told us that once the auction had started we would be able to switch on the "Registered Bidders Only" option, and Mel said she would do this as I raised the first of many glasses in celebration.

A short while later Mel asked me to join her. She couldn't get the option to switch on, and at the moment it was a bidding free-for-all. Bids were already at over $100,000, having started at just $1 only minutes before. The “Registered Bidders Only” option didn’t seem to be available, but I said that it shouldn’t be a problem, as I would just give Matthew a call. Ah, but eBay help was only open during working hours on Monday to Friday. It was now just after noon on Sunday. We tried the online help system, and Mel struggled for a while, messaging back and forth with a help rep somewhere else in the world. She was told that the option had to be turned on *before* the auction started, and couldn’t then be selected afterwards.

No problem, I had said, I would just speak to Matthew on Monday morning and get the issue resolved. I suggested that Mel should join me with the others happily downing the cheaper wine now that the champagne had been consumed.

By mid-afternoon bids had reached around $350,000, and I confidently predicted that they wouldn’t go any higher now. By the time we went to bed the top bid was $650,000.

I had to be up very early the next morning for a TV interview, and with a couple of spare minutes, I decided to take a look at the auction’s progress. I was absolutely astounded to see a bid of $1.9 million. As I sat there in amused disbelief, the screen refreshed, and the bid was now $2 million. Laughing to myself, I shut down the computer and headed for the TV studio.

By the time I was interviewed the bids were at $2.2 million, and I was asked what it felt like to become an overnight multi-millionaire. Let’s all just stay calm here, I had suggested. I hadn’t had a chance to check out the veracity of these bids, and had no guarantee that they weren’t fake. I explained the issues we had had with the registered bidders fiasco.

Later in the morning Matthew resolved the issue, and together we looked at the bids. He explained how I, as the seller, could access full details on any bidder, including home phone number, and I got to work.

I made several amusing phone calls that morning, including one to the aunt of a fifteen year old lad in England. Was he there, I wondered?

“No, he doesn’t live here,” she explained in a broad Geordie accent. “He only uses this number because he doesn’t have a phone of his own.”

“Right,” I sighed. “He has been bidding on a rather expensive item on eBay. Does he often do that?”

“Oh yes, he often buys stuff off the internet.”

“Okay, would he be in a position to pay over two million dollars?”

“What? What do you mean?”

“Well, his current bid in a pretty high-profile auction is $2.2 million. If he doesn’t follow through, I imagine it will be your door that the world’s press will be knocking on shortly!”

“Eeee! I’ll kill the little bastard!”

And so it went on. Eventually, I had weeded out all of the idiots, and cancelled all of the bids that looked in any way suspect. By mid-Monday morning we were back on track, and the top bid stood at $150,000.

It had been fun to be a multi-millionaire though, even if it was only for a couple of hours.

The rest of the auction week was equally incredible and entertaining. There were live TV interviews first thing every morning, and radio and newspaper interviews for the rest of the day. There was a wonderful sense of build-up to the finale, and friends would call round regularly to see how things were progressing.

I arranged a party for the Saturday evening, as a "thank you" to all my friends who had supported me over the previous months. On the morning of the final day of the auction, the house was an absolute mess.

With Evan's help in LA, we had set up a live video feed from the house, and were streaming the last hour or so live over the internet. By 11:30am there was a house-full of friends, many still there from the previous evening. We were live online, had two TV news crews setting up gear in the living room, a Japanese TV crew filming everything that was going on, and a helicopter circling overhead looking for a place to land.

After the initial drama of the $2 million-plus bids, the auction had progressed in a much more sensible fashion. The current high bid was $399,300, just a few dollars short of my unstated reserve price of $400,000. I was hoping, as often happens on eBay, that there would be a final flurry of bids in the dying seconds of the auction, and the price would be pushed up a bit higher.

The clock ticked past noon, and the auction was over. My computer was being fed through the projector onto the large screen on the living room wall, and I refreshed the eBay screen, eager to see the final bid.

Nothing changed! I hit refresh again, and realised that there had been no further bids. The final price was still $399,300, which was just below the valuation of the house alone.

I couldn't believe it. Even with all the worldwide publicity, I hadn't been able to get a bid at the bottom end of the house valuation!

The TV crews were eager to capture my reaction, and I tried to hide my disappointment. Yes, I still intended to sell, and move on, I told them. After all, I now had a list of 100 goals to tackle!

But there was worse to follow. Over the next few days I struggled to get any response from the high bidder, and the ultimate result was that the purchase fell through. And of course, according to eBay's real estate terms and conditions, there wasn't a thing I could do about it. In a couple of interviews I theorised about why this might have happened. Perhaps, like many people, the top bidder had expected the bidding to go much higher, and never expected, or even wanted to be the winning bidder at under $400,000.

Even after the next five bidders had been contacted, I could not finalise a sale. Out of the top six bidders, five were from Australia, and one was from the States. Each eventually came up with a reason why they couldn't or wouldn't follow through on their bid.

Despite all of my best efforts in vetting all potential bidders, I now had no buyer. I had publicly stated that I was going to tackle my list of goals, but with the house still carrying a reasonably big mortgage, it looked like I wasn't going to be able to follow through with my grand plans.

What do I do now, I wondered?

I already had plans in place for the first few months of travel that would follow the auction, and needed to set off in early August. Now without a buyer, all was uncertain again. Could I afford to go without selling the house? What would I do with all the furniture, and the vehicles? If I didn't go, what would I do then?

I considered the possibility of renting out my house prior to my initial departure on my two-year journey. The problem with this plan was that any rent would have only just covered the mortgage I had to pay, leaving me with no monthly costs, but also giving me no net income either. It would also mean that in order to travel, I would have to borrow against the equity I had built up in the property. As I spent this, my mortgage would increase, and I would eventually be paying out more to service the loan than the rent would bring in.

If I was going to set off on my journey, the only real option was to sell, hoping for a quick sale.

But with spectacularly bad timing, my eBay auction, and subsequent planned departure on my travels had coincided almost exactly with the deepening global financial crisis starting to be felt across Australia.

Mel left Perth a couple of weeks after the end of the auction for a long summer with family in Europe, and we said a sad farewell at the airport. Her two girls were very tearful, and I said I might see them soon in France if things worked out. Mel simply told me not to make any promises to the girls that I wasn't certain that I would be able to keep.

PART 2

100goals100weeks

Chapter 1 – Weeks 1 to 10

(3rd August 2008 – 12th October 2008)

Australia – Dubai – France – Italy – Spain
England – Germany – Austria – USA

In the first few days after Mel's departure I fell into a bit of a depression. I really did not know what to do. I missed Mel terribly. I found that I hadn't realised how much I had come to count on her for support, advice, friendship and encouragement. She had become an important part of my life, and I felt a bit lost without her there to speak with.

I wondered a great deal about my decision to take on a challenge that would initially mean I would get to spend a few weeks of summer in Europe with her, but would ultimately take me away from her for months on end.

Mel and I had built an easy-going relationship over the past year, and got on very well together. I was pretty sure that Mel wanted to take our relationship a step further, but there was still something inside me that was not ready for total commitment.

I had managed to re-discover some personal happiness, and since separating from Laura two-and-a-half years earlier, I had once again become the independent, self-confident person I had been before and during my marriage. I had also been happy to live on my own, in order to come to terms with the huge change that life had thrust upon me. I wasn't yet ready to settle down again.

When the idea for attempting 100 goals in 100 weeks had developed, I hadn't really thought too much about how this might affect Mel's feelings. I was excited about the possibilities that the journey offered, and in my excitement, had paid little notice to how Mel reacted when the idea came to me.

However, now that the eBay auction hadn't ended as expected, I still had a house and a mortgage, and all the house contents to deal with. In those last weeks, after Mel left for Europe, I grappled with wavering indecision about what to do.

If I went, things would be very challenging and uncertain financially. If I stayed I would miss out on what would probably be the biggest adventure of my life. If I waited six months or a year, and then set off, I would not have the same offers of assistance that I had received via the website from all around the world.

I knew that if I did not go now, I probably never would. If I didn't book that first flight, I thought to myself, I had a pretty good idea of what my future would hold. I'd settle back into life in my house, settle down to an easy-going life with Mel, and probably get another job driving trucks in a mine! Nothing would have really changed, and putting my life up for sale would have achieved nothing!

If I took that first flight my future would be unwritten.

Eventually I snapped out of my dark mood, made my decision, and started to put some plans into action.

Once the decision was made, the excitement was back, but along with it there was a terrible trepidation about some of the difficulties I might face. My first destination was Dubai, and I had no idea how I would cope there.

I put the house on the market, and many of the house contents up for sale. As long as I could get rid of the car, there was enough space in Mel's garage to store the rest of my stuff. The real estate agent was still hopeful of getting the estimated price for the house that he had originally quoted, even though the current global financial issues were starting to have an adverse effect on the Australian property market.

I spent two frantic weeks packing and tidying, boxing up things that I didn't think I would be able to sell in time. The car sold just days before I was due to fly, and for my last couple of days I rented a large van. With the help of my friend Andy, I moved my remaining possessions into Mel's garage.

On my last evening in Perth I stayed with my friend Em, and her boyfriend Simon. They made a lovely meal, and we shared a bottle of wine. Em asked me how I felt on the evening of my departure, and I struggled to explain the weird feeling of unreality that filled me.

It seemed very much like the time when Laura and I had sold most of our possessions in England before moving to Australia. It was sad to get rid of things that had personal meaning, but in the frantic rush to get everything done in time, there was a strange sense of disconnection.

The last fortnight had been endlessly busy, and had just flown by. There had been so much to do, that the huge scale of the journey upon which I was about to embark didn't often sink in.

Somehow though, I managed to do everything I needed to do, and on the evening of Sunday 3rd August, Em and Simon dropped me off at Perth Airport for my overnight flight to Dubai. Also there to wish me well were friends Marty and Carol, and their newborn girl Maxine.

I felt a strange mixture of sadness to be leaving such good friends, excitement and anticipation about where my journey might take me, and a vague uneasiness about potential problems I might face.

The next morning I landed in Dubai, caught a bus to the city centre, and another out to the youth hostel I had booked for two nights.

Things fell into place easily. The youth hostel was nice, with a lovely warm swimming pool, and Dubai city centre itself was easy to get to and to find my way around. I wondered what I had been worried about.

First goal achieved! Ski Dubai
Tuesday, August 5, 2008
(Dubai, United Arab Emirates)

Well, we're off to a flying start, only two days in, and the first goal has been completed successfully.

Today I caught the bus out to Mall of the Emirates, where SkiDubai is situated. What an awesome place. I met my friend Mark from Perth at the entrance as planned. We had a quick chat, and he headed off for his ski lesson. I paid for two hours on the slopes, and was issued with jacket, trousers, boots and board. Once dressed, I headed straight for the chairlift.

The first couple of runs were a bit shaky. It's been almost three years since I was last on a board (how has that happened?), but it soon started to come back.

The place is pretty big, with a four-seat chairlift, and a single drag-lift too. I had a few goes on the chairlift, but found the drag to be a lot quicker, so managed to fit quite a few runs in.

I thoroughly enjoyed myself, and for a while it was possible to forget that it was over 40°C outside!

Finally I reckoned my time was up, but nobody was checking tickets, so I went for "just one more run". About half an hour later I had to call it a day, as I was meeting friends Jeff and Socorro at 4pm, and was now running late. I got changed very quickly, and dashed off to meet them.

A great indoor snowboarding experience – it certainly beats the old Catterick Army Garrison dry ski slope where I first started learning as a kid.

One goal down, 99 goals left to go!!

I really enjoyed the experience of the huge indoor ski slope, and was immensely proud to have achieved my first goal. I had set off on my journey, despite the difficulties presented by the failure of the eBay auction to result in a sale.

I had also overcome the fear of setting off into the unknown, and was now doing exactly what I had said I would, tackling a list of all the things I had ever wanted to do.

But alongside the pride, there was an overwhelming sense of the hugeness of the task I had set myself. I had achieved one goal, but I had 99 more to go, and two years of travelling ahead of me!

Socorro had contacted me via the 100goals website before my journey began, and explained that she and her husband Jeff were expat Americans living in the United Arab Emirates. They would love to host me there, she had said, and show me around. They met me at the ski slope after my two-hour session, and we drove out towards Abu Dhabi.

I was very touched by such a wonderfully kind offer from people who were complete strangers to me, and I wondered what had prompted them to reach out and offer to help me. They had followed the eBay auction with interest, they told me, and were impressed with my choice of what to do next. They simply wanted to help out, and show me their adopted homeland.

What a fantastic opportunity too. It was very interesting to see the country through the eyes of people who had lived there for several years, and had an insight into the history and the culture.

I found it fascinating to hear their stories of how things worked there, and how different it was to the two countries in which I had lived.

Dubai and Abu Dhabi had turned out to be nothing like the huge challenge I had anticipated, and it was a shame to have to leave, as there seemed to be so much more to see. But my next flight was booked, and I stopped over for half-a-day in Istanbul in Turkey. I was relieved of ten dollars for a tourist visa, which apparently was necessary if I wished to leave the airport. Somewhat suspiciously, this could only be paid in cash! It was worth it though, and Istanbul certainly looked like somewhere to come and take a look at with more time on my hands.

I arrived in France and met with Mel and the girls in Nice, staying with her father in the hills above the beautiful city. It was wonderful to see her again, and the time we spent together was just like a European summer holiday.

The first French goal to address was the enormous bungee jump over the spectacularly deep Verdun Gorge. As we approached the bridge I could feel butterflies of excitement in my stomach.

Mel just looked ill. Despite her fear of heights, she had impressed me by deciding to do the jump too.

Second goal completed! Bungeeeee....
Sunday, August 10, 2008
(Verdon Gorge, France)

We got up pretty early this morning and drove up into the mountains to the north west of Nice. The journey became more and more spectacular the higher we climbed. We passed through beautiful little French villages, and stopped at a boulangerie for a breakfast of fresh bread and croissants.

We finally arrived at the Gorges de Verdon, where the view into the deep valley was pretty daunting. We rounded a corner, and there was the bridge, Le Pont de l'Artuby. It is an incredible place, with a worryingly deep gorge below the bridge.

Crowds were already gathering, and jumping was in progress. My stomach felt a bit queasy. Melanie was looking decidedly pale.

We queued and booked in, discovering that we would have to wait over an hour to jump. We drank coffee at the little café at the end of the bridge with trembling hands, awaiting our turn. It was a long hour and a half!

Finally our turn came, and I was called to gear up. I was feeling pretty good by then, but as I took photos of the guy before me making his jump, my hands were shaking. Finally I climbed the steps and stood on the edge of the bridge, having told myself not to hesitate when they counted "Un, Deux, Trois..."

It was an incredible experience. In many ways it was a bit like a parachute jump - the sudden, smooth acceleration, and the increasing wind-noise as speed picks up - but visually very different. In a parachute jump you never see the ground that close, coming up to meet you so quickly - if you did, something would have gone horribly wrong!

By the time I returned to the bridge, Melanie was ready to go. She climbed up onto the edge of the bridge, and jumped without hesitation.

Fantastic - well done!

The rest of my time in Europe with Mel turned out to be just as much fun. We took a trip into the countryside, where in the small village of Lourges we met up with my cousins Christine and Mike, and Christine's family at a beautiful villa they were renting for the week.

From there we headed up into the Alps, camping for a couple of nights in the beautiful mountain town of Chamonix. We then drove through the mountains into Italy, where we camped again, and dived into the third goal on my list.

Third goal completed! Cristo Degli Abyssi

Sunday, August 17, 2008

(Portofino, Italy)

From Chamonix we drove through the Mont Blanc Tunnel, 17 kilometres long, and came out on the other side in Italy. What an amazing feat of construction!

We arrived in Santa Margherita Ligure at about 5pm. I had imagined it would be a small quiet fishing village nestled on the coast, with perhaps a few tourists wandering around. How wrong I was!

The place was absolutely packed! Cars, bikes, mopeds, cycles and pedestrians all jostled for space in the tiny streets. It seemed like utter chaos! We drove around for some time, but could not find a parking space anywhere. Every conceivable place to park a car was full, as were several places where I would not have thought you could even fit a car. Every other space not big enough for a car was filled with mopeds and scooters.

We tried up a side street, which quickly turned into a twisting road up into the hills, far too narrow to turn around to come back down. We eventually found our way back to the coast, and finally found a space into which we could cram the car. The guy in front of whom we were parking looked very nervous, and actually came out of the shop to move his car a bit to avoid tragedy!

We went and introduced ourselves to Luca at DWS Diving, and got directions to a campsite, which was apparently "almost full". When we arrived at "Miraflores Camp Site", hidden away in an industrial estate, they managed to cram us in on a gravelled patch down at the back of the park. Later that evening, despite being "full", we saw them manage to fit in four more tents and a huge caravan!

To say it was the worst campsite at which I have ever stayed would be a major understatement. We were relieved of 22 Euros for a patch of gravel about ten metres from the freeway that ran alongside the campsite. We had to pay extra for a card to access a hot shower.

The place was jam-packed full. And it was in the middle of an industrial estate. There was a small swimming pool, proudly advertising "Free Entry", but that was locked up before we even had our tent set up!

The only thing the place had going for it was its small restaurant – there was nowhere else to go – they had a captive audience! They did a pretty good pizza, and wine by the carafe was very cheap. There was nothing else to do but hope that enough wine would help overcome the freeway noise!

We drank a fair amount, and began to find the whole campsite experience quite entertaining – it was so bad it was good. After dinner we took a walk through the industrial estate, admired the local petrol station, and then had an early night.

We were glad to pack up and leave early, and headed off to the dive shop. There we geared up and climbed aboard the boat, which took us along the beautiful mountainous coastline.

There was a bit of doubt among the dive crew about whether we would be able to do the dive that we wanted, because of sea and wind conditions. We hassled them a bit, explaining that we had come to see the "Cristo Degli Abyssi" statue, and no other dive would do.

When we got to the site conditions turned out to be fine, and the dive was on! We jumped in, and spent about forty minutes swimming around the coastline.

At the end of our dive, in about ten metres of water, we came upon the three-metre-tall bronze statue of Christ. He gazes up towards the surface, arms spread wide, as if in invitation to join him in the depths. Swimming down towards the beckoning figure is quite surreal indeed.

It is quite breathtaking and beautiful. I was very satisfied to see it at last. I first saw a picture of it in a diving magazine when I was a child, and thought, "One day I will go and see that!" Well, today was that day!

On the boat trip back I am sure I had a big smile on my face. I could see that Mel did.

Back in Nice, Mel's dad put me in touch with the local paragliding club, and I booked in for a three-day introductory course.

Things seemed to be going very well, and so far everything had gone according to plan. I was only two weeks into my journey, and was already booked in for the fourth goal.

Once again, I was surprised at how easy it all seemed, and how much fun I was having.

Fourth goal completed! Paragliding in France
Tuesday, August 19, 2008
(Gourdon, France)

Today was the second day of my paragliding course in Gourdon, in the south of France. I started first thing on Monday morning, along with five other French guys.

Gourdon is another spectacular French village, perched high on a cliff top, with an incredible view overlooking Nice and the Mediterranean far below. This morning I arrived with time to spare, and walked up into the village itself. Because it was still early, there wasn't another tourist around, and I wandered alone through a village that seemed to be from another century.

We practiced on the nursery slopes again in the morning, and then after lunch we headed up the hill to the top. We were all a bit disturbed by both the height, and the strength of the wind. But after watching a couple of others take off, as the wind died a bit, we were ready to go.

When it came to my turn I took off pretty much as we were taught, and was soon soaring over the ground far below. I received instructions through my radio, and followed the flight plan, landing triumphantly five minutes later, away down the hill.

It was a great experience, although over pretty quickly. Because there were constant instructions and things to think about it was hard to take in the view and the experience fully, but I am going back for more tomorrow!

It is very different to parachuting, as the paragliders are much more responsive to small braking manoeuvres, and are designed to fly further and stay up longer. It was quite disturbing to be so close to the ground at times, but not to be within a second or two of landing.

Without the help of the instructors I imagine I would have overshot the landing area by a significant amount, as my approach would have been way too high!

What a wonderful experience! I will certainly be trying this again.

It was hard to say goodbye again to Mel, and the free-wheeling holiday came crashing to an end when we discussed what the next six months of travelling might mean for our relationship.

During the year-and-a-half I had been with Mel I had never made any promises, and had always been honest about how I had felt. I had been upfront about not really wanting to settle down, and that I didn't necessarily feel that I even wanted to be in a long-term relationship.

I still missed Laura incredibly, and although I knew it was wrong to do so, I compared relationships. For reasons I couldn't quite put my finger on, I didn't feel that my relationship with Mel would ever mean quite as much to me as my relationship with Laura had.

We had had the same painful discussion on several previous occasions, when Mel had indicated a desire for more from me. I had had to tell her that I didn't think I loved her, certainly not in a way that I had felt love before.

But one night as we had travelled together in France, we had made love, and basking in the warm afterglow, I had told her that I loved her. When we parted, and I explained that as I travelled I wanted to consider myself single, my earlier declaration just made things more difficult.

As I caught the early morning train out of Nice, heading for Spain, our farewell was sad, and slightly bitter, and I didn't know when, or even if I would see Mel again.

I spent many hours staring out of the train window as I headed south, wondering if I had just made a huge mistake, wondering if I had maybe lost the one thing that I should be trying to hold on to. I never came to any sort of conclusion.

In Spain I met up as planned with Paula, one of my work colleagues from the rug shop in Perth. We had a couple of days in Barcelona, and then made our way down to Valencia, where I was planning to stay with my second website-invite hosts.

I felt a little awkward asking Graham if it was okay to bring another guest along to his family home, but he was kind enough to extend his invitation to Paula for an evening.

Once again, I was curious to know why Graham had made such an extraordinary offer to a complete stranger, but when he showed me his home office space, the posters and notes on the walls quickly provided the answer to my question.

Graham was a very goal-oriented person, and this had also filtered down to his children. He thought it might be interesting to see what impact my visit might have on his family. He also thought it would be fun to help me achieve, and also join in on my next goal.

Fifth goal completed! Tomatina!
Wednesday, August 27, 2008
(Bunol, Spain)

Yesterday I bought a couple of items that would be invaluable for today. The white t-shirt was a bargain at 2 Euros, and the waterproof camera would be very useful.

We set off in good time for Bunol, about thirty kilometres from Valencia. We found a place to park the car, even though there were many more arriving all the time. Graham and his daughter Maria were my companions on this goal, and we walked down towards the centre of the town with the growing crowds.

The atmosphere was very festive, and there was an excitement in the air. The closer we got to the centre of town, the denser the crowds became. We continued to worm our way through towards the centre square. It was packed there, the crowd was surging back and forth, and there was still almost an hour to go before the official start at 11am. It didn't look like I would be able to find Paula and her group in the seething masses.

The town centre was a lot more closed-in than I had imagined, and the narrow streets were packed full – it was almost impossible to move anywhere, and in the surges I lost Graham and Maria. I eventually made my way into the square just off the street. I found a bit of space for myself a couple of steps up off the street, and eventually managed to bag a great vantage point on a wall.

The atmosphere was electric, the crowd was singing and chanting, TV cameras were perched on many of the rooftops, and a helicopter circled around. From my vantage point I eventually spotted Graham and Maria, who weren't far away, and kept an eye on where they were in the surges as the excitement mounted.

At 11am there was a big bang to start the celebrations, and tomatoes started to rain down from people on the rooftops and balconies.

Before long a huge tomato-filled lorry made its way along the packed street, and people aboard it threw tomatoes in every direction. The crowd went wild! Watching the lorry drive through the packed street where a minute before it was impossible to move, I wondered how nobody would be run over.

The lorry was the first of six to pass through the centre, and each one caused an increase in the tomato throwing frenzy. When the fourth lorry tipped up and emptied tons of tomato semi-puree into the streets the scene took on incredible new proportions, the air being filled with a red haze of tomato juice and semi-pulped tomatoes. It was amazing and hilarious to see.

The wall was not the best place to stand, as I felt I stuck out a bit as a target. When the Irish guy in front of me, who was acting as a great shield, gave up and jumped into the crowd, I soon gave up and followed suit, re-joining Graham and Maria.

Eventually we made our way right into the centre of the melee, and found ourselves wading ankle-deep in tomato juice. It was incredibly packed, and as the crowd moved towards the edge of town it was impossible not to be swept along with everyone else. At times it was possible to simply lift up your feet and be carried along.

There was another big bang, and the hour-long food fight was over, but that did not seem to slow anyone down one bit. Eventually we got to a less packed area as the crowd thinned out, and we happily made our way back up the hill out of town.

What an amazing experience! It is well worth going, but one word of advice I would give - take some cheap, but sturdy shoes, and be prepared to lose them. Flip-flops are not the best footwear, and I eventually ended up barefoot - it seemed much safer - although my toes are pretty bruised!

After a quick visit to Madrid, Paula and I flew to London, where my brother Martin and partner Rachel collected us at Gatwick airport. Paula headed back to her home in the city, and I spent a relaxing few days at Martin and Rachel's house in Ealing, just to the west of London's busy centre.

While here I received an extraordinary offer that would allow me to achieve my next goal in fine style, and at almost zero cost.

Did I want a free trip to Paris, home of the Eiffel Tower, one of the goals on my list? I had a train ticket booked within hours!

Goal number 6 completed! Eiffel Tower

Friday, September 5, 2008

(Paris, France)

Well, things took a surprising turn just a few days ago, when I got an email from a company which offers assistance to other companies exhibiting around the world.

Philippe from EIE Global wondered if there was anything his company could do to help me with my goals. He explained that his company specialised in solving problems and overcoming challenges, and suggested that they may be able to help me with some of the challenges I would face in the coming months.

Of course I was interested, and wrote back saying so. We spoke a couple of times, and Philippe suggested that we could possibly meet in Paris, and his company would cover the train cost from London. Would I be able to come over?

"Hmmm, let me think..." I thought to myself. "A free trip to Paris, and I can complete my Eiffel Tower goal on the same trip!" Heck yes, when do I set off?

It's just over two hours from London to Paris on the EuroStar, and I arrived on Thursday afternoon. I had a long chat with Philippe, who kindly offered me accommodation for the evening too. He lives in Fontainebleau, which is a beautiful place. We went out for dinner with a few of his staff, and stopped to take a quick picture outside the amazing Chateau de Fontainebleau.

The next morning at 10am I was at the foot of the Eiffel Tower, at the place I had specified a day or two earlier on the blog. I was accompanied by a different Philippe, one of the EIE staff I had met the previous evening. We were also joined by a website contact, Emmanuel, who came along to climb the tower too.

It was a bit rainy, but we decided we would still climb the steps as planned, and off we went. You can only climb so far, then have to queue for the lift to the top. The views of Paris were magnificent.

It was very strange really, as this was the first time I had ever been there, but it all sort of seemed so familiar. I guess I have seen it in movies and pictures so many times before.

So, much earlier than expected, Goal Number 6 completed, all thanks to my new friends at EIE Global!

I took the opportunity to spend an extra day in Paris, and was keen to meet with another contact from my website. Stephen is an Irish expat, living in Paris with his wife Tiazza, originally from Morocco.

Once again, I was very flattered that a complete stranger would reach out and offer to help me, having seen a news article about my eBay auction, and then taken a look at my 100goals website.

I was thoroughly enjoying meeting so many new people, and was finding that staying with people who actually lived in the places I was visiting was a wonderful way to travel. I really liked seeing a city in a very different way, on a much more local level than I had ever done previously when staying in hostels or hotels.

I decided that I wanted to continue in this vein as much as possible, seeing as much as I could through the eyes of locals, rather than as a backpacker passing through as a cash-strapped tourist.

Back in England I made my way north in the nippy little Peugeot 205 GTi that my brother would usually lend me whenever I returned to England. I stopped off to visit my cousin Christine and family again, now back home from their French vacation.

A free day there with Christine's daughter, Eleanor, resulted in a very entertaining afternoon. Did I want to go and see the Abbots Bromley Horn Dance, she wondered?

Of course I did! I had no idea what the horn dance involved, but Eli's description of an ancient tradition, strangely garbed dancers, old reindeer horns, and beer drinking was too good to be true.

One of my philosophies about this whole journey was to try to experience as much as possible, and in a way I looked upon the list of goals simply as a framework around which to construct a big adventure. My idea was to try to accept as many invitations and suggestions as possible, and open myself to new situations and experiences at every opportunity.

The horn dance was certainly unlike anything I had ever seen before. It was like some strange ritual from a bygone era, with the participants dressed in clothes that made them look like they were ready for a medieval banquet. There was lots of clashing of reindeer horns, and the earnest seriousness of the participants made the whole thing hugely entertaining.

Like many other quirky British events and traditions, the day ends in a headlong dash for the pub. Meeting up that evening with Christine and her two other children, Matthew and Owen, we headed back to town and joined the dancers in the streets, beer in hand.

The next day I continued north to see my mum in Darlington, where I planned to confront a childhood fear for my next goal.

Goal Number 7 causes a bit of a splash!
Sunday, September 14, 2008
(Darlington, United Kingdom)

I am back here in Darlington to put right something that I did not dare do as a youngster. As kids we used to take the bus from Barnard Castle to the bigger town of Bishop Auckland, where they had a great swimming pool, with three diving boards. I used to love the excitement of the jump off the top board. I also used to dive from the lower and middle boards, but never managed to work up the courage to dive from the scary top board.

I was hoping to return home, and finally make the dive off the top board at Bishop Auckland swimming pool, but that is out of the question, as there are no longer any diving boards there!

So this morning, after a false start on Friday afternoon (my friend couldn't make it), I did the next best thing, by going down to the Dolphin Centre, which has a similar set of boards to the ones Bishop Auckland used to have, including the all-important 5m board.

I did a practice dive off the 3m board and then went straight up to the top board. I was hoping that it would now look a lot smaller to me as an adult, and I was planning to march confidently to the end and dive in without hesitation.

But oh dear, it looked just as big and daunting as it did in my childhood days, and there was an element of dithering around on the edge as I plucked up courage. It really was like being a scared child again.

Eventually I launched myself off, and the dive sort of went okay. My top half entered the water pretty cleanly, but my thighs slapped the water a bit. I think lack of confidence had caused me not to dive at a steep enough angle.

There must have been a bit of a splash, because as I climbed out, the lifeguard asked, "Are you okay mate?"

"Yes thanks," I wheezed. I had only hoped to have to do this once, but I was not happy with my performance. I told my friend Notty, who was there to take a couple of photographs of the momentous occasion, that I was going to have to try again to do it properly.

The second time I managed a much more graceful dive. I dived off confidently with no hesitation, and I felt that I entered the water much more smoothly. I felt very proud, and immensely relieved too.

Did I go for another try? No way! One successful dive was all that was required. I had finally done it, and that was enough for me.

Within ten minutes we were across the road in the Boot and Shoe with a pint each. Sunday morning, not even half-past-ten yet, and the pubs are already busy - it's great to be back in good old Darlo!

Heading south again, the feeling of being on holiday was stronger than ever. I stopped off with friends Sie and Marie on the east coast at Whitby, and continued on to my old home town of Scarborough.

This was my second return home since my marriage had ended, and as I had the last time, I found it very emotionally challenging. I had met Laura here on the beach in the summer of 1993, and in 1996 she had spent the whole summer living with me there. The next year, as she finished college we moved in together permanently, and had shared three wonderful years together before finally marrying in November 2000.

The town was filled with memories of the wonderful years we had spent together there, and at every turn I would be reminded of the part of my life that had been stripped from me.

I stayed in Scarborough with my best buddy, and previous business partner, Bruce. He had suffered a similarly traumatic loss himself a couple of years before Laura left me, and we wistfully compared notes.

"Maybe you only ever have one love like that in your life, and maybe you are lucky to have experienced that," suggested Bruce over drinks one evening.

I didn't feel particularly lucky. That night, after a long evening in the pub, left alone in the kitchen when Bruce staggered off to bed, I leant drunkenly up against the kitchen worktop and cried quietly and sadly. Maybe I would never feel that sort of unconditional love ever again.

I crammed a lot into my last few days in England. In Scarborough Bruce and I took his son Tyler to see the spectacular motorbike racing at Oliver's Mount, and reminisced about the days we used to race a sidecar together. I caught up with friends in Bridlington, and down in Cheshire my pal Mark took me for an awesome flight in his microlight.

Back in London I played golf with Martin and Rachel, and repacked, preparing for the next leg of the journey.

As the day of my next flight approached, I felt the trepidation return, stronger even than when I had prepared to leave Perth. At least then I was heading for Europe and England, where friends and familiar places waited for me. This time I was setting off for a five month period during which I probably wouldn't see a single person that I already knew.

It was starting to feel very uncomfortable to consider forcing myself to step back out of my happy English comfort zone, and fly to Germany, then on to the USA.

On my last morning in England I voiced my discomfort to my brother, and he tried to make me feel better, pointing out all the positive aspects of such an adventurous trip. I was also worried about the potential loneliness, and I'm pretty sure he knew this. I was grateful that he didn't mention it.

This is what I wrote at the time, but eventually decided against publishing on the blog:-

1st October 2008 – I have been in the UK for a full month now, which has all been very familiar. I was picked up by Martin at Gatwick, travelled the UK in his car, and visited lots of family and friends. It has been just like a big holiday really.

But this morning, I completed packing my bags, ready to set off. This time there is nothing familiar ahead, nobody at all that I know, possibly for several months! Again I feel that sick feeling of awful trepidation, and voice my concerns. I think Martin might have an idea of how I feel, and says, "Yeah, but it will all be a big adventure too, won't it?" I know he is right, but I feel sad at leaving.

This travelling thing is weird. Looking ahead, it can seem quite ominous, daunting, difficult and challenging. But looking back afterwards, it has been such fun, filled with such amazing experiences, wonderful people, and great places. I have to try to remember this as I look forward. This journey is certainly causing me to step out of my comfort zone again and again. And in doing so, I am certainly experiencing things I wouldn't otherwise.

Some part of me still wonders about the point of all of this. I still miss Laura a lot, and think of her frequently when alone. She is my travel buddy, and without her, this all has a horrible hollow ring to it

In the beautiful German town of Friedrichshafen, after a nice day of easy travelling, I booked into a cosy little hotel. I was looking forward to the next day in Munich, meeting a few new people and achieving another goal. Munich would be fun, I thought, and I was definitely looking forward to New York. But there was still that apprehension. Will it ever go, I wondered?

Goal number 8 – Prost!
Thursday, October 2, 2008
(Munich, Germany)

"Prost" is German for "Cheers", and I have said it more than a few times today, as I achieved Goal Number 8, by attending the Oktoberfest in Munich.

I arrived in Munich shortly after lunchtime, and soon found my way to my hotel, which was only a couple of minutes walk from the station. I was a bit too early to check-in, but could wait in the lobby, where I checked my email, and waited to meet Christophe, from the German magazine "eBay!", and his photographer, Marcus.

When they arrived we talked for a while, and eventually I managed to check-in. I left my bags in my room, which had seemed reasonably cheap when booked on the internet, but turned out to be a broom cupboard somewhere in the bowels of the hotel near the carpark!

We set off for the Oktoberfest, and it was good to have a couple of local guides, although I did take note of the route we took, as I suspected I may be coming back on my own, and perhaps a bit less sober!

They took pictures, lots of them, for their magazine article, and eventually Christophe had to leave. Marcus and I wandered about a bit more, and had a beer - after all, that's what this goal is all about - and eventually he had to go too.

I wandered around a bit more, had a few more beers, and met quite a few very friendly, very drunk, people from all over Europe. I visited quite a few of the beer tents, but they were nothing like I had imagined. I thought they would be pretty basic, perhaps with a bar at one end, and a few tables. They were HUGE! Each tent was immaculately presented, with a well organised system of tables and reservations. In fact, it was pretty difficult to find anywhere to sit, and if you weren't sat, it was pretty difficult to order a beer!

However, once I got to grips with the system I was quite at home, and enjoyed myself to the full.

I came out of one beer tent, after chatting to several German guys for a while, and discovered that it had started to rain. I weaved my way back to my basement room, after stopping for a quick bite to eat.

Goal number 8 completed in fine style, and I still have several more days here yet!

Despite the copious quantities of beer available at Oktoberfest, or maybe because of it, I faced further emotional challenges in Munich.

Later on that first evening, eventually heading back to my hotel on my own, I was feeling very lonely. On my way from the festival I stopped off in the big church just outside the festival grounds.

I am not a religious person, but find these buildings fascinating, always somewhat mystified at the comfort many people seem to find there. I sat alone feeling sorry for myself, crying drunkenly again, and suggested that if there was anyone there, maybe now was the time to offer some help. What was the point of all this? Without Laura, without someone with whom I could share these amazing experiences, what was the point? Anyone there? Any answers? Nothing!

I tried to capture my feelings, recording my thoughts on my mobile phone. Those recordings make very uncomfortable listening now, as I hear the pain and loss and loneliness in my voice. There is a longing for that love again, a desire to be able to feel it with Mel, and an awful incomprehension of how I could have ended up in this situation.

I weaved my way sadly home.

I felt much better the next day, and looked forward to meeting with my friend James from Australia, who I had just discovered was also in Munich for Oktoberfest. I was also planning to meet a couple of girls from Chicago who had contacted me through the website, and were also going to be in town.

That night, with Diane and Dawn, we met up with an entertaining group of English beer enthusiasts, and had an excellent evening.

I asked Dawn my now-usual question about what had prompted her to want to meet up with a random internet stranger, and why she had contacted me.

"Because I get it," was her simple answer.

When I asked her to elaborate, she told me she had also gone through a marriage break-up, and had just wanted to sell everything and leave. She said she completely understood what I had done, and why.

We had more than a few beers, encouraged by the group we were with to enjoy the festival to the full. I spoke with the English lads a bit, and was very amused to find out that most of them had heard of the guy in Australia who had put his life up for sale on eBay.

Later that night, as I weaved my way home, my face ached from laughing so much. It had been a great fun-filled evening, and I was starting to feel much better again about travelling.

The next morning I was collected from my hotel by Peter, an enthusiastic German guy who had wanted to meet up with me, and join me for a small part of my travels.

We got on pretty well, and had a shared interest in paragliding, and all things flying-related. When I asked him my question about his reasons for wanting to join me, this was part of it, but he also seemed to genuinely just want to help me out, and show me his country.

Where did I want to go, and what did I want to do, he had asked me before we met?

One of my favourite movies is "Where Eagles Dare". My father used to love old war movies, and we watched loads of them together when I was young. Some of these are still among my favourites, but "Where Eagles Dare" is definitely in my all-time top ten!

It stars Richard Burton and Clint Eastwood, in a tautly scripted thriller with several intriguing plot twists and turns. Most of the story takes place in the aptly named "Schloss Adler – The Castle of the Eagles" high in the Alps, which is an amazing-looking place.

During the ALife4Sale period, in the run-up to the auction, I had watched the movie again on DVD, and was interested by the "making-of" documentary on the disc too.

When I started compiling the list of the 100 goals I would like to achieve, I offered readers of the blog the chance to suggest and select some of my goals. I had already chosen 95 goals, and opened up the selection of the last five to anyone reading my website.

From the hundreds of suggestions I received I chose twenty possibilities, all of which I was very enthusiastic about. Visiting Hohenwerfen – the real Castle of the Eagles, in Werfen in Austria – was one of the final twenty. Unfortunately when these twenty were voted on, this one did not make it to the top five, which were added to my list to make the total up to 100.

The actual final five which received the most votes were:-

Whitewater rafting

"7 Peaks in 7 Days"

Ride an ostrich

See an active volcano

Spend a night in a haunted house – alone!

When Peter had wondered where I might like to go, I had studied a Google map and found out that Werfen was only a couple of hundred kilometres away. I thought it would be good to go and visit the castle anyway.

Peter had driven for a couple of hours to get to Munich, and seemed more than happy to drive us on to Salzburg in Austria, and then on to Werfen. The castle was quite majestic, towering over the small village, and the dramatic theme tune from the movie played over and over in my head as we toured the spectacular fortress.

We stayed in a small hotel nearby, and the next day visited a spectacular ice cave high in the mountains, before our return to Munich. It was inevitable that we finished our journey together back in one of the large tents at the beerfest.

I was delayed for over four hours in Amsterdam, which meant I arrived later than expected in New York. By the time I figured out the trains to get to my ultimate destination, it was about 10pm, which for me was the equivalent of 4am the next morning back in Europe.

Lilly lives in Long Island, and had emailed to offer me a place to stay with her and her family while I visited New York. When I arrived at their local station her husband Leo picked me up, and at their house I met Lilly herself, and their kids Nicole, Chris and Leo Junior.

We chatted for a while, and they invited me to join them for dinner the following evening to celebrate Leo Junior's birthday.

The next morning I was up early, the jetlag refusing to allow me to sleep any longer, and I headed into the city. Emerging from Penn Station in the centre of New York, buildings towered all around me, and one of the first places I spotted was the Empire State Building.

Above the sidewalk the US flag waved, backlit by the sun rising to the east, and I marvelled at the view. "I'm in New York! In America!" I laughed to myself happily.

Despite never having been before, the whole place had an air of familiarity about it, almost as if I had walked onto the set of a movie. I had seen these familiar streets and iconic buildings so many times on TV shows and in movies.

Inevitably, my random city wanderings took me to Central Park, and eventually back towards Penn Station via Times Square. Here in the huge Disney Store, I bought a present for Leo Junior's birthday.

That evening we all went out for dinner, and I enjoyed my first-ever Long Island Iced Tea, on Long Island! Leo was very excited about his high-powered rocket kit.

Lady Liberty – goal number 9 achieved!

Thursday, October 9, 2008
(New York, New York, USA)

Stephanie emailed me a week or so ago, about meeting in New York, as she wanted to come along when I went to see the Statue of Liberty. She is, or was, a New York local. She now lives in Connecticut, and she gave me a few tips on other things I might like to do while in New York. One of her suggestions was to walk across the Brooklyn Bridge.

So Lilly and I and the three kids were up early and headed into the city on the Long Island Rail Road. We took the subway downtown and under the East River, getting off at High Street in Brooklyn. The walk across the bridge was another experience that had a very familiar feel to it, almost as if I had been here before. It was a beautiful autumn day, and we strolled across with the other tourists, with plenty of time on our hands.

On the Manhattan side we headed south down Broadway, and made our way to the Liberty Island Ferry, where we met up with Leo. Across at Liberty Island we met up with Stephanie by the flag pole as planned, and after introductions all round we went up into the statue pedestal.

The statue is huge, very impressive indeed, and all the more amazing when you look at pictures of the construction, transport and completion of the giant project in October 1886. The view of Manhattan from the pedestal is fantastic, but it's a real shame that it is no longer possible to go up to the crown itself.

Eventually Leo, Lilly and family headed off home, and after a quick walk around the base of the statue, Stephanie and I headed back into Manhattan. After something to eat we went to the World Trade Center Tribute Memorial, which was very moving. We were both very quiet for a while afterwards.

Next stop was the Empire State Building, and we arrived at the observation deck just after dark. It was breathtaking to see the city spread out far below, lit up just like in the movies!!

Finally Stephanie suggested seeing the Rockefeller Centre, where the often-featured-in-movies ice skating rink can be found. It is great having a local guide.

Stephanie headed off for Grand Central Station, and her train home, and on the way back to Penn Station I detoured through Times Square, which looked wonderful at night.

What a brilliant day. I love New York.

I was very flattered that Lilly and her children had come along, happy to join me as I achieved one of my goals, and had chatted to them all throughout the day.

They were fun to hang out with, and they really seemed to enjoy themselves. Later the next day, I chatted with Lilly's husband, and he told me that Lilly had been telling him what a great time they had all had. Leo told me that initially it had only been Lilly who had wanted me to come and visit. He hadn't ever really expected me to show up, and when it became clear that I was coming, he had been somewhat concerned about this stranger coming to his house.

He told me, however, that when I had produced a present for Leo, he had thought to himself that this guy actually seems okay. I was flattered once again.

But I was most flattered by Lilly's 17 year-old daughter, Nicole, who made a candid comment as I was leaving. "When my mum told me you were coming, I did not want you in my house at all," she told me frankly. "I had to force myself to come and say hello on that first evening when you arrived. But after the wonderful day we had in the city, I am so glad you came. It was such fun, and we don't usually get to do things like that. It has been great to have you visit."

I was very touched.

I was collected in the city by Linda, who drove us through the Lincoln Tunnel into New Jersey. Linda had been following my story on the ALife4Sale blog, and when she spotted that I would be heading her way for one of my goals, had offered to help out.

She had also spotted that during the three month run-up to the ALife4Sale auction, I had become a little obsessed with New Jersey-based mafia TV series The Sopranos. I had managed to squeeze in the whole boxed DVD set of six series of the show before the auction began.

She had arranged a tour around many of the filming locations used for the show, and we started immediately on exit from the tunnel where we joined the New Jersey Turnpike.

We saw many locations from the opening credits of the show, and had lunch in a fantastic little diner under a railway bridge that had featured in one episode. But the highlight for me was going to Satin Dolls, better known as Tony Soprano's unofficial headquarters, go-go bar "Bada Bing".

I was surprised to find it actually was a real go-go bar, and it looks almost exactly as it does in the series! Linda suggested that we could go in if I wanted, and there was no holding me back.

The interior was dark and noisy, semi-clad girls danced on the stage, and beer-swilling customers threw dollar bills. We walked right round to where Tony usually sat, and ordered a beer from the scantily dressed waitress. Sat in Tony's seat was a burly-looking guy who was obviously the manager, dealing with a couple of the girls, a wad of bills in his hands! Brilliant!

He just laughed when I asked if I could take a photo inside! "No way, buddy!" Hmm, I thought not!

That night we went for dinner with Linda's brother and his wife – eating Italian, Sopranos-style of course – and later I got to meet Linda's husband Brian, a tough, no-nonsense New Jersey cop who had just finished his shift.

We chatted for a while, and instead of the hotel I was expecting to go to, I was invited to stay in the spare room.

Goal 10 completed! Kingda Ka
Saturday, October 11, 2008
(Six Flags Great Adventure, New Jersey, USA)

We planned to be at Six Flags New Jersey early this morning, but after a bit of a mix up with the tickets, and a return back to the house to collect them, we got there a bit later than we planned.

It is a holiday weekend, and it was also a beautiful sunny day, so the crowds were out. We went straight to Kingda Ka when we got there, but the queue was already 90 minutes long!

Eventually we got to the front of the line, and had to join another small queue to get the front seat.

When the car set off the acceleration along the flat section at the start was incredible, followed by a fast steep climb up to the summit, which is 456 feet tall. The car slowly rolled over the top, and accelerated vertically down again. The ride publicity says that speeds of 128 mph are reached. It certainly felt fast!

The whole ride was over quickly, but it was a pretty intense experience.

We spent the rest of the afternoon in an endless series of queues for other big rides. There were some good ones, my favourites being Superman, and The Great American Scream Machine. Eventually we couldn't be bothered with the queues any more, and called it a day.

I had reached the end of my first ten weeks, and I had completed ten goals. I was on target, and had started to feel much happier in myself. Travelling was proving to be much easier than I had thought it might be, and I had met some wonderful people so far.

The next few weeks were very much unplanned, and I only had one date firmly booked, three weeks away, in Oklahoma. But despite this vagueness, I was now looking forward to the challenges ahead with a much more positive attitude.

Chapter 2 – Weeks 11 to 20

(13th October 2008 – 21st December 2008)

USA

Before leaving New Jersey, Linda took me to the bank to try to open an account. At the time I was withdrawing money from my Australian funds using my ANZ bank card. The problem with this was that each time I took money out, I would get hit with a fairly hefty transaction fee. I would also lose out a little, because the exchange rate the bank offered wasn't always as good when withdrawing cash at an ATM.

A US bank account would mean that I could just do one big transfer, as the exchange rate from Australian Dollars to US Dollars was very favourable, at a fantastic high of 97 cents.

But in the bank, it was clear that my idea was going to run aground quickly. I had to be resident in the state of New Jersey, we were told by the bank's customer service assistant.

"You can just use my address," suggested Linda. Ah, but that wouldn't work, we were informed, as I would have to have some sort of bill at that address in my name. Or perhaps a bank statement, the customer assistant suggested helpfully!

"Oh, what if I had a cheque, payable to me, posted to this address?" I asked. No good. I hoped I was going to really need a US bank account soon, as I was hoping that I would have a big cheque to deposit in the next few weeks.

Brandon, my Hollywood agent – I always laughed when I told people I had a Hollywood agent, as it just sounded so ridiculous – had recently told me that Walt Disney Pictures was going to buy an eighteen month option, which could be extended by another eighteen months if they wished, for a further payment. The option would simply mean that they had secured the rights to the story, and I wouldn't be able to sell it to anyone else. It didn't guarantee that a movie would ever be made, but I was to be fairly well paid for the option.

If the cheque ever came through, and it did seem to be taking a while, then it would pay for most of my travels in the States, and perhaps a bit more too.

I had also asked Linda about registering a vehicle in New Jersey, as I planned to buy something to get me across America. No chance, she thought, without a New Jersey licence. Since the terrorist attacks of 9/11 security was so much tighter, and it seemed that as a non resident, things were going to be more difficult than I had imagined.

In Australia, it is a very simple process to buy and register a second-hand vehicle no matter what your nationality. You can even use a backpacker's hostel as your address for registration purposes if you are travelling.

I eventually gave up on New Jersey as a banking base and motor vehicle purchase location, and assuming that things would be much easier and freer in Canada, bought a ticket for the Greyhound bus.

Goal 11 achieved! Niagara Falls

Wednesday, October 15, 2008

(Niagara Falls, Ontario, Canada)

I arrived on the Greyhound bus in Toronto at about 10pm on Monday, and walked to the backpacker hostel in the city centre. Once booked in I made my bed quietly in the dark, as there were already two people asleep in my room, and then went downstairs for a quick beer.

The next morning I got up, leaving my two room-mates still sleeping, and I met up with Jordan, who had contacted me through the website, offering to show me around Toronto. I checked out of the hostel, threw my bags into the back of Jordan's pick-up, and we were off for a quick drive around downtown Toronto.

The city reminds me very much of Australian cities, not too built up, fairly relaxed, and the people seem very friendly. After some lunch we headed for the CN Tower, which dominates the city skyline. At the main observation deck, I was fascinated by the glass floor sections. To be able to stand on a clear floor and look straight down is very unnerving.

We went higher to the SkyPod, which is the highest man-made viewing platform in the world, at 447m (1,465ft) above the ground. The view is awesome. It was amazing to watch a plane heading directly towards the tower below us, and then turn and land on the runway by the shore.

After descending from the tower, we went for a quick Steam Whistle, the local beer brewed in an old railway turning shed almost right below the CN Tower, which Jordan reckons is the best beer in the world.

We then picked up Jordan's girlfriend, Rachel, and headed for Niagara Falls, around an hour's drive from Toronto, arriving there after dark. I was absolutely amazed to find that the town of Niagara Falls is something like I imagine a mini Las Vegas to be. There are huge hotels, nightclubs, entertainments and attractions, and two big casinos.

When I thought about what I had expected, I had imagined the edge of the falls would be forested, with a scenic drive through the trees leading to a big carpark and visitor centre. Jordan and Rachel were very amused by both my expectations, and my surprise at the garish modern reality.

We went for dinner first, and then headed for the falls. The falls themselves are floodlit at night, and look pretty large, but it is hard to get any sort of perspective in the dark, although the noise gives some impression of the power of the falls.

After a bit of a flutter in the casino we booked into a motel for the night, went back out for a few more beers, and eventually got to bed at around 2am. Really not quite what I had expected of a visit to Niagara Falls, but great fun all the same!

In the morning we went back down to the falls to have a look in daylight, and when I actually saw them I was awe-struck. They really are quite something to see. It is possible to walk right by the edge of the horseshoe section of the falls, and watch the water cascade over the edge right beside you. Very impressive indeed.

My assumption that Canada would be much easier-going in terms of vehicle registration proved to be mistaken. My revised plan was to perhaps buy a campervan, or RV, in Ontario, and then use it to travel down through the States. If all went according to plan, I would eventually head up the west coast before Christmas, and cross back into Canada again, where I could sell the vehicle at the end of the journey.

I even got as far as finding a suitable-looking vehicle on the Toronto section of Craigslist online adverts. It was a mid-sized camper that had done a bit of travelling, and was reasonably priced. It was owned by a Swedish girl who was now back at home, and had left the vehicle with a friend in Canada. She seemed very keen to sell, and I imagined I could get the vehicle for a bargain price.

I started to do some research. My first call was to the Department of Motor Vehicles, who informed me that in order to register a vehicle I would need both insurance and an Ontario driving licence. Okay, no problem, I thought.

I rang a couple of insurance companies, but discovered that with an Australian driving licence, it was going to be difficult to get cover for both Canada and the States. Maybe things would be much easier if I had a Canadian licence issued in Ontario?

I rang the DMV again and asked how I would go about getting an Ontario driving licence. Apparently I would actually have to take a practical driving test, and even worse than that, I would have to give up my Australian driving licence. That was completely unacceptable, as it had my truck driving qualifications attached to it, and I planned to possibly use it again when next back in Australia.

Eventually I decided to give up on the idea of making a purchase in Ontario and caught a Greyhound again, heading for Chicago, start point for Route 66 across America.

In Chicago I stayed with Diane, one of the two girls I had met in Munich at the beerfest. She lived a short distance out of the city, and was easy to find, as her home was close to one of the L stations, Chicago's elevated train network.

In my first couple of days there I started to get myself organised. My first port of call was the local bank, and I was amazed when a friendly manager told me that there would be no problem at all opening an account for me.

I explained that the address I was staying at was just a friend's place, and that my bank card, when ready, may have to be forwarded on to another address. No problem at all apparently. We did all the necessary paperwork and I handed over the $25 minimum requirement to open my new account.

However, I did run into one surprising, and very disappointing issue. I needed to transfer some money from my Australian account to my new US account, as my Disney cheque was still tied up in contractual red tape. I had decided that around six thousand dollars would be enough to hopefully buy me a vehicle, and pay all my expenses until Disney came through. Six thousand Australian Dollars would get me almost the same amount in US Dollars, I thought, as AU $1 was worth US 97 cents the last time I had checked – an all time high, and the perfect time to exchange some money.

But I was amazed when the bank manager told me that AU $6,000 would only get me US $4,000. Surely he had made a mistake? I asked him to check again, and discovered that the exchange rate was now only 67 cents to an Aussie Dollar. What? How had that happened?

In order to end up with the US $6,000 I figured that I needed, I would have to exchange $9,000. I appeared to be $3,000 out of pocket, and had no idea why.

I checked online later, and discovered that only two weeks earlier the Australian Reserve Bank, in response to the much slower housing market caused by the global recession, had lowered interest rates by a full one percent. This had had the effect of devaluing the Australian Dollar against all other currencies worldwide.

This news made things look much bleaker financially for me. I was still paying a mortgage on an empty house. The value of the house seemed to be falling all the time, and house sales in Perth were at an all-time low. There was no sign of a buyer, and now, even if I did manage to sell, the interest on a much smaller capital sum was going to be significantly less. Also, measured in US Dollars, any reduced capital sum I may eventually receive would only worth two-thirds of the value it had a couple of weeks earlier.

There was nothing I could do though, and I bit the bullet, transferring $9,000 to my US account.

My next task was to see if I could register a vehicle in my name if I bought one. I looked online, and found that vehicle registration is handled by an office under the control of Secretary of State Jesse White, a friendly and efficient chap, judging by the look of his website.

I found the address of the office in the city, and when doing some city centre sightseeing, dropped in to ask some questions.

What would I need, I asked, in order to be able to register a vehicle in Illinois? "You need the title documents from the previous owner, and then you just fill in this form, get it stamped here, and pay at that window over there."

What about my Australian licence? "That's fine, no problem at all, sir."

Will I need to have insurance sorted out? "You do need insurance, of course, but we don't need to see it. You can fill in details in that section there if you wish, but you don't have to."

"So just let me get this clear," I said, wanting to confirm what I had just been told. "I just have to pay the registration fee, that's all?"

"Yes, you pay the money, we give you a set of licence plates, and off you go."

This was all sounding suspiciously easy, compared to the challenges I had faced with US and Canadian beaurocracy so far.

With practical matters seeming to be under control, I could relax a little and enjoy some time in Chicago. Diane and her friend Linda took me to my first major ice hockey game, where local team The Blackhawks beat the visitors from Vancouver.

I toured around the city on the L, enjoying the view of the towering buildings from the loop of elevated track which runs through the city centre. Unfortunately it rained on my first day in the city, and the top of Sears Tower was shrouded in mist. I would have to wait for a better day to take in the cityscape from the top.

I met Aileen in the city one evening, after she finished work. She had contacted me through the website, keen to show me around her city. It was cold in the afternoon, and I was relieved when she finally found me. I jumped enthusiastically into the passenger seat of her warm car.

She took me out for drinks to a wonderful bar high up in the John Hancock Building. The view of the darkening city was awesome, and we had a few drinks before heading off for dinner. Later on Aileen took me for a tour of her local neighbourhood, affectionately known as Boystown, due to the huge number of gay bars there. We picked one and went in for a drink, and a game of pool, and were entertained by a camp transvestite singing and dancing competition.

Laughing in the bar that night with Aileen, and some Irish flight attendants we had got chatting to, I told her that it is just such random evenings that make this whole trip so much fun. That morning I had no idea who Aileen was, but by 11pm I was in the campest bar I have ever experienced in my whole life, in downtown Chicago, with a whole new group of entertaining friends! I was enjoying Aileen's company very much.

The next day I did some serious RV shopping, and Diane drove me out to Franklin Park to view a large vehicle that looked like it might suit my needs. It was quite old, built in 1986, but was in great shape.

The current owner had bought it from an older couple, the original owners, who had had the vehicle for twenty years and had used it very little. It still had less than 40,000 miles on the clock. The tyres looked original, and were in pretty poor condition, but otherwise the vehicle seemed very sound.

We haggled a little, and I left a deposit, having secured my new home and transport for a bargain $2,800.

The next day I returned and paid the balance for the RV, and collected the keys and paperwork. That evening I went out again with Aileen, and we bumped into friends of hers at a little bar. They invited us along to a concert the next evening. Chicago was certainly turning out to be a fun city to spend a week in, and Aileen was a fun guide to have.

Back at the vehicle registration office the next morning, I approached the counter with some trepidation, expecting that the paperwork would prove to be much more complicated than I had initially been led to believe. However, everything went exactly as described. I paid my money, and left the office with a brand new set of RV licence plates in my hand.

At the "Secret Machines" gig that night I felt very happy. I had my vehicle, and had managed to find an insurance company that would insure me on an Australian driving licence for a very small extra premium. Aileen and I had grown quite close, and with my arm around her, watching the group on stage, I felt a warm glow of contentment.

On the Saturday Diane had invited me to join her on a big afternoon and evening out in the centre of Chicago. Halloween was fast approaching, and this year would be the 28th celebration of the Annual Tavern Tour. Hundreds of people would be dressed in costume, and I wondered what I should wear.

In England, and in Australia too, most people tend to dress in scary fancy dress for Halloween. There are always plenty of ghosts, vampires or zombies. Here in Chicago it seemed that any sort of costume would do. At the store I decided on a doctor's outfit, complete with stethoscope. But I couldn't resist the fake blood, and bought some of that too, splattering it liberally down the front of my hospital blues.

The afternoon and evening was great fun, and we had plenty of beer. I set myself the challenge of getting photographed with at least three naughty nurses, but could only find other doctors. There were at least eight other doctors on the pub crawl. Throughout the evening I did eventually manage to find a couple of nurses too.

Towards the end of the night I had lost Diane, and was happily dancing in a pub with a couple of the female "doctors" I had met throughout the course of the day. On a trip to the bar I got chatting to Heather, who had only popped out for a quick beer with a friend, and wasn't in any sort of costume. She was lovely, and very chatty, and we talked and laughed for a while. Somehow, and I am a little vague about how it happened, I found myself kissing her.

We went on to a quieter place, as she hadn't yet eaten, and talked some more, and as I had probably missed the last train back to Diane's apartment, Heather offered me her sofa.

We talked a lot through the night, lying together on her bed, kissing occasionally, but things never went any further. I really liked her, and was a little sad that I hadn't met her earlier in the week. I also felt a little guilty about Aileen, but I was pretty sure that both Aileen and I knew we were just enjoying each other's company as I passed through.

The next day I hung around with Heather for a while in the morning, and then headed back to Diane's, where I packed my bags. It was about time to begin my journey across America.

I thanked Diane, and went to meet Aileen again, staying at her new little apartment for my last night in Chicago. What a week I had had.

I waved a sad farewell to Aileen at the railway station, and laden with more bags than usual, I waited for the train. Aileen had given me a large pillow, some sheets and a towel, and a few other practical items to make the RV a little more comfortable.

I had enjoyed her company and friendship, and as I gazed out of the train window, I thought that this whole journey was going to offer a few challenges like this. I was certainly meeting some wonderful people, and making some great new friends. But the very nature of the challenge I had set myself meant that I was always going to have to move on from these new friends within a short period of time.

I hadn't really anticipated that aspect of the journey. I knew I might never see many of these people again.

At the vendor's house the RV started reassuringly easily. I had only driven it once around the block, and hoped it would perform well as I began my next goal, heading for the California coast a couple of thousand miles away across Route 66.

Within ten minutes I had taken a wrong turn, not the best start to the journey! I had to backtrack a few miles to find the highway I wanted. A map book, or maybe a GPS, was going to be my next high priority purchase.

The first day of driving went very well. I began to enjoy seeing America from the highway, as I headed south and west, down through Illinois. As is always the case when driving a newly-purchased vehicle, I listened carefully to the engine, and watched the temperature gauge, hoping that no hidden problems might start to show a few miles from the vendor's house. All seemed good, and by the end of the day I was in Springfield, Illinois, where I parked for the night in the Walmart carpark.

I had been told by a few people that you could park overnight at most Walmart stores across the States, but it seemed that I was the only RV in Springfield that night. I checked with customer services, and they happily pointed me to a quiet corner of the carpark, where I settled in for the evening.

I spent a cold first night in my new home, and made a concerted effort the next morning to figure out how the propane-powered central heating unit in the RV worked. I also bought a good supply of groceries, and got the gas fridge working too.

My other significant purchase was a cheap GPS unit, which I fiddled with, entering the next address on my itinerary, a little detour off route into Indiana.

Goal number 12 has been inked into place!

Wednesday, October 29, 2008
(Ellettsville, Indiana, USA)

The drive from Springfield out into Indiana took a bit longer than expected, and it was mid afternoon before I found my way to Ellettsville. The Magellan GPS did its job well, when I finally figured out how to use it, and I gave Josh a ring for final directions to his shop.

Josh owns and runs "Eternal Ink Tattoo", and he had kindly offered to help out with my tattoo-based goal. I had a very faded tattoo of a lion's head on my left shoulder, originally done when I was in my first year at college. It was now over twenty years old, and no longer looking its best.

Josh looked pretty much as I expected he might, a bearded, tattooed, Harley-Davidson biker-type guy. He greeted me warmly and took me into his shop. We chatted for a while about travelling, tattoos, guns, and life in general, and we seemed to get on very well pretty much straightaway. We seemed to have a lot in common in terms of both experience and outlook.

Josh had a couple of ideas with regard to covering the tattoo with something new. After some discussion, and a lot of leafing through his artwork, I picked another lion's head, but quite a bit bigger and more elaborate than my previous one. It would cover the old one very well, was Josh's expert opinion.

I took a seat and Josh went to work. It's a bit painful, but not too bad, although after half an hour or so I did ask how much longer it was likely to take. The job was finished within an hour. I have to say that the final result looks WAY better than the old tattoo, although when I look at it in a mirror my initial reaction is surprise, as it is quite a bit bigger. I'll get used to it soon though, I imagine.

As I was preparing to leave Josh and Taryn's home, I heard Josh whispering to his wife in the corridor outside the living room. "It's up to you," I heard Taryn say. "It's yours to do with as you wish."

Josh came in to the room, saying that he had something that he would like to give me, and told me the story behind the object that he held in his hand.

"Many years ago, I once lost someone that was very significant in my life, and for a long time I felt lost, with no direction. I too decided to travel for a while, and ended up in South Dakota near the Pine Ridge Indian Reservation, where I met an older Indian lady.

"After telling her my own story," he continued, "she handed me a ring with a peculiar design on it. She explained the meaning of the design, which she called "The Man in the Maze", and told me I had to find my path in life with the help of others around me, both physically and spiritually. Listening to her story and advice gave me the inspiration to pursue my own dreams. Ultimately that led me to what I do now – tattooing.

"Even after I finished my degree, I decided that this is what I was going to continue to do. Several years later I met my beautiful wife, and on the day I met her I took the ring off. For those years that I had been lost, it had represented for me my search for meaning, for my path through life. When I met Taryn I knew that I had found what I had been looking for.

"I don't need this ring anymore, I have been with Taryn for ten years now, and we have four beautiful children and a fantastic life. After discussing the idea with my wife, I have decided that it is time to pass on my ring to a new owner. I want you to have it, as I get the feeling that you are a bit lost, and are looking for your own path through life."

"I hope you would like to wear it. I also hope that one day you feel ready to take it off, and eventually pass it on to someone else when you no longer need it."

It was without doubt one of the most personal and heartfelt gifts I have ever received, and I was very touched. I put the ring on, and it fitted perfectly on my right middle finger, next to my dad's wedding ring on my third finger.

"I hope I do get to pass this on one day, and I promise I will let you know when I do," I said sincerely.

On the drive westward back towards St Louis in Missouri to resume my trip on Route 66, I thought a lot about Josh, and the gift he had given me. I have always tried not to judge people by their appearance, and think I manage to do this fairly well. Josh represented to me once again why this is so important. At first sight, he looks very imposing – a tattooed, shaven-headed, muscular biker – but you could not hope to meet a more friendly, considerate and thoughtful guy.

I stayed in another Walmart carpark in St Louis, and in the morning my trusty new GPS took me directly to the Y98 radio studio, where I was booked in for an early morning interview.

The radio show was fun to do, and the atmosphere was very casual. There were a couple of presenters, and after a chat we took some calls from listeners too.

I had a wonderful day in town, and particularly enjoyed the St Louis Arch, an incredible piece of engineering with a splendid sweeping view over the Mississippi River.

When I checked my email later in the day, I discovered an invite to dinner from a couple who had been listening to the radio show that morning. I met Tara and Tim at a restaurant that had been suggested by the radio show host, and had a lovely evening with them.

That night I slept in the RV in the quiet carpark hidden away behind the restaurant.

I was really enjoying the spontaneous way in which the days were unfolding. It was wonderful that I could end up at dinner that evening with people I had never even known of that morning.

Tim worked for the mobile phone company that I had bought a SIM card from, and a day or so later, I was surprised and grateful that he had somehow added an extra $100 credit to my account. What a wonderful bonus.

The next day I drove "down through Missouri", as per the lyrics of the famous song, and late in the afternoon I crossed into Oklahoma.

I had been contacted by Rose who worked for Oklahoma Travel Services, and we had emailed back and forth quite a bit as I headed towards her state. I had told her that I had an event scheduled in the town of Wagoner in Oklahoma, and she had managed to arrange a couple of nights for me at the campground at the very scenic Sequoyah State Park just near town.

The place was stunning, right on the shores of a quiet lake. There was practically nobody else about, so I picked a scenic site right by the water's edge, and connected the RV to the water and power supplies. This was the first time I had done this, and everything worked perfectly, lighting, heating, fridge and shower. I was very pleased with the RV, and after almost a week on the road, it was starting to feel very much like home.

As I was setting up for the evening, four deer came wandering past. It had been a very warm day, and it was still warm in the early evening, so I went for a refreshing dip in the lake. I then made dinner and watched the sunset in relaxed and peaceful contentment.

Goal 13 comes swooping in

Saturday, November 1, 2008
(Wagoner, Oklahoma, USA)

I was a bit worried about finding the location for trying to achieve my next goal, as I hadn't heard from Aaron, my hawk-flying contact. He had emailed me a few months ago and told me of a hawk-flying event he would be attending on 1st November in Wagoner, Oklahoma, just off Route 66. After a few emails back and forth, I arranged to set off on my Route 66 journey in time to reach Wagoner for the event, and last night made it to town.

In the days leading up to today, I hadn't heard from Aaron, and I only had an email address, no other contact details at all. When I woke this morning I searched through the emails from Aaron for a clue as to when and where to look in Wagoner.

After a bit of rudimentary detective work I found the right place, and introduced myself to the first guy I found with a hawk on his hand. It turned out that Michael had been expecting me, and he introduced me to Sifin, his Krider's Red- Tailed Hawk, an absolutely beautiful bird. Before long he had a glove on my hand, and Sifin was sat there quite happily.

I met a couple of other members of the group, and was introduced to Bob, the leader of the day's activities. We chatted for a while, and he asked what my goal was specifically, which was to have a hawk fly to my hand, land on it and eat something.

"Okay, let's make that happen now," he said, and set me up about 30 metres away with a glove with some meat on it. His majestic female Harris Hawk, Valkyrie, flew from his hand and swooped low to the ground towards me, rising up at the last second to land on my hand and eat the meat. What an incredible sight to see such a large bird coming straight towards you.

Afterwards we headed out into the bush to go hunting with Valkyrie. This involves the hawk flying along on it's own above a group of people, who beat the undergrowth with sticks to try to flush out any rabbits or small game hiding in there.

It was wonderful to watch the hawk and handler work together as a team, with the hawk sometimes following just behind the beaters, or sometimes flying ahead to sit high on a branch and watch the ground in front of the line of beaters as we approached.

Valkyrie did not catch anything on that run through, as we did not find any game. Later in the morning CB's young Passage Red-Tailed Hawk, possibly called Heather, but name not quite decided on yet, caught a small snake and a rabbit. CB's hawk-naming hesitation was caused by the fact that his wife's name was Heather too!

What an amazing experience, and what a privilege to be able to go along and take part.

Later in the day I finally got to meet Rose in person, and thanked her for arranging the beautiful lakeside accommodation for me. She and husband Lance took me on a bit of a tour of the local area, the most unusual site being Route 66 iconic attraction the Blue Whale at Catoosa. It is a pretty run-down, very eccentric, full-size fibreglass blue whale, at the edge of what once might have been a nice lake, but was now a bit of a green slimy swamp. I was amused to find out that some guy had built it as an anniversary present for his wife! She must have been thrilled! Who said romance is dead?

In the evening I drove down to Muskogee where Bob was working with his hawk Valkyrie at the Muskogee Castle Haunted Halloween Festival. I didn't really know what to expect, but was amazed and amused by the huge event. The "castle" was an elaborate reconstruction of a medieval castle and village, staffed for Halloween with many people in both period costume and Halloween makeup. It was lit by fairy lights, and was really busy, filled with families having a frightful time! I sat for a while with Bob, and he took me into Domus Horrificus, a dark indoor maze peopled by all sorts of horrors – great fun!

I stayed overnight again at the State Park, and went to do some more hawk flying the next morning. I was touched by a gift from Michael, who gave me several bottles of his home-brewed mead.

Oklahoma has the most drivable miles of the original Route 66, and I managed to get off the Interstate and follow the original route, taking my time and soaking up some of the atmosphere.

I had been invited to stay with Sue and Nancy, a farming couple who lived and worked in the Oklahoma farming area to the north-east of Oklahoma City. They had a lovely place out in the country and I spent a wonderful couple of days with them, driving quads and tractors, and being as agricultural as I could.

I have never had much to do with farming at all, and once again I felt that it was quite a privilege to be invited to experience something of a lifestyle about which I knew little.

The girls wanted to offer me the chance to do some shooting, and Sue and I went in to town to buy some ammo for both their shotgun and the .22 rifle.

I was amazed to discover a huge gun counter in the local supermarket, and we collected enough ammo to start a small war. At the checkout, I assumed that we would have to show ID, but Sue assured me we wouldn't. We went through the self-service aisle, and the screen pinged, telling us we required further assistance. The staff member merely had to confirm the ammo was being purchased by someone over the age of 21, and never asked for any identification at all.

I was slightly horrified. I knew that the US was very different to anywhere I had lived, but was still amazed that anyone could walk into a store and just buy handfuls of ammo over the counter, no questions asked at all.

However, I thoroughly enjoyed the experience of using the ammo out on the farm at an impromptu range we set up. The pump-action shotgun had a huge kick, and was very impressive.

It was very interesting to be with Sue and Nancy on the day of the presidential election. Freedom to bear arms was one of the hot-potato political issues often mentioned in the run up to the election, but Sue and Nancy's interest lay in the much more tolerant approach to alternative lifestyles that the Obama administration offered if he was victorious.

Sue was up early that morning to cast her vote enthusiastically. I'm not sure how she voted, but I have a pretty good idea.

In Oklahoma City itself I used my GPS to find a Walmart carpark again as my free accommodation base, and met with my next internet contact, Michelle, who wanted to be my local guide.

We met after she finished work, and went to a local pub offering all sorts of beers, including a very welcome selection of English ales. We chatted for a while, and I asked Michelle my usual question about why she wanted to meet and show me around. But as we talked her phone rang, and she had a very quick talk with someone, including something along the lines of, "Yes, fine. No problem."

I laughed. "That was your safety call, wasn't it?"

I had wondered a little about how a girl would feel, going alone to meet some stranger that she had contacted on the internet, and had only communicated with by email. I added a second question to my initial research question. "What do your friends think about you coming to meet some random internet stranger?"

"Well, you're not a completely random stranger, and I have been following your blog for a while. I feel that I know quite a lot about you, and I wasn't particularly worried about meeting you here today. A couple of friends think it's great, but a few think I am a bit crazy too. That call was from one of those friends, just checking that all was okay."

I was flattered that Michelle, much like Aileen, had felt confident enough, just from what she had read on the blog, to meet me in person on her own.

Michelle was funny, and fun to be with, and the next day we toured the city. This included a visit to the Oklahoma City National Memorial, which was built in remembrance of those who lost their lives on 19th April 1995, when a huge bomb had ripped through the heart of the city.

The memorial was very effective, and started with a recording of a radio interview from that morning, in which the bomb blast can be heard. Doors then open, and you walk through into a scene of complete devastation. The whole display is very thought provoking, particularly the letters of condolence from children. Like my visit to the Twin Towers memorial in New York with Stephanie, I was very quiet and reflective afterwards.

When in Indiana I had had a couple of discussions with Josh, the tattoo artist, about guns. I had expressed my utter amazement that he thought it quite reasonable to carry three guns most of the time.

He had a small pistol in his pocket, another little one in his boot, and wore a third, larger gun under his jacket when out and about.

At his home he had several more guns, including a pump action shotgun and an assault rifle. I had told him that I didn't know anybody in either England or Australia whose house I could pop round to and say, "Come on then, get your guns out and let's have a look at them!"

Josh had explained his reasoning, telling me that as he ran a largely cash-based business, he often had to carry significant sums of cash with him. "I work very hard for that money, and it is for my family. I have no intention of letting anyone take that from me," he explained. In states where there are "conceal and carry" laws, and licensed people are allowed to carry a concealed weapon, he told me that there are fewer assaults and muggings. Anyone approaching somebody and threatening them with a knife, for example, wouldn't know if their intended victim might pull out a gun.

I could see his point, but suggested that an opposite view could be argued too. Something like a simple fender-bender accident could easily escalate out of all proportion if both parties pulled out guns. What in England might end at the worst with a bloodied nose, could end up here with a bullet-riddled corpse on the ground.

But despite my amazement at the US gun laws, I had been pretty keen to fire some of Josh's weapons. Unfortunately we hadn't had time. I had mentioned this on the blog, and on the day I planned on heading out of Oklahoma I received an email from Russ, who suggested I could come and fire some of his guns if I liked.

It was too good an opportunity to miss, and I quickly changed plans, confirming that I would meet him first thing the next morning. I called Michelle again, and asked if she fancied another night out with a random internet stranger.

The next day I met Russ, and we headed out to his local shooting range. He professed not to be a "gun-nut", but when he opened the back of his Jeep, I had to say that by any definition I understood, he could be described as nothing other than a "gun-nut"! There was enough hardware there to satisfy any gun-toting enthusiast, and I was keen to try out some of the high-powered weaponry.

I thoroughly enjoyed shooting the two pistols he had brought along. The first was a .45 automatic, with which I had to try the classic TV cop quick reload, dropping the empty clip and fitting a new one as fast as possible. The monster .44 Magnum hand cannon, as used by Clint Eastwood in the movie "Dirty Harry", was my favourite. It had quite a kick-back, but was very accurate.

Before we moved on to a different range to shoot his semi-automatic assault rifle we sat and chatted for a while, and I didn't need to even ask my usual question. Russ had a very similar story to my own, and had gone through many of the same challenges I had.

Although his story was a sad one, I found it very uplifting to find someone that knew exactly what I had gone through, and in some ways was still going through. Russ was a little further down the road than I was though, and had a new partner with whom he was very happy.

I was happy for him, and encouraged by his supportive story, but a little saddened, and perhaps even a little jealous of his new-found happiness.

I wondered when, and maybe even if, I would ever find a happiness like I had once had. I have always believed that happiness comes from within, and have always been a pretty happy person in general. But I think that on reflection, I had been a much happier person during my years with Laura than at any other time in my life.

My journey took me on into New Mexico, where in Albuquerque I met up with Sharon for the day. Once again, here was someone who was very keen to show me around the area in which she lived, and I was honoured again to have a local guide.

Without kind and outgoing people like Sharon contacting me, I would probably simply stop somewhere like Albuquerque for a quick lunch, a quick look around the town centre, and then be on my way again.

Meeting so many local people as I passed through meant that I could get a much better in depth view of the places through which I was travelling.

Sharon took me north to the picturesque town of Santa Fe, where we had a fantastic Mexican lunch, and browsed some of the many art and craft galleries.

On the way back from Santa Fe we stopped in an Indian reservation store. There I found I found a couple of items with "The Man in the Maze" design, and a description of its meaning. I took a photograph of the description, later emailing Josh the picture, telling him that I was still wearing the ring.

This is what the description said:

> *"The man in the maze signifies a spiritual rebirth from one world to the succeeding one. All the lines passing within the maze form a universal plan of the Creator which man must follow on his own road of life. The outer concentric band represents the boundary of his endeavours. Sometimes the person within the maze will be depicted with his arms in a downward position. This signifies that a major project in his life way has been completed. If the arms of the person are in an upward position, this signifies that a new project in his life is being initiated."*

The ring that Josh had given me showed the man with his arms up, which I thought particularly relevant to me, both in the globe-trotting sense and with relevance to my more personal journey too, both still being very much in their early stages.

Further along Route 66 I detoured off the main route to take a look at a huge meteor crater out in the desert. Sat on the rim of the hugely impressive hole, it was hard to imagine the enormously devastating impact that must have caused it.

On the way back to the main highway I pulled over by a couple of rusty old cars I had spotted out in the desert, and wandered over to take a look at them.

They were stripped bare, completely covered in rust, and riddled with bullet holes. I took some photos, and when I looked at them later I was very pleased with one of them. It just seemed to sum up the spirit of the old road across the country, and was exactly the sort of thing that I had hoped I might discover on this journey.

In Flagstaff I was expecting to finally get hold of my bank ATM card, and got to the bank just before closing. Unfortunately, there was no sign of my card! It was late on a Friday afternoon, and I couldn't hang around all weekend to see if it arrived on Monday, as I intended to push onward to see the Grand Canyon. So with the assistance of the extremely helpful staff, I arranged for it to be forwarded further along the path of my journey to be collected later. I would have to continue to use cheques, and carry a good supply of cash.

One huge frustration with this is the American distrust of the customer paying for petrol with cash. In almost all cases, without a credit or debit card, as a cash customer, you have to go inside and prepay. This involves lining up behind any other customers buying stuff, then taking a guess at how much fuel it might take to fill the tank, paying more than this, going back to fill the vehicle, and then returning to line up again to get your change.

With a bank card, you simply swipe it at the pump, and away you go. In most places in both England and Australia drivers are usually trusted enough to fill their tanks and then come in to pay by whatever means they like. However, there are cameras at most places monitoring registration numbers just in case someone does try to disappear without paying.

As a bank customer I felt justified in staying overnight in the bank carpark, and headed out to find a warm pub for the evening. I was lucky enough to find a great Irish bar selling a great selection of Irish and English beers, and even better, they had free wi-fi. I ended up staying there for around six hours, catching up on a lot of email and blog writing, and making some plans for the next stages of the journey. I was pretty tipsy as I headed back to the RV, and my beer jacket kept me warm in the chilly desert night. I was very happy to get tucked up in a warm bed.

Goal 14 completed – Grand Canyon

Wednesday, November 12, 2008
(Grand Canyon, Nevada, USA)

The Grand Canyon is simply stunning. Without a doubt, it meets and surpasses all expectations.

It was a beautiful crisp clear morning as I drove up from Flagstaff. By the time I arrived at Little Colorado River Canyon, just before the Grand Canyon itself, it was lovely and warm. I had been very lucky with the weather, which could have been awful at this time of the year.

It was lunchtime by the time I entered the National Park, and my first view of the canyon left me breathless. It is HUGE! Words really cannot describe this place, and I took many photos to try to capture the majestic grandeur. As always though, I found it impossible to do such a place true justice with a camera.

I eventually drove along to the Grand Canyon Visitor Centre, found a place at the campsite to park up, and caught the free shuttle bus back to the canyon rim to watch the sun set. It was lovely to see, but I felt pretty much alone, as this is the first goal that I have achieved without anyone coming along to join me. As the canyon walls became tinged with orange, I became slightly tinged with melancholy. It would be nice to share this with someone.

I was reminded very much of the words of Christopher McCandless in the movie "Into The Wild", when he finally realised:-

"Happiness is only real when shared."

The next morning I was up before dawn, and wrapped up well, headed back to the canyon rim to watch the sunrise. Absolutely stunning. It was another beautiful crisp, cloudless morning. I really could not have hoped for better weather for this visit.

The words of acclaimed geologist Clarence Dutton, written in 1882, sum up very succinctly my feelings about the Grand Canyon. "The Grand Canyon at first bewilders and at length overpowers. Dimensions mean nothing to the senses; all that we are conscious of is a troubled sense of immensity."

When writing the blog I had made a conscious decision to make it pretty factual, and focus mainly on where I had been and what I had seen.

The blog post from the Grand Canyon was the first time I had really expressed some of my emotions, and mentioned being lonely.

But the blog post only went halfway to explaining how low I had really felt that evening. Seeing the Grand Canyon was the first goal I achieved alone, and as I watched the beautiful sunset on my own, surrounded by couples, I felt an incredible sadness, and a huge empty loneliness. There was only one person in the whole world that I really wanted to be there with me, and that could never be. It felt so wrong to be alone there, and that night alone in the RV I cried sadly.

I was amazed by the wonderful response from many blog readers. I had several messages of support and encouragement, both in replies to the blog post itself, and in email messages too.

At times I often felt like I was just writing the blog for myself, as a sort of diary of my trip, and it was easy to forget that other people were following my journey too. I was very flattered and grateful that more people than I had ever imagined cared enough to write to support me.

I headed to Las Vegas via the spectacular Hoover Dam. I only managed to get a brief view of The Strip as I drove through, as I had a plane to catch to Rapid City, South Dakota early the next morning.

Goal 15 sculpted to perfection – Mount Rushmore

Saturday, November 15, 2008
(Rapid City, South Dakota, USA)

On Friday I made my way to Las Vegas airport, as the day warmed again to reach well into the 70s (degrees Fahrenheit) by mid-morning. After a bit of a delay the plane took off, and I had a great view of Lake Mead and the Hoover Dam as we flew over. A couple of hours later, as we approached South Dakota, I looked down and was amazed to see the landscape covered in snow.

It was dark by the time we landed. On the ground the temperature was below freezing, the wind was blowing hard, and I was still in just a t-shirt! Fortunately I had packed a couple of sweatshirts and a jacket in my small bag.

My plan was to pick up a rental car at the airport, but the prices were somewhat alarming, so a couple of minutes with the phone directory produced a company called Rent-a-Wreck. That's the car hire company I'm after, I laughed to myself! Ten minutes *later Scott arrived at the airport in a nice little Kia, at the bargain price of $32 per day. After a brief bit of paperwork, and a few directions I was off.*

It had been snowing, and the roads were a bit treacherous, but I soon found a motel with a nice diner next door for dinner. I settled in for the evening to plan the next few days, which were starting to look very full. There seems to be plenty to see and do near here.

On Saturday morning the first port of call was Mount Rushmore, to achieve the goal I had come here to complete. Once again, it dawned fine and sunny, and I drove up into the scenic Black Hills of South Dakota. When I arrived at Mount Rushmore, I was told the weather had been horrendous the day before. I really am being blessed by perfect weather!

Mount Rushmore is impressively spectacular, the scale of the accomplishment is quite breathtaking, and very inspiring too. It really is incredible what people can achieve when they have a dream.

I first became aware of Mount Rushmore as a child when my dad introduced me to the Alfred Hitchcock 1959 classic, "North By Northwest", starring Cary Grant and Eva Marie Saint. Well worth watching - highly recommended.

Mount Rushmore was carved by sculptor Gutzon Borglum, and one of the things he wrote about his work was, "Hence let us place there, carved high, as close to heaven as we can, the words of our leaders, their faces to show posterity what manner of men they were. Then breathe a prayer that these records will endure until the wind and rain alone shall wear them away."

The four presidents depicted are, in the order they appear on the sculpture, George Washington, Thomas Jefferson, Theodore Roosevelt and Abraham Lincoln. In order of presidency, the last two are actually the other way around. Their presidential terms of office, and the significance of the inclusion of each as part of the national monument, are as follows:

George Washington - 1789 to 1797
the struggle for independence and the birth of the Republic
Thomas Jefferson - 1801 to 1809
the territorial expansion of the country
Abraham Lincoln - 1861 to 1865
the permanent union of the states, and equality for all citizens
Theodore Roosevelt - 1901 to 1909
the 20th Century role of the United States in world affairs and the rights of the common man

After admiring Mount Rushmore I drove on to see the incomplete sculpture of Crazy Horse, about 17 miles further along the same road. I had had this recommended to me quite some time ago, when I first launched the 100goals website, and at the time had known nothing of it.

Crazy Horse is another breathtaking sculpture, the scale of which is absolutely staggering. Apparently all four president's heads of Mount Rushmore would fit in the area of Crazy Horse's head alone!

It was begun in 1949 by sculptor Korczak Ziolkowski, who died in 1982, and work continues today, funded primarily by paying visitors. Ziolkowski believed that Crazy Horse should be a non-profit educational and cultural humanitarian project, built by the interested public and not the taxpayer. I certainly feel proud to have made my contribution, and would love to come and see the completed work one day.

I loved the HBO TV series "Deadwood", and it was only on the plane on the way up to Rapid City that I found out that Deadwood itself is pretty close by. After seeing Crazy Horse I headed over there, and discovered that the town had had a big snowfall recently, and the streets were piled high with slowly melting snow.

I arrived just in time to see the most spectacular sunset over the city, viewed from Mount Moriah Cemetery, the infamous "Boot Hill" where "Wild Bill" Hickock and Calamity Jane are buried. It was very atmospheric up there as the darkness deepened, not another soul around, snow piled deep on the graves in a silent cemetery that was closed for the winter. I sat quietly for a couple of minutes with Bill and Jane before heading back into town to look for a motel. On the way down the hill I stopped when I saw a deer stood stock-still under a streetlight in the middle of a snowy side street, and we just stared at each other for a minute. What a place!

I couldn't resist going out to one of the casinos that evening to play a few hands of 5-card stud. Fortunately the evening did not end with the pushing back of chairs and the quick-drawing of pistols, just me wandering back to my room through the snowy streets a few dollars lighter. I think I will need to brush up my game before taking on my $1,000 poker game goal!

I first became aware of the Devil's Tower when I saw the movie "Close Encounters of the Third Kind". The main character, Roy Neary, played by Richard Dreyfuss, becomes obsessed with the mountain after a mysterious encounter. It is a very striking peak, and I decided to take a drive into Wyoming to see it.

The first view of the tower in the distance does cause a gasp, and on driving closer, the amazement does not diminish. It is an incredible sight, towering above the forests below. I took a walk around the base, which takes about an hour, and in that time have decided that one day I want to climb the tower and stand on the summit.

In the visitor centre, I found some words which reflected my feelings about the place, and echoed words I quoted about the Grand Canyon too. N Scott Momaday wrote in 1969, "There are things in nature that engender an awful quiet in the heart of man; Devil's Tower is one of them."

On the way back to Rapid City I made a detour back to Mount Rushmore to see the monument at night, lit up by powerful floodlights - quite spectacular. But it was very cold, and I didn't hang around too long, the appeal of a warm motel room was strong!

Monday morning - what's this - clouds? I wondered whether to head out on my planned journey for the day, eventually deciding to do so, hoping the weather might improve.

My first stop was at the historic Minuteman II Missile site about 70 miles east of Rapid City. The tour around the missile control site, and the missile silo which still houses one of the decommissioned missiles, was fascinating, and was very enthusiastically presented by knowledgeable guide Chris. At one time during the height of the Cold War, there were 1,000 of these missiles ready for immediate launch at a moments notice. Each missile warhead contained a nuclear explosive equivalent to 60% of all bombs detonated during WW2, including the two nuclear ones!! There are now Minuteman III missiles out there somewhere ready for use, with even bigger nuclear payloads aboard!

My final place to visit before returning the car and heading for the airport was the South Dakota Badlands. I had only heard the name before, and did not really know what to expect, but what a place! The name comes from the Lakota Indian name for the place, "mako sika", which literally means "land bad", referring to a difficult area to travel through because of the rough terrain.

All in all, I have had a fantastic weekend in South Dakota and Wyoming, and feel I have packed more than I had ever expected into the couple of days I have had here. I just wish that I had come a little earlier in the year when it wasn't quite so cold! But maybe if I had done that, there would have been so many more visitors at these amazing places. At almost every place, a couple of minutes walk away from the visitor centre would mean you could be totally alone in an absolutely incredible place! I think I have been extremely lucky to have such fantastic weather at this time of the year. What a real stand-out weekend!

The weekend in South Dakota and Wyoming had been fantastic, and I had actually really enjoyed travelling and experiencing the time there alone. But I was looking forward to getting back to the warmth of Las Vegas, and heading out to see some of the big casinos there.

Goal 16 achieved - Viva Las Vegas
Tuesday, November 18, 2008
(Las Vegas, Nevada, USA)

Wow, what a culture shock! At lunchtime yesterday I was in the Badlands in South Dakota, utterly alone, hardly a sound except for the slight noise of the wind, Within a couple of hours I was wandering up and down The Strip in downtown Las Vegas!

I arrived in Vegas on Thursday last week, and drove along The Strip in the RV as I came through the city - that was quite an experience - it's pretty busy! I was staying with Simon, an English guy now living in Las Vegas, who had contacted me through the website and kindly offered me a spare room here.

I had had an early night on Thursday, and was up and off early on Friday, heading for the airport and my South Dakota weekend away, so had not really got to see downtown properly. As I flew back in last night, I called Misty (more about her to follow shortly...), and she picked me up as she was heading for work in a restaurant in The Palazzo. I left my bags in her car, and went to wander around.

The place is quite extraordinary, pretty much as I expected it to be, but ...

...once again I was achieving a goal on my own, and somewhere like Vegas really does need to be experienced with other people. It would be much more fun to be with a group of mates, going to play poker

or roulette, or with someone special to go out to a restaurant and maybe take in a show. I wandered around, enjoyed the sights, and ventured into several casinos. I had a bit of a play on the slot machines, but was sort of relieved when Misty finished work at 2am, and I hitched a lift back to Simon's house.

I think perhaps I was pretty tired after a very long day, but after having seen some incredible natural (and carved) scenery over the last few days, the whole experience in Las Vegas had a bit of an air of unreality and falseness about it. I was interested to see both "Paris" and "New York New York" casinos, but having been to both cities recently and seen the real thing, I felt a bit of disappointment. Perhaps I just slightly cheated. I don't know why really, but ultimately I think I felt slightly underwhelmed by the whole experience. I am glad to have seen and experienced the place though, and definitely think it would be a completely different experience with a group of friends. Maybe one day...

It wasn't all disappointment though. There was a Sopranos slot machine in one casino, and they bring you free beer while you are playing.

In Las Vegas everything is larger than life, even the gun stores, and I had seen several adverts for one particular store that offered the opportunity to shoot fully automatic machineguns. It sounded like too good an opportunity to miss.

Simon and Myles were keen to come along, but were happy to watch me get relieved of a significant amount of cash in order to shoot an AK47, a pump action shotgun, and a Heckler & Koch MP5. What fun!

We ended up out in the older part of Las Vegas for the evening. Following the lead of my experienced local guides, I sat at a 1-cent-a-game machine with a couple of dollars of change, and ordered as many of the free drinks as possible from the passing waitresses. A decent tip to one of the girls ensured that the drinks kept on coming. What a great system!

I was very keen to meet Misty again, as she had created something about which she had told me quite a bit, and I was very much looking forward to actually seeing the results of her efforts. She had got in touch with me in the early days of the original press coverage of my up-coming life-sale, suggesting that she was going to do a painting inspired by my decision to sell everything and go travelling.

It was wonderful to finally see the actual painting she had created, based on something I had decided to do halfway around the world from her. I'm not sure which of us was the most excited.

She had offered to take me on a proper guided tour of The Strip, as she didn't have to work at the restaurant that evening. She was keen to show me some of her favourite poker rooms – she often did quite well in tournaments, she told me. We had a great night out, riding some of the rides on top of the Stratosphere Tower, visiting many of the famous landmark casinos, and valet parking whenever possible. What an awesome Las Vegas guide! It was a much better experience than the solo tour I had taken a couple of nights earlier.

It didn't take too long to get down to Los Angeles, and my GPS took me straight to Evan's house. At last I got to meet the guy responsible for the initial suggestion that had ultimately led to my decision to spend two years travelling the globe.

Evan had to go down to San Diego for the weekend, and I hitched a ride with him, keen to catch up with an old college buddy who now lived there.

I hadn't seen Tim for over twenty years. We had originally met at a college party in the north-west of England, drawn together by our shared interest in motorcycles. We lost touch when Tim moved to the States, to eventually become a commercial pilot. I had tracked him down through a mutual friend who was still in touch with him.

When he answered the door, we both laughed, each of us saying that the other hadn't changed a bit. I think we were both being kind! I was very pleased to find that Tim was still passionate about his motorbikes, and it wasn't long before I was thrashing his Ducati down the freeway. "Just don't cross into Mexico on it," he suggested. The border was only a tempting fifteen miles or so away, but I had left my passport in the RV.

Goal 17 blows into place – skydive wind tunnel

Saturday, November 22, 2008
(Perris, California, USA)

I am a fairly regular skydiver, and in the five years or so since my first jump, I have now done about 130 altogether. There are a couple of skydiving goals on my list, and one was to skydive in a vertical wind tunnel.

In Australia there isn't any such facility at all, the nearest one being in Kuala Lumpur in Malaysia. However, there are plenty of them here in the States, and a small detour on the way back up to LA from San Diego took us to Perris Skydive.

My friend Evan, who did a lot of the internet publicity for my "ALife4Sale" website was keen to come along, but when he found out that he could do a real tandem skydive there instead, he lost all interest in the wind tunnel. We went our separate ways for an hour or so as we both headed off to do our respective training.

The wind tunnel was a very interesting experience, and is very similar in feel to a skydive, but quite different visually. You have the same feeling of being supported by the air, the same pressure on arms, body and legs, but in a skydive there is so much space around you. Unless you are skydiving with other people it is very difficult to know whether you are falling down straight, or backsliding, or falling slow or fast. But in the tunnel there are walls and windows all around, and they provide a great reference point.

I was pretty pleased with my performance, and managed to stay in the middle without too much difficulty. I quickly managed a few turns, and a few moves vertically up and down the tunnel.

Each person in the group has a minute, then flies to the door to get out, and the next person gets in. The time goes pretty quick, but you can fit quite a lot in. My second minute was really good fun, as I played with fall-rate, moving quickly up and down the tunnel.

I only had two minutes, at a bargain price of $35, and could have happily done more. I can see how time in the tunnel would be a great skydive training aid, but it is great fun too!

Back in LA, I dropped Evan off at the airport, as he was flying home for Thanksgiving week. In his car, which he had kindly lent me for the week he would be away, I headed down to the beach at Santa Monica, end point for my journey across America on Route 66.

Goal 18 – Get Your Kicks on Route 66

Monday 27th October to Sunday 23rd Nov 2008
(Illinois – Missouri – Oklahoma – Texas –
New Mexico – Arizona – California, USA)

I imagine the majority of people will be most familiar with the Rolling Stones' version of the song "(Get Your Kicks on) Route 66". The song was actually written way back in 1946 by American song writer Bobby Troup, and recorded in the same year by Nat King Cole. Since then there have been over sixty recorded versions of the popular song:

Well if you ever plan to motor west
Take my way that's the highway that's the best
Get your kicks on Route 66

Well it winds from Chicago to L.A.
More than 2000 miles all the way
Get your kicks on Route 66

Well it goes from St. Louis down to Missouri
Oklahoma City looks oh so pretty
You'll see Amarillo and Gallup, New Mexico
Flagstaff, Arizona don't forget Winona
Kingman, Barstow, San Bernardino

Would you get hip to this kindly tip
And go take that California trip
Get your kicks on Route 66

I had set off from Chicago almost a month earlier, and had taken that lyrically-suggested California trip, passing through all of the places listed in the song on the way. I had stuck as much as possible to the original Route 66, and on the way had discovered a happy new life on the road in the RV that had now become home. I was a little sad that the trip had ended as I finally arrived at the ocean on California's beautiful west coast, but I was happy that there were still more open roads ahead

I bought myself a coffee and sat at the beach thinking over the whole trip and many of the experiences from the past month. I think before I started, in my mind the trip was about finding as much of the original road, and actually driving upon it. But on reflection, I think it became much more about the people I have met on my journey, and the experiences that they had offered me along the way.

I have met some wonderful people who have been incredibly kind and hospitable, especially in light of the fact that to them, I was initially just a random internet stranger. I will be eternally grateful to everyone that I met along Route 66 for making it such a fantastic journey.

I have also seen some incredible places on the way. A couple of places that particularly stand out are the Arch at St Louis, the Grand Canyon, Mount Rushmore, and the Devil's Tower.

I ended my journey on the beach at Santa Monica by dipping my feet in the ocean. I wandered along towards the pier, happily watching all the people cycling, skating, playing volleyball, or heading for the surf. I felt pretty happy to have arrived, and am pleased that it doesn't really feel like the end of anything, as my travels now continue up the west coast towards winter in Canada. I am thoroughly enjoying this whole adventure, and am not ready for it to end just yet!

Afterwards, I headed down to Venice Beach, which had a great hippy-type street market, selling all sorts of arty stuff, beads and trinkets. After a drive down to El Segundo (I just liked the name!) I headed north up Route 1, the Pacific Coast Highway, through Malibu, and up through the mountains back to Evan's house. What a lovely drive up the beautiful California coast.

I am now living in the RV on Evan's driveway, and one of his housemates, Wade, asked if I fancied going ten-pin bowling. We went to the local bowling lanes, and I topped off a great day in LA by bowling a personal best of 170!

I was achieving goals at a great rate now, and the next morning I headed in to Hollywood to complete my third goal in the space of three days.

Goal 19 achieved – The City of the Angels

Monday, November 24, 2008
(Los Angeles, California, USA)

Wow, three goals achieved in three days! I'll be finished by Christmas if I can keep this up!! On Saturday I experienced indoor skydiving in a vertical wind tunnel, yesterday I completed my journey across Route 66 by finally arriving at Santa Monica, and today I headed into Hollywood to complete my goal of seeing Los Angeles.

Evan has very kindly lent me his car for the week while he is away, and my first job this morning was to fix the cigarette lighter socket, which wasn't working. Without that I am unable to charge my GPS, and heading off into downtown LA without it would have been foolish, to say the least. It didn't take me long to have the whole centre console of Evan's car stripped out. It took a bit longer to get it all back together – but don't worry Evan, it's all working well now!

Once sorted, I was off, and got parked at the Kodak Theatre on Hollywood Boulevard. The first thing I wanted to do was to see the Hollywood sign up on the hill, which is for me the iconic image of LA. Just around the corner, there it was, high up on the side of the Hollywood Hills.

I took a wander along Hollywood Boulevard, down Vine Street, and then back westward on Sunset Boulevard. I was surprised to find that among the glamour and the glitz there are quite a few closed down businesses, and that parts of the area are pretty run-down. However, at the westward end of Sunset Boulevard, where it becomes Sunset Strip, it becomes pretty exclusive and expensive.

In the evening I met up with Ari. He lives just off Sunset, and works as a voiceover artist, doing voices for movie trailers, adverts, and any other project requiring voice acting. His is one of the voices you hear dramatically touting a new movie over a montage of the most exciting scenes... "New from Home Cinema International, a heart-warming movie about... etc." He had contacted me through the website, and offered to buy me a pint - how could I possibly refuse?

We met in the Trocadero on Sunset, and after a couple of beers we headed to Sushi On Sunset to eat, which was absolutely fantastic. The Firecracker Chicken was the highlight of the menu. I was incredibly grateful when Ari picked up the bill, as I reckoned it would have cost about a week's worth of my travelling budget!

Every now and then I keep realising what I am doing, and where I am. This evening, sat eating dinner I had another one of those moments. "I am sat in an incredible restaurant on Sunset Strip in LA, eating dinner with a Hollywood actor!!"

What an amazing experience!

Life was surprisingly easy for me in LA. I had the RV parked on Evan's driveway, connected to power from the house. I had access to a shower inside, and I had Evan's car with the GPS now installed, so could get around fairly easily.

I tried to make the most of my time, and met up with several people who had contacted me, offering assistance or support, or simply wanting to meet for a beer.

My next appointment was one that was intriguing me. I had heard several times from Yvette, who seemed quite inspired by my 100goals idea. She had goals of her own, and was also working on her own, blog-based quirky project.

She was divorced, now single, and was writing a book about dating in the modern, internet-driven world. Her plan was to have at least one date per month, a new adventure every month, and to write something on a monthly basis too.

Her book would be written about the twelve month period over the course of 2008, and her ultimate goal was to fall in love by the final chapter in December. Pressure was now on, as it was already late November!

I had hoped that Yvette was going to join me for the trip to the Grand Canyon, but things hadn't worked out at the time. It turned out, however, that she was going to be in Los Angeles at the same time as me, staying with her sister for Thanksgiving.

We had managed to arrange a date for the Tuesday evening, and Yvette had organised tickets for the recording of a TV comedy show at one of the big movie studios.

With nothing much to do in the afternoon I gave Yvette a call, and invited her to come along for a drive in the Hollywood Hills, along the hopefully scenic Mulholland Drive.

Our afternoon went well, and we had dinner later. Unfortunately, at the TV studios, things didn't go quite so well, and we joined a huge line of people waiting to go in. It turned out that many more people were given tickets than there were seats available, to ensure that they had a full studio. Among many others, we were turned away when all seats were filled.

Yvette was disappointed, as she needed to fulfil her "adventure" quota for the month. Thinking quickly, I suggested we could go down to the beach, where we could ride the big Ferris wheel at Santa Monica Pier.

Yvette thought it was a great idea. We drove to the coast, parked the car, and made our way to the garishly flashing wheel at the end of the dark pier.

It was raining slightly, the pier was cold, damp and deserted, and the big wheel flashed its glamorous invite in complete silence! It was closed! There was no adventure to be had here! We gazed off the edge of the pier, and wondered what to do. Yvette suddenly suggested skinny-dipping. "I've never done that before!" she exclaimed excitedly.

"Good grief! How do you get this far through life without ever having been skinny-dipping?" I asked in amazement. "That water is going to be pretty cold," I added, common sense coming to the fore.

Ah, but adventure was required, and adventure would be enjoyed, so on the shore we dipped our toes in the dark chilly waters. "It is very cold, isn't it?" Yvette agreed, starting to appear much less enthusiastic.

I made my decision, and stripped off quickly, running past the dithering Yvette into the cold water. The initial shock was nasty, but once in it didn't seem too bad. I called for Yvette to join me. She undressed in the darkness, and plunged in bravely, but was out again pretty quickly. She was ecstatic though, as not only had she tried something she had never done before, she had also pushed herself way out of her comfort zone with a relative stranger. She certainly felt that adventure had been achieved!

We went for a drink further along the coast to celebrate, chatting comfortably about our respective adventures, and our book-writing goals.

As I dropped her off at home later that night, I asked if a kiss was included in the date, and Yvette said she certainly hoped so.

The next day I experienced another of those incredible, rare moments of clarity, when once again I suddenly realised where I was, and what I was doing. I thought about the amazing chain of events that had brought me to this moment. I was doing something that I could have never imagined in my wildest dreams, and I laughed in amazement!

I had arranged to meet my very own Hollywood agent, Brandon, at a restaurant of his choosing on the top floor of a fashionable Beverley Hills store. As we sat having lunch, he had pointed out a well known movie director also dining there. He also told me that one of the Monty Python team had been in just before I arrived. What a great place.

We ate and chatted, and after lunch he produced my option cheque from Walt Disney. Although not a huge payment by movie industry standards, it was the biggest cheque I have ever had given to me. On our way out, as I opened the front door, we bumped into Eric Idle as he was heading back in to the store again.

I had a wander around the trendy designer shops of Rodeo Drive, where for possibly the only time in my life I felt like I had every right to be there – I was possibly one of the only people there that afternoon with a movie studio cheque in my pocket.

There was no parking charge as I exited from the store's parking garage, as I had dined in the restaurant upstairs. I turned right onto Beverley Hills Drive, pushed my way over into the left lane to make a left on to Rodeo Drive, as my GPS suggested, and it just hit me! "Look at where I am," I thought. "Look at what I am doing!"

I was sat in a car at the junction of Beverley Hills Drive and Rodeo Drive, having just had lunch with my very own movie agent, and I had a fairly substantial cheque from Walt Disney in my pocket. Just one year before I had been driving a truck in a mine in outback Australia!!

Isn't it fascinating how the course of a life can unfold in such unexpected ways?

That evening I had a second date with Yvette, and suggested that I cook for her in the RV, which was still parked on Evan's driveway. This had started to feel a bit like a real home, as I had a permanent electric connection, and access to water and a shower. As I had Evan's car at my disposal too, the RV didn't actually ever have to go anywhere.

I made Yvette a meal with some of the home-raised lamb that Sue and Nancy had given me from their farm in Oklahoma, and we drank the last remaining mead given to me by Michael at the hawk-flying gathering.

We talked late into the evening, and that eventually led to more kissing. But things wouldn't go any further, Yvette told me firmly. Sex without love was not something she was interested in, and as my plans took me onward again in a day or two, I was obviously an unsuitable prospect in this regard.

I was respectful of her decision, and eventually dropped her off again at her sister's house, and we promised to stay in touch. I was particularly interested to see if her book ever made it to print, and if I managed to get a mention in it!

Yvette had invited me to her sister's house for Thanksgiving, and I had received a second invite via the website too, but my third offer was the most intriguing. As this offer was also directly related to one of my goals, it was the obvious choice for the Thursday afternoon and evening.

The experience that night turned out to be one of the best examples I have of achieving a goal in a way that far exceeded my expectations. I got to spend some of the afternoon and all evening with probably one of the best, if not *the* best juggler in the world! Once again, this is something that would have never happened if I had not set off on this incredible journey.

Happy Thanksgiving Day! Fiery Goal 20!

Friday, November 28, 2008
(Los Angeles, California, USA)

LA just keeps offering one amazing day after the next. Thanksgiving Day was absolutely brilliant!

One of my goals is to juggle with fire clubs. My dad taught me how to juggle three balls when I was young, and later he bought me a set of juggling clubs. I am not very good with them, as I don't really practice enough, but have always fancied trying to juggle with fire clubs.

I added this goal to my list, and recently, as I approached Los Angeles, I was contacted by Mark Bakalor, who lives and works with a juggler called Vova Galchenko. Vova, Mark told me, is one of the world's greatest jugglers. He was recently featured in The New York Times and has been on The Oprah Winfrey Show, BBC, ESPN, Ellen DeGeneres Show, The Today Show and US news program Nightline.

Mark invited me to their family home for Thanksgiving Day, and gave me the address to put into my GPS. Driving out there was an experience in itself, as "Maggie" directed me out into the beautiful Santa Monica Mountains above Malibu. As I approached, and the GPS said I was there, I looked up the hillside at the most amazing house perched high above. That can't be it, I thought - it was! The place was stunning.

I met Mark and Vova, and the whole family covering four generations, all gathered for Thanksgiving dinner. I learned a bit of Vova's background story. He had left Russia at the age of fifteen along with his sister Olga who was twelve at the time, and had come to America in search of a better life. Vova and Olga were already an incredible juggling partnership, and had performed many shows, but it was when Mark encouraged and assisted Vova to enter a competition to make a video for a Fat Boy Slim song that things really started happening.

Here I was, in the house where the video was made, throwing clubs around with the guy that Time Magazine called "one of the greatest jugglers in history", and The Today Show called "the best in the entire world"!

After a wonderful Thanksgiving meal, we juggled some more, the fire clubs came out, and the frustrating practice started. Vova, of course, made it look very easy. I discovered, however, that in the dark it is very hard not to concentrate on the flame, and seeing the handle of the club as it comes over the top is much harder than in daylight.

However, with a lot of practice, and a bit of lighting from inside the house, I started to make a couple of catches. The general opinion of all the jugglers there, which included Vova, Mark, and his dad Barry, was that to be considered a successful "juggle" you had to perform an amount of catches which is double the number of items you are juggling. An added bonus would be to catch the final item to "look cool".

I tried many times, and found it a lot trickier than I had thought it would be. However, thanks to the patience of all there, I finally managed to do six or seven catches in a row. I kept at it, and eventually managed a run of six with a final catch at the end. As I caught the final club, I heard Vova saying, "Oh no, don't catch it!" It was the only time he hadn't been filming me, so I had to do it again!

Although I am happy that the goal has been achieved, there is still room for improvement (a lot of room for improvement when you see what Vova can do!) before I will be satisfied. I do intend to keep practicing, and hope to do some more fire-club juggling in the future.

Over the weekend I played tourist in LA, visiting The Griffith Observatory, The Getty Villa, and several other landmark locations. At Santa Monica I visited another website contact, an artist called John. Having been inspired by my ALife4Sale eBay auction, he had decided to sell his artistic lifestyle, and was offering his home in a trailer park right across the road from the ocean.

I wondered how his sales effort was progressing, particularly in light of the unsuccessful conclusion to my auction. So far he hadn't been successful in securing a buyer.

John had previously been a successful businessman, and had decided upon a radical life change at the age of 47. Since then he had been making a living as an artist, selling his enormous portraits to many famous people, and creating eccentric works with all sorts of unusual items. He was currently working on some interesting pieces, involving sticking small children's toys in wooden frames, and then painting the whole thing matt black.

He was very relaxing to be around, and seemed very content within himself. I think that he really didn't consider what he did to be "work", and as far as he was concerned he hadn't done any work now for 18 years. Most days, he said, he would just do whatever he fancied; take a run along the beach, check out the second-hand shops for potential art supplies, or maybe go to visit one of his daughters. "Or stick plastic dinosaurs into a wooden box?" I suggested.

"Exactly," he laughed.

Evan returned from his week away, and I collected him at the airport. In my last couple of days there we visited The Getty Museum, which had been closed when I had tried to go earlier, and hung out with his house buddy Wade, and a few of their friends.

I was sorry to have to finally disconnect the RV from its temporary home on the driveway, but it was time to start heading north as winter approached. My next destination was San Francisco.

I had selected the Walmart carpark in Oakland for my first overnight stop, and called Susan, who had offered to show me around her city. She gave me directions to meet in the centre, and I found the nearest station, catching a BART train into the city.

Susan had suggested that I meet her at one of the stations in the city centre, and I was surprised at the number of homeless people hanging around by the station entrance. A few volunteers were handing out warm soup, and I started chatting to one of them.

One of the goals on my list was to work in a homeless shelter on Christmas Day, and I planned to be in Vancouver over Christmas. Did they have any contacts up there, I wondered?

By the time Susan arrived I had a steaming cup of soup in my hands, and my introductory question sounded a little odd as soon as I asked it. "Do you want some carrot soup?"

Susan showed me around her neighbourhood, which is very gay-friendly, and for the second time in as many months, I found myself in a bar that I wouldn't generally tend to frequent.

We had a great evening, and Susan was fun to be around. She had a great sense of humour, and the best throaty laugh I had ever heard. I was pleased that she had nothing planned for the next day, and agreed to meet me to act as my tour guide again.

It was a busy day. We rode the trams up and down the impressively steep streets, visiting the famously twisting Lombard Street. From there we walked down to Fisherman's Wharf, stopping to look at the sea lions at Pier 39. Susan did a marvellous impromptu impression of the sea lions, bursting into her fantastic laugh at the end. I was really starting to like her very much. We walked through Chinatown, then up Telegraph Hill to Coit Tower, with its wonderful city and river views. Susan had to leave shortly after that, and we waited together for her tram to take her home.

As the tram arrived it seemed very natural to kiss her goodbye, and as I headed off for my evening journey to Alcatraz Island, I had a big happy smile on my face.

Goal 21 completed - San Francisco
Saturday, December 6, 2008
(San Francisco, California, USA)

For me, the Golden Gate Bridge has always symbolised San Francisco, and when I added seeing the city to my list of goals, I imagined either walking across, or at least driving across the bridge.

Once again, I was keen for others to come and join in, and Cindy, her husband Steve, and their chatty young son Trevor came to pick me up at Walmart first thing in the morning. We headed to the city, and parked in the carpark at the southern end of the bridge. We were a little later than planned, but of the others who may have been coming along, it looked like nobody had arrived.

It was sunny and reasonably clear weather, but there was quite a cold wind, so we all wrapped up well, and set off across the bridge. There are some great views of the city and the bay, and I could not help making comparisons with Sydney and its Harbour Bridge. Both cities are beautiful places.

There was a lot going on around the bridge. Helicopters and airships flew over and around it. Kiteboarders, windsurfers, sailing boats and canoeists passed under. Only a few other hardy walkers and cyclists shared the wind-swept path crossing the bridge with us though.

Afterwards we were all happy to get back in the car and warm up, and lunch in the Buena Vista waterfront café was very welcome.

Susan was busy that day looking after her neighbour's two kids, and hadn't been able to join us to cross the bridge, but I managed to meet the three of them briefly in the afternoon. After a few days living in the RV, I felt that I could use a shower, and asked if it would be possible to visit her home to do so. She seemed hesitant, as she lived in shared accommodation, but called later to let me know that she had spoken to her neighbours. I was relieved to take a very refreshing, and much-needed shower in their house, which was undergoing extensive reconstruction works.

San Francisco is a truly wonderful city, and had many experiences to offer. One of the more unusual was a day sailing on the bay with the San Francisco Bay Area Association of Disabled Sailors. I was contacted by Isabel, who had invited me to join them on the Sunday morning to go sailing on the bay.

It wasn't very windy, but once underway, we headed out under the Bay Bridge and down towards Alcatraz, enjoying the view of the city on the way. I took a turn at steering the boat, and had an absolutely marvellous day. It was quite an inspiration to be among people who refused to let their personal challenges interfere with their enjoyment of their chosen hobby.

That evening was my last night in San Francisco, and Susan came to meet me again. We sat for several hours in the RV talking late into the night. We enjoyed an easy, comfortable evening, ending up curled together on the RV sofa. As I drove over the Golden Gate Bridge the next morning I felt sad to be leaving both San Francisco and Susan behind.

Once again I was made aware of one of the more difficult aspects of this journey. Before I started I hadn't really anticipated that I was always going to have to move on from great people and places just as I was starting to feel at home with them.

I continued northward up the west coast, thrilled but slightly worried too by the incredibly scenic coastal highway. It twisted and turned alarmingly up and down beautifully forested valleys carrying roaring streams and rivers to the ocean.

The large RV made the drive tricky and I eventually decided that it would be much better for fuel consumption, and much safer too, if I headed inland and followed an easier route. I made a detour through the aptly-named Avenue of the Giants, where enormous redwood trees towered majestically overhead.

By evening I had reached the Oregon border, where in a convenient casino carpark I met up with Debbie and her partner Jeff. Debbie and I had been in contact for a while on the internet, and she had suggested that I should call in at the beautiful Gold Beach area of the Oregon coast, where I could possibly achieve a couple of goals.

I wasn't quite sure what Debbie had in mind for my visit, but I was developing a very easy-going approach to the whole journey. I was trying to be as flexible as possible, wanting to take up as many offers and invites as I could as I passed through.

Prior to my arrival, Debbie had been very busy, and had arranged a busy schedule for me. After a fantastic beer and pizza dinner we went to look at the local park Christmas lights, which were pretty spectacular for a small town. Debbie then took me to what would be my accommodation for the evening, the ominously-named Ghost Cottage.

There I met Kelli and Riley, the owners of the ghostly cottage, and we all took a walk through the dark woodlands outside. My room for my stay there was a comfortable guestroom which was supposed to be haunted!

I was pretty shattered after my long drive, and slept soundly that night. I woke a couple of times in the night, and listened for any noises, but soon fell asleep again. I woke feeling very refreshed, but slightly disappointed that I had not experienced anything other-worldly. At breakfast Kelli assured me that I would meet the other "residents" that night, when it was planned that I would spend a night alone in the house!

Debbie had arranged a jet boat ride for me up Rogue River that morning. Ryan, a friend of a friend of Debbie's, picked me up from Ghost Cottage at nine, and after fuelling the boat we drove upriver to Lobster Creek where we launched it. We wrapped up well, put in earplugs, and once the engine warmed up we headed upstream.

Ryan's boat was designed and built as a two-seater racing machine, and was very fast. We skipped across the surface of the water, and as we approached the first small rapids I thought Ryan might have to slow down, but he just gunned it through and we continued onwards at high speed.

The scenery was absolutely beautiful, and twelve miles further upriver we entered an area officially listed by the government as "wild and scenic". What better way to enjoy wild and scenic beauty than powering through it at top speed, in a highly tuned racing machine?

We raced onwards, the view becoming ever more spectacular as the river narrowed, and twisted and turned, and we blasted up through more rapids. It was very cold, with the temperature just above freezing, and with the added wind-chill factor of travelling at about 60 miles per hour, I think my head was as cold as it has ever been. But I had a huge smile on my face the whole time.

About 40 miles upriver we stopped at Paradise Lodge, an isolated resort which can only be reached by either boat or helicopter. It was a lovely place, closed now for winter, but offering what I imagine would be wonderful summer accommodation. We chatted to the owner, warmed ourselves inside briefly, and then headed back downriver.

On the return journey Ryan offered me the opportunity to drive, and I soon had the boat hurtling downstream at top speed, guided only by the occasional pointed direction from Ryan through a trickier rapid.

It was one of the most thrilling rides I have ever experienced, and was something that was completely unexpected and unplanned. Once again I marvelled at the way in which the journey was unfolding, and the experiences that it was offering me.

I was certain that the exhilarating ride was destined to become a memory that would put a big smile on my face for many years to come!

Goal 22 is tamed – horse riding at sunset

Tuesday, December 9, 2008
(Gold Beach, Oregon, USA)

As soon as we arrived in town Debbie came to meet us, and whisked me away for the next activity, which was actually on my list of goals.

I have tried horse riding a few times, and am happy to admit being a bit nervous of them. They are just so big and powerful, and it seems to me that if they get the idea into their head that they want to do something, what can you do to stop them? I had a bit of a nerve-wracking experience on a horse on holiday in Tunisia once, when it bolted, scared by a motorbike, but managed to live to tell the tale!

My goal, therefore, has been to have the confidence and ability to gallop a horse along a deserted beach at sunset. Ideally this would be a romantic ride with a perfect companion, but this part of the picture I had mentally painted for myself was not a necessity for the completion of the goal. My companion on the ride was to be Paul, and he had promised that romance would not be a part of the ride!

We met up with Paul, who seemed very blasé about galloping on a horse. "Just tell her to go, and you'll be fine," he said. I wasn't convinced, but he wasn't advocating weeks of costly lessons, as most people to whom I have mentioned this goal seem to do. It was almost sunset and there was a beautiful beach just across the road. This was my chance!

We walked the horses down to the beach, and got there just before sunset. It was beautiful. My horse, a girl called Booty, seemed very steady and relaxed. When Paul spurred his horse on, Booty followed suit with a word of encouragement, and before I knew it we were galloping! I'm sure I didn't look very stylish, but I felt pretty comfortable, and after a quick few words of advice from Paul we were off again.

We tried swapping horses, and I climbed aboard Bo, a Formula 1 of the horse world, now warmed up and ready to go! And go he tried to do, until the saddle slipped a bit, and I found myself on my backside on the beach! I wasn't badly hurt, but there is now a big and painful bruise developing! I got back on Bo briefly, but I think he knew I was nervous now, and I soon elected to swap back.

We galloped again, heading back for the stables as the sky turned a brilliant orange behind us. What an absolutely perfect way to achieve another goal.

Afterwards we all went to a local restaurant for dinner, meeting Jeff, Kelli and Riley there too, and the freshly-caught local crab was delicious. Later we headed back to Ghost Cottage, and Kelli and the others left me on my own there for the night.

To be continued...

I was a little nervous, but quite excited about the rest of the evening, as I prepared to take on the challenge of one of the extra five goals that had been picked by blog readers before my journey had commenced.

Before Kelli left me alone for the evening, she told me that she had been chatting on the phone to a friend of hers who did tarot card and spiritual readings, and they had been discussing me. I was a little mystified as to how someone could perform a spiritual reading, over the phone, for someone they haven't even spoken to, but I withheld my scepticism.

Kelli told me that her friend had said that she felt I had another goal, one which wasn't written as part of the list of 100, one that was more important than any of the other goals, hanging over everything that I did like an umbrella.

Before Kelli had even finished speaking, I knew exactly what her friend was talking about. I knew, and had probably always known, that my unwritten, unspoken goal was that a new love would enter my life, and fill that dark hole that my wife's absence still left.

This was the first time that I had fully realised and acknowledged this truth. However, my sceptical side still insisted quietly that you didn't need to be psychic to figure out that a man travelling the world alone after his divorce might just be open to the idea of a new romance!

Ghostly Goal 23 completed
Wednesday, December 10, 2008
(Gold Beach, Oregon, USA)

Ghost Cottage has an interesting history, and apparently has quite a reputation in the local area. Debbie had introduced me to Kelli and Riley, who live there, and on our first evening together they told us tales of things they had seen, felt and heard in the house. They seemed to be a reasonable and sane couple, and that night I went to bed with an air of expectation, but as reported in yesterday's blog, heard or felt nothing.

Bill was a previous owner of the house, born on 6th December 1945, and died at the age of 32 in late 1978. As reported in the local newspaper, The Curry County Reporter, he died of head injuries caused by a car accident when on a hunting trip with friends. However, all is not as it seems, and Bill now haunts his old home, with a tale to tell, somewhat similar to the movie Ghost. Apparently in town, what really happened to Bill is fairly common knowledge. Kelli and Riley moved here in 2006, and a ghostly Bill told Kelli the true story of the night he died. With his group of friends on a hunting trip, all of them having had more than a few drinks that night, they decided to throw axes at a tree. Unfortunately in the drunken confusion Bill was hit by a thrown axe and died. His death was covered up by his friends, who put his body in a car, rolled it down a hill, and reported the accident.

Bill has told Kelli all of this. She has had many facts confirmed, particularly by people at the hospital who examined Bill's dead body, and with many of Bill's friends in town. Apparently she knows all sorts of little details that she could not know any other way. Bill is not upset about the cover-up, but that his favourite pickup truck was sold, not to one of his friends as he would have liked, but to a complete stranger! This pickup truck buyer eventually married Bill's widow, who had received a large life insurance payment. The romantic interloper then bought a plane and set up a local business with the proceeds of the insurance funds. He then proceeded to rip off many of the local people, a lot of them Bill's old friends. The pickup truck buyer apparently died on the anniversary of Bill's death, by flying his plane into the side of a mountain. Bill is currently writing a book, dictated to Kelli, who acts as his secretary.

Last night I was left to my own devices, and from about 9:30pm onwards I sat in the house alone, writing some stuff on the computer. I didn't put any music on, just worked in silence, the only noise being my slow pecking on the keyboard. A couple of times I had to go outside to get something from the RV, and it was cold, quiet and dark out there.

By midnight I was ready for bed, but before turning in for the night I wandered around the house a bit. As Kelli had suggested, I talked to the ghosts, and asked Bill if he could make some noise if he was there. I also, as suggested, played guitar a bit, and invited the lady ghost who lives in the back bedroom to pluck a string on the harp in there. Finally I turned the house lights off and took some photos in the dark. Before bed I went to the bathroom with the door shut, lit just by candle light, another of Kelli's suggestions.

Nothing! Nothing at all! I was disappointed. Although I had felt some trepidation about the evening alone, I was keen to experience something unusual or unexplainable. The only thing that did make me jump a bit was a scrabbling noise at the patio window as I had worked on the computer. Just a possum, my logical mind says.

I wonder if people are like radio receivers, and I am just tuned to the wrong channel. I guess for now I remain an open minded sceptic!

Continuing north, my next planned stop was in Portland, but I started to run into some vehicular issues shortly after leaving Gold Beach. The weather had turned colder, and the RV seemed to be struggling to keep the engine battery fully charged. The red light on the dashboard forced me to find an auto electrician, who did some tests, and pronounced my alternator dead.

I decided to continue onwards, hoping that the remaining charge in the battery would get me to my destination. I had a couple of appointments to keep in Portland. My first was with David, who had been a competition winner on my ALife4Sale website.

In the run-up to the auction I had made a video to show my entertainment system at the house, and it had featured several movie clips. I had decided to run a little competition, and David had been the film buff who had managed to name most of the movies in the video. His appropriate prize had been the book "1001 Movies You Must See Before You Die".

He had been kind enough to invite me to stop off with him and his family as I passed through. The RV made it, but at his house I didn't dare turn the engine off, fearing that I wouldn't get it started again. After a couple of quick phone calls, he had me follow him to his local mechanic. There, after a few sharp intakes of breath, a lot of head shaking, and a few quick tests with an electric meter, a second opinion confirmed the death of my alternator.

I left the RV there with a request for a speedy (and inexpensive!) repair, but when I called to check progress the next day, the news wasn't good. I needed a new water pump too.

David and his family showed me a wonderfully warm welcome, and I got a fantastic tour of Portland. The next evening we met David's buddy Marc, who features regularly on a local radio show. I soon found myself at the station, headphones on, for a live on-air interview.

We toured the fascinating Portland Underground, where poor unfortunates in previous centuries had been press-ganged into labour aboard ships leaving the city, after attending illegal bars, opium dens and brothels hidden away under the streets.

As I prepared to leave the next day, David's daughter Amy made me a very touching presentation. She had emptied her piggy bank, and wanted to give me all her pocket money to assist with the expenses of my forthcoming travels.

With a lump in my throat I explained that I thought I had enough money to manage, that I was very grateful, but that she should keep her pocket money for something that she needed. She still insisted that I take something, and pressed a handmade card upon me, with a dollar bill hidden inside it. I was very touched by her selfless generosity.

When the bill for the RV repair was eventually presented, it was over $700. Maybe I should have accepted Amy's gift, I thought in mild amusement. I had no choice other than to bite the bullet, as I needed to press onward – my second Portland appointment was fast approaching.

At the airport I met up again with Heather, who I had first met on my last night in Chicago. We had stayed in touch by email, and Heather had been planning a few days away. We had managed to arrange a few days together.

This had all been arranged before I had met Susan, and since leaving San Francisco, Susan and I had also kept in touch. She had been suggesting that I should maybe come back down to San Francisco to spend some time with her. I was still also maintaining contact with Mel in Perth.

Oh dear, it was all starting to get a little complicated, and I wondered if I should be feeling guilty. I decided that I really didn't need too feel too bad. Mel and I had made no promises to each other, and I had indicated that I planned to consider myself to be single as I travelled. Susan was lovely, and I wondered where that might lead. Heather also had a strong appeal for me.

I felt that part of my journey was about rediscovering my passion for life, and for me a part of that was about enjoying the warm company of new companions. As Kelli's spiritual friend had suggested, there was an overall goal that hadn't been written as one of the list of 100 goals. I did hope that from my journey I might perhaps find a new partner – somebody that I could feel as passionate about as I had done about my wife.

I thought Mel had come very close to that, but I also knew my actions spoke louder than words. If Mel had been the one, I don't think I would ever have been as enthusiastic about embracing a project that would take me away from her for two years. I liked her, even loved her, but I didn't think that was enough for me. There seemed for me to be a small indefinable something that was missing.

In Seattle, Heather and I stayed with friends of hers, and went to look around the scenic city. Our touristy activities had to be confined to mainly indoor locations, as the weather had now turned much colder, and snow carpeted the ground. We took the elevator to the top of the Space Needle, admiring the snow-shrouded city from high above, and walked to the infamous Pike Place Market, where we were entertained by the fish-throwing antics of the vendors there.

Our long weekend seemed to fly by, and I dropped Heather off at the airport for her flight back to Chicago. We had had a lot of fun together, but the romance that I had thought might blossom hadn't done so, and I had made a definite decision about Susan – I was going to go back to San Francisco to see how things might develop between us.

I had booked a flight from Seattle back to San Francisco for the following evening, and had a day to hang around. I tried to bring my flight forward, wondering if I could get away that evening, but the cost to do so was more than the ticket itself had been.

Eventually I settled for a cold night in the RV, still parked in the short-term parking lot at the airport. The next day I moved to long-term parking, barrelling the RV through a rather large snowdrift to get it parked in a far-flung corner of the carpark, where the long rear end wouldn't inconvenience anybody else. That evening I flew south again.

My next firm date was Christmas Day in Vancouver, so I could easily manage to fit in six warm days with Susan, who was house- and pet-sitting for a friend in a small apartment near the coast.

I was very happy to be back with Susan again so soon, and I felt that it was good to give this relationship a chance to develop. If I didn't, I reasoned, I would never know what may have been possible, and I would never know if I had met and then left someone who may be the person I should be with.

There must have still been an element of guilt though, or as I tried in vain to convince myself, some consideration, as I didn't make any mention on the blog about my return to California. I was aware that I was selfishly trying to keep all options open, by not being completely honest and open about where I was. Susan referred in amusement to my lack of information on the blog as "going dark". I certainly felt like I was acting slightly duplicitously.

The week with Susan was wonderful, and I soon forgot my guilt as I threw myself into living in the moment. We shared a lot of laughs, and had an incredible amount of fun together doing very little really. This wasn't like being a traveller or a tourist. For a while this was like being one half of a couple again. We went shopping together, watched TV, played games, and spent a lot of time in bed!

Leaving San Francisco the second time, to fly back up to icy Seattle, was much harder than driving out over the Golden Gate Bridge had been just a couple of weeks earlier.

Chapter 3 – Weeks 21 to 30

(22nd December 2008 – 1st March 2009)

Canada – USA – Hawaii – Japan – Australia

After a pretty tiring journey through slippery, snowy conditions I made it to the Canadian border, where I was questioned at length about where I was going and what I was planning to do. I think the fact that I had an Australian passport, a vehicle registered in Illinois, and only US$30 in my wallet raised a few suspicions!

Things went from bad to worse when I was asked if I knew anyone in Canada, and where I would be staying. "Yes," I answered confidently, sure that I was on safe ground now. "I know a couple of people in Vancouver, and am staying with one of them."

"And their names are....?" the border guard asked, pen poised to add more notes to his already lengthy jottings.

"Well, one is called Christina, I can't remember her surname. And I am staying with Denise, or maybe it's Debbie, I'd have to look on the computer."

"And how do you know these people?"

Oh dear! "Erm... from the internet."

"You haven't met them?"

"No, no. They contacted me through my website." The safe ground was crumbling under me quickly now.

"And the name of the website is...?" he asked, pen poised again.

"100 goals 100 weeks dot com," I answered proudly, trying not to laugh at the absurdity of the situation.

"Riiiight...! And you have 100 goals, do you?"

"Yes, yes I do."

"And what are you intending to do in Canada?"

"Well, on Christmas Day I am going to work in a soup kitchen, and..."

"Do you have a work visa?"

Oh dear!

Eventually I managed to convince them that I wasn't Public Enemy Number One and made it through, pressing on in darkness to Vancouver. I finally made it to Denise and Duncan's house with the assistance of the ever helpful GPS. Their road hadn't been ploughed, and as I approached their house I spotted an unused parking spot covered in snow. I managed somehow to slide the RV neatly through the deep snow into place.

I enjoyed a few very nice days in Vancouver. Denise and Duncan had a basement apartment that they had invited me to use, as they were between tenants. I had my own bathroom and the luxury of endless internet access.

I also met up with another website contact, Christina, and a few of her friends for a night out. That night I went home with my face aching from laughing. I met up too with Jason, who had offered to help me out in a couple of weeks when I planned to go snowboarding at Whistler.

I ate Christmas dinner with Denise and Duncan, pleased to have someone to share the day with, and honoured that they wanted me to join them too. In the early evening it was time to head out to address my next goal.

Goal 24 completed – Merry Christmas!
Thursday, December 25, 2008
(Vancouver, BC, Canada)

Being away from home for Christmas can be a bit of a challenge, although I don't actually really have anywhere to call home anymore! But I have often thought about doing something different one Christmas, and the idea of volunteering in a homeless shelter has always appealed. It also seems particularly appropriate this year, as I am semi-homeless myself, albeit by choice, rather than due to unfortunate circumstances.

Vancouver is cold and snowy, and has a huge homeless population. I have talked with a few people here about the problem, and it seems that homeless people in Canada tend to end up in Vancouver, as it is warmer than most other places. Good grief – it's freezing cold here at the moment.

The problem is huge, and was tragically brought to the headlines just a few days ago, when a homeless woman burned to death trying to keep warm, by using a candle in her makeshift shelter.

The problem is only expected to get worse, with numbers of homeless here predicted to triple by the start of the Winter Olympics in 2010.

Over the last couple of days I managed to track down a shelter that still wanted volunteers for Christmas Day, and was scheduled to help out from 8pm until midnight. As I headed down there I felt a bit guilty about the huge, delicious Christmas dinner I had enjoyed earlier with Denise and Duncan.

It was a cold and frosty night. I drove carefully into the city, parked the RV, and made my way to "The Dugout". I arrived just before 8pm and entered the front door of the shelter, which looked like a very busy café, with a huge long line of people stretching out the back door.

I looked for my contact Jackie, and soon found myself serving mashed potatoes, as the long line of people waiting to be fed continued to file past the counter. I chatted with the other volunteers to either side of me (peas and carrots to the left, and gravy to my right) and to the people in the queue.

There was a really festive atmosphere, and everybody was having fun. I enjoyed meeting the people we were there to help, but I could not help being staggered by the amount of people that filed through. They had been serving food since 7pm, and we continued to do so almost until 10pm. Jackie estimated that we had fed between 300 and 400 people!

I think the experience is something that will stay with me for a long time. It certainly has given me food for thought, no pun intended.

However, I am a little ambivalent about the conflicting feelings the evening has caused. On one hand I am very pleased to have achieved another goal, and glad to have helped out on Christmas Day. However, I am also troubled by the fact that I can just walk away and get on with the rest of my life. The people there simply do not have that option.

I talked with Jackie for a while about some of the problems she and her volunteers face, as they try to feed these unfortunate people every day. I am amazed and awed by their dedication, and their selfless generosity. It was an absolute privilege to work with these people, even if only for a few hours, and to meet many of the people they are helping, who I would normally pass on the street with hardly a second thought!

Very thought provoking indeed!

Once again, I marvelled that this adventure just seems to keep on offering increasingly amazing and wonderful experiences. Christmas Day had offered an opportunity to do something that had really challenged the way I thought about (or perhaps hadn't really thought at all about) some issues. An evening spent with people who I hardly spared a second glance for had stopped me in my tracks, and really given me something to consider at length. The immediate impact was that I suddenly had a very clear realisation of how lucky I really was, and how little my worries and woes were when compared to things many people have to deal with on a daily basis.

On the flight to Whitehorse the next day I watched the movie "21", staring one of my favourite actors, Kevin Spacey. One of the big questions asked by the main character of himself is "Am I just chasing what I think I want, and ignoring the things that perhaps are really important to me?"

I asked myself the same question, and wondered about the point of all of this travelling. Maybe what I wanted was a simple settled life, like I could perhaps have with Mel and her girls in Perth. Or maybe I could have just stopped in San Francisco with Susan, and stopped chasing this goal-achieving nonsense. A lot of it is certainly great fun at the time, I thought, but is it what I really want? Could all this travelling ever really result in meeting someone who would be the next love of my life?

I didn't know the answer.

Goal 25 – VERY cold!!

Saturday, December 27, 2008
(Whitehorse, Yukon Territory, Canada)

The flight from Vancouver to Whitehorse was only slightly delayed, as our plane had to join the queue to be de-iced, something I have not experienced before. When we finally descended through the clouds the landscape looked white and bleak. Due to another late arrival at Whitehorse, we were unable to de-plane via the air bridge, and had to walk across the tarmac. The temperature was -25 deg C, but I was surprised that it did not feel too bad.

I was met by Moe, who has long been encouraging me to come and visit to go dog-sledding. After a quick drive around town we headed out to her home and kennels. She lives in a log cabin way out in the woods, self-built over the winter of 2005.

Life up here is quite different to anything I have ever experienced before. The cabin does not have running water or mains electricity. Daylight lasts about six hours, from around 9:30am to 3:30pm, so head torches are worn pretty much most of the rest of the time. By the time we got to the cabin it was already dark, and we went out to feed the dogs. Later on we played air hockey with Moe's neighbour Kim, and it all got very competitive.

The next morning we fed the dogs again, and Moe picked the ten that would be our team for the day. They were bundled into the dog box on top of the truck, along with a huge amount of gear, and we were off into the wilderness.

Moe had geared me up with a big coat and waterproof trousers. We made a quick stop at a neighbour's kennel, on the edge of an amazingly beautiful, frozen lake, to collect some snow boots for me. We drove on and parked on the side of a snow-covered road that appeared to be in the middle of absolutely nowhere. We pulled the sled off the roof, and started gearing the dogs up.

Putting the harnesses on was fun, and the dogs seemed very well trained, and quite happy to have a fumbling stranger attempt to prepare them. Moe had eight dogs harnessed by the time I had managed to gear up the other two.

We clipped them onto the gang line, which is attached to the sled, and the dogs seemed very excited, howling and barking, and pulling at the rope. I sat inside the sled, and Moe removed the anchor from the snow. Silence descended, and all the noise from the dogs stopped as they pulled as one.

We gilded along, the only sound being the runners of the sled rails on the snow, and the rattle of snow on the sled cover kicked back from the dogs' feet. We travelled quickly at first, but the dogs soon settled, and steadied to a more even pace. I sat happily watching the snow-covered world glide by.

About twelve miles down the track we veered off the road into the trees, following a narrower trail into a clearing, where we turned the team around. After a few dramas getting back on the track, which involved us both rolling around in the snow as the sled went over, we were heading back. Once sorted out, Moe pulled the dogs up and we swapped places. I stood on the small footpads on the rails, and felt like a real musher.

I didn't have much to do really, as the dogs knew where they were going. My main role was to slow the sled a bit on the downhill sections, so the dogs didn't have to go too fast. I couldn't help giving them a shout of "Mush, mush!" on a flat section, which did spur them on a bit.

The whole experience was incredible, the surroundings beautiful, and I was so pleased to be able to try out something so different to anything I have done before.

Dog sledding in the wilderness was another absolutely awesome and challenging experience. My earlier questions and doubts as I had flown up to Whitehorse had all disappeared again in the enthusiasm for the journey, and the people I was meeting along the way.

Moe's house turned out to be all I had hoped it might be, and more, but also had several features I hadn't ever considered. The house itself was a secluded log cabin hidden away in the forest. The setting was very scenic, and I imagined it would be a very atmospheric week staying in such a location.

But I had never imagined that the cabin would have no electricity and no mains water supply.

Moe had a generator, and a couple of big batteries to store power. The generator would run a battery charger which would top up one of the batteries. She would then have to swap the batteries over to charge the next one. When charged, the generator could be switched off, and an inverter would change the stored 12 volt battery output to 115 volts to power lights, computer, and the internet connection.

The system seemed incredibly inefficient, and I suggested at least joining the two batteries in parallel, which would mean there would no longer be a need to swap them over every couple of hours.

Water had to be brought in from the local community centre, about eight kilometres away. About ten large plastic containers had to be taken in the truck, and filled with water from a warmed supply that was available inside the small garage. The water supply was warmed to prevent it freezing in the pipes. At minus 35ºC, there is no other unfrozen water anywhere nearby.

With no piped water in the cabin, there was of course no bathroom, no shower, and no plumbed-in toilet. The nearest available shower was at the swimming pool in town, 50 kilometres away.

The toilet at the cabin was a wooden outhouse, which meant, in temperatures well below freezing, that journeys out there had to be swift and efficient. The small cubicle had thin wooden walls, coated with a thick layer of ice, and the toilet seat was fashioned out of polystyrene, as a wooden seat tended to ice over too.

I wondered what the big stick standing in the corner was for, but didn't ask. After an early visit to the outhouse in the dark, I figured out what the function of the stick might be. In the dark, with my head torch to light the way, I couldn't help myself, and like a ghoulish onlooker at a car crash, I had to look down the long-drop hole, against my better judgement.

The pit was quite deep, but rising up majestically from the bottom was a towering thin spire. What was happening was immediately obvious. With the aim point being the same at each visit, new additions were added to the top of the frozen pile below, and in turn became frozen there too. As in limestone cave formations, the stalagmite continued to grow, and eventually would get too tall. The frozen outhouse stalagmite had to be toppled occasionally, hence the big stick!

Fortunately it wasn't a job that had to be attended to during my brief stay.

Moe and I had only exchanged brief emails before I had arrived, and I didn't even know what she looked like until I had stepped off the plane and met her. In the short emails she had managed to fit in a couple of what appeared to be slightly suggestive comments. I hadn't been sure if my interpretation had been correct, but a couple of days into the week in Whitehorse, I discovered that they certainly had been considered and intentional comments.

From the first night at the cabin I had been attracted to Moe, but had no idea if she felt the same way. On the day after our dog-sledding adventure we had laid around on her bed in front of the stove, reading and chatting. That night I had wanted to kiss her, but had no idea how an approach might be taken, and at the end of the evening, simply said goodnight, and went upstairs to bed.

The next morning I had come back down again, and laid on her bed beside her. We spent much of the day chatting and reading, and I eventually built up the courage to ask what might happen if I tried to kiss her. Things went pretty smoothly from then on!

She later told me about her plan, which had involved me from the start. She called it the "Imported Lover Project"!! The idea was that I was there purely for the week, and part of my role was to provide physical intimacy, but nothing more. Moe had recently been divorced too, and missed the physical side of having a partner, but really didn't want anyone permanent in her life at the time.

I was obviously a "safe bet", as I had things to do and places to go, and there was no danger of me hanging around.

This arrangement suited me fine, but as the days went by we only managed to get out with the dogs one more time, spending a lot more of our energies on "Imported Lover" activities.

I liked Moe, but accepted that this was never going to come to anything. Once again I was happy to live in the moment, and enjoy the shared companionship and closeness.

During one conversation I suggested something that we might do the next time we met. "No, no, no!" said Moe. "I've explained this. There will be no 'next time'. When you leave here, that's it. No email, no phone calls. Over and done, no more contact at all."

"Er, okay," I said.

When we said farewell at the airport as she dropped me off, I intended to stick to our agreement, although I had really enjoyed the time I had spent with her.

Back in Vancouver a day later, just before I was due to set off for the ski slopes of Whistler, I received an email from Moe, with the intriguing subject line: "I hear you laughing as you see my name on this e-mail."

Apparently the ILP had been deemed a complete failure:

Progress report on the Imported Lover Project: January 1, 2009.
Project successful, plan implemented and conducted as expected.
End result: complete failure.
Female study subject unable to retain required non-attachment.

I was flattered and surprised. Moe's tough and uncompromising exterior had proved to be a big front, and she suggested that there really was no reason why we couldn't stay in touch. After all, she reasoned, who knows what the future holds?

My travels had once again allowed me to meet another inspiring, intriguing, and wonderful person, and this further opened the doors of future possibilities, I thought happily.

Goal 26 achieved – more fun in the snow

Saturday, January 3, 2009
(Whistler, BC, Canada)

The last time I was on a snowboard was five months ago, back in August last year, when I achieved the very first of my 100 goals, by snowboarding on the huge indoor ski slope in Dubai.

That was a brief session of only two hours, and is the only time I have been on a snowboard in the last three years.

Before coming up to Whistler, about two hours north of Vancouver, I should have perhaps done a little more exercise in preparation for the slopes than I actually have. I don't think that sitting in the driving seat of the RV for hours on end is the best form of snowboarding preparation!

When I came up to Whistler yesterday with Jason and Jonathon, I guess I was not quite as fit for boarding as I could have been. They are both keen skiers, and even though I got the impression that they were taking things easy for the day, I struggled to keep up with them. By the end of my first day on the slopes my legs were like jelly!

However, I still had an awesome day! The snow was good, although still a bit thin in places. We covered both sides of the twin resort, spending time on both Blackcomb and Whistler itself, which is made very easy by the new Peak 2 Peak gondola joining the two summits.

Visibility was pretty good, and for a few minutes it looked like the sun might try to come out, but it never quite made it. Later in the afternoon it got a bit windier, and temperatures at the top of a couple of the chairlifts reached -17 deg C. With the wind-chill it felt even colder. And I thought I had escaped this sort of thing when I left Whitehorse!

At the end of the day, after a bite to eat, Jason and Jonathon dropped me off at the hostel I had booked into for a couple of evenings, and then they headed for home. I am planning on staying up here for a couple of extra days.

I was up early today and back out onto the slopes first thing. It was very quiet for the first few runs before the resort started to fill again for the day, and I had some great runs while my legs still felt in reasonably good shape.

As the day wore on visibility reduced, the snow started falling, and my last run of the day was down an almost deserted stretch of piste covered in fresh powder – fantastic!

There is a lot of fresh snow on the ground this evening, and tomorrow, my last on the slopes here, should be a great day.

As I left Vancouver the weather had improved a bit, and much of the snow had gone, making the journey back to Seattle much easier than the trip north had been.

Romantic life was continuing to be a little complicated now, as Susan and I had arranged to meet in Seattle, and she would join me for the journey back to San Francisco.

My next destination was Hawaii, and as yet I hadn't booked a flight from mainland USA. Original plans had been to sell the RV and fly out of either Vancouver or Seattle, but a few more days with Susan would be fun. As I planned to return to the States again in the future, I decided to keep the fairly reliable RV, and looked for a place in San Francisco where I would be able to store it for approximately six months.

The journey south was beautiful, and we stopped off at a couple of nice RV parks in off-the-beaten-track towns on the way. Back in San Francisco I found a storage place who very kindly offered free storage for the RV in return for a link on my website. I was happy to oblige.

Susan and I talked at length about my journey, and I got the impression that she would like me to hang around for a lot longer. She pointed out that I could stop my journey at any time, that I didn't have to complete it if I didn't want to, and that I didn't have anyone to answer to for any decision I made.

She was right of course, but I asked what she thought I might do in San Francisco. I had no work visa, so if I could work at all it would have to be off-the-books illegal employment in a coffee shop or something. That wasn't the life I had set off in search of. Susan didn't like my answer, or the fact that my decision, reasonably easily made, was to continue on my journey.

As I left San Francisco for a third time, the plane banked to the left, and from my window seat I had an incredible aerial view of the whole city below. I could see the bay and the Bay Bridge that I had sailed under. There was Alcatraz Island, and then the Golden Gate Bridge as we continued to bank left around the city.

I looked down and imagined I could make out Susan's neighbourhood far below, and as the plane started to head out to the west, I thought sadly that living there and working in a coffee shop might not be too bad at all.

I was struggling again with moving on. Would this ever stop? I felt like I was torturing myself endlessly. But in my heart I knew that I still wanted my adventure to continue. As it had been when I had chosen to leave Australia, my enthusiasm for continuing the journey spoke volumes to me about my readiness to settle down. Perhaps I knew that I still had some answers to find before I would feel ready to settle in one place, or with one person.

I had nothing at all planned for Hawaii – no accommodation arranged and no activities booked. I had only a couple of email addresses of people who suggested that we could meet up at some point. Life was going to be a little trickier without the RV. I had got used to having a home on wheels, and would miss the ease and convenience that it afforded.

Once again however, and without too much effort on my part, events conspired to work out for me in quite an extraordinary way, and everything just seemed to fall into place nicely for me.

Debbie in Oregon had been putting her incredible organisational talents to good use again, and having lived in Hawaii before, she still had some friends and contacts there. She put me in touch with Becky at the Big Island Visitor's Bureau. By the time I had caught my transfer flight from Oahu, Becky had arranged free accommodation, a free tour to see the volcano, and a couple of interviews with local newspapers too.

Goal 27 achieved – Kilauea volcano

Saturday, January 17, 2009
(Big Island, Hawaii, USA)

I was up very early this morning and packed my stuff for the day in darkness, before driving the 20 miles back to town. There I met up with Danny, the guide from Hawaii Forest and Trail who would be taking a group of twelve, including myself, on a tour of the Kilauea Volcano.

This had been organised by Becky at the Big Island Visitors Bureau, in response to contact from Debbie in Oregon about my visit here.

As we drove across the island, Danny told us stories of the history and culture of Hawaii, as well as facts on volcanoes, and the formation of the Hawaiian Islands chain.

Our first volcano stop was to overlook the huge Kilauea Caldera, a crater which is three miles long and two miles wide. Smoke seeps out of cracks in the floor, and the whole scene is quite other-worldly.

Next we took a walk through a lava tube, which is formed when flowing lava develops a skin over the top, but continues to run underneath the surface, forming a tube of flowing molten rock. When the lava stops flowing, an empty rock tube remains, and these can often be miles long.

We also took a look into the smaller Kilauea Ika Crater, and behind that we could see the huge plume of sulphur dioxide which the volcano has been producing for months.

Our final stop of the day was to see the spectacular point where flowing lava reaches the sea. At the water's edge, the lava instantly boils the seawater, which causes a huge steam cloud. We were very fortunate to be able to see this, as it has been occurring at this point only for a matter of weeks. For the previous few days the wind has been blowing in the wrong direction, and the road has been closed due to the danger. However, today the wind shifted, and the road was opened again – perfect timing. Where the lava meets the water there are often explosions, with new rock being thrown high in the air.

As the lava meets the water, it is cooled and solidifies, and becomes new rock, and the Big Island continues to get bigger - what an amazing process to see in action. This newly solidified rock becomes the youngest piece of land on the planet.

The whole experience was quite incredible, and the views stunning. It is truly awesome to see the newest piece of land on the planet being formed right before your eyes.

Hawaii also offered a chance to consider more spiritual matters, as I had been invited to stay in wonderfully quirky alternative accommodation. Barbara is owner and operator of the beautifully situated Dragonfly Ranch, and despite being fully booked at the time, was happy to find some space for me.

My “bedroom” was a wooden platform high up on the hillside above the main house, overlooking the forest and ocean. On the floor of my platform bedroom was a brightly coloured labyrinth. I chose to lay out my sleeping bag right at the centre of the swirling design.

My shower was outside, hidden among the lush forest foliage. At night under the hot water, in complete darkness, I could gaze at the millions of stars in the clear sky above.

Visitors to Dragonfly Ranch were varied, fascinating and entertaining. There were sound healers, tarot card readers, mystics, and psychics of all kinds, most offering some kind of reading or healing therapy, many of which I had never even heard of before. I realised that this was a very unique opportunity, and decided for once to suspend my scepticism and disbelief in all things supernatural, and simply see what this experience had to offer.

The place was incredibly peaceful and relaxing. I tried a tarot card reading, read several of the books available, and sat for a mystic reading where the reader passed on messages from departed loved ones.

At the end of my stay, for me the jury was still out, but I had seen something quite extraordinary during the mystic reading with down-to-earth documentary maker Troy. He had spoken about a couple of ancestors who I hadn't really recognised, and then towards the end of the reading, he said we would ask my spirit guide to come forward. As if on cue a small gecko wandered across the table towards us, one of its front legs missing. Troy pointed the brightly coloured creature out to me, and as we watched it deftly caught a passing fly.

Apparently this creature represented the wounded aspect of my personality, but its ease at catching its meal as it flew by also indicated that I wasn't going to go hungry in the future – things were going to work out for me.

I took a couple of photos of the bright green lizard, which was very obliging, even with my camera only inches from its nose. The most incredible thing was when I put my finger on the table in front of it, it confidently walked over and rested its chin on my fingernail. I was stunned.

Spirit guide, or tame, hungry lizard? My sceptical side argued for the latter, but this creature seemed to take a real liking to me, showing no fear at all. It hung around while we chatted, and at the end of the reading, it wandered to the edge of the table and disappeared into the foliage.

I didn't quite know what to make of the fact that the one tattoo that Laura had had was of a gecko too?

On the Monday morning, as I sat in a beachfront café overlooking the beautiful ocean, my phone rang and I found myself chatting to one of the dive masters from Jack's Diving Locker, where I was booked in for a night dive with manta rays that evening. Oh no, I thought, it's going to be postponed again, as it had been for the last couple of evenings, because of poor visibility.

But no, Matthew had seen me on the front page of the local newspaper, West Hawaii Today, and had been intrigued and inspired by my story. Did I want to go on a "black water dive" after the manta ray dive that evening, he wondered? It wouldn't cost me anything, and would be one of the most memorable dives of my life, he promised. I had no idea what a black water dive was, but the obvious answer was a resounding "Yes!"

As Matthew and I talked, the waitress in the café caught my attention, waving the newspaper at me. "Is that you?" she mouthed. I was stunned to see myself sharing the front page with Barrack Obama, who was to be inaugurated as President the very next day.

"Obama: 'Anything possible'", said the main headline in huge type. I couldn't agree more, as I considered the amazing list of experiences with which my days in Hawaii were filling.

Goal 28 - amazing underwater ballet

Monday, January 19, 2009
(Big Island, Hawaii, USA)

Almost seven years ago Laura and I took a trip up the west coast of Western Australia, only a couple of months after moving there from the UK. It is a beautiful stretch of coastline, and way up north there is a little place called Coral Bay. It is possible to go diving with manta rays there, but at the time our finances were pretty stretched. We decided not to do the dive, and save our money to go whale shark watching instead. I have always wanted to do a dive with manta rays since then, and imagined it would happen on another trip up the west coast of Oz.

However, two people informed me of the possibility of manta ray diving here in Kona, on the Big Island. Kathy suggested it as a possibility, and Melissa sent me a link to Jack's Diving Locker, where she had done the manta dive a couple of times.

Jack's Diving Locker offer a night dive with the manta rays, and I contacted them to book for Friday night. Unfortunately the weather prevented any diving that evening, and over the weekend, so the trip had been re-scheduled for tonight.

The whole trip started just after lunch, when I went to the dive shop to get a lift out to the harbour. There we were all geared up, and around 4pm we headed out of the harbour, a little nervous as we had just seen a big swordfish towed in to be weighed with a couple of huge shark bites taken out of it!

The first dive was a daylight dive on the reef. Our guide Joe took our little group of six around and showed us all sorts of multi-coloured fish, and a couple of moray eels too.

After a quick bite to eat as the sun set, we geared up again, with torches this time. We dived down to about 40 feet, and joined a circle of other divers on the bottom. We waited for a while, and suddenly a manta gracefully swooped into the circle and swam around, feeding on the plankton drawn by the lights.

It wasn't a huge one, perhaps 8 feet from wingtip to wingtip, but it was so graceful and spectacular as it glided around the circle, swooping again and again right over the heads of those with the brightest torches.

I moved around the circle to join Keller, one of our group's instructors, as he had some very bright lights. The amazing creature passed a couple of times less than a foot above us.

Eventually our circle broke up and set off to explore the reef. Towards the end of the dive there was only Joe, myself and Jason, one of the other customers left with air, and the manta rejoined the three of us. It swept by so close, and on one pass rubbed right across the top of my head.

On the surface Joe climbed aboard the boat, and the manta joined Jason and I again, right below us. We held on to each other so we didn't drift apart and shone our torches together to gather the plankton. The amazing huge creature did beautiful back summersaults right below us, coming within inches as it turned over and over, like an incredible three dimensional underwater ballet. I could have stayed for hours watching it, but we were eventually called in to the boat to head back to shore.

What an incredibly moving experience, to be so close to such a gentle giant.

That night the black water dive turned out to be very much as Matthew had promised, one of the most memorable dives I had ever experienced. Just a couple of hours after seeing the beautiful manta rays, and sharing the front page with the new President, it all added up to one outstanding day.

On the boat there were only three of us, photographer Steve coming along to record the dive too, and after a quick briefing we headed out into darkness about three miles offshore. There they geared me up with a flashlight, clipped me onto a weighted line hanging fifty feet down into the dark waters, and asked if I was happy to head on down alone. Apparently at night all sorts of creatures from the depths come up towards the surface.

I'm generally not one to back down from the challenge, and in I went, despite feeling quite apprehensive. It was very dark as I descended alone, and as I arrived at the bottom of the line, I looked up and could barely make out the boat far above. All around was completely black, and shining the light down between my feet revealed nothing at all as far as the beam of the torch reached. I was very aware of the fact that there was about a mile deep of black water below me.

Occasionally I would see a small fish pass through the light far below, and it was very difficult not to let the imagination run wild. I was glad when Steve joined me with his camera.

There were some very unusual creatures to see, some very small, some a bit bigger, none of them like anything I have ever seen before! They were incredibly beautiful, and in the torchlight, lit up in the brightest iridescent colours.

We stayed down for as long as our air lasted, around 45 minutes, and eventually returned to the surface cold but elated at having experienced something so unique. It took me quite a while to get to sleep in the early hours of the morning at the silent backpackers' hostel that was my home for the night!

Becky had been busy in the Big Island Visitor's Bureau, and had arranged several fantastic adventures for me to try out during my time on the island. I had been invited on a submarine journey, diving to over 100 feet down the seawall, and had also enjoyed a thrilling ride on the ocean in a Zodiac inflatable with a monster outboard engine.

We had spotted a whale spouting, seen spinner dolphins, and snorkelled on a beautiful reef right where Captain Cook had met his untimely demise at the hands of the irate locals in 1779.

While waiting for the last of the snorkellers to return I chatted with Kyle, skipper's mate aboard Captain Zodiac, asking him what had brought him to Hawaii, and how he had ended up working aboard the zodiac. "Oh, I don't work here. I just help out now and then because it's fun." What did he do as a job, I wondered? "I'm a helicopter instructor. I work at a flight school out at the airport."

"Oh really? One of the goals on my list is to get my hands on the controls of a helicopter," I told him.

"Oh really?" he replied. "I just happen to have a free slot on Tuesday morning."

"Oh really? I'll be at the airport on Tuesday, as I fly out that afternoon."

"Well it looks like we are going to get another of your goals ticked off before you leave the island then, doesn't it?

Goal 29 – take the controls of a helicopter
Tuesday, January 20, 2009
(Big Island, Hawaii, USA)

I woke early this morning at the backpacker's hostel in Kona, where I had to sneak in quietly last night at around midnight, still wide awake and excited by the evening's diving activities. When I climbed out of the bed the floor felt like it was swaying slightly – I think I spent a bit too long aboard various swaying vessels yesterday!

I got up and found the TV on quietly in the common room, with only one other person watching the inauguration ceremony for the new president. We sat and watched while the rest of the hostel still slept. My timing was perfect, as I was just in time to watch the last couple of speeches, and then the official swearing-in.

After breakfast I walked up to the main highway with my bags, and stuck my thumb out again, heading back to the airport. I had to wait awhile in the hot sun, but eventually got a lift with Kevin, who took me right to my destination – Mauna Loa Helicopters flight training school.

After a quick briefing, Kyle took me up on a flight along the coast in a little red Robinson R22 two-seater helicopter. We took off and hovered a couple of feet off the ground at the airport while we waited for clearance, and Kyle bravely let me try to hover the helicopter. He had to step in quickly on the controls a couple of times, as the machine swayed about all over the place, with very little in the way of positive control from me at all.

Once cleared we rose quickly and followed the main highway south, and at 500 feet Kyle handed the controls over to me to try straight-and-level flying, which was a little easier. He still had to step in to make corrections, but as time passed he did so less and less, and I started to get a bit of a feel for it.

I was slightly alarmed when Kyle let go of everything, and picked up my camera and started snapping away, but I concentrated on what I was doing, and seemed to manage okay.

We continued south along the coast with me at the controls for quite a bit of the time, with regular verbal input and occasional manual input from Kyle. At the point where we were due to turn around we found the Captain Zodiac boat near the cliffs. Kyle flew us around it a couple of times as I filmed and waved.

On the way back Kyle demonstrated a dead-engine landing, and then helped me on the approach to the airport. I tried hovering again, and did slightly better than my first try, but it is quite alarming how quickly the thing can get out of hand. One over-correction and the unstable machine was all over the place, with the incredibly cool and patient Kyle quickly stepping in to sort out my mess.

This brings my time on The Big Island to an end, as I am now sat at the airport itself, just along the road from the helicopter school, waiting for my flight back to Oahu. I have had an extraordinary time here, and have experienced so much here in such a short time. Much of it is thanks to Debbie, her wonderful organisation, and her initial contact with Becky at the Big Island Tourism Bureau.

I still continue to be amazed, excited and immensely grateful for the way things just seem to work out so well for me. For example, the set of connections that today led to achieving Goal 28 started with Debbie's interest in my goals way back in June. I then got to meet her in Oregon, and achieve a couple of goals with her help. She happens to have lived in Hawaii, and made some enquiries here on my behalf. This led her to Becky, who I did not even meet. Becky arranged, among other things, a trip on Captain Zodiac's boat, which wasn't one of my goals, but sounded like great fun. On the boat one of the staff just happened to be a helicopter instructor, and in our random chat this came up! And he had some free time just hours before I am due to fly out. Wonderful!

Hawaii - what a beautiful place. I love it here, and I am sure I will be back sometime soon.
Aloha!

I wondered again about the amazing string of wonderful people, lucky contacts, random conversation, and fortunate timing which had allowed me to achieve another goal unexpectedly.

Not only had I had control of a helicopter in flight, but I had done it over the spectacularly beautiful coastline of Hawaii, once again achieving a goal in a way that far exceeded my hopes or expectations.

I marvelled at the incredible string of co-incidences that have conspired to allow this to happen. I thought of a couple of documentaries I had watched recently, and some discussions that I had with Moe while in the wilderness of Canada just a week or two earlier.

Maybe if you put an idea out there with enough conviction, larger forces than we understand go to work to help that idea become reality. At times I certainly felt that this was the case, and my time on The Big Island has caused me to question some of the things I have always taken for granted.

Or is that just Dragonfly Ranch exerting its subtle alternative influence over my thinking?

On Oahu I had been invited to stay with Matt and Jackie, who had moved a few months earlier from Washington DC to fulfil their dream of living in Hawaii. Being goal-oriented people they were happy to help me on my way, and I was given a couch to sleep on in the front room of their apartment. The balcony outside my window literally overhung the water's edge just south of Waikiki Beach, and facing west, offered some beautiful sunset views.

Both Matt and Jackie were keen to join me for the next goal on the list, and we wandered up the beach in search of the boat operator we needed.

Goal 30 - Hawaii Five-o

Saturday, January 24, 2009
(Oahu, Hawaii, USA)

I remember as a kid watching Hawaii Five-o, and thinking that it looked fantastic - it was always sunny - but the downside was that the place seemed to be riddled with crime!

I have always wanted to visit the beautiful Hawaiian island of Oahu, and so far I have managed to stay out of harm's way. One of the things that I most wanted to do when I got here was to ride the surf at Waikiki in an outrigger canoe, just as I remembered from the dramatic opening scenes of Hawaii Five-0.

This morning Matt, Jackie and I wandered along the seafront to Waikiki, and chatted to Uncle Gill from Star Beach Boys on the beach there. He soon had us sorted out with a captain, and with a couple of additions to our crew, we were off into the surf.

Fifteen bucks for about half an hour out there seemed very reasonable, and we caught three long waves, with time for a quick swim in the beautiful warm water before the last ride in.

What a beautiful day, and what a beautiful place in which to achieve goal #30.

The rest of my time on Oahu was just like a holiday. I had completed all the goals I had planned for Hawaii, and even achieved an extra, unscheduled goal too. I had a few days left, and a few people to meet.

Julie and Karen took me on a tour of the island. Shannon, a friend of Steph, who had joined me to the Statue of Liberty in New York, took me to a beach on a golden sunrise morning and we took turns paddling out on her paddle board.

I took a bus down the coast to the beautiful Hanamau Bay, and spent some time wandering around Waikiki and Honolulu.

Matt and Jackie took me to see the spectacular Diamond Head volcano crater, and we climbed up to the rim, where we admired the sweeping views up and down the coast.

Pearl Harbor was a more thought-provoking visit, and once again Matt and Jackie were wonderful tour guides.

During the occasional break from my busy Hawaiian tourist schedule, I sat happily on the balcony at home chatting with my hosts. It was all very relaxing, but there was work to be done too, and I spent quite a bit of time planning and organising on the internet. My next stop was going to be a lot more of a challenge.

On the day I was booked to fly from Hawaii to Japan, the next goal practically fell into my lap, achieved with very little input from myself.

Goal 31 – Paula Campbell is in the top ten!
Monday, January 26, 2009
(Internet)

Today is Australia Day, when the whole country celebrates it's identity as a nation, and commemorates the arrival of the First Fleet in 1788, the unfurling of the British flag at Sydney Cove and the proclamation of British sovereignty over the eastern seaboard of Australia.

I don't think there could be a better day than this to announce that Goal #31, getting my Australian buddy Paula Campbell into the top ten in a Google search for her name, has been achieved.

Paula is currently living and working in London, and I am sure that she will be celebrating Australia Day today, somewhere in the big city with her fellow countrymen and women. Happy Australia Day Paula!

Huge thanks are due to Anthony Merizzi, who is the web genius who has somehow made this happen. He somehow discovered this goal in my list of things I wanted to do, and made it a pet project of his own.

I really thought that this might be one of the harder goals to achieve, and did not know where to start. Anthony has achieved it relatively easily, despite there being a very well-known singer called Paula Campbell too.

Anthony runs his own Search Engine Optimisation business, and if you need help in this area, he seems to be pretty good at it!

Happy Australia Day everyone!

For the first time in several months I felt the familiar twist of apprehension as I boarded the plane for Japan, and headed for a country completely unfamiliar to me. However, this time it felt nowhere near as bad as either of my previous departures, initially from Perth to Dubai or later from England to Germany and the USA.

I felt that I had gained a huge confidence in myself over the past months, and was much better at travelling now. I had faced and overcome many problems on my travels so far, and was sure that I could handle anything that was thrown at me.

I also knew that almost everywhere I had been, and hopefully in most of the places to which I was yet to travel, I would be hanging out with some great people, and making some wonderful new friends. The people that I was meeting along the way really were proving to be such an integral part of the whole adventure, as much as any of the goals on the list.

Konichiwa – Goal 32 achieved in Tokyo

Wednesday, January 28, 2009
(Tokyo, Japan)

Konichiwa! (kon-nee-chee-wah)

I arrived at Tokyo airport yesterday afternoon, and found an ATM to get some Japanese Yen. The maths took a while, as I tried to figure how much Y10,000 is worth. I didn't want to get it wrong, and withdraw ten bucks worth, or try for a couple of thousand by mistake either! I am reasonably confident that I have about $400 worth of Yen with me now.

I found the bus that I needed to catch, bought a ticket with a couple of minutes to spare, and travelled for a couple of hours through the centre of Tokyo and out the other side.

At the bus station in Shin Yurigaoka I called Connie, who had offered me accommodation with her family. I eventually met her husband Kazuyuki at the station, and took the metro with him to their home in the suburbs.

There I met Connie, and their four children, three boys, aged 12, 9 and 6, and a girl aged 3. We went out for dinner, the young daughter happily chatting to me on the way in the back of the car in a confusing mixture of Japanese and English. She had me laughing delightedly, as she seemed quite surprised at my lack of understanding. She tried teaching me the Japanese words for the colours of the traffic lights we passed, but I struggled to remember the words later.

This morning I was wide awake at 3am, body-clock still on Hawaii-time, and did some planning for the day. After an early breakfast with Kazuyuki, I gathered some things, and headed into the city.

Tokyo's railway system is mind-boggling, and although the section of system I was on seemed relatively easy to navigate, the ticketing system is a minefield of possibilities. Several different companies seem to offer several different options and services. The complicated train system map initially took quite a while to figure out too.

Eventually I made it to the city, just in time to meet Kazuyuki for lunch. He showed me a nearby capsule hotel and he tried to book me in for the evening. Oh dear, everything had been going so well. Kazuyuki was too honest when asked if I had any tattoos! Unfortunately I found that a goal achieved earlier was now in conflict with this goal at this particular hotel. Kazuyuki's only possible explanation was that maybe they had had trouble with tattooed gang members previously!

According to the list of restrictions, it would also be an issue if I turned up "deeply drunked"!

We got directions to another capsule hotel nearby, where the possibility that I may be a tattooed thug didn't seem to be an issue, but my lack of ability to speak Japanese would be. However, Kazuyuki saved the day by translating the many rules, and left his mobile number with the manager in case I proved to be too troublesome!

For the rest of the afternoon I wandered around happily soaking up the atmosphere of the city.

There are some amazing sites, and some completely unexplainable ones. I imagine that I wandered most of the afternoon with a look of puzzled amusement on my face. The huge array of schoolgirl and nurse outfits in one shop window was eyebrow-raising!

I took a look in a few electronics stores, where I found myself in gadget heaven. The range of technology was fantastic, but the prices seemed a bit higher than they had been in the US. My purchase of a new computer may have to wait for a while yet.

Eventually I managed to tear myself away and headed to my accommodation where I tried out the tiny cubicle, and made use of the communal baths and sauna. The capsule hotel is for men only, no women allowed. The choice of stations on the tiny TV in the cubicle reflected this, with channel 21 offering "adult-oriented content"!

I headed back out for a bite to eat, and a wander around gazing at the bright neon lights. I strayed into a video games arcade which spread out over six floors, filled with an array of amazing games I have never seen before. Somehow I ended up in the extremely busy red light district, and must have stood out like a sore thumb, as I seemed to get a lot of invites into little clubs hidden away down dark, narrow staircases.

The whole place really comes alive and is so vibrant at night. I could have walked around for hours. It is quite fascinating and so different from most places that I have experienced. Eventually though, I headed "home" for an early evening. I am still trying to get over a last lingering bit of jetlag, and this morning's early start, I think.

Now it's time to complete the goal, by sleeping here tonight. I might just check out Channel 21 again though first!

Oyasuminasai. (oh-yah-soo-mee-nah-sigh)

I spent another couple of days with Connie and family, and tried to get out and about as much as possible to explore Tokyo. At first, as I had passed quickly through Tokyo on the bus from the airport, I had thought it looked like many other big cities. But when I ventured out, I found it to be quite an unusual place. It was so different from anywhere else I have ever been.

A blog reader had made a comment about Tokyo, saying, "The thing about Tokyo, for me, was I never, ever forgot for even a moment I was in a foreign country!"

I too found that it was impossible to forget that here I was truly a stranger in a strange land.

Most of the signs and written materials are in Japanese writing only, so it is impossible to know what many shops contain from their names, or the advertising outside. The train system is equally confusing, although if you look around carefully you might just find a map with tiny lettering that you can understand, if you can get close enough to squint at it.

The restaurants are particularly entertaining and unusual, and often feature one innovation that really goes some way towards overcoming the linguistic challenges faced by the foreign traveller. Outside the restaurant they don't simply show pictures of the dishes they offer, but have full scale plasticized versions of the foods on offer, proudly displayed in show-cases outside the restaurant. Unfortunately, for me it often had the opposite effect to that intended, as it all looked disturbingly unappetising, being so shiny and, well, plastic-looking!

One of the places I was keen to find was a store called Daiso, which is the Japanese equivalent of a dollar-store, although is obviously referred to as a hundred-yen store in Japan. In San Francisco, Susan had introduced me to her local branch of her favourite Japanese store, gleefully showing me some of the amazing and entertaining items that can be bought there. She was so excited when she heard I was going to Tokyo, and insisted that I should visit the main store there.

After my night at the capsule hotel, I figured out how to get to Harajuku, a trendy teenage shopping area south of Shinjuku, which is the busy central area where I had spent the night. It was only a couple of stops on the underground, but it probably took me longer to get a ticket and figure out where the platform was than it did to make the journey!

Once there, I quickly found the Daiso store, with its four floors filled with eccentric Japanese stuff you never new you needed. Fascinating!

I initially only had two goals planned for Japan, but an email tip had alerted me to another possibility. Further internet research, and a few email enquiries had led me to an ex-US marine running his own dive company in Okinawa. He suggested a further potential goal achievement that we could add to the list of possibilities.

I was going to have to be very organised, as time was going to be a little bit tight, so I set about trying to arrange flights around Japan. I had to factor in all sorts of variables, including accommodation availability during the Yuki Matsuri festival, transfer times across Tokyo from one airport to another, and of course my final booked departure flight from Japan.

I had been given the number of a travel agency who might be able to help me, and once I found an English speaking assistant there, things went pretty smoothly. I was soon on my way to Okinawa.

Doug had been stationed in Okinawa when in the US military, and had stayed there after he was discharged, opening a dive shop and charter business. I dropped my bags off at the hotel he had booked for me for the night, and he and a dive buddy collected me at reception. We went for a meal and a few beers in an extraordinary restaurant, built high in the branches of an enormous fake tree. Why a restaurant in a huge fake tree, I asked them? "This is Japan, man! Why not?"

Goal 33 glides into view – hammerhead sharks!

Tuesday, February 3, 2009
(Yonaguni Island, Japan)

I once saw a documentary about the Galapagos Islands, and was amazed by the huge schools of hammerhead sharks that gather there at certain times of the year. Without knowing any more detail than this I added seeing this spectacle to my list of goals, and it duly became part of my list of 100.

I received an email from Philip in mid-December, suggesting that I might be able to achieve this goal while in Japan, so I did some research. There are actually three known major places in the world where these gatherings of hammerheads occur, the other two being the Caicos Islands in the West Indies, and at Yonaguni Island, here in Japan.

With a week or so available in Japan after a bit of juggling around with dates and flights, I contacted Doug of Reef Encounters in Naha for further details. I managed to eventually arrange three days down in Yonaguni. This involves flying Tokyo to Naha, about three hours, Naha to Ishigaki, about an hour, and then a final half-hour hop to Yonaguni itself.

On the flight from Hawaii to Tokyo I watched a fairly routine action movie. As my second choice, I picked a documentary called Sharkwater, which was fascinating. It isn't the usual sensationalist shark-attack frightener, but a well balanced and thought-provoking documentary. It explains how illegal and uncontrolled long-line fishing in certain parts of the world is devastating shark populations, with potentially catastrophic environmental results.

One grave concern is that by removing a top predator from a balanced eco-system, species further down the food chain can then multiply unchecked. If these are eaters of plankton, one of the major producers of oxygen on Earth, results could be disastrous.

The documentary detailed the staggering numbers of sharks, including hammerheads, killed each year in

Caicos. They are harvested simply for their fins, to make shark-fin soup, or for traditional cures. Often the fins and tail are cut off the shark while still alive, and it is simply tossed back into the water.

Perhaps if this continues unchecked, there will soon be no more schools of hammerheads to go and see! Fortunately, in Japan, this is not currently a problem, and the sharks can gather here unmolested.

After an overnight stop in Naha I flew first thing down to Ishigaki, and from there across to Yonaguni, the most westerly point of Japan, quite close to Taiwan.

It is a small island, and reminds me very much of some of the small islands I have visited in Thailand, but without the rampant backpacker tourism. It is quite tropical, but very run-down, and it really feels like being at the end of the line – there is only one flight in and out each day.

I was met by Chie, one of the dive guides from Sawes Diving. Along with Akiko, another girl who had flown in on the same flight for a few days of diving too, I was taken for a quick lunch before the afternoon's diving began.

Our first dive was a reef dive, to check we were both reasonably competent. We went out from the small harbour on the dive boat, and entered off the back, heading for the bottom pretty quickly as there is a strong current. We saw a turtle pretty much as soon as we entered the water, a couple of eels, and a vast array of tropical reef fish as we drifted along with the current.

Our second dive was with a larger group, ten of us in total, looking for hammerheads. We entered in deeper water, swam down to about 15 metres, and hovered there drifting along with the current, looking around for shadows in the water. At first the bottom was not visible, and we just hovered in this complete blueness. As it got slightly shallower I could just make out the seabed far below, perhaps another 30 metres or more down. We were drifting at quite a fast pace, I was surprised to see.

We looked around for a while, and Akiko and I spotted a hammerhead in the distance at the same time. It looked pretty big, but was a long way away, and it glided past and out of sight. I spotted it again a minute or so later, and it disappeared again. That was it for that dive, but I was very pleased to have seen one, at least.

After dinner I was dropped off at my accommodation, a small, backpacker-style guest house, and settled in for the night. I got chatting to some of the other guests, who turned out to be quite a large college group. I spent a fun evening drinking beer and sake, and playing cards.

The next morning I was collected at 8am for the first dive, another deep water drift. It was uneventful for about twenty minutes, until I turned around, and right behind Akiko spotted a group of five hammerheads, one pretty close. I had borrowed a camera for the dive, and managed to get one picture, the only one of a shark taken on that dive! I was very pleased.

Before lunch we took a bit of a tour around the island, which didn't take long – it's only a small place.

After lunch we went out again for two more dives. The first was very uneventful, with no sharks being spotted at all. The last dive of the day was much more exciting, however. A couple of minutes after dropping in I spotted several of the group turn and head off to the right at speed. When I turned there was a large group of hammerheads just disappearing into the shadows. Later Chie, who had spotted them before me, estimated that there were about thirty of them.

A minute or so later Chie spotted one shark returning, and pointed it out to me. We were on the right of the group, and the shark was over to our right, approaching us slowly. I had the camera set for video, and started filming as I swam towards it. It passed slowly in front of me, coming quite near, and as I got closer it turned and casually swam away.

They really are pretty shy, and seem to keep their distance, and it is awesome to see them so close. There is no fear involved, despite their size, as they are so wary around divers.

What an excellent dive!

February 6th was a date I had been looking forward to for a while. I had been travelling for six months at this point, and was still the slightly dismayed owner of an empty property back in Perth.

But that, along with my precarious financial situation, was about to change.

Goal 34 – A Life Sold!

Friday, February 6, 2009

(Perth, Western Australia)

The start of this whole 100goals adventure is rooted back in my earlier project, which was to sell my "life", in order to free myself up to travel, and make a fresh start.

Unfortunately the "ALife4Sale" eBay auction did not go quite as I had hoped, and ultimately the sale fell through.

I had already decided that I wanted to try to achieve my 100 goals in 100 weeks, and for a while wondered if it was going to be possible. After all, I still had a house and all my possessions. I would still be paying a mortgage and paying all of my travel costs, with no form of income at all. The maths really didn't add up!

In the end I had decided to go, and put the house in the hands of a real estate agent, hoping it would sell quickly. Once again things did not work out quite as planned. At the time I put my house on the market, the worldwide financial mess was just starting to affect Australia, and property was not moving at all.

Over the past few months I have had to drop the asking price a couple of times, as values have tumbled. Eventually I received an offer, and a sale was agreed upon. This is, however, for significantly less than I had originally expected.

Today the sale was finally settled, and I believe the balance of funds has been paid into my account, after my mortgage and loan have been paid off. This finally frees me considerably, as I now have no mortgage outgoings, and actually have some cash in the bank, although not quite as much as I had initially expected.

I guess that this is as close as I will get to achieving my goal of selling my life – I sold my car before I left on my travels, now the house is gone, and I have relatively few possessions stored away – so with no ties, and cash in the bank, I am free to go where I want and do as I please, which was my original aim.

I estimated that if I had simply sold my house a year earlier, instead of choosing to follow my eBay auction idea, I would probably have sold the house for $50,000 more than I was now receiving. But I tried not to look at it in terms of losing $50,000. I had still made a very good profit over the original land and build cost, and the alternative path that I was now following was much more exciting and fulfilling.

It was still tough to think that a year earlier I could have had an extra $50,000, locked in a term investment at almost double the interest rate that I could currently secure. I would have been making three times as much in interest, which could have carried me so much further.

I wondered again about the incredibly bad timing of some of the larger events affecting my decisions, and yet was still proud of all I had achieved so far, despite these challenges.

On my return from Yonaguni, Doug invited me to stay in the spare room in his Okinawa apartment, which was very obviously a diver's crash pad. Okinawa saw quite a bit of action in WWII, and the seabed is still littered with wartime debris. There was evidence of this all around the apartment, most noticeably in the bathtub, where I had to stand astride a huge shell casing to take a shower. The casing had perhaps come from a deck cannon on a destroyer, Doug thought, and had to sit in fresh water for several weeks to prevent it from simply crumbling away in fresh air after sitting on the seabed for over sixty years.

Doug suggested that we attempt another of the goals on my list, and early in the morning a small group of us gathered at the dive charter boat and set off out to sea.

Goal 35 – Thar she blows!
Saturday, February 7, 2009
(Okinawa, Japan)

Doug lives pretty close to the ocean in an area to the north of Naha called Sunabe. He is also close to one of the US Air Force bases here, and I was amazed by the amount of aircraft flying in to land and taking off from the base. It is pretty much non-stop. Apparently rents are cheaper the nearer you get to the base. No wonder, the noise from the fighters taking off is pretty loud.

Down at the seafront yesterday, I saw quite a few people with cameras with huge lenses attached. Doug later explained that the relatively new F-22 fighter plane was flying in and out of the base, and there was a high demand for pictures of it for military enthusiast publications. "Of course, there's also the Korean and Chinese spies down there taking snaps too!" he told me.

Doug runs his own dive charter business, Reef Encounters, and had arranged the trip down to Yonaguni for me. He then said that on the way back through Naha, if I wanted to try to swim with whales, he would do his best to help, as it is currently humpback season in Okinawa.

This morning we were up early, gathered full diving equipment from the dive shop, and headed down to the harbour. Once aboard Reef Encounter's boat Doug steered us out offshore. Miho suggested we should gear up in our snorkel equipment, as we were approaching a popular whale spot. On deck, Casey was already prepared, and Mike and I put our gear on as Jim fiddled with his camera. Jim would be trying to get pictures of any or all of us with a whale if at all possible.

Doug soon spotted a whale, and brought us onto what we hoped was its course. We dropped into the water, and finned like mad to where we hoped we might see it.

I ran into problems immediately, as when I cleared my snorkel and took a breath in I got a huge mouthful of seawater. I tried clearing it again, and the same thing happened again. I was a bit more careful to avoid taking too big a breath the third time I tried, and it was pretty clear the snorkel was broken, taking in water at its base.

Nobody saw the whale, and we all climbed back aboard for another try. The second time the whale surfaced not far in front of the boat, and kitted out with a fresh snorkel, I jumped in again. We all finned like mad, but only Casey reported seeing the tail in the distance. I was starting to think this was going to be a tough, exhausting day.

Back aboard the boat we trolled along slowly, and suddenly there was the whale again, about twenty yards away from the back corner of the boat. We all dropped over the side, I turned around in the water waiting for the bubbles to disappear, and I imagine my eyes opened wide in utter disbelief.

The whale was right there! It was right in front of us, no more than ten yards away! It was incredible! She had a calf with her too! We swam towards them slowly, and I could see Jim just in front of me taking pictures. I swam around him, getting closer to the whales. I watched astonished as the mother rolled onto her side, putting herself between me and the calf, and looked right at me. I could see her huge eye, and could actually see it flicking from me to Mike beside me, then back again.

They swam in a lazy circle around us, appearing to be as interested in us as we were in them, and I managed to get within three or four yards of them.

At one point I was so close that with a couple of fin kicks I could have probably touched the tip of the mother's pectoral fin. I reached out, and must have been a bit too close, as she curved her huge tail towards me. I took this as a fairly obvious warning, and backed away a bit, heeding Jim's earlier advice that mothers with a calf tend to be very defensive, and therefore potentially dangerous.

From then on, I tried to keep at a more sensible distance. She kept the calf shielded from us most of the time, either keeping herself between us and the youngster, or keeping it down below her.

We watched for a few minutes, as we all went around and around. I reckon the baby would have been about nine feet long, the mother maybe twenty to twenty-five feet long. She had barnacles on her fins and tail, and quite a group of remora sucker fish with her. She was so impressive to see.

It was one of the most incredible moments of my life, and I tried to take it all in. Eventually mum had seen enough of us, took a straight course, and with a bigger sweep of her tail picked up some speed. I finned hard to try to keep up, but they soon disappeared into the blue distance.

I climbed aboard the boat absolutely speechless, and Miho said, "Let me get a picture – look at your face!" We were all very excited. Jim took a look at the pictures on his camera, and looked very satisfied.

We tried again, but I think she had had enough of us, and proved to be very elusive. Completely satisfied that we could not possibly have a better encounter, we headed off to go diving.

The dive site we went to was fascinating. Okinawa saw a lot of action during WWII. We moored just above a reef off one of the main beaches where the US troops had made a first landing. The previous day, the military had just detonated a WWII mine that Doug and his team had found not long before on the seabed. Doug and Jim were keen to take a look at the site where the mine had just been detonated. Along with us was Take, to document for a TV show the damage done to marine life.

We descended to the reef, which sadly was littered with dead fish, unfortunate modern-day victims of an explosive relic from sixty-five years ago. Take found a piece of the body of the mine, all ripped and twisted out of shape by the blast. Remnants from the war littered the seabed, and Jim had warned me not to touch anything at all, as there could still be live munitions down there. One interesting find was a group of four Coke bottles, date stamped 1944. They were presumably tossed off the back of some US battleship, last handled by a wartime sailor all those years ago.

That evening we celebrated with a big Japanese meal, and a lot of Japanese beer!

Swimming with the humpback whale and her calf had truly been one of the most outstanding moments of my life. It was the most incredible sight I have ever seen! The experience was so stunning and moving. It still brings a tear to my eye when I try to describe how amazing it was. We were so close that we could see her eye move from person to person, and could tell exactly who she was looking at as we all swam around each other.

If my journey were to come to an end right now, I thought, and I achieve nothing more from my long list, these precious, extraordinary few minutes would mean that everything had been worthwhile.

Once again, random events, brief contacts and the incredible kindness of strangers had offered me the opportunity to achieve a long-held ambition in a way that far superseded anything that I had ever been able to imagine.

Isn't life truly wonderful, I thought? A couple of years earlier, how could I ever imagine that life might lead me to this point, experiencing this moment of complete elation, among people that I hadn't even met a couple of days earlier?

Sapporo, in the north of Japan, was a frigid contrast to the shorts-and-t-shirt summery weather of Yonaguni and Okinawa, so far to the south. In the space of one day it felt like I transited from mid-summer to the depths of winter.

Goal 36 – Yuki Matsuri

Monday, February 9, 2009
(Sapporo, Japan)

Two flights took me from Naha up to Haneda, Tokyo's domestic airport, then on to Sapporo. It was late afternoon by the time I arrived. A train into the city itself, and then another out to where my hotel was situated meant that it was early evening by the time I got settled in.

I think I had been lucky to find a hotel room, as I had left it a bit late, not really being sure of my Sapporo dates until I worked out the Okinawa trip. Mark's Inn was reasonably inexpensive, and pretty comfortable. Best of all, it was only a five minute walk to the Yuki Matsuri, the famous Sapporo Ice Sculptures Festival.

I hadn't eaten since breakfast, and went out to find something. I considered walking up to see some of the sculptures, which line Odari Park, just to the north of my hotel, but it was snowing pretty hard when I went outside, and I decided to leave it until morning.

I was glad I did, as it dawned a beautiful sunny morning. After a late breakfast I walked up through Susukino, where there are some smaller ice sculptures. Eventually I arrived at Odari Park, and was very impressed by the size of some of the sculptures there, some as big as a house. There are so many, and they are so intricate and detailed. They looked stunning in the bright sunlight, and I wandered happily up and down the mile-long length of the incredible display.

In the afternoon I took a bus out to a third festival site. I returned to the city in time to go up the big tower at the end of the park, and take some pictures in daylight, before waiting for darkness to fall to see the whole place lit up like a winter wonderland.

Sadly, that's now the end of my visit to Japan, which has been so interesting. Time to move onwards again, back to Australia next....

I flew from Sapporo back to Tokyo, and crossed the city again to the international airport. From there I took a flight to Cairns on the north east coast of Australia, and finally a third flight in thirty hours took me south to Sydney.

Mel had flown across from Perth to meet me, which was wonderful, and I was looking forward to spending some time with her. However, the main activity that I had planned during our couple of days in Sydney was a much less appealing prospect.

My father died at the age of 61, taken by cancer which had started in his lower intestine. Despite a couple of operations, it had soon spread to liver, kidneys, and beyond, out of control.

I had written shortly afterwards about the experience of seeing him fade away over a relatively short period of time, and had reflected upon the loss many times in the years since then. He had written up a huge list of wonderful adventures, planned for his years of productive retirement, but he never made it that far. I guess we never know what surprises life has in store for us.

His early death, at a relatively young age, had impacted me greatly, and I think had a lot to do with my decision to get on and enjoy life now while young and fit enough to do so. I would worry about the future when it arrived.

Towards the end of 1993 I can remember my father grumbling occasionally of stomach pains, but he wasn't a person to complain too much, and he simply got on with life. He was 60 at the time, just about to turn 61, and was looking forward to retiring to travel the world in a few short years.

Christmas in Darlington that year was the usual family affair. My brother Martin was home for a couple of days, and in time-honoured fashion we went out for a drink on Christmas Eve. As usual we promised mum that we would not drink so much that we would be too ill to face the Christmas dinner she would be making. However, as usual the Christmas spirit was upon us, and on Christmas morning we both felt quite queasy, although probably not quite as bad as the year before.

On Christmas Day we spent the morning opening our presents. While I tidied up and mum, assisted my Martin, made the lunch, dad had a snooze by the fire. As he slept my cat curled up beside him to share the warmth.

My dad was a really energetic, and I suppose slightly eccentric father, and it pained me to see him so ill and listless. He had been diagnosed as suffering from cancer of the bowels a couple of months earlier, and although he put a brave face on, I knew it had shaken him very badly. He was often in considerable pain when he moved, and had been pretty much confined to the house lately by his illness, which for him was very frustrating.

He had been very active before becoming ill, and was a regular badminton player, windsurfer and motorcyclist. When I look back over my life, I realise how much I have to thank my father for, and what a huge influence he has had on the person I have become. Instead of the usual family-type beach holidays we were often taken on multi-activity adventure holidays as children.

It was on these excursions that I discovered my love for climbing and caving, orienteering and hill walking, skiing, camping, canoeing, sailing, and a range of other activities. At the age of twelve, although I didn't know it at the time, my future had been shaped by the holiday on which we had been. My interest in outdoor activities was eventually to lead on to a teaching degree at Liverpool Polytechnic, specializing in Outdoor

Education, and from there into working in centres just like the one we had been to on holiday all those years before.

At the age of sixteen my father treated me to the finest birthday present I'd ever had. After a day of training I made a parachute jump from 2,500 feet. However, my dad didn't just come and watch, like most of the other fathers that I knew would probably have done – he came and did the parachute jump with me.

He had done a course on hang-gliding, had dabbled in the world of dinghy sailing, was a keen and competent snow-skier, and had travelled around Eastern Europe on a motorbike. He had enjoyed a very full and active life. Christmas that year was tinged with sadness at seeing my dad so ill.

In mid January I was back in Darlington again when dad was taken back into hospital for a further operation. He had been whisked to hospital on New Years Eve in terrible pain, and had had an operation to remove part of his colon. It seemed that this had not been completely successful, and further surgery was required.

My dad died on January 22nd 1994. He never really fully recovered from his second operation, and as the doctor explained to us, there was no further help they could give. He had been heavily sedated and had simply faded away.

Our family doctor had explained to my brother and I that bowel cancer has a genetic aspect to it, and suggested that from the age of 40 onwards we would be well advised to have regular colonoscopies.

As one of my goals, I had wanted to do something in my father's memory, and chose to try to raise a large sum of money for a bowel cancer research and awareness charity based in Sydney. It is the second-largest cause of cancer deaths in Australia, and yet if caught early enough, is one of the most easily treatable forms of cancer, with a 90% success rate.

A little later than planned, at the age of 45, I had finally managed to get around to booking myself in for my first screening. I was not looking forward to the process. For a day-and-a-half I didn't dare wander far from the Sydney hotel bathroom, as laxatives did their work to clear out my innards. I couldn't eat anything either as I was only allowed to drink water. It was a pretty miserable couple of days, and although I could laugh about it, Mel decided she would do some city sightseeing on her own.

In conjunction with the charity, Bowel Cancer Australia, I had hoped to make the occasion a bit of a fund-raiser, but again, with uncannily poor timing I had arrived back in Australia just after some of the most devastating bushfires in living memory. All news and fundraising efforts were rightly being aimed at helping those most affected by the disaster.

At least I got a clean bill of health, and another five years before I have to go through that experience again!

The end of my time in Japan, my return to Australia, and eventually back to Perth, where little had changed in my absence, brought to an end my first round-the-world journey. This offered some time to reflect on the first seven months of what was still a huge journey ahead.

I felt a wide range of mixed feelings. I was excited to be back on familiar territory, and pleased to be back to the warm Australian summer after a wintery few days in Sapporo. I was relieved to be among old friends again, people who knew my background, and didn't ask all the usual questions I had got used to answering during the previous months. I was also relieved that I was not going to be spending money endlessly every day.

I was also a little sad that the travelling was over for a while, as I had thoroughly enjoyed the total freedom and independence that travel gave me. There was also a good measure of guilt too, as I settled in to Mel's house. I was very mixed up over the decision to stay with her. I really enjoyed being with her and the girls, but had also enjoyed the company of others while away.

I was also very enthusiastic about my planned Australian goals. My rough outline plan was to try to get a job driving dump trucks in a mine again, hopefully just on a three- or four-month contract, and top up my funds. I hoped I could land a job with a 9 days on/5 days off roster, commonly referred to as a 9/5. An 8/6 would be even better, or there was one place that I wanted to try that I knew ran a week on/week off roster.

Three or four months of hard work would mean I could save at least $20,000. I would only have to pay a bare minimum of tax, as that would be the only income I earned during the whole tax year. I would have a decent amount of time off, in good-sized periods, which would mean I could still address the goals I needed to work on. By the end of June I would be well cashed-up again, and ready for the next part of my travel-based goals. It was a perfect plan, or so I thought.

When I moved in with Mel there was an initial awkwardness between us. I felt somewhat dislocated and out of place, and struggled to settle into a regular domestic life. We argued about silly things quite often during those early days. She spent a lot of time thinking I might leave at any moment, and I too often considered other accommodation options. After a while though I settled, Mel and I fell back into our familiar easy companionship, and all was good again for us.

I was eased through these slightly turbulent early days in Perth by taking a road trip down south.

Goal 37 - outback adventure

Wednesday, February 25, 2009
(Israelite Bay, Western Australia)

Back in 2000, after my first couple of extended travel trips to Australia, I was still living and working in the UK. Laura and I were seriously considering the possibility of moving down under to live. We had a map of Australia on the wall with our two previous trips highlighted on it.

One evening we were discussing travels with my friend Richard, who had been to Australia many times, and had lived and worked in Perth for some time. "If you have liked what you have seen of Australia so far, you will love Perth. You should try there first," he advised.

We continued to study the map, and he pointed out some nice places to visit to the south of Perth. We spotted a small place on the map, to the east of Esperance, quite remote and alone at the end of a long road along the southern coast. "I never went to Israelite Bay," he laughed. "That's a long way from anywhere."

"Maybe one day we'll go and see what's there," Laura had suggested. And seven years later, when it came to writing out my list of 100 goals, I decided that I still wanted to go and see what was there. I had no idea. So with a few days to spare this week, I decided it was time to go and find out.

My initial plan was to borrow my friend Chris's camper van and spend a couple of days driving down to Esperance, and then along the coast from there. On Sunday evening Mel pointed out to me that the map showed the track to Israelite Bay as suitable for four-wheel drive vehicles only! Oh dear, it looked like a bit more planning than I had originally anticipated would be in order.

I had to set off on Monday if I was going to go, and I was still a little undecided. I needed to be back in Perth for Thursday evening, and it might be a bit of a rush. I rang a couple of vehicle hire places in Esperance to see if I could rent a 4WD for the trip to Israelite Bay. The first couple of responses were discouraging, to say the least. "We wouldn't rent anything to go out there, it's pretty rugged going!" Hmmm.

Finally I found a place that would rent me an older Toyota Land Cruiser for the journey, and rang my friend Andrew to see if he would be interested in accompanying me on the journey. Despite the short notice he decided he would like to come along. We abandoned the camper van idea, choosing to go in his car instead, taking a couple of tents with us.

We drove for about four hours on the Monday afternoon, camped overnight in a bush rest stop, and headed on in the morning towards Esperance. We took a small detour on the way to see the very picturesque town of Hopetoun on the south coast.

In Esperance we got ourselves organised for the 4WD trip the next day, confirming with the hire company a pick-up time for the next morning. That evening we fished from the jetty, with a reasonable amount of success, catching our supper of squid, herring and yellowtail. There are a couple of friendly sea lions that live under the jetty, and Andrew bravely hand-fed a fish to one of them. When he did so without getting bitten, I thought I would have a go too. I am not sure who was the most nervous, but the sea lion got another fresh snack, and then just stared at me, hoping I might have more.

We spent another night at a bush camp near the town, and in the morning went to pick up our 4WD vehicle. There had been some sort of a mix-up. The Toyota was nowhere to be seen, and instead we were given an immaculate new Nissan Patrol, with dire warnings about how we should treat it. I was a bit disappointed, as I would have much preferred the older vehicle that we wouldn't have to worry about quite so much.

We drove eastwards out of Esperance, and travelled about 100km on a good sealed road, followed by another good gravel track for a further 50km. We were making great time, but then the road ended, and a tiny sandy track lead off into the bush. We were still over 50km from our destination, and the going was about to get quite a bit rougher.

Within the first kilometre we were getting bogged in deep sand, but once we put the Nissan into four wheel drive and locked the front hubs, we had no further issues. At one point we got a bit over-confident, and I got us bogged in a deep muddy hole, but we soon managed to reverse out of trouble.

It took us just over two hours to complete the last 50km, and it was great fun. At Israelite Bay we had a look around the ruins of an old telegraph station, and drove to the beach where we had lunch. Goal achieved!

We had only rented the Nissan for the day, as it was hideously expensive to hire. We didn't have too long before we had to set off back, as it was going to take another three hours for the return journey.

We also had a bit of a detour planned on the way back. "Don't take it on the beach!" the hire company rep told us! Riiiiiight....

After a much needed visit to the car wash, which included picking out some seaweed from under the chassis, we dropped the Nissan off. We then put in a couple of hours in the car in the direction of home. The next morning we continued northwards, taking a slightly different route back, stopping off at Hyden to visit the very impressive Wave Rock, another West Australian attraction I have always wanted to see.

We finally arrived back in Perth late Thursday afternoon, and the first order of business when I got back was a shower, much needed after four days in the bush!

The whole trip was a lot more challenging than I had ever expected it to be, and I learned quite a few lessons from the journey. Firstly, a bit more research is always a valuable thing. If I had simply set off, assuming that all was going to be easy, then I imagine at best I would have turned back defeated, at worst my friend's camper van would be completely bogged in deep sand miles from anywhere!

Secondly though, I thought a lot about other people's attitudes and advice, and decided that it is often wise just to ignore them. Quite a few times, when we told people where we were going, and what we planned to do, we got responses such as, "That's a long way to go in one day!" or "It's pretty rugged out there!" or "Why go all the way out there, there's nothing to see!"

Ignoring all this, we set off regardless, and had an incredible day out there. For me, the goal was a much greater adventure, and much greater achievement than I ever expected it to be.

The trip to Israelite Bay was another goal tinged with a little sadness, as I did not achieve it in the company of the one person who I had always imagined would be there with me on that particular journey.

But the trip had turned out to be a fantastic couple of days, and had been much more challenging than I had ever imagined it would be, therefore ultimately much more satisfying too.

Maybe I was finally approaching a readier acceptance of the fact that Laura was no longer a part of my life, and never would be. I hoped that I was going to be able to stride confidently into a happier future, pleasantly at ease with my new-found acceptance.

Chapter 4 – Weeks 31 to 40

(2nd March 2009 – 10th May 2009)

Australia

My return to Perth for an extended period of time was still causing some emotional upheaval and confusion for me. I missed the travelling, the freedom, the adventure, and the excitement of new places, people and experiences. But it was nice too, to be back among friends, and to have a bit of time to relax.

I received an invite and free ticket for a weekend-long personal development course, and decided to attend. The weekend was extremely challenging and thought-provoking. One decision prompted by the course was that I needed to talk again to Mel about our relationship, and what I felt about it. I was still feeling guilty about my travelling liaisons.

We had had the same conversation several times before, and I found it incredibly difficult to tell someone so wonderful that I perhaps didn't feel about her the quite the same way she felt about me. There was some discussion of my "adventures" while away, and I told her that if she wanted to ask, I would answer any questions truthfully. It was a difficult conversation, but at least we both knew where we stood.

Other things weren't going too well either. My plan to get a job back in the mines wasn't quite working out as I had hoped. I had put in several applications, and been in touch with several contacts, one of which looked like it was almost certain to end with an offer of employment.

Howeever, due to the global economic downturn, even mining in Western Australia was finally feeling the pinch, and in the months I had been away several mines had closed down. Now, in contrast to seven months earlier when I had left Perth, instead of jobs galore, there were more drivers looking for jobs than there were seats in trucks.

With a gap of over a year since I had last driven a truck, I was pushed to the bottom of the pile of job applications, and even my almost-certain job offer fell through.

Following suggestions from several people on the website, I had put in an application for "The Best Job in the World", and thought that I must have been, almost without doubt, one of the best qualified people for the position.

The job entailed being a "caretaker" on a tropical island off the east coast of Australia, and involved blogging about the experience, making videos, and acting as a media representative for tourism in Queensland. For a six-month contract they were paying $150,000.

I was obviously pretty enthusiastic, and threw myself into the application process with gusto. I had been blogging for a year now, made many videos, and was an old hand at TV, radio and newspaper interviews! Surely the best job in the world had my name written all over it? My revised plan would be to take a six-month break from my 100 weeks, add the extra $150,000 to my bank account after lounging around in paradise for a while, and then simply resume where I had left off.

The application had to be in the form of a one minute video, and I started mine with footage of a live breakfast TV interview, followed by a montage of some of the most outstanding moments from the last six months. “If you want to know what I can do with your six months.....” my video suggested, “.....take a look at what I have just done with my last six months!” There was a link to the website, which mentioned blogs, videos, and press coverage. I had ticked every one of their boxes in fine style!

If I could get the position, all my financial worries for the 100 goals would be over. I would be able to finish them all in style and comfort, and I would get a bonus six months in paradise.

The selection process involved cutting 30,000 applications down to 50, and I had to deal with the disappointment of not making the final cut.

No mining job, no “Best Job in the World”. My original plans had been to work until July, then head for Spain, but with no income I decided that it may be a better plan to set off on the next part of the journey sooner, and worry about finances later. I started planning for the next trip, while continuing to work on some of the Australian-based goals.

Goal 38 - this never happened, but....

Friday, March 13, 2009
(An undisclosed location!)

Okay, so this never happened, but if it ever did happen, it might go something like this:-

I hoped to achieve my goal of topping 150 mph, or 250 kph, on a motorbike in a fully legal fashion while in Germany last year, where on certain autobahns any speed is allowed. However, it proved to be a bit trickier than I had imagined to get my hands on a fast bike there. I only had limited time available to me, and a lot of beer to try out at Oktoberfest, so this particular goal was shelved at the time.

Back in Australia it is easier for me to get my hands on a fast bike. A very good friend, who wishes to remain anonymous, offered to lend me his bike, the make and model of which he would prefer to remain undisclosed too! All I am at liberty to say is that I could borrow, should I ever wish to do so, a very black bike that is quite a bit quicker than mine.

If I was going to do this on roads where this sort of thing would be frowned upon, I would pick a time very late at night. I would perhaps meet with a couple of friends at 2am by a long straight stretch of very quiet, very deserted freeway.

We would take a steady ride down that freeway for a couple of junctions, just to check that it was clear of any obstructions, debris, or anyone that might not approve of our activities.

I would then leave these people at a couple of strategic points on the route, and go back up the freeway to the planned start point. If by a pre-arranged time I had not received any text messages indicating otherwise, I would be clear to set off.

I would accelerate hard down the slip road onto the freeway, and be surprised how quickly the bike got to 200 kph on the digital readout. There would be 5 kilometres of straight road ahead, with only one junction on that stretch, and on the bridge my friend would have a video camera rolling.

I would tuck down behind the fairing, trying to hold as streamlined a position as possible as I wound the throttle right to the stop. I would try to cast a quick glance at the speedo every now and then to see the numbers still slowly increasing, past 230kmh and climbing towards 240.

Over 240 kph the bike would be nearing its limits, and progress up through the final numbers would be slow. Just before the first bridge the speedo might climb to 243 kph, and I would hurtle under the bridge, and gradually start to slow down, feeling a little disappointed.

At the end of the run, I would probably stop for a quick chat with my friend waiting at the second bridge. After a quick discussion on the phone with my other assistant, we might all agree that it would be worth a try in the other direction. There may have been a slight headwind as I was coming down the freeway. This would now be a tail wind heading back.

On the second run the bike would accelerate again quickly, and start to struggle again at around 240 kph. Perhaps with the slight tail wind, the numbers would keep climbing slowly, and before the mid-point of the run the display would show 253 kph. With another kilometre to go before having to back off, I might just see 260 kph flicker on the digital readout, before winding the throttle back, whooping with excitement, and beginning to slow down, back to the 100 kph speed limit before reaching the exit ramp.

Of course, none of this ever happened, but if I was going to do it, very early morning on Friday 13th would be an appropriate time to give it a go!

If I ever did get around to doing something like this, I would like to point out the following. I realise that 260 kph is not all that fast compared to some of the modern superbikes on the roads. I have seen some incredible videos of people riding in traffic on busy roads at speeds up to and over 300 kph. However, I am not that crazy, or that skilful on a bike, and know my own limits.

If I was going to do anything like this I would first of all ensure that I did not endanger any other road-users, by picking a completely empty stretch of road. I would like to try to make the whole thing as safe as I possibly could for myself too. After all, I still have a lot more goals to achieve yet!

At the end of my first thirty weeks of travels, goals and adventures, I received an email from Penny in England. She told me how much inspiration and enjoyment she was getting from following my travels online. I had received several emails of a similar nature, and was very flattered that other people found inspiration in what I was doing.

Penny made some very insightful comments and observations on my journey and my experiences so far, and wondered if I had had any time to reflect on everything I had achieved. I hadn't made much of an effort to do anything specific about this, and had only enjoyed a vague sense of satisfaction about all I had done to date.

Prompted by her suggestion I decided that March 14th would be the perfect day for quiet reminiscence, being a year to the day since the ALife4Sale website went live, and this whole rollercoaster ride started.

It had been quite an adventure. When I had decided to sell my life and move on, hoping to make a fresh start, I had no idea that I would be travelling the world for the next two years, trying to pack a lifetime's worth of experiences into 100 weeks. I had done some exciting things, and seen some incredible sights. I had visited new countries, and made new friends. If I was inspiring others as I did so, that was a wonderful bonus.

Penny had also wondered if one of my unwritten goals was a desire for my adventure to lead me to sharing my life with someone really special. I was open to this possibility, but the thought created a conflict inside, when I thought about what being back in Australia meant, in terms of my relationship with Mel.

I had thought long and hard about how we were together. I was pretty sure that although I enjoyed being with her, she wasn't the person I was looking for. However, I couldn't find any logical reason why that might be.

I was very pleased that once more I had laid my cards on the table with Mel, explaining again that although I enjoyed my time with her immensely, I didn't know if we had a long term future together.

If that wasn't enough, I had told her, I would leave now and set us both free. Neither of us wanted that, we decided eventually, happy to share each other's lives for now, avoiding the loneliness we would both have to face as an alternative.

Without the structure and pressure of flights to catch, new people to meet, or locations to reach, I found my rate of goal achievement dropping off a little. I struggled to maintain my motivation. It was easy to just drift along day-by-day, go out on the motorbike, and hang out with whoever wasn't at work that day.

I needed to get on, so I enrolled for kitesurfing lessons, and signed up for a four-week didgeridoo course. I managed to get back in the air again a couple of times too, but my skydiving goals eluded me, as weather factors, or absences of jumping buddies put plans on hold.

I discovered that a couple of friends from Canberra were heading out on a road trip to the dusty outback, and pretty soon had made arrangements to meet them at the airport in the red centre of the huge Australian continent.

Goal 39 - rock of ages
Friday, March 27, 2009
(Uluru, Northern Territory, Australia)

I have called Australia home for over seven years now, and have travelled around here quite a bit. I have seen quite a lot of the country, but am also aware that there is much more that I have yet to see.

Australia is made up of six states and two major mainland territories, namely Queensland, New South Wales, Victoria, South Australia, Western Australia,

Tasmania, Australian Capital Territory, and Northern Territory.

The only one of these that I haven't set foot in at all is Northern Territory, and I understand there is much to see there!

Australia has many well known icons, one of the most familiar being, I imagine, the Sydney Opera House. Ayers Rock, or Uluru as it tends to be known now, is another famous Aussie icon. It was officially given the dual name of "Ayers Rock/Uluru" in 1993. This was changed to "Uluru/Ayers Rock" in November 2002 following a request from the Regional Tourism Association in Alice Springs.

When I discovered that friends Pam and Ces were driving up from Adelaide to Uluru, then onward to the west, it seemed like an ideal time to finally head to Northern Territory, and go to see the iconic rock.

I flew from Perth direct to Ayers Rock airport, and had booked a spot at the Ayers Rock Resort campground. I was lucky enough to get a window seat at the front of the plane, and had a great view of the rock as we came in to land.

Pam and Ces picked me up at the airport, and once set up at the campground we headed out into the sand dunes and I got a closer look at the rock than I had from the plane. Even at a distance of around ten kilometres it is impressively large.

Later we went to see the rock as the sun set behind us, which was very atmospheric.

The next morning Ces and I were up early and drove into the national park itself to see sunrise. We joined busloads of other sightseers at the sunrise viewing area, and as it got lighter, I started to get an impression of just how incredibly big the rock is when viewed close-up.

I have wondered for quite a while about whether I should climb the rock or not. The traditional Aboriginal owners ask people not to, as it is a sacred site. Many people now choose not to climb, but quite a lot still do, and eventually I decided that I would try to do the climb. Although I would wish to respect tradition, I still feel that everyone should have the freedom to enjoy nature as they choose, as long as it is in a non-destructive way.

However, it turned out that I had no choice in the matter, as it was too windy on the rock, and the climb was closed.

That afternoon we walked around the base of the rock, which is a fantastic 10 kilometre walk, offering some stunning views of this incredibly atmospheric and beautiful place.

With the goal of seeing the rock achieved I had time to explore the area a little more. Pam, Ces and I explored the stunning Kata-Tjuta area, also known as The Olgas. This is a spectacular area consisting of 36 huge rock domes, the tallest, Mount Olga, being higher than Uluru. We also spent some time relaxing, lounging around in the sun by the pool at the campground.

I was still keen to climb Uluru. Our park pass for the Uluru-Kata Tjuta National Park was only valid for three days, and I had got up at 5:30 in the morning and driven into the park three mornings in a row in an attempt to be able to do so. For three mornings the climb had been closed due to strong winds at the summit.

Yesterday morning, armed with a couple of extra passes that had been kindly left behind at the campground kitchen by a departing camper, Pam and I headed into the park again. Before dawn it was just as windy as on the previous mornings, but incredibly, the gate was open, and the "Closed" sign was nowhere to be seen.

Determined to be well up the rock long before the ranger returned and had a re-think, I quickly applied some sunscreen, grabbed my water bottle, and set off hot on the heels of three Japanese girls.

Halfway up the first section of the steepest part of the climb I passed the Japanese girls, and was now at the head of a growing straggle of climbers slowly ascending. I pushed on in the growing dawn, keen to be the first to the summit. The climb was steep and tough going at first, but levelled halfway up into a much gentler gradient.

Not long after I got started the ranger appeared at the foot of the climb, and it was closed again, and no new starters were allowed, Pam told me later.

Most of the final part of the climb was still in the shade, and the wind was quite strong, but easily manageable. I finally climbed into the sun and reached the summit marker, and admired the vast sweeping view.

I had about ten minutes alone at the summit before the next climbers arrived, and quickly took a few pictures while nobody else was in sight. Then I just sat quietly and soaked up the stunning vista. I was incredibly pleased to be able to do the climb, and glad that my persistence had finally paid off.

I still wonder a little about the rights and wrongs of climbing the rock when the traditional owners request that people do not do so. I think for me I made the right decision - it was a wonderful experience.

By the time I climbed back down and returned to the carpark there were several buses and a lot of cars, and many disappointed people who would not be climbing today.

After another relaxing day by the pool we wandered up to one of the lookouts to watch the sun set over the domes of Kata Tjuta in the distance. Absolutely magnificent!

Today I fly back to Perth again, but have had a wonderful time here at Uluru. It really is well worth coming to see.

My success at climbing the rock against the odds was, to me, a wonderful example of how perseverance and sacrifice can pay off. By getting up early each morning four times in a row, when I could have happily lain in bed, I managed to achieve something that only a handful of other people did during the time I was there.

The dedication to achieve this was also worthwhile, because in the near future, proposed new regulations may well make the possibility of climbing the rock a thing of the past.

Goal 40 – didgeridoo dawn
Sunday, March 29, 2009
(Uluru, Northern Territory, Australia)

I have been attending a didgeridoo, or yidaki (see below) class at Didgeridoo Breath in Fremantle, and over the past few weeks have progressed fairly well under the expert guidance of Levi, the didge teacher there. In the first lesson I managed to get the feel of the technique of "circular breathing", which means that a continuous note or rhythm can be played without having to stop to refill the lungs.

I have practiced as regularly as possible over the last few weeks, and can manage a couple of decent-sounding rhythms. I am really enjoy playing. The practice didge is merely a piece of plastic plumbing pipe, but sounds pretty good. However, after each lesson, a few of us would try out some of the didges in the shop, and when you find one that suits you, the sound is rich and deep and awesome. One day I might treat myself to one of these top-quality didges, but in the meantime, I decided to buy myself a cheap didge that I planned to bring out to Uluru with me.

I feel that to class my didgeridoo goal as complete I needed to come and play it out in the Australian wilderness, and thought that Uluru would be the ideal place to do so. Unfortunately, I discovered that the didgeridoo is originally only from Arnhem Land in the far north of Australia, and only spread to the central area about 150 years ago.

Regardless, it still felt pretty special to climb up to the top of a sand dune just before dawn yesterday morning, and sit playing my current favourite rhythm. The magnificent Uluru filled the view in front of me, just to the right of the slowly rising sun.

There wasn't another soul around, and it was a wonderfully peaceful and relaxing way to achieve my 40th goal.

On my return to Perth at the beginning of April it was time to make some firm decisions. I booked a flight to France for May 11th, only six weeks away.

Mel was surprised and upset that I was going quite a bit earlier than she had expected. Again I found myself apologising for my desire to travel, and the apparent ease with which I made the decision to change plans and choose an earlier departure.

Blowing in the wind – gusty goal 41 completed

Thursday, April 2, 2009
(Perth, Western Australia)

Perth has a long sandy coastline, and in summer has a regular afternoon onshore wind, making it an ideal kiteboarding location. A drive up the coast on any summer afternoon will show how popular the sport has become, as kites regularly fill the sky over many of the beaches.

I have watched these people on several occasions, and been impressed with both the speed that they can travel, and the height they can jump from the waves. I have often thought, "I would like to be able to do that... it doesn't look too hard!"

I remember one trip up the coast to Lancelin, about an hour and a half north from the city, when my brother was visiting from the UK. We sat on the beach analysing what the kiteboarders were doing, and both being reasonably competent on a snowboard or a wakeboard, reckoned we had it figured out!

When I made my list of 100 goals, I decided it was time to learn the sport. On my return to Perth I booked some introductory lessons with Kite Boarding Perth, who are based at Mullaloo Beach, in the northern suburbs of Perth.

My instructor Tony took me through the basics of kite care and safety. He showed me how to set up the kite on the beach, and how to pack it away again. We then moved on to launching the kite and controlling it in the air. I had done quite a bit of practice with the small trainer kite I had bought, so managed fairly well with the bigger kite.

Midway through the second lesson, I was just about to get into the water to practice using the power of the kite to drag along through the water (it is much safer to do than on the land), when the wind dropped, and we had to call the lesson off.

Over the next couple of days the winds didn't improve. Towards the end of the week I had to set off for Uluru, so it was a while before I got back to the beach. A week later, after my trip into the desert, the winds picked up on Tuesday, so my final lessons were scheduled for the next two afternoons.

I practiced dragging through the water, and re-launching the kite when it landed on the water. I also tried out the power-stroke which pulls you up out of the water onto the board. In the final lesson I was ready to add the board into the equation.

On my first couple of attempts I floundered around in the water trying to control the kite with one hand, the board with the other, all the while being dragged slowly through the waves. It was very frustrating! But on my third try I got everything into the right position. With my feet on the board, I manoeuvred the kite into the power-stroke, and before I knew it, I was up on the board, riding across the waves. "Yeay! Now we're kiteboarding!" I heard Tony exclaim via the helmet radio I was wearing.

It only lasted a few seconds, as in my excitement I forgot to keep the kite in the right place. I lost power, my board sank, and I ended up back in the water.

I had a few more tries, with mixed success, before the lesson ended. I made my way to the beach completely exhausted, but very satisfied.

Tony was happy to issue me with my International Kiteboarding Organisation Card, Level 2i, which means I am now considered to know the safety requirements and the basics of the sport.

It is certainly a sport I wish to progress with, but at the moment it is possibly not the right time to do so. The summer is coming to an end here, and I am heading off on my next travel adventure soon. If I bought some gear now it would just sit in storage for the next 8 months, so for now I will have to put this hobby on the back-burner. I hope I might get some chances to practice my new-found "skills" while travelling.

I appreciate that my skills are at a very low level at the moment, and there is no way I could call myself a competent kiteboarder, but Tony said that I now have all the knowledge I need to progress. "It's all just practice now," he said.

In terms of goal completion, I achieved very little in the remaining weeks in Perth. I started going to poker competitions at the local pubs, and really enjoyed the steep learning curve I had to climb. If I was ever going to hold my own in a high-stakes game I had a lot of work to do. After a couple of weeks of fairly regular games, I entered the West Australian State Championship, and of 470 entrants, I made it to the top 50 before being eliminated. Maybe there was some hope of playing at a high level without being too badly scalped?

Towards the end of my three months back in Australia I planned a trip north to see the enormous whalesharks at Ningaloo Reef. Whaleshark season is from April until June, so the timing was perfect.

I sent a few emails to the whaleshark boat tour operators in Exmouth, enquiring about prices and availability. I managed to book a flight back from Exmouth to Perth at a reasonable price, but flights north out of Perth were outrageously expensive. I looked at other possibilities, eventually finding a car hire company who had a vehicle in Perth that they needed delivering back to Exmouth. For a very small hire charge, and fuel costs only, I could drive, taking a couple of days to enjoy the journey up the coast. This was a much more appealing prospect than yet another expensive short-hop flight.

Mel had decided to join me in Exmouth for a couple of days too, and booked flights which fitted around her work commitments.

Goal 42 – gentle giants

Thursday, April 30, 2009
(Exmouth, Western Australia)

I was up before the sun rose again this morning, and prepared for an early pick up to go on a whaleshark tour. A couple of weeks ago I had emailed all of the whaleshark tour operators in Exmouth, explaining what I am doing, and that one of my goals is to see a big whaleshark.

I was surprised to only hear back from two of the six Exmouth-based operators, and can only imagine that they are all fully booked and need no further customers this season! However, I did hear from Kat, who is manager of Ningaloo Blue. She said she would be happy to book me on one of their tours, and would happily offer a repeat option if a big whaleshark was not spotted. She was very helpful, and enthusiastic to assist in any way she could with my goals. I had no hesitation in choosing to book my day with her.

I was picked up at the entrance to the caravan park, along with Stony, who was on the same tour. Along with a group of 15 others we were driven about 30 kilometres to the boat launch point around the cape. There we were ferried out to the big boat via a small zodiac inflatable.

After an initial snorkel practice on a shallow reef we headed out to the deeper waters outside the main reef, where we awaited sightings from the spotter plane, which had started patrolling at 10am. The small plane works for all of the tour operators. Once a whaleshark is spotted all the boats in the vicinity get to share time with the creature in the water.

We didn't have to wait for long before the first whaleshark of the day was spotted by the plane, and we raced off to find it. Two other boats were already there. As we approached the plane spotted another whaleshark, and we were off again, aiming to be the first boat to meet this one.

Whalesharks are not related to whales at all, but are fish, and breathe through gills like any other fish do. They are the largest species of fish in the world, and regularly grow to lengths of 12 metres or more. They are filter feeders, eating plankton by swimming along with their mouths open, filtering the tiny creatures from the water as they go. They are known as gentle giants, and are very tolerant of swimmers in the water with them.

As the whaleshark approached we quickly geared up in our snorkel gear and jumped in. It was very exciting waiting in the water, knowing this huge thing was heading our way. Suddenly there it was!! It wasn't a fully grown one, but was still over 6 metres long and very impressive as it swam straight towards us. We got out of its way, and then swam along beside it. It was quite an incredible and breath-taking sight.

After a hundred metres or so our group stopped. The second group jumped in to meet the huge creature as it continued on towards them, and the boat picked our group up. This continued for a while as the shark continued on its course, seemingly oblivious to the excitement around it. We got to swim with it three or four times before taking a break.

After a morning snack, we swam with the same shark again, the two groups taking turns as before. A younger one was spotted nearby, and we headed off to take a look. It was smaller, but still very impressive. It was much more curious that the bigger one.

Our second group was first in the water this time, and I climbed up to the bridge of the boat to see if I could get a picture of the shark in the water. All aboard were amazed as the whaleshark headed directly for the back of the boat, through the group of swimmers in the water, and came to within a metre of the stern of the boat. It was like a scene out of "Jaws", but without any of the fear of being eaten!

When I got to swim with the smaller shark, it was travelling fairly quickly, and I was pleased to be one of only a couple of us who managed to keep up.

Although I did not quite get to see the 10 metre-plus whaleshark I had hoped to, I certainly feel that I can call this goal complete. I got to spend quite a bit of time in very close proximity to the biggest fish I have ever seen in my entire life. Fantastic!

The long weekend with Mel had been like a holiday, and we came back feeling very relaxed and content. But back in Perth my imminent departure hung over us like a dark cloud as the inevitable day drew closer.

Chapter 5 – Weeks 41 to 50

(11th May 2009 – 19th July 2009)

France – England – Spain – USA

I had only managed to achieve five goals in the previous ten weeks, but was still slightly ahead of schedule, having now completed 42 of my list of 100 challenges and adventures.

I was keen to get on, looking forward to travelling again, but felt a vague apprehension, similar to that felt before previous departures. After almost three comfortable months in familiar surroundings, once again I had to face the trepidation of dragging myself out of my comfort zone. However, I was finding that the more often I forced myself to do so, the easier it was becoming.

I set off on my second round-the-world journey almost 40 weeks to the day after my first departure. This time Mel dropped me off at the airport and we said a sad and slightly strained farewell. I told her I would probably see her again before Christmas, but had no idea how much things were going to change for me on a personal level during this second journey.

My second voyage got off to a poor start when I left my battery charger, with my spare camera battery in it, hanging from a wall socket in Perth airport

Later in the day, with about 6 hours to kill in Hong Kong, I relaxed in the departure area. As the final call for the red-eye flight to London Heathrow was made, I casually strolled up to the gate.

"No, no, no! You are on the BA flight." What?!! There were two flights to Heathrow, both leaving at 23:55? Yes, and my gate on the far side of the airport was probably receiving its own final boarding call! So I found myself, confident, cool, experienced traveller that I thought I was, sprinting through Hong Kong airport as midnight approached, with disastrous financial scenarios running through my head!

However, I took the time to confirm the gate number at the first departures board that I passed, and was incredibly relieved to see that the flight was now scheduled to leave at 00:35. I was glad to be able to walk the rest of the way to the gate. I really needed to get back into the travelling mindset.

On the flight to Europe I watched the movie "Benjamin Button", and paused it, writing down a quote which really captured the slightly melancholy mood I felt.

"For what it's worth, it's never too late, or in my case, too early, to be whoever you want to be. There is no time limit, stop whenever you want. You can change or stay the same. There are no rules to this thing.

You can make the best or the worst of it. I hope you make the best of it. I hope you see things that startle you, I hope you feel things you never felt before, I hope you meet people with a different point of view. I hope you live a life you're proud of, and if you find that you're not, I hope you have the strength to start all over again."

It was true, I reflected – I could stop whenever I wanted – and had been tempted to do so a couple of times so far. I knew that my journey was certainly taking an emotional toll at times, but I was happy that I had seen things that had startled me, felt things that I had never felt before, and met many people with different points of view.

One of the things I felt most proud about was that when I had needed to, I had had the strength to start all over again.

I arrived in beautiful sunny Nice in the south of France, and was warmly welcomed by Pierre, Valerie and family. They had invited me to stay with them for a day or two as I visited Cannes for the famous film festival there.

Little did I know that I was about to experience another amazing tale of goal over-achievement, as another fairly random set of contacts led from one step to the next. The result was an experience at the Cannes Film Festival that I really had no hope of achieving, and yet did in the finest style possible. It is amazing what you can achieve when you put an idea out there, and open yourself to gratefully accepting help from others.

Goal 43 - Cannes-tastic!

Thursday, May 14, 2009
(Cannes, France)

Wow! As an example of how you can expect the events of a day to unfold in one fashion, but a couple of things change, and the course of the day takes you in quite an unexpected direction, yesterday is certainly going to be hard to beat!

I woke early again, feeling slightly feverish, and wondered casually if I might have caught the swine flu virus already. When I passed through Hong Kong, the airport resembled a hospital wing. About a third of the travellers were wearing surgical masks, notices everywhere displayed dire health warnings, and temperature testing stations were set up in several locations for paranoid incoming travellers.

I was looking forward to a quiet day at Valerie and Pierre's apartment, and wanted to catch up on some emails. My main priority was to try to sort out some new accommodation, as Valerie and Pierre have family arriving today, and they need the space.

I had had some contact from people who suggested that they may be able to help out. So far nothing had been confirmed, so I re-emailed a couple of people. My first contact was Rikki, whose company, Exhibition Consultants International, builds stands for the film festival, among other things. He had been told about me by Philippe from EIE Global, who helped out with my Eiffel Tower goal back in September last year.

My second contact was Adrian, who first contacted me via the website, when I first started my goals quest. At the time he was living in Cannes, but has since moved to London. He still has many contacts here, and thought he could possibly find some accommodation for me in Cannes itself.

Adrian was quickly on the case, and put me in touch with Lao from Cannes-based accommodation agency Azur Alive. Lao said that he would be glad to help, offering to let me use one of their apartments at no charge! Marvellous! I arranged to meet him at 3pm that afternoon.

Almost straight afterwards Rikki called me. Although he had been unable to track down any accommodation, he had a contact from the UK Film Council who would like to meet me in the afternoon, with the possibility of a ticket to a screening. It looked like things were coming together, perhaps.

After a quick shower and shave, Valerie dropped me off at the train station, and I met Lao at his office. He took me to see a lovely fourth floor apartment right in downtown Cannes, and left me with the key. I can use the place for about 5 days, and then he will find me another.

Next I went to meet Rikki in front of the Palais. He produced a pass for me, and we went through security, into the festival building itself. I almost felt like my goal had been achieved, as I was already somewhere that the general public could not access.

We walked through the huge marketplace area, where stands from movie production companies from all over the world are set up, promoting their latest releases to movie buyers. We made our way to the International Village area, and at the UK marquee Rikki introduced me to Tina from the UK Film Council.

She is Head of Industry Relations, and as well as helping me with my goal, hoped that the Film Council might benefit from some publicity too. She rang a couple of people to set up some possible interviews, and offered me a ticket to the movie which was going to screen that evening at 10:30pm.

At first I didn't quite grasp the significance of the ticket I was given, but when Rikki saw it, he was amazed. The movie being screened was the premiere of the first movie in the Film Festival competition. It was called "Fish Tank", written and directed by Andrea Arnold. Andrea won the Prix de Jury in 2006 with her first movie "Red Road", and "Fish Tank" is her highly anticipated follow-up.

Because the UK Film Council co-funded both of these movies, they had some pretty good tickets for the screening, and my seat was in the "Orchestre" section. "That's right at the front, up the red carpet and in through the main door," Rikki exclaimed!

"You have got a tuxedo, haven't you?" Tina asked.

"Er, yes," I answered, trying to sound confident.

Somewhat coincidentally, Eric, a Hollywood producer had called the day before I left Australia. He had put me in touch with an actor/writer /filmmaker who would be here in Cannes. I had managed to speak to Bobby earlier in the day, and was hoping to meet him later. He had suggested that if I managed to get a ticket, I could borrow his suit, if he wasn't using it at the time.

I tried Bobby a couple of times, but his phone was off – he was obviously having a busy first day. I went looking for a suit hire shop, and soon found one pretty close to my apartment. At 7pm I gave Bobby a final try, and upon discovering that his phone was still off, I went ahead and was relieved of 90 Euros for the hire of a tux and shoes for the evening.

I was going to have to stay in Cannes for the night, as the movie would finish long after the last train, and I called Valerie to let her know. At the apartment I showered and washed as best I could, but had no toiletries at all with me. I had no more cash either, as it had all gone on the suit, and a sandwich for dinner. The apartment was so completely empty that I had to dry off after the shower with handfuls of toilet paper! All my stuff was still back in Nice.

Eventually I suited up and headed down to La Croisette, the seafront area. I wandered around soaking up the atmosphere, which was electric. I joined the line of other smartly dressed movie-goers, and made my way through several security and ticket checks. Many others with different coloured tickets to mine were directed off through side entrances. I kept waving my silver ticket about, and kept getting waved through, until I was at the foot of the red carpet. To either side were huge crowds of press photographers. They didn't take any pictures, obviously waiting quietly for the real stars to arrive.

The walk up the carpet was wonderful, and I stopped at the top to look back down. Many other movie-goers were taking photos, despite warnings on the ticket that photography was not allowed, and I joined in too. What a wonderful atmosphere!

My ticket granted me access through the main doors, where a friendly escort greeted me and guided me right to the front of the cinema. She told that I could sit wherever I liked. I picked the front row!

On the huge screen in front of me the scene outside the cinema was displayed. I watched others arriving and climbing the red-carpeted steps, as the seats slowly filled around me. Eventually the director, Andrea Arnold, arrived with some of the stars from the movie, and I followed their progress on the big screen as they made their way up the steps outside. The press photographers were a little more enthusiastic than when I had passed them!

It was interesting to watch a live feed of their progress through the lobby area, and then turn around to see them come into the room, greeted by a huge round of applause.

When we were all eventually seated again the movie started. It is a very English, very gritty study of a girl growing up on a rough housing estate in southern England, and was very compelling and well acted. At the end there was a huge standing ovation, which was fun to be part of.

Afterwards, we had to wait for the stars to go back down the steps, and then followed suit. I met a Chinese girl who appeared to be on her own too, so we swapped cameras and took plenty of pictures of each other. She seemed to be as thrilled and excited as I was to be there.

Around 1am I wandered back to the apartment through the busy streets with a huge smile on my face. What a way to achieve my Cannes goal! I couldn't possibly have imagined being so successful in acquiring a ticket for a screening. What a dream come true!

Valerie had contacted local English-speaking Riviera Radio on my behalf, and this morning I was scheduled for an interview with them at 9am. I put my suit on again – I had paid 90 Euros for it and was determined to get value for money!! – and headed down to the huge Hotel Martinez on the seafront. There I met Peter, who transmits live daily from the lobby there, and was soon live on air. It seemed to go pretty well, and when I eventually got back to Nice Thibault, Valerie and Pierre's son, said he had heard the interview. He thought it had sounded great.

What an amazing 24 hours! What an awesome way to achieve a goal! What an adventure!

From Cannes I headed up into the hills above Nice to visit Mel's father, where we had stayed the previous summer, as I tackled some of the first goals on the list.

Inspired largely by being with Mel for a while, I had been trying to learn some more French. My basic schoolboy ability was far short of fluent, but over the previous months I had tried to get Mel and her kids to talk to me as much as possible in French. I had been practicing as much as I could on my travels too.

During my previous visit to Jean-Claude's house, there had been a gathering of a few of his friends one evening. I had tried to keep up with the conversation as best I could. One lady asked me if I spoke much French, and I haltingly explained that I could manage a little. As the rest of the gathering listened in, I said that I could manage if people spoke slowly enough, but when a lot of people spoke at once, I couldn't keep up. When I said that the last thing I had understood properly was the lady's husband saying, "Ah, putain!" distastefully, as he tried the Turkish aniseed drink I had brought with me from Istanbul, I got a big laugh. "Putain" is a French word which roughly translates into "fuck" in English, in this case, as in "Oh fuck, this stuff is awful!"

I reckon that if you can get a good laugh at a French house, with French people, speaking in French, then you can claim at least a basic level of fluency!

Goal 44 – Je parle Francais (un petit peu!)
Sunday, May 24, 2009
(Various French-speaking locations)

There are quite a few goals on my list that are very difficult to quantify in terms of when they are achieved. For example, I recently marked my goal of learning to play the didgeridoo as complete, but I really am still a beginner when compared to some of the Aboriginal didge masters I have seen or heard.

But my playing has improved considerably, and I continue to practice when I can. I learned the technique of circular breathing, which is something I have been unable to do for a long time, although I would never dream of claiming to have mastered the didgeridoo.

As with any such skill, I don't think there is ever a point when you stop learning and trying to improve. That is how I view life too, always trying to learn how to play the game a little bit better than you could previously!

My "Learn to speak conversational French" goal is another that is difficult to decide exactly when the goal has been achieved. But over the past year I have had quite a lot more interaction with the French language than I have had in all the years since I left school.

I really do feel that I have improved. My friend Mel in Perth is originally from France, so I have had some help from her. I spent a couple of weeks in France last year at the start of the 100goals trip, and did my whole paragliding course in French. I met French football coach Philippe Troussier in Japan, and we had quite a lengthy chat in French, with which I was very pleased. Doug and Mike, who were there as that interview and chat was filmed, both reckoned that I could have claimed my French goal as completed there and then!

Now I have been back in France again for the last couple of weeks, visiting the Cannes Film Festival.

I have managed to do pretty-much everything I have needed to in French in the time have been here. I have made all of my day-to-day purchases without resorting to English, and have successfully managed less common transactions too, such as hiring a tuxedo!

But it was actually while wearing the tuxedo that I made my greatest steps forward in conversational French! The movie I watched, called "Fish Tank" was a gritty, real-life, English-slum-housing-estate drama, and as such was liberally sprinkled with some choice expletives!

One of the best things about the movie was that it was subtitled in French, so the local audience could appreciate it too. I thoroughly enjoyed the movie, but was somewhat distracted by trying to remember some of the more choice phrases in French.

The next time I spoke to Mel, I ran some of my new vocabulary past her, and she was pretty impressed at my top-level French swearing ability. I have two particularly high-level French swear words in my vocabulary now, and have been strongly advised not to try to fit them into any sort of French dinner table chatter!

While I will be the first to admit that my French conversational abilities are somewhat stilted, on a one-to-one basis, I am certainly able to communicate at a reasonably satisfying level. I can't possibly keep up with a group of French people chatting together, but can often get at least a good idea of what they are talking about.

This morning I fly out of France, having completed my last French-based goal. I don't imagine I will be back here, or have much more opportunity to speak French for the rest of my 100 weeks, so I am quite happy to finally tick this one as achieved.

I will however always continue to practice and try to improve my French, as I would like to become much more fluent.

"Merci beaucoup," to all who have helped along the way.

Back in England again I stayed once more with my brother Martin and his partner Rachel in London. Martin ended up being a somewhat surprised participant in my next, dangerous downhill goal.

Goal 45 – chasing cheese
Monday, May 25, 2009
(Brockworth, England)

After the early start in Cannes the previous morning, the last thing I wanted to do yesterday was get up again at 5:30 in the morning. But I had been in touch with the organisers of the infamous Gloucester Cheese Rolling Festival, and they had told me that the only way to be certain of competing was to be there early, and line up with everyone else. There is no entry fee, no paperwork to complete, and no guarantee of taking part in the event.

Martin, Rachel and I headed westward out of London along the M4, and made it to the small village of Brockworth by around 8am. We found a place to get a coffee, and waited for the carpark field to open.

Our first view of the hill, as we drove out of the village, had us slightly worried – it looked very steep. It wasn't until we actually arrived and scrambled up to the top that we realised just how steep it really is.

At the top of the hill Martin and I joined a crowd of others sat waiting for the first race. Tension and excitement was already building, and it wasn't even 10 o'clock, still over two hours to go before the action started!

Eventually, when the burly security guards and event organisers arrived, we were all shepherded off to the side of the run. We formed some semblance of an orderly line, and sat to wait out the next couple of hours.

We had managed to get a pretty good position, and I was reasonably confident of making it into the first race. There are only five downhill races in the day, four for men and one for women, and the number of competitors is strictly limited to fifteen per race.

As the morning progressed the hillside filled up, and an estimated 5,000 people vied for position to get the best view of the upcoming events. The place was packed, and the line of potential competitors behind us was steadily growing. We had certainly been wise to arrive early, as there were going to be many disappointed people.

Just before the event was due to start a light rain began to fall, making the whole hillside much slippier. About five minutes before midday they let the first fifteen people through the little gate and onto the flatter area at the top of the hill. Both my brother and I made it through, despite the chaos at the front, as everyone tried to get in for race number 1. Martin had said he was only there to keep me company in the queue, but had become more enthusiastic as the morning had progressed. He still looked a little surprised to be lining up next to me though!

There was a huge cheer from the crowd as we lined up, and my heart was hammering – there was a real danger that this could end very painfully! After brief instructions on how the start would be conducted, the cheese was rolled, and we were off!

I think in my younger years I might have been a lot quicker than I was yesterday, but in my middle-aged years common sense has obviously finally kicked in a little. I ran with slightly more caution than many of the other young guys, most of whom were probably at least 20 years younger than my brother or I.

I still found myself tumbling and sliding, completely out of control. It was impossible to stay on your feet, as the slope was so steep, and by now quite wet and slippy. Somehow though, I managed to make it down in one piece, my number one priority, but was one of the last in my race across the line. It's the taking part that counts, I told myself proudly at the bottom of the hill.

The atmosphere at the bottom was fantastic as the winners collected their prizes and certificates, and we shook hands all round with the guys with whom we had run. It was only later, as the adrenaline began to wear off, that I started to feel the cuts and scrapes on my arms, and the ache in my left shoulder. Compared to my brother though, who had chosen to wear shorts for some reason, I was relatively unscathed.

We stayed at the bottom of the hill, and had an excellent view of the next two races. I think that if I had seen the carnage on the hill that race 2 produced, I might have been a lot less inclined to run myself. One of the guys looked like he possibly dislocated or broke his shoulder, and there was quite a break before race 3 started, as he was carted off to hospital.

Back at the top of the hill, after race 3, there was another long break as another casualty was transported away – the rumour that ran through the crowd was that he had fallen out of a tree! He was taken away down the main slope, a tricky rescue operation in its own right, his neck immobilised to prevent possible further damage.

After race 4 we made an early exit to avoid the worst of the traffic chaos that would obviously follow as everyone headed for home, and got away pretty quickly.

As pretty much all eccentric UK Bank Holiday Monday activities do, the day ended in a trip to hospital for the unfortunate few, and a headlong dash to the nearest pub for everyone else! What a fantastic day! I have no idea how this event continues to run without the Dept. of Health and Safety stepping in!!

The cheese-rolling adventure led to another unexpected experience, when I was contacted by CNN International, based in Central London. Would I be interested in doing an interview on their morning show?

I was picked up from Martin's house early in the morning and chauffeur-driven to the studio. When I had tried to get in the front seat of the car, the driver had insisted that I sit in the back, and I felt quite the celebrity being rushed through the quiet early morning streets of London.

Little did I realise that I was soon going to be in the back of another chauffeured vehicle, this time with a real celebrity.

I had been at work for a long time on the next goal, and had been told by many people that this was going to be a tough one to achieve. This had only served to strengthen my resolve to succeed, and I had persevered with efforts to make contact, following any and all possible avenues that I could think of.

Eventually my persistence had paid off, and the goal was achieved relatively easily too, via probably the simplest method that I tried. The people who had suggested that meeting Sir Richard Branson would be one of the hardest goals to achieve were amazed when I succeeded, as was I, and once again things worked out far better than I had any right to hope or expect.

Goal 46 - Virgin territory

Sunday, May 31, 2009
(London, England)

I have long been an admirer of Richard Branson, and have mentioned him in several of my previous blog posts. It was with great excitement that I headed into central London this morning with my brother Martin.

While back in Australia I had done some internet searching, and had found email addresses for several people at Virgin Blue, the Australian-based Virgin airline. I sent a couple of emails, and got a reply suggesting that I might be able to meet Richard next time he was in Australia. Unfortunately that wouldn't be until November 2009, and I was not sure that I would be back in the country by then.

However, my email had been forwarded to a Virgin PR person in the UK, and I followed up by emailing her. I got a response from Richard's personal assistant, who said that Richard would be happy to meet me when next possible.

While in Cannes, I heard rumours that Richard may be heading down to Monaco, which is just along the coast, for the Grand Prix. I had sent another email to his PA, explaining where I was, and that I would also be in the UK for the following few weeks. I was amazed to get a response from Richard himself!

He invited me to the unveiling of a plaque to commemorate the life of WWII fighter pilot, Douglas Bader, and suggested that I could then jump in the car with him afterwards as he headed for the airport.

Martin and I arrived in the city in good time, and waited in the small city centre mews as the TV crews and the crowd gathered, watching the plaque get polished in preparation.

Eventually Richard arrived, and when he appeared to have a relatively quiet moment I took the opportunity to introduce myself. In terms of my hopes and expectations for this goal, I had already achieved what I set out to do, but Richard confirmed that I could join him after the ceremony for the trip to the airport.

The ceremony was interesting, and if you don't know the story of Douglas Bader, it is well worth reading. Despite the loss of both legs in an aeroplane crash in 1931, he went on to become one of the most successful war-time fighter pilots. There is also a movie about his exploits, called "Reach For The Sky", which I watched again just last week. A very inspiring man!

Richard was there because he wanted to support the "Douglas Bader Foundation", which exists to advance and promote the physical, mental and spiritual welfare of persons who are without one or more limbs, or otherwise physically disabled. He was also there because he had met Douglas Bader while he was a boy, as Douglas and his aunt Clare had been close friends. He told the amusing tale of how, as a mischievous 7-year-old, he had stolen Douglas's artificial legs while he was swimming, and had been chased by an irate legless Douglas dragging himself along after him!

After the ceremony was over, Richard made his way back to his waiting car, and I joined him. After a quick photo we headed towards Heathrow.

We spoke about many things, and I thoroughly enjoyed the half-hour I got to share with him. He is very down to earth, and easy to chat with. I asked him about his current ventures, and was particularly interested in recent progress with the amazing Virgin Galactic project.

He asked many questions about my goals, and I told him of a couple on which I am currently working, including my fundraising efforts for Bowel Cancer Research, and my attempt to gather 5 Ian Ushers in one place!

He made a very kind offer, and said that he would donate $500 to the Bowel Cancer Research and Awareness Institute, for every Ian Usher that I managed to gather!!

I was immensely grateful to Richard for fitting me in to his busy schedule, and allowing me to complete another goal in a manner way beyond any of my expectations. It really is quite amazing what you can achieve when you make an effort.

For a while I had been getting very frustrated about some of the plans I was trying to put into action. I seemed to have so many things on the go at once, but didn't seem to be achieving anything. I felt a little like a comedic plate spinner in a circus, dashing around from pole to pole, giving each one a quick wiggle to speed its plate up again, before spotting the next plate about to crash down.

I suppose progress is often like this. For a long time it can seem as if nothing is working and it can be very tempting to give up. However, I have learnt it is often the case that this is the time when you have to push on just a little bit further. Sometimes something that you did earlier may be producing results that you haven't yet seen, and success may already be barrelling towards you. In my case it was coming on an incredibly rickety moped.

For quite some time I had been trying to get in touch with an operator of a "Wall of Death". There are only a couple of them remaining in England, touring as fairground attractions, and I had seen several shows as a kid at the Newcastle Town Moor Fair.

The amazing spectacle involves a vertical-sided circular wooden arena, approximately thirty feet across, in which daredevil motorbike riders transition from ground level onto the vertical sides of the wall. This is accomplished via a small forty-five degree ramp at the bottom of the barrel. With enough speed, it is possible to ride around and around inside the huge barrel, heading higher and higher up the circular wooden wall.

I had done a good deal of internet research, and tried to contact the owners of both of the still-operational walls. After the poor response to the six emails I had sent to the whaleshark tour operators in Australia two months earlier, perhaps I shouldn't have been surprised when neither of the "Wall of Death" operators replied to me. I really don't understand why businesses don't reply to their email enquiries.

I did some more internet research, and in the process came across a YouTube video of a guy in England who had made his own wall, constructed from wooden pallets and plywood, and built in a field near his home.

I emailed Colin via his YouTube page, and was pleasantly surprised to get a very positive response from him. I called in to see him as I headed north to visit my mum, and made arrangements to visit again on my return south.

Death defying goal 47 - Day 1
Saturday, June 13, 2009
(Stamford, England)

What a day! I was up pretty early, and packed my bags again, ready to leave Darlington once more, and head south on the next leg of my adventures. After a quick farewell to my mum, I hit the road. Two and a half hours later I arrived again at Colin's house at Stamford.

Colin Furze is a very interesting guy. He owns a homemade "Wall of Death", built in a friend's field, and was kind enough to allow me to come and have a try at riding it. I had called in on my way north a week and a half ago, and was quite alarmed at the run-down appearance of the wall, but excited too at the prospect of having a go on it.

Over the last week, Colin had cleaned out most of the thistles from the bottom of it, and prepared two Honda scooters for the day.

Getting the bikes into the interior area of the wall was treacherous enough, involving a precarious ride up the steep ramp, stopping just in time to avoid plunging into the deep hole at the top. I wisely left this tricky operation to Colin.

Once inside the wall with both bikes, Colin fired one up, and headed around and up the wall. He said he was pretty rusty, as he hadn't ridden the wall for a year and a half, but I watched in amazement as he worked his way pretty quickly up on to the vertical section several times.

After a bit of fiddling around with the older, tattier looking bike, which we couldn't get started, Colin foolishly offered to let me try on the better bike. This was the first mistake of the day. My theory was to attack the wall with confidence, much as Colin appeared to, and I did so. This was the second mistake!

Before I had managed the second circuit, I had the bike onto the vertical section, but having never experienced such a thing, my natural motorcycling reaction was to try to get the bike upright. Before I knew it, I was sliding down the wall behind the bike, which had obviously lost all traction! I scraped my arm a bit, but otherwise was okay.

Colin pretty quickly put some extra effort into getting the older bike running. He succeeded this time, and after a bit of a pep-talk, I was off again. The idea is to progress upwards a bit more slowly at first, and lean more.... much more.

I really had imagined that it could not be too hard to do, but was a bit frustrated at my slow progress. It is SO much harder than you can possibly imagine! After three or four circuits you end up incredibly dizzy and disorientated. The hardest part is to overcome the natural reaction to want to be upright.

But I persevered, taking regular breaks to stop the mental spinning effect. The wall itself is very ramshackle, and pretty bumpy, and there are quite a few potholes in the 45 degree-angled section. The vertical wall is a lot smoother, apparently, but it is a huge mental hurdle to get up there.

After a couple of hours, I was getting up onto the vertical for short stretches, which I tried to make longer and longer. But the whole experience really is very visually and physically disturbing!

By the end of the day, I was confidently riding at the transition point between the 45 degrees and the main wall. I was also getting up onto the vertical section regularly, but could not quite stay up there!

Now, relaxing afterwards, I feel a strange mixture of elation and frustration. In a way, I am enjoying the fact that this is a much, MUCH harder skill to master than I thought it would be, but am also disappointed by the fact that I still haven't done a complete circuit on the vertical wall.

However, like many things in life, if it was easy, everybody would be doing it, wouldn't they? I feel that I can say that I have achieved my goal of riding a "Wall of Death", but I want to do better. I still have more time tomorrow to crack it!

Death defying goal 47 – Day 2
Sunday, June 14, 2009

A barbeque with a few beers, and a reasonably enthusiastic game of back garden badminton was the ideal end to the first day of death-defying wall-riding. Colin and Charlotte's spare room had a very comfy bed, and I slept pretty well. However, each time I rolled over in my sleep, my scraped arm, from my initial crash earlier that day, woke me up, which was slightly frustrating.

On Sunday morning we went around to Mark's house to watch the motorcycle MotoGP from Barcelona, which had an incredibly exciting finish. Valentino Rossi and Jorge Lorenzo fought an astonishing battle for the whole of the race, and to huge cheers in the living room, Rossi snatched a well-earned victory at the final corner.

After a quick bite to eat we loaded the bikes back onto the truck, and headed out to the wall again. Once the bikes and tools were lowered back in, some repair work was carried out to the dodgier sections of the lower parts of the wall. Finally, cameras were set up and fiddled with, and it was time to get back on the bike.

My idea was to make the first couple of circuits slow and steady until I got the feel for it back, but things didn't quite work out as planned. In quite an impromptu fashion, Colin and I ended up with both bikes running, and with a nod at each other we both set off from opposite sides. I knew I had to get up the wall quickly and keep my speed up, and I was very quickly back to the transition point where the wall became vertical, aware of the noise of Colin's bike opposite and behind me. We managed a couple of good dual efforts before going back to the safer solo rides.

Once again I tried to creep further and further up above the transition to vertical, with similarly frustrating results as the day before. I could feel myself getting better bit by bit, and my confidence was building, but I knew time was running out. I had still not ridden around the wall in the way that I had imagined it beforehand.

One of the other guys, Lee, came down to give it a go, riding in the opposite direction to everyone else. With a background in BMX riding, he quickly managed to get the hang of doing big arcs up onto the wall, like riding a bike ramp.

Spurred on by his quick successes, I pushed myself harder on the next couple of turns. I got a couple of good rides around, and on the next try Mark, who was operating the video camera, reckoned I had done a full circuit entirely on the vertical section. There was a cheer from above, but Colin looked doubtful as he reviewed the video footage.

"What do you think?" he asked me, handing me the camera, and I watched through the viewfinder.

"It's still not good enough, is it?" I said quietly to Colin.

"I thought you'd say that," he replied.

But something in me had clicked, and Colin and I talked about pushing up with the lower handlebar. He explained that the first time that you felt yourself actually hold the bike up on the wall when its weight wants to pull you down, and it stays where you want it to, everything mentally falls into place.

The next couple of times on the wall I was conscious of keeping the throttle open, and pushing on the lower bar. I made a couple of much better circuits of the wall, creeping up higher for longer, until I made what I thought was an excellent double circuit.

Colin, who had been watching from the top of the wall for a while, came back down, and I managed another good lap on the vertical. I was so pleased, and quickly gathered my spinning thoughts, setting off again. This time I could keep the bike up for a much longer period, and my confidence soared. I had cracked it! It felt absolutely awesome, and I was incredibly thrilled.

Just in time too, as Colin, who decided to have another quick go himself, found himself struggling to keep control of the bike. No wonder, we discovered, as he brought it down looking very discouraged – it had a flat rear tyre. The day was over!

We packed everything away, dragged the bikes back out of the wall and put them on the truck. There was quite a crowd now, and a lot of chatting and laughter, and I thanked everyone profusely. I couldn't really find the words to properly express to Colin how grateful I was to him, but I think he knew, and I imagine my face said more than words ever could. He and his wonderful friends had pretty-much given up a large chunk of their weekend to help a complete stranger achieve a goal. Although I am sure they had enjoyed themselves, I was quite overwhelmed by their generosity. It really was one of the most outstanding weekends of the trip so far.

As I drove away I felt very proud, and very satisfied within myself. I thought a lot about what I had just achieved. I had seriously underestimated how difficult a skill it would be to learn, and was pleased that even after an early setback, scraping down the wall without the bike on my first attempt, I had not given up.

I had managed to push past the fear and the frustration, and the spinning disorientation. I had stuck at it, pushing myself when it might have been easy to give up, call it a day, and say that I had given it a good try. Ultimately I had succeeded in what I had imagined doing, and the feeling was absolutely wonderful. This goal is certainly, by a long way, my proudest personal achievement so far.

Just a few days before, I had been asked in a radio interview why I chose to have some of these crazy, dangerous goals in my list of 100. As I drove away from Colin's "Wall of Death", I thought to myself that if I could just take some of what I felt right then, bottle it up, and give it to them, I could simply say, "There, that's why I do these things!" What an awesome weekend!

Thanks to Colin for the generous provision of a "safety tie", which all riders of his wall are required to wear! Why? "Well, you've got to look your best, don't you?" was the closest I got to an answer that made any sort of sense. As I left at the end of the weekend, I asked if Colin needed his tie back. "Keep it as a souvenir," he said, "as long as you promise to wear it at the movie premiere if your film ever gets made!" I kept it as a souvenir, and I will keep my promise too, if I ever get the chance!

Riding the "Wall of Death" was an achievement of which I am immensely proud. It was so much harder than I ever thought it would be, and so much scarier too. It would have been easy to give up after the first day, and call it a goal achieved, but I knew I could not do that. Once again facing up to a challenge, facing the fear, stepping out of my comfort zone, and ultimately managing to do what I said I would gave me one of the most satisfying feelings of achievement that I have ever experienced.

Ultimately too, I was so pleased that I hadn't managed to organise a ride on one of the more professionally and sturdily constructed walls. Colin's wall had been much more of a personal experience, with a guy much like myself, who simply wanted to squeeze as much fun out of life as possible. Colin, and his wonderful group of friends, weren't the type to say, "Wouldn't it be great to build a 'Wall of Death?'" and then do nothing about it. They were the sort of people who had ideas and put them into action. They were very inspiring to be around, as well as great fun too!

When I reflect back on that weekend, the wall-riding was, of course, a hugely important part of the experience. But the people I met there, their outlook on life, and their enthusiasm to help a stranger fulfil an ambition were ultimately more important aspects of the pleasure of achievement.

Colin's "safety tie" came in handy again, shortly after its successful protective qualities had been proved on the rickety wall. I had booked another thrilling activity that I had always wanted to try.

I had hoped to be able to talk my way into an experience with one of the touring display teams, but once again, responses to my emails had been non-existent.

However, I hadn't given up, and eventually found a guy operating out of a little airfield near London. He was the only person I ever discovered that was offering wingwalk flights that you simply paid for.

The legal aspect of his operation was interesting. What I had booked wasn't simply a thrill ride. I was going to be a trained wingwalker, performing in my own demonstration. I think he had to describe his business in this manner for insurance reasons.

The "training" was minimal, consisting mainly of being strapped in on a tiny seat on the top wing of the beautiful biplane, and being asked if I had any questions.

Goal 48 – Wingwalking
Saturday, June 20, 2009
(London, England)

My early accident on Colin's "Wall of Death" last weekend could have been much worse! The first attempt ended with me sliding down the rickety wooden wall which is filled with rusty nails and dodgy screws, and yet a bit of a graze on my arm was the only injury sustained.

Colin reckoned I was relatively unscathed only because I was wearing the safety tie that he had insisted on, and suggested that for any further dangerous activities, wearing the tie might be a wise choice.

So before climbing up onto the top wing of the Boeing Stearman PT17 Kaydet biplane, I made sure I was appropriately attired. Pilot Mike told me I would be his first-ever tie-wearing customer!

Wingwalking UK is based at a small airfield on the east side of London, and it had taken me about an hour and a half to get there, driving around the M25, London's huge, traffic-clogged, orbital ringroad.

I met Mike, and after a very quick briefing I was up onto the top wing, strapped in. As we trundled over to the runway I nervously checked the straps again – they felt good and tight, but there didn't seem to be enough of them for my liking.

As soon as we got a clear runway, Mike gave me a shout, and we were off. Almost as soon as the plane took off, Mike banked it over to the right, and we swooped in low over the airfield.

We went through a routine of turns and swoops, and I was amazed at how low to the ground we passed over the field. Mike later told me that he is licensed to fly as low as 30 feet during a display. It felt very quick being so close to the ground.

Towards the end of the sequences, we climbed up to about 500 feet. Mike tipped the little plane towards the runway in a steep dive, gathering speed, and then pulled up into a climb and another dive – it was like being on a huge rollercoaster.

The whole display lasted about 15 minutes, and I could have happily stayed up there for much longer, it really was quite an incredibly free feeling. What an incredible view too!

It was quite similar to the thrill of a skydive, but for a more extended period. By the end I was feeling pretty relaxed and confident.

Afterwards Mike presented me with a certificate, and I hung around to watch the next person's flight.

It was fantastic to be right under the plane as it flew over at speed, just 30 feet above.

After the wingwalk I had to dash back around London to drop the car off at my brother's house, and then catch the underground into the city to meet some other Ian Ushers.

I had tried everything I could think of over the course of the previous week, in order to gather five of us. By Saturday morning I had three other Ians confirmed, making a total of four including myself.

I had been in touch with four or five other Ians from various parts of the country, but all had other engagements, or London was too far for them to come. I had hoped to be able to get the four of us in a car and drive to briefly meet one of the other Ians, but hadn't been able to get in touch with him to make arrangements.

Eventually I had to accept defeat on this occasion, and be happy with meeting three other Ian Ushers.

Ian (London) Usher had arrived at the pub just before me. We got a couple of pints and sat down for a chat with the first other Ian Usher we had both ever met.

Shortly afterwards Ian (Portsmouth) Usher arrived, followed minutes later by Ian (Bristol) Usher. We had a couple of rounds in the fantastic old Glasshouse Stores pub, and got to know each other a bit.

We all got on pretty well, and the other Ians had some funny stories about how my eBay antics had impacted them. Ian from Portsmouth is about the same age as me, and had had many old friends contact him, asking if he was okay, and why he was selling everything.

Ian from Bristol is an artist, and when setting up his website, his web designer couldn't understand why they couldn't get him a good ranking in a Google search. He finally discovered why... "Oh, that's unlucky! You've got the same name as the guy selling his life on eBay! That makes things much trickier."

The fire alarm went off just as we were finishing our second round, and we all ended up out on the pavement, pints in hand, until things were sorted out. We decided that it would be a good time to head off to the Roundhouse in Covent Garden. The new owners, Fuller's Beers, had offered each Ian a socially responsible two free pints of beer. You can't turn down free beer!

As the afternoon turned into evening the beers continued to flow, and we did a lot of laughing at unusual and entertaining situations that could occur. I mentioned that I had hoped to drive the four of us to meet a fifth Ian, but if I had borrowed my brother's old car, which overheats in busy traffic, I could picture a scene when we break down in central London. When the police turn up to sort it out, imagine them asking who was driving...

"Name?"

"Ian Usher."

"And the others here? What's your name?"

"Ian Usher."
"Right! And you?"
"Ian Usher"
"Hmm, you?"
"Ian Usher"
"Right, you're all under arrest!!"
Even though it didn't actually happen, we thought it would make a great scene in a movie!

Eventually Ian (Bristol) had to leave to catch the last coach home. Ian (London) was next to head for home. Ian (Portsmouth) and I headed for the tube. I dashed headlong onto mine which was just about to leave.

Unfortunately by then I was pretty drunk! We had had a good long afternoon and evening, and I did not check the destination of the train. I also did the usual late night comedy trick of falling asleep almost immediately.

The Piccadilly line splits into different directions before my brother's house, and when I woke the train was at a station I had never heard of before. It took a few drunken minutes of studying the tube map before I figured out where I had gone wrong. Fortunately trains were still running back towards the city, and I backtracked, and eventually managed to find my way home. It took me almost two hours to do a journey that should have been about 40 minutes!

I woke with a fine hangover the next morning... I'm never drinking again, I promised myself, as I have done many times before, and as I am sure I will do again in the future!

I was a bit disappointed that I hadn't managed to achieve the goal of gathering five Ian Ushers – how hard can it possibly be to get five guys together in a pub? But I was extremely grateful to the other three Ians for coming along to meet a group of strangers that possibly had nothing in common, other than a name! It was great that we all got along so well, and had a great evening. Hopefully I will still get to achieve the goal at a later date.

My friend Simon, who wrote the very first press release about "ALife4Sale" back in March last year, and started the ball rolling on the huge amount of international coverage that my auction received, now lives down in Devon.

With a few days to spare before heading off to Spain, I packed some stuff in Martin's trusty car again. Martin and I headed west out of London, his only packing consisting of a box containing a little food and a lot of alcohol. Martin has a ticket for the huge Glastonbury music festival that weekend, and was meeting up in a motorway services area with his friends, who had rented a camper van for the event.

Martin's pals soon showed up, and he moved his gear into the camper van. I continued south, eventually crossing Dartmoor to find the secluded little cottage where Simon and his family live. I hadn't been there long before Simon's trials motorbike was wheeled out of the garage, and we were thrashing around the abandoned quarry behind his house.

I have never been particularly good on a trials bike, and watched in amazement as Simon rode the bike up and down some impressive gradients. I managed a couple of slightly lesser hills, but sensibly knew my own limits, declining to come down the bigger, steeper section that Simon encouraged me to tackle.

The next day I headed out onto the hills to try to toughen up my legs in preparation for my "7 Peaks" goal planned for late August in Colorado. I walked to the top of the moors behind the house. The weather was lovely, and the views were spectacular.

Encouraged by my first foray into fitness, I got up early the next couple of mornings, and headed out onto the hills again on increasingly ambitious circuits. I spent a couple of hours on day two wandering around the hilltops, known locally as tors, and thoroughly enjoyed the silence and tranquillity.

With seven hours to yourself on the high moors, there is plenty of thinking time. As I walked around my self-created challenge of visiting "10 tors in 1 day" on my third day of fitness training, I thought a lot about what the future may hold for me.

One of the questions that I would get asked most often is, "What will you do once your 100 goals challenge is over?" I didn't really have an answer. I was asked the same question many times during the build up to the eBay auction, and until about a month before the sale began, I didn't have an answer then either. All I knew at that time was that I wanted to do some travelling.

But it was the question itself that had eventually helped provide the answer about what I might like do after ALife4Sale was over. "What will you do after you sell your life?" Often my answer was, "Whatever I like!" What did I want to do, I had asked myself? I had started to write a list of some of the places I wanted to go, and some of the things I wanted to do, and with a couple of other little triggers, "100 goals in 100 weeks" was born.

I had been asked a couple of times, in the days I spent in Devon, what I planned to do when my journey was over. I suppose the question was on my mind a bit as I wandered the moors from tor to tor.

Once above the walls of the farms the moor opens up, and the choices available in terms of route are endless. There are a few well defined paths, but for the challenge I had set myself, these paths did not always lead in the direction that I wanted. Most of the time I had to strike out across boulder-strewn moorland, my target tor visible far in the distance, but the route between where I was and my final destination unclear.

I would set off knowing exactly where I was going to get to, but had only a vague idea of the exact route I would take to make the journey. With head down, watching the uneven rocks ahead, I only ever really had about three or four steps ahead clearly planned. After taking these steps, the choice of route for the next few steps became clear.

Sometimes, when the ground became clearer, the path for quite a way ahead was obvious. But on occasion the path that had seemed so obvious turned out to be boggy and impassable, and some back-tracking and re-planning was necessary.

As I walked this slowly unfolding and often changing path, I thought about what a good metaphor it would be, not only for my progress throughout my 100 goals challenge, but also for life itself. In both cases we have a pretty good idea of the ultimate destination, but the path between here and there is often unclear.

It is only when we make a start towards the goal we wish to achieve, and we take those first few steps, that the next part of the path reveals itself to us. Sometimes there are dead ends, and we have to back-track. As we do, so long as we keep our focus on the end goal, we are still progressing towards it, even though it may not feel like it at the time.

My thoughts wandered to one possible future course that a friend had suggested to me only a few weeks earlier. “Maybe you could do inspirational talks, about goal setting and achieving! You will certainly be able to consider yourself some sort of authority on the subject after this!” My walk across the moor, I thought, might make a good analogy to use in such a talk: how life’s often hidden path only starts to reveal itself to us once we begin to walk it.

I had no idea how I would even begin to attempt to become a motivational speaker, but if I chose to follow that particular path, I would just need to take the first step in that direction, and expect the path to reveal itself to me step by step.

The goal I most feared, one of the first things I ever remembered saying that I would do one day, was now fast approaching. I had booked a cheap flight from Birmingham to Biarritz in the south-west of France. The journey involved catching a train from London up to Birmingham, and another overnighter on an airport bench. I spent the day in scenic Biarritz, and caught the evening bus down to Pamplona in Spain.

Graham, who had hosted me the year before in Valencia when we had gone to the Tomatina festival, had contacted an Irish guy now living in Pamplona, suggesting that he might be able to help me out.

Michael was running an accommodation agency in the historic city, focussing primarily on the upcoming San Fermin festival. He had contacted me, offering to find somewhere for me to stay in the city centre.

He had originally intended to put me up in his spare room, but by the time I arrived in Pamplona, he had managed to rent this out too.

Michael therefore had a cunning plan. He introduced me to Mikee, one of his clients from San Diego, who had booked an apartment for a week. Mikee had a few friends arriving over the next few days, and until they arrived, had a couple of spare beds. He was happy to let me stay for a night or two, and we hung out together drinking beer for a day or so until his pals arrived.

I met the others in his group, which included his brother Willy, and friends Nick, Fipps and Ivy. A day later another buddy Kurtiss showed up too. I volunteered to move out and find somewhere else as the apartment filled up, but the group would have none of it. I ended up being squeezed in to the upstairs bedroom, and welcomed into the group for the rest of the week.

Goal 49 – run for your life!
Wednesday, July 8, 2009
(Pamplona, Spain)

I had a bit of a siesta yesterday afternoon, and in the evening headed back out with my American housemates, who were hitting the town again. I had one quick beer with them, and then made my way through the packed main square to Michael's apartment, where I was due to be interviewed by John, from website BullRunning.com. John was also planning to run for the first time in the morning, and we discussed possible places to start, and tactics for survival. We had pretty much come to the same conclusion as to where we might start.

After the interview, which was very easy-going and relaxed, I made my way through thronging crowds to the Cuitadela, where there is a fireworks extravaganza every evening. It is competitive, and the Italian team put on a great show.

Back at home I got a reasonably early night, along with half of my housemates, who had also finished the evening at a sensible hour. The rest of the group, however, had partied on. At around 4:45am, they were insisting on a house meeting, scheduled for 5am, from what I could gather! I don't think anyone else made it to the meeting, and I don't think I missed much, as it all went quiet again soon after that.

I had set my alarm for 6:15am, but was woken up at 6:35 by Nick, who was on his way out. I checked my phone, and was amazed to find, on the morning of one of my major goals, I had set my alarm for the evening, instead of morning!

I dressed in my red and white gear after a quick shower, and down in the busy main street I soon bumped into John. Before long the street was cleared of revellers and runners alike, and we were shepherded into a side street. We made our way through little back streets, trying to get in to the town hall square again, to re-join the pack of runners.

The streets outside the run were packed, and it was difficult to even get into the main streets. When we finally made it through the crowds of on-lookers, back onto the bull-run route, we were absolutely squeezed in tight as the main street got a final cleaning. Tension was mounting, and there was an incredible air of expectation.

At about ten to eight we were allowed to spread back into the main street, and John and I picked a spot just before the ominously named Dead Man's Curve. Our plan was to round the corner just as the bulls started running, stay well to the right as they swept wide around the corner, and then join them for the run straight along Estafeta.

However, any sort of planning in such a crazy, excited, scared crowd like that, is hopeful at best.

The first rocket went off, a huge cheer went up, and you could really feel the fear and excitement in the air. As the second rocket went off, indicating that all the bulls are out of the pen and running, John and I joined the crowd. We pushed-shoved-jogged our way around the corner, and that was the last I saw of him. It was packed, and wild.

I made it about five yards along the street, and then tucked in at the right side, pretty much at the front of the crowd backed against the wall. People were streaming past in front of me, and the speed and panic increased as the bulls approached. I watched in amazement as the lead animals hurtled around the corner – they were huge. As soon as they drew level with us I heard myself shouting "Go, go, go!" and ran out, along with a large part of the crowd I was with, and we joined the run. I knew all the bulls hadn't gone past, as there had only been about six or seven in the first group. Therefore there were more still behind us. They must have got separated earlier on.

Now, running in the middle of the street, it was just a matter of making sure I didn't fall over. I had to try to get back towards the side before the next bulls came barrelling through. While that seemed like a good idea, it is not how things worked out at all.

In the middle of the running hoards, three or four people went down in front of me. I jumped and veered left, and just made it around them, but was off balance. Another person fell in front of me, impossible to avoid, and I tripped over the top of him. I was now on the ground, pretty much in the centre of the street. All I could do was curl up and hope for the best. I looked up, just in time to see one of the huge brown and white guiding steers thunder by just a foot or so away. I stayed curled up, as the crowd of runners was now passing over and around me. To try to get up would be impossible. Eventually the crowd thinned a bit, and a couple of guys gave me a shout and dragged me to my feet.

I rejoined the runners, trying to quickly take stock of myself, and decided that I was relatively unscathed. I continued to follow the route with the rest of the running crowd, eventually making it into the bull ring at the end. The ring was packed, and people milled around laughing and whooping, obviously thrilled and excited to have completed the run. I too felt elated and thrilled, and somewhat lucky too. "Next time," I thought, "I really must try to stay on my feet!" That thought was immediately followed by, "What next time? I'm not doing that again. That has to be the craziest thing I have ever experienced."

In the ring the craziness continued. For the entertainment of the packed audience, bullocks are released into the ring one at a time to run riot among the runners brave enough, or foolish enough, to want to stay in there. I stayed in for a few minutes, but when the first bullock came charging past, the crowd surged back, and I decided enough was enough.

Watching would be a much better option that staying in the ring.

A wise choice, I decided, as over the next twenty minutes or so, I saw at least three people transported away on stretchers.

I eventually made it back home around an hour and a half after the run, buying some breakfast supplies on the way. As I made a sandwich, I was surprised to find that my hands still had a slight shake to them, as the last of the adrenaline wore off.... or maybe it was just the strong cup of coffee I had just had on an empty stomach kicking in?

How do I feel afterwards, I asked myself? This was an important goal for me, one I have wanted to fulfil longer than any other. I have been promising myself for over thirty years now that one day I would come and do this. Well, of course there is a huge sense of closure and achievement. I also feel proud to have once again done what I promised myself I would do.

Of course, the whole event was incredibly thrilling too. I can see why people keep coming back to do this again and again! I had promised myself though that once would be enough for me!

I managed to set my alarm correctly for the next morning, and was up early again. The only others up and about were Fipps and Ivy. Fipps was planning to run with the bulls, so Ivy and I went down to the bull ring to watch the end of the run. Despite being over an hour until the start, the place was already packed, but we were lucky to find two seats in a great location.

There are two big video screens high up in the arena. When eight o'clock finally came around the first rockets went off, and we could watch the run live on the big screen. It was great to see the crazy progress through the streets. As the bulls on the screen approached the ring outside, people were streaming through the tunnel into the ring right in front of us.

There was a huge cheer as the bulls burst through the fleeing people. They scattered to left and right, as the bulls passed through the centre of the ring, disappearing almost directly under us into the stalls under the stands. People continued to flow in to the bull ring. Eventually the gates were closed and the bullock madness began again. My favourite comment of the day: Ivy – "It must be some sort of guy thing, because I don't know what would make ***anyone*** *think that* ***this*** *is a good idea!"*

Fipps enjoyed himself, and escaped relatively unscathed, tripping once and gathering a couple of scrapes as trophies of the morning. Well done!

We had two new arrivals at the apartment yesterday, when Mike's friends Muna and Carmen arrived in the morning. This brought the occupancy total up to an impressive nine, although Kurtiss was scheduled to leave later in the day, bound for Barcelona and then home to San Diego. He had tried to leave a couple of days earlier, but he and Mike had only managed to get as far as the first bar. Kurtiss had given up on the idea of the flight he had booked, and stayed for a few more days. He was determined to escape today.

Muna and Carmen had brought a couple of bottles of duty free, and before long shots of Jack Daniels were being handed round. I managed to stay sober enough to wander off to the square near our apartment, where there is wi-fi access. I tried to sort out my own onward travel plans, which are as yet unconfirmed. I am trying to arrange another goal while here in Spain, but things are still in the balance.

As the day progressed, most of the household tried to stay relatively sober. Both Mike and Willy were keen to run in the morning, and the rest of us were keen to go back to the bull ring to watch the morning entertainment again. Apparently though, we didn't quite manage to stay sober enough. When Ivy, who was the only person out of the original group who hadn't yet run, suggested that she might do so in the morning, we were all impressed. So much so that

Fipps, Nick and myself offered to run again with her if she decided to do so.

At decision time at 6:30am, Ivy decided we were going to join the run. I emptied phone and money from my pockets, and wondered what on earth I was thinking! Was I really going to go back and do this again?

We walked down to the town hall square, and were onto the run streets by 7am. Mike and Willy, along with Muna and Carmen, headed off down towards the steep early section of the run. This is the fastest part, just after the bulls come out of the holding pen. The rest of us headed in the other direction, around Dead Man's Curve. We picked a spot against the wall that would hopefully be off the main track of the bulls, and yet offer a great view as the bulls came sweeping wide around the corner.

The plan was to have as safe a morning as possible, stay up against the wall with a buffer zone of other people in front of us, watch the bulls and faster runners go past, and then join the stragglers in relative calmness.

After picking our spot, we headed back towards the town hall square, to avoid being swept out of the main street by the police when the final cleaning took place. As we waited, packed in, tension mounted, and Fipps started to feel very ill. His eyes were swollen and red, and his lips were swelling, and he thought he was having an allergic reaction to something he had eaten. His wise decision was to pull out while he still could, and when we met him back at home later, he was pleased he did. Anti-histamines that one of the others had at home had slowly fixed him.

That left Nick and I, along with Ivy. At around ten to eight we were released back into the main street, and we went to take up our chosen position. Again tension cranked up another notch, at last the first and second rockets went off, and the bulls were on their way.

People streamed around the corner faster and faster, and a couple of people squeezed up in front of us. I still had an incredible view as the bulls thundered around the corner against the opposite wall. Quite a few people went down among the bulls, and the corner was very chaotic, but the bulls passed through cleanly and were gone. We waited a few more seconds for the chaos to die down a bit, and joined the runners, who were still streaming past.

Further along the run, we approached the closed gate across the main street, about two thirds of the way along. The gate is used to prevent any bulls turning around and returning back along the run, which would be devastating. As we drew closer there was shouting and excitement, as three of the massive, but relatively docile steers were herded along, approaching us from behind. As they approached the still-closed gate, now hidden by hoards of runners who hadn't been quick enough to get through, panic broke out, and people ran in every direction as the steers reached the back of the crowd. We managed to avoid most of the trouble, as we were still a little way back. Eventually the gate opened, and order was quickly restored.

Another successful and, for our entire apartment group at least, injury-free morning. However, when we watched the re-runs on TV back at home, others had not been so lucky. The reason that the gate we were stuck behind had been closed for so long, was that one of the back-marker bulls had stopped, turned around and gone pretty wild. Several people had come to grief. One guy had been impressively tossed right over the bull's head, and the bull had then turned around and continued to attack him while he lay on the ground. I am pretty sure he was okay, but he will have a few wounds, and some amazing video of his impressive tussle with the huge creature.

Once again, what a fantastically terrifying and thrilling experience. Never again? Well, who knows? I don't any more – I can see that this could be very addictive. For each run you have done you can add a knot to the tassels of the red sash that you wear as part of your San Fermin outfit. Mine now proudly sports two. Apparently there are some regular runners with sashes that have so many knots they can't fit any more on there!

There is a sad footnote to the day though. Unfortunately there was a death during this morning's run. "Daniel Jimeno, a 27 year-old Spaniard, was gored in the neck after one of the bulls veered into a group of runners, a Navarre regional government official told reporters."

This is the first death in fifteen years by goring. The incident, which happened towards the end of the run, has been reported and shown many times already on Spanish TV, and is hardly even noticeable on the video. It really does bring home the true nature of the dangers involved in this crazy event.

I don't think I can paint a vivid enough picture, with words, to explain just how huge and crazy and exciting the whole event is. It is the biggest celebration I have ever seen, in terms of numbers of people, area the festival covers, amount of bars in every street, volume of alcohol consumed, size of rubbish piles in the morning, number of bands marching through the streets, scale of fireworks displays, and of course, the incredible excitement and danger of the main attraction. I think the atmosphere and scale of the festival is hard to imagine unless you have been to Pamplona during San Fermin. I understand now why Hemingway was so fascinated by this incredible spectacle.

This takes place, not just over a few hours, or a single day, like the Tomatina that I attended last year. It goes on, absolutely non-stop, for over a week. Day and night, asleep and awake, drunk and sober, terrified and elated, all merge into one week-long whirl of sensory overload that is hard to process.

Believe me, if there is one thing you really should experience at least once in your life, this is it!

Viva San Fermin!

Running with the Bulls in Pamplona gave me such an incredible feeling of closure, after over thirty years of promising myself that one day I would do so. There was a huge feeling of pride at eventually doing what I had always said I would do, despite the fear. I had been quite terrified of what achieving this goal involved and had just wanted to get it over and done! Yet after the first run I had joined in again for a second time, on the fourth day of the festival. There had even been some talk with Mikee about running again on my last morning there, as we watched from Mike's balcony as the runners gathered again below us.

Of all my goals, I think this particular event was the one which scared me the most. Many of the other riskier goals have some element of control. For example, skydiving has potential risks, but these can be minimised by careful gear selection and maintenance, and by practice and training. Running with the bulls is something that is almost completely out of your control.

This is where all of my goal-setting had begun, when I had watched that Hemingway documentary as a child. Over thirty years later I finally managed to do what I had promised myself for so long. And I had had one of the most thrilling, amazing, fun, wild, exciting weeks of my life!

I had been in touch with Mel fairly regularly as I had been travelling again, but communications in Pamplona were quite tricky. I could charge up the battery of my laptop at the apartment, and not too far away in Plaza San Francisco, if you sat in the right corner of the square, you could pick up a free wi-fi connection.

Several other travellers would gather there on the wooden benches in front of the church, laptops on their knees, to check their email and make their travel plans.

As well as trying to enjoy the San Fermin festival to the full, I was also trying to organise my next goal, which was proving to be very tricky to arrange. Potential plans had changed many times over the previous weeks, and it now looked like I was going to have to make my way to Algeciras. Other than knowing it was somewhere in Spain, I had no idea where Algeciras was!

Struggling to see the laptop screen in the bright sunlight, still slightly hung-over from the previous night's celebrations, I started to make some new plans. All flights from anywhere near Pamplona, as the end of the festival approached, were either fully booked, or laughably expensive. Maybe I could catch a train from Pamplona, or a bus, perhaps? Algeciras was very close to Gibraltar, I had discovered, and I considered the possibility of a flight from there back to London.

My laptop battery power was below 25%, when Mel popped up online. I connected via video chat, and could just make her out on the screen in the bright afternoon sun. To hear what she was saying I had to hold the laptop up to my ear, as I hadn't brought any headphones with me. I tried to explain over the noise of another marching band, warming up over on the other side of the square, that I couldn't be on for long. I received a very terse reply, followed immediately by the internet equivalent of a telephone handset being slammed back onto its holder.

I emailed a quick apology, trying to explain the challenges of communications at the craziest festival I had ever been to, but heard nothing back for a couple of days.

When I did finally get a reply, it was a heartfelt message telling me how she had finally realised that she would never be the main priority in my life. She said that she had always known this, and in all fairness, agreed that I had been pretty clear about this too. She had hoped that things might change, and now saw they never would. It was time to call it a day, and move on, she said.

In my reply I didn't argue. I simply tried to express my regret at how things had worked out for us, how I couldn't be the person she wanted me to be, and how wonderful a person I truly thought she was. I hoped she would find everything she was looking for, but she was certainly right – I was not going to be that person at this point in my life.

I was saddened by the loss. For two years Mel had been an incredible partner, friend and supporter. But I knew I had to let her go, now that she was ready to do the same with me.

Goal 50 - Greenpeace - persistence pays off

Sunday, July 12, 2009
(Algeciras, Spain)

This morning the alarm on my mobile phone woke me again, just after 6am. I have been hearing a little too much of that alarm recently! But this morning was going to be the only opportunity in the foreseeable future to achieve goal #50.

I have been quietly trying to organise this for many weeks now. I decided in early June, when I had a bit of spare time on my hands, to email Greenpeace, to try to find out the location of their flagship vessel "Rainbow Warrior". I was surprised to receive two telephone calls almost straight away, one from Jane in the San Francisco office, and one from Oscar in head office at Amsterdam.

Oscar was keen to help me out, and told me that at the time, the ship was docked at Seville in southern Spain. Was I free between 21st and 27th June? I certainly was, as that was just after my wingwalk and Ian Ushers night out, which were both scheduled for the 20th. I looked at return flights from the UK, and found that I would be able to go and return at a fairly reasonable cost. But Greenpeace plans changed unfortunately, and "Rainbow Warrior" had to move, and I missed out at the time.

Oscar sent me new schedules, and thought there might be another opportunity to catch up with the ship in Malta around the 23rd of June. Flights would be a bit more expensive, but still within the budget, so I prepared to make my bookings. However, Greenpeace plans changed again, and I would no longer be able to join them in Malta, Oscar had informed me.

The new schedule would give me a chance to catch the ship in Palma, on the Spanish Mediterranean island of Mallorca, but not until 3rd of July. This was the day before I was due to fly out of the UK to Biarritz, heading for Pamplona, and once again I researched flights. I would have to change the flight that I had booked, fly instead to Mallorca, visit the ship on the 3rd, then fly Mallorca to Madrid, and finally catch the bus up to Pamplona. I could just do it, I thought.

But as the day drew nearer, I waited to get the go-ahead from Oscar. Eventually, while walking up one of the ten tors I climbed in Devon, Oscar called me. Believe it or not, he said, plans had changed again! "Rainbow Warrior" would not be in Mallorca, but instead at Tarifa on the southern tip of mainland Spain. When I got back from my walk, I checked flights again on the internet, and thought all would work out well. I almost went ahead and booked, as Oscar was very confident. I'm glad I didn't!

That's right! Plans changed again, and I would no longer be able to meet the ship at Tarifa. I was practically at the point of giving up. In the end I headed for Pamplona as planned, and thought that it was a shame not to have achieved this goal, especially when I had the time on my hands to be able to do so.

While in Pamplona, I tried to stay in contact with Oscar. He eventually confirmed that the only dates he could get me on board the ship were 17th and 18th

July, again in Palma, Mallorca. Oh dear! I had a ticket from London to Florida booked for the 16th, an underwater hotel booked for the 18th, a flight to Mexico on the 21st, a tour to Chichén Itzá on the 22nd, and a flight to San Francisco on the 24th. Would I be able to change my plans, Oscar wondered. Erm, I don't think so!

Oscar also put me in touch with Marta, the Spanish Greenpeace press officer. I think he was as frustrated by the endless changes as I was. I now asked Marta where the "Rainbow Warrior" would be prior to the 15th. She told me there would be only one opportunity to meet it, on the morning of the 12th at Algeciras, for only a few hours as it made preparations to move on again.

After a long journey from Pamplona, fraught with difficulties, I finally arrived in Algeciras last night at 10pm. This morning I headed out to find the ship, following vague directions Marta had given me.

It was a beautiful quiet morning as I strode along the deserted breakwater of the huge port, and just before 8am, I found the "Rainbow Warrior".

I met Marta, and was taken aboard, and she showed me around the deck area. I was so happy to have made it, and to finally get aboard. We chatted for a while, and I was introduced to several of the crew. Marta handed me over to Isabel, another Spanish press officer, as she had to go to a meeting, and we headed below decks. The ship seems to be incredibly well organised, and everything has a place and a system.

For a while I was allowed to wander happily on my own. I looked around the wheelhouse, and examined the iconic rigid-inflatables that are considered to be one of the best-known images of Greenpeace's work. They are called Avon, Hurricane, Novi I and Novi II.

I chatted to several others of the crew, and Mehdi, who is chief mechanic, asked if I wanted to give him a hand with some maintenance he needed to do. I jumped at the opportunity, happy that I would be able to say that I worked aboard the 'Rainbow Warrior", even if only for half an hour. By now it was lunchtime, and Marta came to find me, laughing that I had already been put to work. Apparently you can't sit around on "Rainbow Warrior" for too long without being given something to do.

After lunch I took a final quick look around with Marta, snapped some final photos, and said my goodbyes. Ah, but I wasn't going as soon as I thought. Spanish national TV station TVE was filming a documentary on board, and wanted to interview me about my reasons for this being one of my goals.

I told them how impressed I am by the incredibly brave work Greenpeace does down in the southern oceans every southern summer, when the Japanese come to slaughter the humpback whales there, and how I have been a supporter now for several years. I was also interested in seeing the "Rainbow Warrior", because it is actually the second ship bearing that name. The first one was bombed and sunk in Auckland harbour in New Zealand in 1985, by the French secret service, as at the time Greenpeace were protesting French nuclear tests. On board the current vessel I saw the ship's bell and a pair of binoculars that had come from the original ship.

I got a picture taken with the film crew, and by then one of the most interesting items on board had been uncovered. Dave, the wooden dolphin on the front deck was built by crew members, and is rumoured to contain a secret. Some say it is a message for the world, others think it is a bottle of rum. Marta imagines that it is both of these.

The whole visit was very interesting, and I got a little bit of the sense of family aboard the ship from some of the crew I met. I feel very honoured to have been offered the opportunity to achieve this goal, and once again, in a manner much exceeding my expectations.

I will not even try to explain any of the campaigns Greenpeace is currently working on, or that "Rainbow Warrior" in particular is involved in.

Their website will do a far better job than I ever could. Take a look at greenpeace.org, and should you feel it worthwhile, feel free to offer them your support.

Finally I would like to finish with something that I just learned today – how the "Rainbow Warrior" got its name. It comes from a quote from Native American Cree Indians, which reads as follows:

"When the world is sick and dying, the people will rise up like Warriors of the Rainbow..."

The Cree Indian symbol is proudly displayed on board.

With my Greenpeace goal achieved, I had a couple of days in hand before my flight back to England, and I spent some time exploring the spectacular rocky outcrop of Gibraltar.

At the end of a long hot day climbing up the steep cliffs, admiring the sweeping views from the top, and being entertained by the antics of the monkeys trying to steal food from the tourists, I sat in a bar enjoying a well-deserved cold beer. I sat quietly, feeling rather reflective, watching the world pass, and thinking of Mel and the happy times we had shared together. I was hit by the lyrics of one of the songs playing on the juke box. Bruce Springsteen mournfully suggested:-

You and me we were the pretenders,
We let it all slip away,
In the end what you don't surrender,
Well the world just strips away.

Had I just let the best part of my life slip away? I had to accept that the loss had been an inevitable consequence of the choices I had made, something that was always destined to be stripped from me when I had decided I wanted to travel for two years.

Chapter 6 – Weeks 51 to 60

(20th July 2009 – 27th September 2009)

Mexico – USA – England

I flew from Gibraltar to Gatwick Airport, just to the south of London, arriving in the evening. My next flight left early the next morning, and I was glad I had had the foresight to pack my larger bag and leave it with Martin and Rachel. They very kindly came to drop the bag off for me, and we went out to find a pub close to the airport to have some dinner.

I did a quick re-pack, organising a bag of bits and pieces from Spain that I wouldn't need for the next leg of my journey. Martin took that home to store for me until my next visit to the UK.

They dropped me off again at the airport at around 11pm. I set the alarm on my phone, found a quiet corner of the airport, and laid my sleeping bag out for the night. I was getting used to being able to sleep anywhere at any time.

My flight in the morning was part of a package deal holiday. Before going to Spain I had searched for the cheapest way to get to Florida, but mid-July is the start of the British holiday season, and for some reason all one-way flights seemed to be very expensive.

Based on previous holiday experience, I searched for fly-drive holidays. I was amazed to find a week-long holiday, including round-trip flights and car hire, for significantly less than a one-way flight. The choice had been easy.

The nine-hour flight dragged, and I slept lightly on and off, but eventually it was over and I arrived at Sanford near Orlando. At border control I was taken to a small interview room. I began once again the process of trying to explain why I didn't have a job, why I had entered the States several times over the past year, how I had a US bank account, and a US address associated with that. Where would I be staying, and who with, they wanted to know? My answers – in an underwater hotel and then with strangers who had contacted me via the internet – did not help my cause! Eventually, after looking at my website, the agents seemed to believe I was neither a terrorist, nor planning to stay in America longer than I should, and I got my passport stamped again.

Beyond customs I was met by Cari, who had driven over from Tampa. She had been following my travels on the blog, and when she had found out I was heading her way for my next goal, had been very keen to be my local Florida guide.

We picked up my hire car, and I was treated to a luxurious couple of days in Florida, including a massage at a spa, and a visit to SeaWorld. Heading south, Cari stayed with her family, and I called in on Nancy, who had invited me to stay over on my way down to the Florida Keys. Nancy is the mother of Linda, who had previously acted as my host and guide in New Jersey, when I went to ride the enormous rollercoaster, Kingda Ka.

Cari didn't continue with me any further south, staying with her family, and in Key Largo I had to achieve another goal on my own.

Goal 51 – 20,000 Leagues Under The Sea

Sunday, July 19, 2009

(Key Largo, Florida, USA)

Well, it wasn't quite 20,000 leagues, more like 20 feet under the sea, but it was still a boyhood dream come true.

Nancy gave me a quick tour around Fort Lauderdale yesterday morning, and then dropped me off to collect my car. It took me a couple of hours to drive down to Key Largo, where I soon found Jules' Undersea Lodge, just off the main highway. After some brief paperwork, I was ready to go, and geared up with scuba equipment. No wetsuit would be required, as the water was almost as warm as a bath.

Jason, my instructor/hotel guide, showed me the surface control room and explained the communication systems with the lodge below. He put the belongings I would need down below into a small waterproof case, and we entered the lagoon.

I spent twenty minutes or so exploring the area, while Jason prepared the hotel, and unpacked my gear down there. I made my way through the rather murky water to the hotel itself, and swimming below it, came up into the wet room via the moon-pool entrance. It was a very atmospheric moment, something I had imagined doing for such a long time.

After Jason gave me a quick tour, he left me alone and I was free to explore, rather like an excited child! The place was great, an odd mixture of old, practical functionality, and modern comfort.

Jules' Lodge was originally built as an underwater research station, and was used as such between 1972 and 1975. In the early 80s it was converted to its current use. Just under the veneer of comfortable hotel, inside many of the cupboards, there are valves and pipes and pumps all humming and buzzing away.

I made myself comfortable, and at 6pm Jason brought dinner down, again in a watertight case. He made the final preparations in the microwave in the small kitchen. It was all quite a bizarre experience. He then left, and I started watching an entertainingly terrible underwater movie called "Leviathan", in which the inhabitants of an underwater mining base are troubled with alien issues.

Once dinner had settled, I geared up and went for a dive in the lagoon. It was wonderful to exit through the moon-pool and already be at a depth of 20 feet. I spent some time examining the hotel itself, fascinated by the structure. It is quite impressively big outside, compared to the smaller space inside. It was built with all sorts of ballast tanks, so it could originally be floated into place. The tanks were then flooded to sink it into position, much like a submarine. It is quite an extraordinary feat of engineering.

Later, when it went dark, I went out for a second dive in the now very gloomy and eerie lagoon. Jason had told me that a couple of nurse sharks sometimes came in at night to sleep under one of the piers, but I couldn't find them. I followed a lobster around the seabed for a while, and got quite disorientated in the dark, but eventually found my way back "home".

I slept really well, and woke in the morning just as the large bedroom porthole window was beginning to lighten. I helped myself to breakfast and coffee in the small but well organised kitchen, and Jason gave me a call to come and collect me.

I had been living under the sea for around 18 hours, and as I surfaced, I wished it could have been much longer. It was so atmospheric, and so unique.

On the return journey northwards I had a couple of interesting experiences. Back with Cari at her family's home, I met her brother, Richard, who helps out with a large private collection of big cats and other unusual creatures. I was very enthusiastic about going to take a look, and got to stroke a tiger, and hold a small crocodile.

Further north we stopped at Kennedy Space Center, timing the visit perfectly. It was the 40th anniversary of the day that man first set foot on the moon, on 20th July 1969. All visitors on the special day got a piece of a huge commemorative cake that was shared out.

My final obligation on the east coast of Florida was to drop my car off again at the airport, where we picked up Cari's car and headed westward for Tampa.

Goal 52 – 7th Wonder – Chichén Itzá

Wednesday, July 22, 2009
(Yucatan Peninsula, Mexico)

I flew from Tampa down to Cancun on Tuesday, and made my way to the hostel I had booked, managing to check in just before lunch time. I got settled in and read about two pages of my book before I fell asleep. I woke at 7pm, having slept deeply for about 6 hours. Over the past few days I have been battling jetlag, and have not been sleeping too well, but I felt great when I woke up in the evening.

I didn't get much of a chance to have a look around Cancun, but did go out for some dinner, then slept again. I think I was pretty run down.

In the morning I went to the reception of the nearby Soberanis Hotel, where I was picked up for my tour of Chichén Itzá. We gathered several more tourists from other hotels, and eventually set off on the two-hour drive to the Mayan pyramid. We stopped for a while for a period of enforced tourist shopping, but the racks of tacky Mexican souvenirs soon drove me out onto the main road for a wander around.

We arrived at Chichén Itzá itself at around 1pm, and were issued tickets. Slightly dismayed, I found myself as part of a large tourist group, following a flag-waving guide. However, the historical background was very interesting, and after a while we were set loose to explore on our own.

The first thing that you see as you enter, after running the gauntlet of enthusiastic local vendors, is the spectacular central pyramid. That, however, is only one part of the whole incredible place. Between 600 and 1200 AD this area, whose name means "at the mouth of the Itzá (a family name) well", was a thriving Mayan city, home to an estimated 50,000 citizens.

There are many structures, including a huge gaming arena called the ball court, where a game which resulted in sacrificial beheadings of the losers (or possibly winners) was played. There is an enormous area made up of a thousand pillars, which was a covered marketplace. There are many other buildings too, thought to include an observatory, nunnery, church, and much more.

Also fascinating was the deep Sacred Cenote, a deep limestone sinkhole, where it is thought that sacrifices, including human ones, were made. All sorts of artefacts and human remains have been found in the water there.

Once released from the tour group, it was easy to wander away from the crowds. As is often the case in these places, if you are prepared to do a little extra walking, you can find yourself totally alone. I wandered through quiet remains with nothing but the sounds of the jungle around me, and it was easy to imagine how it might have been when the Mayans lived and thrived here.

It was the central pyramid that drew me back to the more crowded areas. It is a beautiful building, but even more so when the extraordinary geometrical and astronomical principles built into the design are explained. There is an incredible precision to the design that means that on the equinoxes, the sun lights the structure with an almost unbelievable accuracy, to produce the effect of a snake descending the side of the pyramid.

Time passed quickly, and I headed back to the tour bus for the next part of the trip. We were taken to another cenote nearby, and had time to go swimming in the cool fresh water of the amazing limestone sinkhole. Trees grew around the edge with huge long roots trailing down to the water. Small black catfish swam around in the clear water, and people jumped and swam.

I took some pictures, and then went to jump off the high walkway. I soon wished I hadn't! Something hurt my left foot as I hit the water, and as I climbed out, I discovered that my big toe was bleeding quite badly. Something black was buried in the underside of it. It was quite painful to stand on, and all I can think is that I landed on a fish as I plunged into the water. I thought at first I might have broken my toe, but it is a lot less painful today. However, I will certainly have to remove the suspected fish spine that is still in there!

Back at Chichén Itzá we watched the evening sound and light presentation. The equinox sunlight effect of the descending snake is reproduced artificially, and must be quite something to see for real. How did they manage to build so precisely?

What a fascinating place to see, and well-deserving of its place as one of the "New Seven Wonders of the World".

This goal was one of the last ones added to my list of 100, after another of my goals became impossible when the business shut down. Fly-by-Wire in New Zealand had offered what looked like an amazing adrenaline experience. Strapped onto an aeroplane-like craft, powered by a huge fan engine, you would swing out over a wide canyon, the flying craft suspended from above by a long cable. This allowed you to swing back and forth in spectacular fashion, controlled by steering yourself with the huge fan. I think the business had run into some financial issues.

I had discovered that when my journey ended, if successful, I would have seen six of the "New Seven Wonders of the World".

Chichén Itzá was the 7th Wonder missing from my list. When Fly-By-Wire ceased to exist, seeing this amazing place was immediately added as a worthy substitute goal. Coming here today means that I have now seen three of the seven - four more to go, all of which are on the list.

I have one day left in Cancun, which I will spend hobbling around the downtown area exploring. I then fly back to the States to try to convince them to let me back in again.

I woke in darkness with a vague, but horrible sense of uneasiness. What had woken me? Where was I? What time was it?

Slowly the dream came back to me, bit by bit, and I pieced it together in my mind. She was going to a new job today, but I hadn't even known she had a new job. "Let me ask you something. Were you going to tell me?" I had asked.

"Of course," she answered, but she wouldn't look at me as she spoke.

As she tried to leave I held her, and asked her to look into my eyes. Her gaze kept sliding away. "Is there anything else you need to tell me?" And then more directly, "Is there anything wrong with us?" But I didn't need to ask. I already knew the answer.

I lay alone in the darkness in the Mexican backpacker hostel. I thought this sort of thing was over. After a seven month wait, I was going to see Susan again today, and I was excited. But here was Laura, back in my dreams again, over three and a half years after we separated.

I had been reading Franz Wisner's book "Honeymoon With My Brother", and its wonderfully descriptive account of the loss of his wife was bringing a lot of things back to the surface for me again. It was pretty obvious to me that I still loved Laura, and at times, when travelling alone, I still missed her terribly!

For the past months, when alone it has been Susan I have longed for. In the underwater hotel it was her that I imagined down there with me. When I had wandered around the spectacular ancient site of Chichén Itzá however, it was Laura that my soul longed for. She was my long-time travel partner and backpacker buddy. She was the one that I could spend endless months with and never tire of her company. She was the one I was supposed to be with.

I wondered if I would ever find anything like that again. I am okay on my own. I can get along quite happily in a relationship, as I did for two years with Mel, but it's the small things that always get to me. An irritating turn of phrase, an annoying small habit, a blank stare when I say something that I think is funny, and I know in my heart that this relationship will never be as good.

I know it is wrong to compare. Each relationship is unique and different. I know too that it is unfair to compare a relationship that has only begun recently to something that had thirteen years of history behind it.

Compare or not, I also knew that so far I have not found anything that came close to what I had. I wondered if I ever would. Maybe I would just have to be content with something else, something different, and yes, maybe something less. Perhaps, as Bruce had suggested, I have been lucky to have had that incredible relationship once in my life.

At times I think too that I may have been cursed to have had it.

I had thought Laura was long-gone from my dreams, but here she was again, as real as ever, and as emotionally unbalancing as ever. I had thought that Mel, or even Susan had replaced Laura now as the person I felt was missing from my life.

I was going to see Susan again before the day was over, something I had been really looking forward to. Things were apparently quite simple now, and I no longer had to feel any guilt. Susan was now the only female remaining in my life that I had any real romantic connection with. Yet as my birthday in San Francisco approached, I felt extremely unsettled and somehow off-balance.

In San Francisco things didn't go too well from the start. I was tired and jet-lagged when Susan finally met me at the airport, and our first evening together was slightly awkward.

The next day was my birthday, and I was still feeling a little emotionally volatile. We went out for an Indian meal that evening, and with Susan drinking very little, I had far too much wine, polishing off the better part of two bottles on my own.

The large intake of alcohol, coupled with my delicate emotional balance, tipped the scale later that evening. We ended up in a heated discussion about relationships, where I had stayed while in Australia, and what we meant to each other. I ended up pouring my heart out about how much I still missed Laura. Susan angrily suggested that this wouldn't be the best way to impress the next girl I met.

It was looking like I had already ruined another relationship. I eventually fell asleep wondering where I kept going wrong.

I stayed in San Francisco for about two weeks. Susan and I eventually got onto a more even keel, but it felt as if perhaps some permanent damage had been done to our relationship. We never quite managed to rediscover the easy happiness that we had shared the last time we had been together, the previous year. In Susan's super-tidy home, I felt like a slightly inconvenient intruder.

We argued occasionally, and at times I looked forward to heading off on my own. I got out as much as I could, walking and running the steep hills of the city in an effort to get toughened up for the physical challenges that lay ahead.

It wasn't all bad, and at times we got on well and laughed together as we had the year before. I felt happy again to have someone with whom I could share some fun.

I picked up the RV from the storage unit where it had been parked for the previous six months, and was incredibly impressed when it started straight away. I had anticipated a couple of hours of tinkering with spark plugs and jumper cables to get it going. It needed a little repair work to some of the water system pipes underneath, as I had done some damage over rough ground near the Grand Canyon the year before, but eventually I was ready for departure.

Susan and I had discussed travelling together for a couple of weeks, as she had no commitments at the time. I had wavered between wanting her to come along, and thinking that things would be better if I travelled alone. My thoughts at any given time depended upon whether we had been arguing or laughing recently.

As the day to set off came closer we decided that we should go together. I made a last few purchases for the RV, and Susan packed her bag. We met at a station on the outskirts of the city, and headed out on the open road, aiming for the wide open spaces of Nevada that evening.

Goal 53 – Bonneville Speed Week
Wednesday, August 12, 2009
(Bonneville Salt Flats, Utah, USA)

After he left school my friend Bruce flew from England to travel around the States. While driving across America from east to west, crossing Utah, he spotted several race cars on trailers travelling along Highway I-80. When he saw a couple turning off and heading out onto the large expanse of salt, he followed, and found himself at Bonneville Speed Week. Since he told me about that many years ago, I have always wanted to come and see for myself. More recently I watched the movie "The World's Fastest Indian", which tells the story of New Zealander Bert Munro, and his journey to Bonneville glory. This merely fuelled my desire to come, and today I have finally made it.

We actually arrived yesterday, and saw a bit of racing, but really had no idea what was going on. After a night high in the mountains in Nevada at another small rest area the previous evening, we drove down into Wendover, just on the Nevada/Utah border. We refuelled, and found a great little information bureau, where I could access the internet and check email. Linda told us of the attractions that Wendover has to offer, and we went to take a look around. The salt lake is so big and flat that from a viewpoint above the town it is possible to view the curvature of the Earth, which is pretty amazing to see. Just out of town we also took a look at the airforce base museum, where bomber crews trained for dropping the Hiroshima and Nagasaki nuclear bombs that ended WWII. Also there was the plane that was used in the movie "Con Air", which was fun to scramble around in.

Eventually we headed out to the flats, and were allowed onto the salt without charge, as we had arrived so late in the afternoon. We watched a few vehicles rocket past the pits at high speed, and wandered around the Impound area, where potential record breakers were stored for the evening. To gain a record, a vehicle must first qualify to do so on one run, by going faster than the old record. The vehicle then goes into Impound, where it can be worked on for a period of up to four hours. The next morning a further hour's work can be done before the vehicle has to back-up the record-breaking run with a second pass. The average of the two runs is then taken as the official time. This makes records hard to beat, because as well as one-time speed, consistency and reliability are also required.

Last night we parked out on the salt along with perhaps another hundred RVs and campers, and watched "The World's Fastest Indian" on the computer. This morning we were up very early to secure a fantastic front row parking spot at the start line. It is possible to sit in the RV and watch the amazing action.

The atmosphere is fantastic, everyone is incredibly friendly and helpful, and many people have been very patient in answering my endless questions. The whole style of racing is much more laid-back than anything I have ever experienced, as each run is against the clock, rather than other vehicles. Starting speed and early acceleration are not too important, top speed is all that counts. Most people are here to try to beat their own personal bests.

One of the most exciting runs to see was 71 year old Connie on a huge motorcycle. She beat her own personal best of 211 mph by a significant margin, achieving 229 mph. Apparently, her 82 year old boyfriend also rides the bike occasionally!

There are some absolutely incredible vehicles here. Just wandering around the start line listening to the engines fire up, and watching the cars and bikes accelerate away, is such a thrill.

I have already started wondering how I might make it back here, and what sort of motorbike I would like to bring to have a go on. "Certainly, you should give it a go," one guy that I chatted with encouraged me. "First step is to pick up a rule book to find out what you would need to do!" That's exactly what I did. Maybe one day I will be back here to race something myself, if finances ever permit! In the meantime I am very happy to be here as a spectator.

It is wonderful to have Susan along as my travelling companion. As always, it is so much more fun to experience an event like this with someone else, than it is to do so alone.

At the end of our second day at Bonneville we went in search of a nearby cave that Linda at the information bureau had mentioned. As evening approached we decided to stay overnight where we had parked. We made a campfire and ate dinner sat outside. As the fire died we pulled the mattress out of the RV and lay side-by-side in the desert, looking at the vast canvas of stars above us.

On the road Susan and I got along much better. The easy-going friendship started to re-form, as we laughed together, and enjoyed the journey. I think we were better together when we weren't in Susan's home. I no longer felt like I was upsetting her ordered lifestyle. I think she felt much more relaxed too. Whatever the reasons, I was once again thoroughly enjoying her company, and was glad she had come along.

We crossed into Utah, and booked into an RV park in Salt Lake City. We discovered that we had arrived just in time to catch a free shuttle bus into the city centre, to see the Mormon Tabernacle Choir practice.

Tiffany had contacted me through the website many months before, suggesting that I should contact her if I was ever heading to Salt Lake City, and I had got in touch with her again just before we arrived. We planned to meet up with her the next day, and she said that she wanted to introduce me to someone very special.

Clay is an incredible guy, and has faced more challenges in his life than I ever hope to. Fifteen years previously, riding his motorbike one night, he had hit a horse that had somehow got loose and was in the middle of the road. He had broken his back, and has been confined to a wheelchair ever since. He has no use of his legs at all, and restricted use of his arms and hands.

But he hadn't let that setback stop his adventurous lifestyle. He has become involved in the world of rockcrawling – extreme four-wheel drive motorsport over some of the toughest terrain possible. Not only has he done well in this tough world, but with a specially modified vehicle, he manages to compete at a professional level, with no concession given for the physical challenges that he faces.

He enjoys all sorts of other physically challenging activities, including hunting, and was very keen to show me his recent tandem skydive video!

He has developed his own line of snowboard gear, and was working on a TV show that he wanted to produce, which would pair able bodies extreme sports enthusiasts with physically disabled enthusiasts who were not prepared to let their own challenges slow them down. The pilot episode featured some amazing footage of a guy in a wheelchair doing all sorts of stunts in a skateboard park, and unbelievably, being towed up and off a motorcycle jump by a freestyle motocross rider.

Clay also works as a motivational speaker, giving talks on the challenges he has faced and overcome, and the attitude needed to succeed when the odds are stacked against you. I quizzed him a little about this, having considered it as a possibility at the end of my journey, and he seemed very enthusiastic about my potential to follow such a course.

It was an honour to meet Clay, and see how much one person could cram into his life. It certainly put some of my challenges into perspective, and gave me a renewed positivity about what I could achieve.

Goal 54 – Bobsleigh ride

Saturday, August 15, 2009
(Salt Lake City, Utah, USA)

Tiffany offered to take us up to Park City, where Utah's Olympic Park is located. She was running a little late in the morning, but all worked out well. When we arrived the bobsled had not yet started operating, as there was an aerial ski jump display just about to begin. What great timing!

There is a fantastic ski jump training facility, with a couple of huge jump ramps, and several smaller training jumps of various sizes. These all feed into a large pool, so landing errors don't result in broken bones! The display team consisted of quite a few Olympic team members, and was very spectacular. The height of some of the bigger tricks was astounding. I have added another goal to the bottom of my list, and would very much like to come back here one day to do their beginner's training course.

After the show we jumped in the minibus which took us to the top of the bobsled track. Susan and I were the only ones going to do it. Tiffany unfortunately has a recent neck injury (so she said!), and her two kids Ben and Hannah did not seem too keen either. I'm not surprised! It looked very fast judging by the run we saw set off before us.

All the waivers were signed, and we were issued with helmets and instructions. We climbed into position behind our worryingly young driver, Carter, and clipped ourselves in. The lights turned green, our helpers pushed, and we were off!

The ride started slowly, and the first two or three corners were pretty tame. As we picked up speed quickly the corners became tighter and longer, and the G-force was very strong. We were thrown from side to side, and in front of me I could see Susan's head forced down onto her chest, which gave me a great view forward. The corners looked amazing as we banked around them high up the wall.

Carter did a great job, and very soon we ended up at the bottom of the track, still in one piece. What an incredibly thrilling ride. I seriously considered a second go, and would have definitely done so if I could have taken my little camera with me in the camera glove I made for it, but they wouldn't let me! I can see why though – it's a pretty wild ride, and you really do have to hang on tight!

Afterwards we went on both of the steep zip-lines they have there, one of which comes down at about 55 mph over the 120m ski jump. We also tried out the toboggan which has small sit-on carts that run down a fast, twisting stainless steel track, very similar to the one I tried in Chamonix last year.

Olympic Park is a fantastic place, and Ed at the front desk was kind enough to offer us a great discount. I really hope to be back soon to try some ski jumping, and maybe the winter bobsled ride too.

Susan flew home from Salt Lake City the next day, and I spent a long day at the wheel, covering 400 miles across Wyoming. I ended up in Laramie, where I stayed with six other RVers at the Walmart carpark there. I considered pushing on for the final two hours that it would take me to get to Boulder in Colorado, but it looked like a big storm was approaching. After eating dinner I really did not feel like any more driving, so settled in for the night.

The next day dawned fine and bright, without a breath of wind, and I headed south to the Colorado border. The scenery changed almost immediately from the high flat plains of Wyoming to more mountainous terrain. The drive from Laramie to Fort Collins was beautiful, the road smooth and winding, and the views spectacular.

In Boulder I met up again with Yvette, who I had spent some time with in LA, on my previous visit to the States. She put me up for the night, and gave me a wonderful tour of the local area the next day. I managed to get some laundry done too, and gave the RV a much-needed clean-out.

A few months earlier, I had just about written my next goal off as being impossible, as both location and dates for the event had changed since 2008. I was already committed to being in Colorado on the new dates. The event took place in the UK, so for a time it had looked like this was going to be the goal that would mean that it would be impossible to complete all 100 goals. If I didn't manage to attend this year, there was no possibility to achieve the goal in my self-imposed timeframe, as in 2010 the event would take place after the end of my 100 weeks period.

However, I had been extremely lucky, finding a bargain price flight from Denver direct to Heathrow, leaving on the Wednesday night, returning on the Monday. With a little flexibility, and some creative juggling around with dates, the challenge was still on!

I parked the RV at long-term parking at Denver airport, and boarded my flight for a long weekend back in England.

Goal 55 – Fly like an ostrich!
Sunday, August 23, 2009
(Worthing, England)

I flew into Heathrow, and stayed overnight with Martin and Rachel. The next day I drove down to Bognor Regis, and then along the coast to Worthing, new home of the birdman competition since the fire on the pier at Bognor in 2008. I had been contacted by Michelle in Worthing, who had very kindly offered assistance and a place to stay for the weekend.

Saturday was a beautiful sunny day, and Michelle and I wandered down to the seafront for day one of the Worthing Birdman Competition. There are three classes of flyer, the most serious being the Condor class, who usually have hang gliders, sometimes specially modified for the competition. The second group is the Leonardo da Vinci class, who have more homemade contraptions, but still with the potential to fly a significant distance. Both of these classes would be competing on Saturday. The third class, in which I had entered, the Kingfishers, would not be "flying" until Sunday.

I could therefore happily enjoy Saturday's competition as a spectator. What a lovely day it was too. The sun was out, the beach was packed, big screens were set up for viewing the action, and the whole place had a great carnival atmosphere.

We watched a couple of flights from the beach, and then wandered out along the pier, surprised at how close we could get to the action. We eventually headed up the stairs to the bar on the second floor in the pavilion at the end of the pier, where the balcony offered an excellent vantage point.

The wind was in the right direction for the flyers, blowing straight onto the platform, and there were some spectacular flights. The most amazing was by Steve Elkins, who flew an incredible 99.87 metres, easily beating the previous record. He must have been very disappointed to fall 13cm short of the target distance of 100m, which would have won the £30,000 prize that is on offer!

Later on in the evening, Michelle dropped me in Brighton, and I met up with Martin and Rachel. They had come down to show support for my flight the next afternoon, and were out and about on the town with friends Rob and Suzanne. We had a great evening, although I went steady with the beer, as I had a big day the next day! The flyers' platform certainly looked unnervingly high, but I was nervously looking forward to my own "flight" from it.

The next morning I had to drop my "craft" off at the pier before 11am. I then had to be dressed in costume by noon for the judging of the Kingfisher class. The theatre on the pier where the mayor and others came to judge us was filled with a variety of entertaining costumes. These included a guy in a huge crocodile outfit, Laurel and Hardy, naughty nurses, and many others.

At 12:30, there was a mandatory safety briefing for all of the "flyers", including the 18 serious flyers from the day before. They would be making their second attempt today. Our group of 20 or so Kingfishers were looking forward to our first "flights". The atmosphere was fantastic, and humorous comments from many of the contestants made the briefing very entertaining.

At 1pm the "flights" began, with a guy in Hawaiian hula girl outfit and a body board plunging off the platform into the water below. He was followed by more spectacular plunges by other crazily dressed competitors. I took my place in the queue behind "Del Boy" Trotter from UK comedy "Only Fools And Horses". He had a complete mock-up of Del's famous car, which failed to fly any further than any of the other Kingfishers, disintegrating on impact with the water.

It was my turn next, and I waddled up the steep ramp to the platform in my costume. I had opted to "fly" sat astride an ostrich, and had worked on the costume a couple of months before, with much sewing assistance from my mum while last in England. I had also found the perfect pair of ostrich feet flippers while at a car boot sale down in Devon, back in June.

Each contestant was interviewed on camera at the top of the ramp, the pictures being transmitted on the big screens up and down the beach, and streamed live on the internet too. I was asked quite a few questions about both ALife4Sale and 100goals. I was trying to explain my fundraising goal, when I was informed that my time had begun, and I had thirty seconds left!

I barely had time to waddle to the end of the platform, and wanted to take the time to actually look off at the height of it. "5 seconds!" I was informed as I looked off the edge. It really was a spectacularly high jump! "Go, go, go!" I heard, and I flew – well, plummeted really! It was a long fall, and I hit the water pretty hard, but the ostrich costume protected me well.

The safety boat arrived and I was dragged aboard completely waterlogged! We waited for the next competitor, who had managed to split his lip and was bleeding a bit. I saw him interviewed later on the beach, and he was still shaking!

I got changed, thrilled by the jump, and went to watch the last of the Kingfishers, followed by the more serious flyers. ("Are you suggesting that we are not serious?" a guy in an outrageous drag outfit, beside me at the safety briefing, had asked loudly!)

Unfortunately the wind conditions were not as good as the previous day. Nobody managed a flight anywhere near as spectacular as Saturday's fantastic efforts. The sun was out though, and the spectators didn't seem to mind.

Worthing Council did an absolutely awesome job of organising a fantastic event, which all seemed to go very smoothly. The English summer weather was perfect for the whole weekend, other than wind direction on the second day, and the crowds were huge.

It was fantastic to have a group of friends join me for the day, including one of the Ian Ushers that I had met in London a couple of months earlier. As is usually the case, the eccentric English weekend culminated in a trip to a crowded bar.

I now have to dash back to Heathrow, and will be back in Colorado tonight. Quite surreal.

I drove the RV from Boulder down to Colorado Springs, and met Val, his wife Brenda, and their dog Buddy. I had been in contact with Val since the start of my 100goals journey over a year earlier. Val had made a suggestion for one of the final five goals that I had others select for me.

In Colorado there are 53 peaks that are over 14,000 feet tall, the Colorado 14ers. Val is working on a long-term goal of his own, aiming to visit the summit of them all. One thing he had always wanted to try was to climb seven of the summits within one week, and so the “7 Peaks in 7 Days” challenge had been born.

It was about 10pm when I arrived at their house, but on UK time that was about 3am the next morning. I was on some time zone somewhere in between, and as Val and Brenda chatted to me, I could feel myself zoning out a little. I was utterly exhausted, and eventually I had to make my apologies and head for bed.

Val is an extremely efficient organiser, and after an easy first day of sightseeing around Colorado Springs, we began our first day of the seven-day challenge.

Pikes Peak was an easy start to the week, but things were going to become a lot harder as the days progressed. Quite a group of Val’s friends and colleagues also came to join us for the day.

Day two was much tougher, and although the climbing wasn’t too hard, I struggled badly with the altitude. We were over 12,000 feet for several hours, and I obviously hadn’t acclimatised enough in the short time I had been in Colorado. We managed to collect three summits on the second day, Lincoln, Democrat and Bross, but by the end of the day I didn’t really care one way or another.

Altitude sickness is horribly debilitating, and is somewhat similar to a really bad hangover. The body isn’t receiving enough oxygen, and the resulting mixture of throbbing head, nausea, and complete lethargy saps the will to continue. It was only with the support and encouragement of several members of the group that I got through the day.

The sickness quickly disappears as you drive down to a lower altitude, and I was relieved to return to the condo that we were using as a base for a couple of nights.

Day three took us high into the mountains, as we travelled from one part of the state to our next climbing location. In much more remote territory, and with a group reduced to a core of just four of us, myself and Val, along with Val's climbing buddies Tim and Eric, we did a bit of sightseeing. We stopped off at an amazing old dilapidated mill, way up in the mountains, and visited a tiny town called Crystal, where only a handful people live through the summer months.

We camped out in the forest below the trailhead that night, setting up our tents before heading down into the scenic town of Ouray for a couple of beers. Our mountain for the next day was the spectacular Mount Sneffels, and a few more people met us early in the morning at the trailhead.

With a day's rest after my tough second day, I felt much better. I think my body had started to condition itself to the altitude, as I had no problems at all on the steep rocky climb.

That evening we relaxed at a hot springs resort, then drove over the incredible Engineer Pass, which tops out at around 12,800 feet. One of Val's work colleagues, a gung-ho young guy called Loren, decided to take his Subaru Legacy, an ordinary car whose only advantage was All-Wheel Drive, over the pass too. I have never seen such a feat, and was immensely impressed that he made it over the tough terrain with the loss of just one fog lamp.

It was late when we got to our chosen camp spot, and we decided to simply sleep on camping mattresses in the back of the two pick-up trucks in which we were travelling.

On day five we summited our sixth 14er, Wetterhorn Peak, after a longer, tougher climb again. That left us with a couple of days, and only one more peak to go. With a day in hand, we decided to fit in an extra goal, as everything was going nicely to plan.

Goal 56 - Whitewater rafting

Monday, August 31, 2009
(Canon City, Colorado, USA)

Our day off from slogging up the mountains was far from relaxing. After a great night's sleep at the Days Inn, and a fine breakfast we made our way to Raven Rafting, situated at the head of Royal Gorge on the Arkansas River. There we met Diane, Val's cousin, who would be our fifth rafting team member for the day.

We were geared up, some opting for wetsuits, other tougher locals happy to simply wear shorts and t-shirts. I went for the warmer wetsuit option! A short minibus ride took us to our start point, and we launched pretty quickly, our guide Carrie happy to give us our instructions and safety talk once we got moving.

The first rapids were pretty shallow. We scraped and bumped down them, and started to get our paddling teamwork together. We had arrived pretty much at the end of the rafting season, and the river was low, the flow being about 280 cfs (cubic feet per second). In June, when the river flow is at it highest, the flow can be over 3,000 cfs! However, the lower levels would make the trip quite technical, and would mean we would actually have to do a lot more paddling to make our way through.

As the walls of the gorge narrowed and we entered the canyon, the rapids got bigger. We started to drop into some more exciting, tricky sections. At one point we got well and truly stuck. Carrie later told me that I needed to write in the blog for anyone familiar with the river that we were "left at Bird Drop (oops!) in Sledgehammer Rapid!" I guess we weren't meant to go that way! It certainly took some teamwork to get us out again.

The scenery was very spectacular, and the steep-sided canyon had all sorts of interesting and unusual features. A railway ran through the gorge, and the train passed by a couple of times, filled with waving tourists. There were remnants of a wooden water pipe that used to run along the canyon wall just above the river, a leftover from a past era of mining here, now just a skeletal framework. There was a steep cog railway up out of the gorge, a swinging thrill ride that hung out high above us over the steep cliffs, and the highest suspension bridge I have ever seen!

Halfway down the river there was an opportunity to get out of the rafts and do some jumping off the cliffs, which was fun. Well done to Diane, who pushed herself to make the jump, and did so in fine style.

After tackling the remaining exciting rapids we began the easier final approach into Canon City. I got to have a try at steering the raft, calling out the instructions for the rest of the crew. I enjoyed my brief stint as captain, although I don't feel I was quite awarded the same respect from my crew members as our guide Carrie!

That night we made our way back up into the mountains, up a 4WD track out of Westcliffe. This one, believe it or not, made the previous tracks look relatively smooth. We found a fantastic campsite just below Colony Lakes, and made a campfire. I made the most of a couple of hours of down-time, trying to catch up on writing about the previous days' adventures, which seemed to amuse the others. I admit it must look unusual to be sat in the middle of the wilderness with a computer perched on a log, but it's been a busy week, and you have to fit blog-writing in whenever possible!

The weather had been extremely kind to us. I explained to Val that over the past year I had been incredibly lucky, getting just the weather needed to make each experience as pleasant as it could possibly be. We had done very well throughout the week, and had only seen one really cloudy day. Once again, on the final day of the week-long challenge, the weather couldn't have been more perfect.

7 peaks – Day 7 – Goal 57 finally achieved!

Tuesday, September 1, 2009

(Crestone Needle, Colorado, USA)

We didn't quite manage the early start we had planned, but were still on the trail towards South Colony Lake, at the foot of the Crestones, before the sun came up. Once more, it looked like the weather was going to be kind to us, and we would have a full week of perfect conditions.

Above the lake the climbing soon became steeper, but the four of us made good progress towards the saddle. Above that, the path became even steeper and rockier, and the hugely enjoyable climbing began.

The easiest route suggested climbing to about 13,800' up the east gully, then traversing into the easier top section of the west gully. There is another, slightly harder climb which continues up the east gully. I was climbing well, and felt pretty confident on the solid rock, and elected to continue straight up. I climbed fast, now above the others, and decided I wanted to be the first to the summit for my final peak. I pushed on, panting hard.

It was such a fantastic climb, in perfect conditions, on great, solid foot- and hand-holds. Despite the effort, I had a huge happy grin on my face. At the summit, I had about four or five minutes before Eric arrived, followed by Val and Tim. I signed the summit log book, and for a short time, I was the only person who had been on the summit of Crestone Needle during September!

The weather was perfect, not a breath of wind at the summit once again. However, the view was quite hazy, we suspected because of huge bush fires currently burning to the west, in California.

We sat in quiet reflection on the summit, our goal achieved. We were soon joined by Laura, who Val knows from his work, and her brother Brian. They were planning on continuing onward across a very steep looking traverse to Crestone Peak. We had also considered the same route, but had decided we would probably return the way we had come.

However, after some discussion, and a bit of time spent surveying the route, Val, Eric and I decided to join Laura and Brian. Tim, who has already done all of the Colorado 14ers, decided to head back down our ascent route. We all wished each other well.

The descent off the needle was a steep down-climb on good holds, with quite an intimidating drop below. Our group managed without needing to resort to the ropes we had, and we continued down and across the steep terrain towards the next summit.

Navigation through the steep crags was tricky, and we headed down one steep gully and around towards the next. There was more up and down climbing, and eventually we were almost below the summit of Crestone Peak. I elected to stay on the steeper, but solid rock and climb up, rather than head around to the next gully. Followed by Eric, we headed upwards, and reached the peak without too much difficulty, on great climbing holds in a fantastic location.

The others joined us, and there were congratulations all round. After a quick bite to eat it was time for the journey down, which took us down a steep, loose gully. This was probably the most dangerous part of the day, as occasionally a slip would send a rock cascading down towards those below. All went well though, and after another steep climb down and out of the gully, we reached better terrain, and slightly easier conditions along a rocky ridge.

I really was at the end of my stamina, and the journey back to the vehicles looked like an endless trudge ahead. I was amazed and very impressed when Laura and Brian decided to collect a third 14er, heading up the steep but easy slopes of Humbolt Peak.

We eventually reached the vehicles, and after a tortuous journey down the rough track, we made it back to Westcliffe. There we treated ourselves to a well-deserved beer and burger.

What a long, hard day! We were away from the vehicles for almost 12 hours, most of which was pretty tough going. Eventually though, we have not only managed to achieve the goal, but over-achieved by managing 8 peaks in 7 days. I think we all felt justifiably proud of ourselves.

I have had an amazing week here in Colorado, which really is a stunningly beautiful place. Despite all the miles we have driven, the tracks over which we have battled, and the trails we have climbed, I feel like I have only just scratched the surface of this incredible place.

This goal has certainly been the one which has required the most consistent and long term effort. I started my journey to fitness by cycling and swimming while in Perth. I spent time in the gym with Martin and Rachel in London, walked over Devon's beautiful tors and climbed the steep hills of San Francisco. After much preparation I was ready to tackle the steadily increasing set of challenges here in Colorado.

Over the course of the week-long challenge, I had been joined at one time or another by around thirty people, including the three with whom I had spent the whole week - Val, Tim and Eric. This sets a new record in terms of numbers of people joining in with a goal. Colorado really must be one of the fittest places I have ever visited!

Great people, great place, great fun.

Back in Colorado Springs, I learned a little of what relaxing in Colorado involves, particularly for Val and his buddies. Freshly returned from our seven-day marathon, Val suggested that we go and try out The Incline, a mile-long steep climb over wooden railway ties that used to carry a cog railway high into the mountains. Val had been working on trying to beat his personal best time, and break the thirty minute barrier. I set my target at fifty minutes for my first attempt, and managed a very respectable 47 minutes.

A party was organised too, with many of the people who had joined us on the mountains, coming together at the end of the challenging week to relax a little. At the party it was decided that we should go skydiving the next morning, and at around noon the next day, a group of us headed out towards the airfield.

The views from the plane over the Arkansas River, where we had rafted a couple of days earlier, and the Royal Gorge Bridge, were awesome. I managed to fit in a couple of solo jumps, as others in the group did tandem jumps with the instructors.

It wasn't all high-adrenaline adventure in my last few days in Colorado Springs though. I had met Kris, one of Brenda's work colleagues, and another very inspiring person. Kris has battled arthritis since the age of seven. She has had several operations and many other challenges to face, and yet is an incredibly upbeat and positive person.

We spent the best part of a day together, and I discovered that she is working on developing a motivational speaking career. This was something I had vaguely considered when back in England, and then again when I met Clay in Salt Lake City. I had many questions for her, and like Clay, she seemed very positive about my potential to do something similar, based on my challenges, travels and adventures.

I enjoyed my last days with Val and Brenda, and their wonderful circle of friends. I didn't particularly feel a pressing urge to move on, as my next firm commitment wasn't until late October, a couple of months away. I had a few goals that I wanted to address between now and then, but none had any sort of fixed date. I also wanted to spend some more time with Susan, hoping to continue the renewed happiness we had discovered once again on the road together.

Eventually it was time to say my goodbyes, and hit the road. I headed north once again, and then turned east across Colorado, stopping overnight at the beautiful Hanging Lake. I just pulled up in time, and as I turned the engine off, I could hear a terrible bubbling, knocking sound from the front of the RV. A quick scan of the dash confirmed my fears, the water temperature was way up in the red, and a look under the bonnet revealed parts of the fan belt scattered around the engine bay. It was already dark, so the problem would have to wait until morning.

A bodged repair job with some thin rope I had got me halfway to the next town. After the engine had cooled for an hour or so again, I made it the rest of the way. I was incredibly lucky to find a guy who could fit a new belt, as it was Labor Day holiday, and practically everywhere was closed. He certainly seemed to add a Labor Day tax to the price he charged me, but I didn't have much choice really.

Eric was one of the other three who had climbed all seven peaks with me. I had enjoyed his company immensely, as well as getting to know his wife Jackie and their kids Brian and Dylan. I stopped off with them at their home in Grand Junction. The next day Eric, Jackie and Dylan joined me on the next part of the journey, which took us along the Colorado River, and into Utah. Dylan, who was six years old, came and sat with me in the RV as we travelled along, and chatted away happily about all sorts of stuff. It was nice having company again as I drove.

Arches National Park is simply stunning. We parked the RV and drove around the park in Eric's truck, stopping off at the various lookout points and natural formations. Sunset was beautiful, and we sat quietly together as the slowly sinking sun lit up the spectacular rock formations.

After dinner in the nearby town of Moab, Eric and family headed home, and I parked for the night on the banks of the Colorado River.

The next week or so took me through some of the most spectacular country I have ever seen. I headed down through Monument Valley, backdrop for many western movies, and continued to follow the winding course of the Colorado River.

I had stocked up on food, and each night I could park wherever I wanted, and enjoy the scenic splendour all around. I crossed into Arizona, passing through the town of Page, site of the huge Glen Canyon Dam at the head of Lake Powell.

I stopped off to see the Grand Canyon again, this time from the North Rim. I was overawed once more, as I had been on my first visit to the southern side, almost a year earlier.

There is something about the enormous majesty of the Grand Canyon that for me causes a deep introspection. On my own again, watching the sun set over the timeless landscape below, I felt the familiar loneliness that had troubled me at the South Rim on my previous visit.

The words of a Richard Ashcroft song, always at his lyrical best when most reflective, floated through my mind:-

Old river,
And your restless wonder,
And your graceful leisure,
Rolling to the sea.
Many men have stood like I am,
Gazing out and wishing for someone.

It was slightly ironic, however, that it wasn't actually possible to see the Colorado River from the viewpoints at the North Rim Visitor Centre! That night I parked the RV in the forest just outside the Grand Canyon National Park, and made a little campfire, and felt much more at ease with being alone than I had when last there.

I stayed an extra day and night there, enjoying a long walk through the forest to the East Rim of the canyon, and another beautiful evening in the forest. I enjoyed the solitude, and felt that for now I had reached a resigned acceptance of being alone. I was still wishing for someone, but that would come in its own good time, I hoped.

My next stop was Zion National Park, back in Utah again. This offers some of the most incredible scenery, and caused me to linger another day longer than originally intended.

The days of freewheeling travel in the RV were immensely satisfying, and I could have spent so much longer walking and climbing in these beautiful areas. My goals seemed to have taken a bit of a back seat, as the journey itself became reason enough to drift happily through these stunning places. The goals were still there, however, and the bright lights and excitement of the Las Vegas poker rooms were calling to me. I contacted Val and Brenda's nephew Justin, who had climbed a couple of the seven peaks with us, and arranged to stay with him for a night on the outskirts of town.

Poker in Las Vegas - Day 1
Wednesday, September 16, 2009
(Las Vegas, Nevada, USA)

I left Justin's place, on the west side of the city, shortly after he went to work. After doing a bit of grocery shopping, I headed in towards The Strip. At the Sahara it was quite obvious that the RV was not going to get into the low clearance parking garage, but the valet parking guy directed me to Circus Circus, where there was plenty of open parking space.

Back at the Sahara, I paid my $45 and drew seat 7 at table 2. With twenty minutes to spare I found my *way out to the swimming pool area for a short while, and then took my seat at the table. With 4,000 in chip money in front of me, I began to play. It was quite a luxury to have a dealer, as in most of the pub games I had played in Australia, everyone had to take their turn to deal. It was also nice to have someone bring you whatever you wanted to drink. I stuck with coffee at 11am, but many others chose more alcoholic options.*

I didn't get much in the way of decent cards for the first hour, and found myself reverting to my old ways, playing very conservatively. My chips were slowly nibbled away, but I made it to the break, as a couple of the more aggressive players around me were busted out.

At one point I had another one of those moments of wonderfully satisfying clarity, when I realised where I was and what I was doing. I had just won a hand, and was stacking my newly-won chips, when it hit me! "I'm in Las Vegas, playing in a poker tournament," I thought excitedly, "and I know what I am doing too!"

However, it soon turned out that I didn't know what I was doing. I had two pairs, aces and queens, and ended up "All In" with the meagre balance of my chips. I was beaten by a flush that I hadn't even spotted as a possibility. What an amateur mistake!

Oh well, it was good fun to sit back down at a table and play, and I am really looking forward to tomorrow's game at The Rio. I only have three episodes of the 2007 World Series Of Poker, which was played at The Rio, left to watch as part of my homework!

Afterwards I made my way to Sam's Town Hotel, Casino and RV Park, a couple of miles out from The Strip. It's a pretty nice place, and is only $18 per night for the RV. There is a nice pool to lounge around during the afternoon, and a free shuttle bus to The Strip. What a bargain!

Poker in Las Vegas – Day 2
Thursday, September 17, 2009

Day 2 didn't start so well. I took the shuttle bus from Sam's Town RV Park to The Strip, and walked to The Rio in good time for the start of the noon tournament. I was dismayed to find that the tournament now started at 11am, and I was too late to enter. The next one was not scheduled until 7pm.

I wondered what to do, and eventually decided to head back to Sam's Town for an afternoon of lounging by the pool. I would then drive in again for the 7pm tournament, as I am really keen to play at The Rio, home of the World Series Of Poker.

The shuttle wasn't an option for the evening game. The last one back would be too early for me, unless I managed to get knocked out of the 7pm tournament very early, which wasn't part of the plan!

I returned to The Rio at around 6:30pm. I couldn't find a space big enough for the RV in the parking lot there, but managed to park easily in the huge Gold Beach casino parking lot just across the road. I registered for the $70 tournament, drew seat number 6 on the only table to be used, and sat down to play at 7pm. With a couple of early bust outs and a couple of later arrivals there were about twelve people in the tournament, the smallest competition in which I have ever played.

I think I played quite a bit better than yesterday, and won a couple of decent hands, remaining competitive for a good while. I won a great "All In" hand against three others, with my pair of queens, and had a pretty good stack for a while. Unfortunately I lost about half of my chips in an unlucky hand just before the ten minute break, but did survive to return to the table.

Shortly after the break I had two possibilities for a straight, eight cards in all, and called what I thought was an "All In" bluff. Neither of my cards came up, and I was beaten, ironically, by a pair of queens. I left the table with only four players remaining.

My wallet is $70 lighter, but I had a brilliant evening. I loved playing in the home of the World Series Of Poker. Poker really is an exciting game, and in terms of thrill for your dollar, I reckon it beats many of the adventure activities on which I have spent similar sums of money. It is a different sort of thrill though – a longer, lower level, but constant tension and awareness of nerves and concentration.

I am excited and nervous about tomorrow. It will only be the second time I have sat down to play in a cash game, the first time being in Deadwood last year, where I blew $60 pretty quickly. I know a bit more about the game now, and am hoping that my conservative style of play will serve me well at a cash table.

As Kenny Rogers' train-travelling gambling buddy told him:-

> *You got to know when to hold 'em, know when to fold 'em.*
> *Know when to walk away and know when to run.*
> *You never count your money, when you're sittin' at the table.*
> *There'll be time enough for countin', when the dealin's done.*

I hope I can figure out when to hold 'em, and when to fold 'em tomorrow night!!

Poker in Las Vegas – Day 3 – Goal 58 achieved!
Friday, September 18, 2009

What an evening! I am quite drained by my time at the poker table tonight. This evening's game certainly took me well outside of my comfort zone. After a lazy afternoon by the pool I took the 4:30pm shuttle into town, and made my way to my chosen game at The Wynn.

The walk from the shuttle stop was a nervous one, as the money with which I had chosen to play, although not absolutely devastating if it did all go, was certainly a sum that would be uncomfortable to lose. Most of my poker experience is in very cheap tournaments, and I didn't really know what to expect of a bigger cash game. So with some trepidation, I put my name on the list for a seat at a table. My choice *was a Texas No Limit Hold 'Em $2/$5 cash table, without an upper limit, so I could "invest" a sum of $1,000. I had to wait nervously for a while for a seat, and eventually sat down to play just before 6pm.*

I surprised myself a little by playing fairly aggressively with the first couple of hands, when I received some decent cards. However, I lost both of the hands I got involved in pretty quickly, and was down by about $300 within the first ten minutes. I settled down though, and decided not to let the early setback get to me. Half an hour later I won a pretty good hand, bringing me almost back to my starting point.

From then on I played fairly steady, winning a few, and losing a few, but my chips slowly dwindled. At one point the crunch came. A brash young Australian guy across the table from me, with a huge stack of chips, went "All In". After a brief moment of hesitation I called him, reasonably confident, with a ten in my hand to go with the two other tens on the board. The Aussie guy had the fourth ten, and we split the pot, both profiting fairly well from other players bets.

I felt that this was the moment when my goal was achieved. The last of my money had been at risk, and I was pretty proud to be still in the game afterwards.

I ended up down by the time I had to leave, having lost over half of my stack. When I cashed in I collected over $400, a little less than half of what I started with. However, I am generally a "glass-half-full" type of guy, and in this case, I reckoned anything that I carried away from the table was a bonus.

It is pretty clear to me now that I am no poker genius. At tonight's table there were guys who had a much better idea of what they were doing than I did. Others can see things that I simply miss, or discuss finer points of betting strategies that I only half-understand. I certainly have no misconceptions about winning the World Series any time soon. However, I did have a fantastic time, and I know I will be taking part in many more, but less costly, games. I am glad to have experienced the excitement of a game at this level, and do think that I got great value for money in terms of thrill and experience.

After I cashed in my remaining chips, I tried to find my way out to the street, but got completely lost in the huge place. These casinos are deliberately designed to let you find your way in, but make it very difficult to ever find an exit, I am sure! Eventually, with a little help, I found my way out, and just made it to the Riviera in time for the last shuttle back to Sam's Town. If I had missed it, the taxi fare would have made serious inroads into the remnants of my capital!

Back at Sam's Town, I went into the casino there to grab a celebratory beer. I somehow found myself at the poker room, wondering how much the 11pm poker tournament might cost me! "What are you thinking?" I asked myself. "Quit while you're ahead - well, not exactly ahead - but at least while you are no further behind than you need to be!"

I really didn't think the $50 entry fee would be a good investment. In the end, I think I made a great value-call by investing a further $3 in three more beers and heading back to my RV to watch a movie.

I followed the familiar route down from the mountains into California, and felt a warm glow of happiness to be returning to the sunny state, where I would be meeting again with friends from my previous visit.

Goal 59 – ten out of ten!
Monday, September 21, 2009
(Various worldwide locations)

From Las Vegas I spent a long hot day on Saturday driving down to Los Angeles, where I turned up at my friend Evan's house. He had moved since I had last stayed with him, and now lived in a lovely location right by the beach, about 50 miles north of the city.

Evan was away for the weekend. He had left me the keys for his apartment and car, and a note asking if I could pick him up at LAX airport at 10pm the next evening. On Sunday afternoon I went to meet another internet contact, Chris, and his mate Nick, in The Corner Office sports bar in Costa Mesa. I managed to gain a slightly better understanding of American football, but am still somewhat confused by all the plays.

After the game, we arranged to meet again the following weekend, if we didn't manage to catch up during the week. I made my way to the airport, where I was pleased to see Evan again.

On Monday I borrowed Evan's car once more, and went to meet Andrew, who had just flown in from Australia. Andrew had joined me on my trip to Israelite Bay earlier in the year, and had planned to join me in Las Vegas, but unfortunately had not been able to make it.

We wandered around Hollywood Boulevard and then took a drive out to the coast at Santa Monica. From there we drove up Highway 1 to Malibu, where we watched the sunset over a huge field of commemorative flags at Pepperdine University.

I was very much looking forward to meeting Eric, who I have spoken with several times on the telephone. That evening Eric had chosen Dukes Restaurant, right on the water's edge at Malibu as our rendezvous. They did a great Hawaiian chicken.

Eric is a TV producer, and I had had an amusing conversation when I spoke to him the first time, right at the very end of the ALife4Sale auction, about three or four minutes before the auction closed. At the time of the conversation there were three different TV crews in my living room, a news helicopter flying overhead looking for a place to land, and a live internet video feed from my house. When I think back about that time, it all seems so long ago.

After I finished ALife4Sale, and wrote out my list of 100 goals, I decided that I would like to meet some of these people who had contacted me to offer support, or ideas, or encouragement during that process. There were about twenty people on that list, and I have now met ten of them, Eric being the tenth. In actual fact, I must have met at least fifty people, maybe more, who knew of me and contacted me because of either ALife4Sale, or 100goals. This goal has been well-and-truly achieved!

The ten people that I have met that were on my original to-meet list are as follows, in the order I met them:-

1). Misty wrote to me to tell me she was doing a painting inspired by my life for sale idea, and I got to meet her, and see the picture, in Las Vegas in November 2008

2). Evan helped me a lot with PR for ALife4Sale, and we became good friends. We met and went to Perris Skydiving in California, where Evan did a tandem jump, and I tried out the wind tunnel.

3). Yvette writes a couple of blogs herself, and made a few comments on my ALife4Sale blogs. She also was trying to achieve a new adventure each month in 2008. Her idea was that one of her adventures might be to try to meet me, and we went for an evening out in Los Angeles when we discovered we were both there in November 2008.

4). Brandon, my very own Hollywood agent, was introduced to me by Evan, when several people were asking about movie rights early on in the flurry of media interest in the ALife4Sale story. I finally met Brandon in person when we went for lunch in Beverley Hills.

5). John emailed me to tell me that he was using my idea as inspiration for his own life-sale, and offered his home and lifestyle, living and working as an artist by the beach, on his website artistlifeforsale.com. I experienced a little of the life that was in offer when I visited him in Santa Monica.

6). David was the winner of the video clips competition I ran in the final days running up to the auction. He chose the book "1001 Movies You Must See Before You Die" as his prize. We kept in touch, and I met him and his family in Portland, Oregon as I passed through.

7). Moe had offered to take me dog sledding in the wilderness if I fancied a change of pace after selling my life. That idea subsequently went onto the 100goals list, and became a wonderful reality when I flew up to Whitehorse in Canada for an amazing week.

8). Matthew was my dedicated eBay help representative for the whole of ALife4Sale, and we talked a lot during that time. We finally got to meet when I was in his hometown of Vancouver.

9). Richard has always been a figure I have admired, and was quite an inspiration for my final decision to go ahead with ALife4Sale. Although I did not speak to him during those months, I did blog about him, and finally got to meet him briefly in London.

10). Eric seems to have a remarkable ability to call me just as something big is happening. He called during the final minutes of the auction, as a news helicopter circled over my house. The next time he called, many months later, he caught me on the evening before I was due to set off from Australia, on the second part of my 100goals journey - great timing!

There are so many others that could have been on this list. I have met many people over the past 14 months, and I imagine there are many more wonderful people to meet before this adventure is over. Thanks again to everyone who has offered help, support and encouragement on this amazing journey. It would never have been possible to have achieved so much without your kindness and generosity.

Top marks - ten out of ten to you all!

I had a relaxing couple of days hanging out with Evan by the beach, and meeting various people for coffee, drinks or dinner in and around LA.

However, it was time to start getting serious about my next goal. My Hollywood acting career was about to be launched.

Chapter 7 – Weeks 61 to 70

(28th September 2009 – 6th December 2009)

USA – Mexico – China – Thailand – Christmas Island

I had to be in Burbank in the morning for a sign-up session for movie extras, so decided to stay in Hollywood overnight at one of the backpacker hostels there. I caught up again with Ari, the voice-over guy, who came out to meet me for dinner. He arrived on a Segway, one of those weird contraptions with a small platform that you stand on, and a single steering column which you hold on to. Dinner was very nice, but I was far too distracted by my desire to try out the Segway, and before long I was hurtling up and down Sunset Boulevard on it.

The next morning at Burbank, I realised that the goal of being an extra in a movie might be a little trickier than I had anticipated. I had tried all my own contacts, including my agent Brandon, as well as a couple of producers who had contacted me when I put my life up for sale, but so far had had no luck.

At the casting agency I wasn't even allowed to enrol. As I didn't have a US work visa, I wouldn't be able to be paid. If I didn't get paid I wouldn't be employed, and therefore wouldn't be covered on-set by insurance. If I wasn't insured, then I wouldn't even be allowed on-set!

The agency directed me to a couple of smaller agencies just across the road, but I had the same issues there. I tried to explain that I didn't need to be paid, but there was apparently no way around the problem. Maybe, someone suggested, I could try for a role in a student film. It wasn't exactly the Hollywood blockbuster I had been hoping for.

All I wanted in order to achieve my goal was a small part in any sort of scene. Part of a crowd at a big game. A dead soldier on a battlefield. Third man in line at the bus stop. Anything!

It seemed like it was going to be a lot harder than I had first thought, but I wasn't ready to give up yet.

I tried a couple of other casting agencies, and kept an eye on Craigslist for upcoming casting calls. At the end of the week, when I managed to get another invite to a casting agency, I neglected to mention my work visa situation!

When I saw a similarly full room to my previous casting agency rejection, my hopes faded. However, when I had a brief one-on-one interview, things looked much more positive. I was lucky enough to be interviewed by the agency manager, and her first interview question was a simple request. "Tell us something about yourself."

This was my chance! I quickly and succinctly explained my eBay auction, my subsequent decision to travel the world with a list of lifetime goals to achieve, and finished with the fact that one of my goals was to have a small part in a Hollywood movie. My explanation prompted a couple of further questions, but it seemed like I may have found the right person. We got to the tricky part about my work status, and Ema brushed over that, suggesting it wouldn't be a problem if I didn't mind not being paid. Could I come back on Monday, she wondered, to get some photos taken, so she could set up a talent file?

Wow! In the space of half-an-hour I had become a Hollywood talent. Driving out of the city afterwards, I reflected on how perseverance can really pay off. I had needed to find that one person who would be enthused by my story, and would want to help. Ema seemed to be that person. She had promised that she would make it her goal to make my goal happen.

Although this was Tinseltown, I hadn't quite made it to the A-list just yet. Let's not get too excited!

Goal 60 – helicopter skydive
Sunday, October 4, 2009
(Elsinore, California, USA)

I took the RV into Beverly Hills yesterday, and parking it proved to be a bit of a challenge! My movie-extras interview went well, and plans have now had to change a little, as I need to be back first thing on Monday for my photo shoot! My original idea was to head onwards down to San Diego after a weekend of skydiving at Lake Elsinore, but I will have to postpone that for now.

I got to the dropzone yesterday afternoon. By the time I got paperwork sorted out it really wasn't worth hiring a rig for the rest of the day, so I happily watched the action.

It is the biggest and busiest skydive meet I have ever attended, and is largely aimed at female skydivers. The event is called "Chicks Rock!", although there are also plenty of guys here to jump too. They were running three large planes yesterday, and had a big meal and 70s theme party in the evening. Today they ran two planes, as well as a helicopter.

This morning I had to get up early and join the queue to hire a parachute for the day, and then wait for the helicopter jumps to start. There was a bit of a mix up initially, as we were booked on in groups of four, but the helicopter could only take three people at a time. However, in the re-shuffle I was bumped up from load 9 to load 5, and geared up when the time came.

The helicopter was pretty small, with open sides, and I squeezed in behind the pilot, the other couple taking the two left seats. We took off, and the small machine climbed pretty quickly, and it didn't seem very long before we were above 4,000 feet, where the pilot gave us a two minute warning.

I was first to exit, and when given the go-ahead, climbed out of the door and stood on the skid. I gave the others a quick nod and tried to take in the experience, but couldn't hesitate too long. I jumped backwards, and watched the helicopter appear to accelerate upwards as I fell away from it.

It is quite a different experience to jumping from a plane, as at first there is no wind. Before you pick up speed you really have very little control over how you fall. The feeling of falling from a stand-still is quite intense. As I gathered speed though, the familiar feel came back, and after a very short freefall I threw the pilot chute. Once the parachute was open, I got my bearings and made a pretty good landing on the narrow landing area.

Later in the day I did a couple of enjoyable fun-jumps from the plane at 12,500 feet. Chatting with a few of the other helicopter jumpers later, I discovered, somewhat ironically, that Perris Skydiving, just down the road, where I tried out their wind-tunnel last year, has someone who organises skydives from a hot air balloon. Well, my US funds are a bit tight now, but if I manage to sell the RV in time, I might just see if I can fit a balloon jump in before I leave the States at the end of the month! We'll see. Regardless, I am elated to have achieved this goal in such a great place.

On my return to town I went and had some photos taken at the casting agency, and was told to wait for a call. I decided that I would keep trying other avenues just in case nothing came from this one.

I had also decided that it was the end of the road for the RV. I advertised it on the website, and in a couple of places online. I had had to park the RV in the city a couple of times now. The huge vehicle was a bit of a handful in LA's crazy traffic, so I rented a reasonably cheap car for the next week, and moved the GPS over from the RV. I was now ready to face the manic city centre traffic.

I was very fortunate, and sold the RV pretty quickly to a single mum who was going to live in it at a friend's house. I managed to recoup almost everything I had paid for it, falling just a couple of hundred dollars short of my original purchase price. Apart from an alternator, a water pump and a very expensive fan belt repair, my home for six months of the last year had cost me very little.

With a few days on my hands, and the acting career off to a slow start, I did some more catching up. Clay, the pro-rockcrawler from Salt Lake City, had emailed to say he was working at a four-wheel drive expo at Pomona, so I took a drive out to visit him there.

He managed to get me in on a staff pass, and was busy signing large posters of himself, so I went for a wander around. When he finished we grabbed something to eat and headed for the bar at his hotel. He was obviously very well known in the off-road circles, and I was very interested when he took quite some time to chat with a guy with whom he had only corresponded online. The guy had recently been incapacitated in an accident, and was now wheelchair-bound. Clay had a lot of advice and support to offer.

Clay had a suite at the hotel, paid for by his sponsors, and suggested I could use the spare bed, which meant we could share a few more beers at the bar.

Back in LA the next day, I tried my hand at voiceover work with Ari, in his home-based recording studio. We mocked up a voiceover for a movie trailer, and edited it over the film. I was quite proud of the results.

I headed down to San Diego for the weekend, and caught up with several of the group with whom I had shared so much fun in Pamplona. It was great to catch up again and laugh over some of the stuff we had done, and some of the things we had seen there.

I stayed with Fipps's parents, who had used my blog postings while in Pamplona to follow their son's progress. Dennis's hobby was wood turning, and I was fascinated with the process of making beautiful wooden pens from simple blocks of wood.

I went lobster fishing with Willy one night, and caught dozens of the things. Unfortunately not one of them was big enough to keep, but he gave me a couple out of the freezer, caught on a previous outing.

Of course, I also drank quite a few beers with Fipps, Ivy, Willy and Kurtiss. Both Mikee and Nick were working overseas.

What a wonderful weekend, and what a great group of people.

Goal 61 – "and……Action!"
Wednesday, October 21, 2009
(Los Angeles, California, USA)

It has taken quite a while to achieve this goal, but perseverance has finally paid off. I'm glad that I scheduled enough time in and around LA to be able to do this.

As I drove back from San Diego yesterday, my phone rang. Angie from One Source Talent asked me if I was still in town, and if I was still trying to achieve my goal to appear as an extra in a Hollywood movie. I had not heard anything from them since I registered a couple of weeks ago, and thought I might not hear from them before I head off for Mexico. I am registered with another agency too, and am promised a role with them, but the scene they are shooting, set in a nightclub, keeps getting pushed back. I was starting to get worried that time might run out there too.

It was with great relief that I accepted a background role as a guest at a bed and breakfast establishment, to be filmed on location in Malibu, for a movie called "Storage".

I received details and directions by email from Alesia, and was told to bring three wardrobe choices of casual clothes. That's fortunate! The only clothes I have are all pretty casual!

This morning however, I had second thoughts about my wardrobe, deciding that most of the stuff I have is far too casual (meaning almost worn out!) The two smarter shirts I have managed to borrow are probably too dark (a light shirt was specified). So I made a quick stop at a thrift shop in Oxnard before heading down the coast.

I found the location, a lovely house in the Malibu hills with a beautiful outlook, overlooking the hills to the ocean. I found Alesia and a few other extras, and introduced myself. We were shown where to change, and from our clothes we had brought, our outfits were chosen. My new thrift shop shirt fit the bill perfectly! Two-and-a-half bucks well spent!

There was all sorts of activity going on, and calls for silence every now and then as a scene was filmed. I got to meet the lead actress, Sarah Jones, and took advantage of the photo opportunity.

Eventually it was time to film our scene. We were seated on the balcony at tables, set up as a restaurant at a bed and breakfast place. My table consisted of three of us, and we were given a bit of background as to who perhaps we were – I was one half of a couple who were meeting our nephew in LA.

For the scenes we had to mime conversation, but keep silent as the sound from the lead actors was being recorded. We shot the scene three or four times, and then took a break as something else was filmed. It was fun sitting around chatting with the other extras, and finding out what other roles they had played. I had photos taken with the rest of my co-stars – well, co-extras, really – and with my on-screen "wife" Deebye!!

Later we shot the scene again from the reverse angle, pretending again to chat, eat, and sip wine.

It was all great fun, and I loved every minute of it. I chatted with a few of my co-extras about my goals, and why I was there today, and marvelled once again at the journey on which all of this is taking me.

Here I was, in the hills of Los Angeles, filming a scene for a Hollywood movie!!

I had dropped in again to see John, the artist who had decided to follow my example, by putting his whole artistic lifestyle up for sale on the internet. It appeared that he had had as little success with his sale as I did with mine. He was still in his mobile home overlooking the beach at Santa Monica.

He didn't seem particularly worried that he hadn't managed to sell, and looking out at his beautiful view, I could see why he wasn't concerned. John didn't strike me as the type of guy that would be bothered by much. After all, the toughest part of his day seemed to be if the glue didn't hold together properly on his current piece of artwork.

I had been keen to speak to him about his daughter, and the outdoor sporting goods store that she ran in Ventura. On my previous visit John had mentioned that they often had speakers in the store. If I could arrange to do a presentation, as well as being a good first try-out at public speaking, it would also be the perfect occasion to achieve another goal.

Goal 62 – "If you can keep your head..."

Saturday, October 24, 2009
(Ventura, California, USA)

My dad has been a huge influence on much of my attitude to life. His death, at a time long before he should have left us, certainly influenced my belief that life is short. My strong opinion is that if there are things that you want to achieve, you really just need to get on and do them.

His favourite poem, "If..." by Rudyard Kipling, has become one of my favourites too, and offers some excellent fatherly advice. It therefore became one of my goals to learn this wonderful piece, and to be able to recite it from memory.

In order to achieve this goal properly, I really felt that I needed to recite the piece in front of an audience of strangers. The opportunity to do so presented itself, when I was booked to speak at an outdoor sports equipment store about my adventures.

John's daughter Ashley had suggested that I might like to speak there, and a date was arranged. I have been doing some hasty poem revision in preparation, as well as wondering what on earth I am going to say on my first public speaking engagement.

Somewhat nervously I headed to Real Cheap Sports in Ventura this morning, and got set up with a computer and projector, so I could show a few selected photos from my travels.

By 11am there were ten people in the audience. I was pleased to just creep into double figures, and I made a start. By the end there were a few more late arrivals stood at the back of the group. It was a good sized group for the first try at telling my story, as it was pretty casual and relaxed. I already knew a couple of the people there, so didn't feel too pressured or nervous.

By the time I got into it, I really enjoyed doing the talk, and could quite fancy doing a bit more of this sort of thing. I felt it went pretty well myself, and all the feedback I received seemed positive, although I don't know if people were just being polite! I hope not.

I kept it short, with an intro about myself, and a bit of background on the ALife4Sale beginnings of my journey. I then talked about four of my big highlight goals:-

Swimming with whales
Riding the "Wall of Death"
Running with the bulls in Pamplona
Climbing 7 peaks in Colorado

I also talked briefly about my last goal, acting in a movie here in LA, and then suggested that I was hopefully ready to achieve goal # 62.

I got Carina, who had emailed me during the week, having heard about me via Real Cheap Sports email list, to act as video camera person. I launched into my recitation. I had one brief moment of hesitation, which gave me concern for a second or so, but quickly got back on track! I think it went okay.

I am pretty sure that the poem is now fairly well embedded in my memory, and intend to keep it there by occasional practice. It is a great thing to have as a party-piece if I ever need it again.

After the talk I was very surprised and flattered to meet Doug. We have talked a little on Facebook, and he has been following my adventures since the ALife4Sale days. He had driven from Bakersfield to come to the talk, about a two hour drive.

After the talk I chatted for a while with some of the others who had come, and then Doug offered to take Evan and I out for lunch. We asked Ashley for a recommendation, and when we picked Mexican, she and her husband and John also decided to join us. What a great way to celebrate goal #62.

A couple of people have been instrumental in helping me to learn the poem. Kelli, who I met last year at her ghostly cottage in Oregon, gave me a beautiful calligraphy copy of the poem. Cari, in

Florida, gave me a beautifully printed and presented version of the poem when I was there to visit the underwater hotel. This has been either on the dashboard of the RV, or in the top of my small back pack for the past three months now. It is looking a little worn, but has been the best help ever in learning this poem.

Thanks also to my dad of course, for first introducing me to this timeless advice.

If... by Rudyard Kipling

If you can keep your head when all about you
Are losing theirs and blaming it on you,
If you can trust yourself when all men doubt you
But make allowance for their doubting too,
If you can wait and not be tired by waiting,
Or being lied about, don't deal in lies,
Or being hated, don't give way to hating,
And yet don't look too good, nor talk too wise:

If you can dream – and not make dreams your master,
If you can think – and not make thoughts your aim;
If you can meet with Triumph and Disaster
And treat those two impostors just the same;
If you can bear to hear the truth you've spoken
Twisted by knaves to make a trap for fools,
Or watch the things you gave your life to, broken,
And stoop and build 'em up with worn-out tools:

If you can make one heap of all your winnings
And risk it all on one turn of pitch-and-toss,
And lose, and start again at your beginnings
And never breathe a word about your loss;
If you can force your heart and nerve and sinew
To serve your turn long after they are gone,
And so hold on when there is nothing in you
Except the Will which says to them: "Hold on!"

If you can talk with crowds and keep your virtue,
Or walk with kings – nor lose the common touch,
If neither foes nor loving friends can hurt you;
If all men count with you, but none too much,
If you can fill the unforgiving minute
With sixty seconds' worth of distance run,
Yours is the Earth and everything that's in it,
And – which is more – you'll be a Man, my son!

The next few weeks were starting to look like a bit of a logistical nightmare, as several goals approached that all had set dates. The major problem was that in the middle of the up-coming festivals was a natural event that was controlled by the phases of the moon, and the arrival of the rainy season on Christmas Island.

The spectacular migration of red crabs across the island to the sea could take place either in November or December, and almost always takes place on the high tides caused by the new moon.

This meant that while other dates were fixed, I had to remain totally flexible about which way I planned to tackle the goals, and therefore which flights I would need to book.

Only one flight date was pretty fixed. I had booked a flight for early November to Kuala Lumpur in Malaysia. From there I could either head south to Christmas Island if the crabs were on the move, or north into Thailand if it looked more likely that they would migrate in December.

Since selling the RV, I had been living on Evan's sofa in his apartment by the beach for the last few weeks, and I decided he perhaps needed a break from me. I booked a flight up to San Francisco, bidding farewell to LA, and my blossoming Hollywood career.

I stayed again with Susan, and spent a lot of time on the computer trying to sort out the next few weeks. I kept in regular contact with the Christmas Island National Parks Service. It eventually became clear that the rains hadn't arrived in time for the crabs to make the November migration, so December was almost definite now.

Finally I could book some flights, and make some formal arrangements. The new schedule meant that I had a bit of a hole in my calendar from early- to mid-November, and some quick research unearthed some very cheap flights from Kuala Lumpur to China. Maybe I could fit in another goal during this time.

I would need a Chinese visa, and only had a couple of days in San Francisco in which to get one. I spent several frustrating hours in the Chinese embassy trying to deal with the confusing beaurocracy. Could I show them my flight details and hotel booking? I hadn't booked them yet, as I hadn't managed to secure a visa. Ah, but you must have a booking first. If I made a booking, would I be guaranteed a visa? Ah, so sorry, no visa guarantee!

I had nervously made flight and hostel bookings for Beijing, and had to pay a surprisingly reasonable fee to have my application expedited. I was very relieved to get my passport back with a 30 day visa stuck inside.

Back at Susan's apartment we fell back into our somewhat argumentative routine. By then I think we both knew that we were never going to make it as a couple. We both managed to rub each other up the wrong way too often. At times I found her to be incredibly frustrating, as she took so long to do anything, and everything had to be done in such a particular manner. I am ashamed that my frustration was often too much to contain, and I hated myself when I let my annoyance show.

I thought many times of a song I had once introduced Laura to long ago, telling her that the lyrics explained how I felt about her. More importantly, I explained, it put into words how I felt about myself when I was with her:-

And now I believe in love, I believe in love,
You're the reason why I can,
'Cos when I look at myself in the mirror,
I see a better man.

When I was with Susan, I didn't see that better man in the mirror. I was sad that we couldn't make things work out for us, because she was such a wonderful, caring person. However, I was also a little relieved to fly down to Mexico before the end of the month.

Goal 63 – Día de Muertos

Sunday, November 1, 2009
(Oaxaca, Mexico)

After my trip to Monte Alban on Friday, I took a wander around the city of Oaxaca, enjoying the festive atmosphere. The sand paintings and decorations are very eye-catching.

Later in the evening I had a couple of beers and quite a few shots of mezcal, the local drink somewhat similar to tequila, with a group of other travellers in the courtyard of the hostel. I had a slow and easy start yesterday.

I set off late morning to try to find my way to a nearby town called Tule, on the advice of fellow traveller and hostel resident Rebecca. I tried for some time at the crazy, run-down bus station to find the right bus, but my poor Spanish provided confusing results at best. Eventually I gave up and jumped in one of the shared taxis with a group of locals. I was pleasantly surprised that the 13km journey only cost me 8 pesos (about 70 cents).

There isn't much to see at Tule, other than the spectacularly huge "Arbol de Tule", a tree estimated to be over 2,000 years old, and still doing well. It absolutely dwarfs the church in whose grounds it stands. It was nice to sit in its shade, and contemplate the history that has happened during its lifetime.

Back in Oaxaca, I took some photos of the large sand paintings/sculptures in the Zocalo, the main centre square of the city, while it was still light. Later in the evening I met with Rebecca, Mark and Karen, and another five travellers, and we set off for Panteon General, the main city cemetery. On the way we came across a comparaza, a big parade of people in Halloween costume, accompanied by an exuberant marching band, and joined them for a while.

The cemetery itself, lit by candle light, was very atmospheric. Preparations were being made for a concert later that evening, as an orchestra and choir arranged their seating.

I had read a lot about a cemetery further out of town in a place called Xoxocotlan, (pronounced Hoho-cotlan, or simply Hoho, with a throaty Spanish accent on the h's!) and was very keen to go there. Most of the rest of the group were happy to stay in town, and in the end only myself and Finnish traveller Essi went to find a taxi, which proved to be much easier than we had expected.

We entered through the gate of the cemetery, and were quite awe-struck. The scene was beautiful, very much as I had imagined it might be. As far as you could see there were graves covered in intricate flower decorations, and lit with candles. Family groups sat around many of the graves or tombs, all ages represented, from oldest great-grandparents to sleeping toddlers.

At many graves the mood seemed to be quiet and reflective, but elsewhere celebrations were in full swing. Fireworks would shoot into the air, bands played, and there was much laughter and cheering.

I talked for a while to one guy sat with his family at his father's grave. He explained that they came to be with their relatives, to let them know that they were still cared for, and on this one occasion each year were welcomed as they came back to join their family once again. Many people bring the deceased relative's favourite food or drink for them to enjoy, and there was plenty of mezcal being drunk.

I found it all surprisingly emotional. At times I was saddened and reflective, at other times laughing and clapping along with others as one of the bands played a deceased relative's favourite tunes around the grave.

We wandered around until midnight, and then went into the thronging little market area to find something to eat, heading back afterwards to wander the graveyard some more.

The whole experience was fascinating and thought-provoking. I was intrigued by the different attitude to death, and less sombre celebration of the lives of people who have passed on.

I was grateful to Essi, who was a perfect companion for the evening, sharing my thoughtful and reflective mood. I was very pleased that she had also wanted to make the extra effort to visit this touching event. I think it would have been a bit more challenging and confronting to be there alone.

I had found the ceremonies in Mexico to be much more emotional than I had expected they might be. Once again my experiences prompted thoughts of my father, who had died many years earlier.

On my last night in Oaxaca, Essi and I were invited to join a group heading out to another cemetery, in a little village out in the country somewhere. I had politely declined, wanting to spend some time on my own. Essi opted to join the group, and we shared out the flowers we had bought, along with a couple of candy skulls and a candle each. I took my small supply and walked alone through the dark streets to the main cemetery at the edge of the city.

I walked around the brightly lit and gaily decorated centre section as I had a couple of nights before, and then made my way out to the darker recesses on the outer fringes. Some of the graves bore candles and flowers, others dark and unmarked. I wandered quietly until I found a grave that appealed to me, and made my own little private shrine, including a picture of my dad that I had printed at an internet café.

I hoped the current occupant didn't mind me using his final resting place for my own purposes. I sat quietly and wondered what my dad would have made of my current adventures. I thought that he might have been proud, and perhaps a little jealous too.

I don't really believe that there is anything left of him to watch over me, or to see any of what I am doing, but it felt nice to sit there and think fondly of him, and the impact he has had over the course of my life. Whether he was watching or not, all these years after he had gone, his life still continued to influence mine, and the choices I made.

I thought I might have trouble renewing my US visa again, for what would be the fourth time in just over three months. I had flown out to Mexico, returning just a few days later, carrying only hand luggage. At customs the questions started, but when I mentioned the Dia de Muertos the agent became very enthusiastic, asking me how it had been. He told me that he wanted to go himself next year, and I was soon waved through with a new stamp in my passport.

I only had one more day with Susan, and we parted as good friends. We both knew that any relationship had probably been doomed from the start, our incompatibilities outweighing the good side of what we had found together.

I had been in and out of the States for the past three months or more, and it really was starting to feel quite like home. Over the previous fifteen months of travel, I had spent almost half of my time in and around the USA.

I was flying from San Francisco down to LA, then onward on a 14 hour flight to Taipei, on again to Kuala Lumpur, and on again finally to Beijing. It felt a little like I was leaving home.

Despite not having a house or apartment of my own, I have made my home here for a month or more, with Evan in LA, and with Susan in San Francisco. I was going to miss being here.

Although things didn't quite work out as we hoped, and Susan had become more of a friend than anything else, I still felt a saddening loss at seeing her drive away to work that afternoon. I felt empty and sad as I left a couple of hours behind her, travelling much further away than her.

This sort of adventure is all very well when meeting interesting new people, doing exciting new things, and seeing fascinating new places. Soon though, those new people tend to become good friends, new places become comfortable and familiar. Time rolls on, and time to leave comes all too soon. With it comes the excitement of the new again, but always tempered by the loss of the friendly and familiar.

It is very much a double-edged sword. It is wonderful making such good new friends, but very hard to leave, with no idea of when, or even if, I will ever see them again.

I had a night and a day in Kuala Lumpur, between my flight in from the States, and my next flight out to China. I took the bus into the city centre. I have passed through Kuala Lumpur and stopped over there a couple of times before, and I love the place.

When Laura and I first started travelling to Australia in 1998, Malaysian Airlines were offering some of the best deals. Included in the price of the return from England to Australia was a free return flight from Kuala Lumpur to anywhere else in Malaysia that the airline serviced. For the price of the return ticket, you could have a stopover in KL for a few days, then fly to another fascinating place like Penang, or Borneo, and spend some time there too. We had always taken that option, and always enjoyed our days in KL.

Again Laura's ghost was there with me. She was there in front of the first hostel we had stayed at in the city, the photo of her in front of the door crystal clear in my mind. She was there sat across the table from me eating roti bread and drinking sweet tea. She was there at the top of the KL Tower, admiring the view to the mountains across the busy city.

It seemed though, that time was working its slow magic, and the memories only prompted a sad smile. The past was gone, and I was much more at ease with the new life I had now chosen for myself.

The next day I arrived in Tianjin in China. I had flown in on a cheap airline that used a satellite airport a good distance away from Beijing, but it was easy to find a bus to the train station in Tianjin city centre. My train to Beijing didn't leave for a while, and I went in search of some breakfast.

The tiny little café I found was a bit of a challenge, as nothing was in English on the menu, but I was saved by some pictures above the counter. I ordered something that looked like it might be made from eggs by pointing at the picture, but when it arrived, its ingredients were a complete mystery. I don't think there was any egg in it at all, but at least it was filling.

I caught an incredible high speed train into the centre of Beijing. The train travels over 100 kilometres between the two cities, but does it in less than half an hour, reaching a top speed of well over 300 kph.

I got a little mixed up with the subway system in Beijing, getting off at the wrong stop. I eventually had to give up and catch a taxi. Even then, with my hostel address written down, it was tricky to find the place, as it was hidden away down a tiny back alley.

I finally arrived, about an hour later than planned, feeling a little guilty, as I had arranged to meet Lancy there at noon. Lancy was another internet contact who had offered to be my Beijing guide, after she had found out about me in one of her English classes. Her teacher had given her an English newspaper article to summarise, and it had been about this guy in Australia putting his life up for sale on the internet. She had been interested in what had happened next, and following my blog, had discovered that I would be coming to China for one of my goals.

The hostel looked very homely, with a covered central courtyard filled with tables, chairs, couches and many plants. I was pleased that Lancy was still there. After I dropped my bag off in a comfortable little bedroom upstairs, we headed out to take a look around the city.

The hostel was very central, and a short walk took us to a busy shopping area. Just behind that there was an extensive system of ornamental lakes with cycle tracks weaving around them. On the winding pathways, vendors were selling all sorts of weird and wonderful items.

Beijing reminded me a little of Japan, in that it was so different from a western city, different even to an Asian city like KL. It was much colder after the tropical warmth of Malaysia. The temperature in the afternoon was around 12°C, and would drop to near freezing in the evening, Lancy told me. It seemed like a busy place, but apparently would get much busier, as it was Sunday afternoon, which is of course relatively quiet. It is, like Kuala Lumpur, a fascinating mixture of sleek modern and old traditional. There are interesting sights at every turn, such as people playing chess or mah jong at street-side cafés, or a street vendor making intricate animals on sticks from toffee.

Everything was so strange and foreign, and very little was signed in English. Food stalls sold a confusing array of mysterious dishes, and Lancy and her friend Jenny had me try all sorts of different things.

We wandered happily, and I soaked it all up and chatted with the girls, who were wonderful hosts. At times I would feel my head swim a little with tiredness, but it was all too new and exciting to miss out on. At one point I suddenly felt that familiar thrill of realisation again. "I'm in Beijing! In China!!" I thought excitedly.

Later in the evening the girls dropped me off back at home. I was amazed once more at how quickly I could start to refer to a new place as home, even though I had spent only a few minutes there. Wherever I lay my hat... (or in my case, my rucsac!) The girls went to catch their bus, and after quickly checking my email, ten minutes later I was fast asleep on my bed!

Lancy had been right about it being quiet on the Sunday afternoon. On Monday morning, when I walked out of the little alleyway down which my quiet hostel was hidden, my senses were assaulted by the apparent chaos. I could not believe my eyes. The place was a melee of cars, buses, trucks, bicycles, mopeds, motorbikes, hand-carts, and many other contraptions that were some kind of home-made hybrid of two or more unusual donor vehicles. It was wild, and my first street-crossing was a nervous affair.

Slowly it all started to make some sort of sense, and I found that I could predict, with at least a small degree of accuracy, the direction from which the next thundering wave of vehicles might come.

Lancy had to work over the next few days, so I played tourist around Beijing, visiting Tiananmen Square, the Summer Palace, the Forbidden City and Olympic Park. I figured out the subway system, and a couple of bus routes which would get me home again. My confidence in getting around this strange place grew.

I was perhaps a little over-confident when I borrowed a rickety old bicycle from the hostel to go out for dinner one evening! I threw myself into the whirl of early evening traffic madness. The ride was terrifying and exhilarating in roughly equal measures, and I survived only by picking one of the skilled local cyclists and following their lead at the enormous free-for-all junctions!

Here are a few other random observations taken from one of the blog posts I wrote at the time about my fantastic days in Beijing:-

Foreigners pay a different price for many things. I bought some fantastic bread this morning at a tiny little window outlet. The woman in front of me got three spicy hot bread rolls, gave 2 Yuan, and got some change. I bought two rolls, gave 2 Yuan, and got nothing back but a confused look. Upon my return later in the afternoon, I bought three rolls, and the asking price was 6 Yuan. This is the point where I made a stand, and simply paid 3 Yuan, which was accepted without question. I am pretty sure I still overpaid. It is one of the tastiest breads ever, and 3 Yuan is 45 cents, so I'm not complaining!

Spitting is a national pastime. Male or female, it doesn't seem to matter. The more hawking and guttural noise you make before the big spit, the better! You can spit anywhere – footpath, road, temple – it doesn't seem to bother anyone!

Public toilets can be pretty hit and miss, literally! Many are squat hole-in-the-ground type, and accuracy seems to be a bit of an issue with some of the locals! Another very important lesson to learn is that each cubicle (that is if you are actually in a toilet block with the luxury of a cubicle at all) does not have its own supply of paper! Don't discover this by trial and error! Collect your paper from the communal paper dispenser before heading for your cubicle.

I visited one toilet today, optimistically labelled as 4 Star by the Beijing Tourism Administration. (It is obviously somebody's job to go around giving out star ratings for toilets!!) I couldn't help but notice this, as the sign was proudly displayed above the single paper dispenser that served both ladies and gents toilets!!

Beijing was fast becoming one of my favourite cities ever! It is such a wonderfully fascinating and endlessly entertaining place. Something as simple as getting a bus from one place to another can become an adventure in its own right. With the appropriate adventurous attitude, and plenty of time on your hands, it's all great fun, as a bus ride to anywhere in the city costs the equivalent of 15 cents. One journey right across the city on the subway is only 30 cents, and if public transport fails you, a taxi home will be a couple of bucks at the most.

Goal 64 – Walking on the Chinese Wall

Thursday, November 12, 2009
(Beijing, China)

"He who has not climbed the Great Wall is not a true man."

Mao Zedong.

Well, I guess finally I can truly call myself a man now, as today I got to climb and walk along the Great Wall of China at last.

I was hoping that Lancy was going to be able to join me for this goal. Unfortunately she was at work during the week, so we had planned to go out to one of the older, less touristy sections of the wall at the weekend. To do this involves catching a local bus (or going on an organised tour) to the start point. From there you walk a 10 kilometre section of the wall, and organise return transport from the end (or catch your tour bus back!)

But mid-week, the forecast was for the weather to get much worse, with predictions of heavy snow to come. In the end, I had to make a practical choice. I decided to at least go and see the wall today. There is a much more accessible section, apparently frequented by hoards of tourists, but from pictures I had seen, it still looks quite spectacular. If the weather deteriorated later, making a weekend trip impossible, at least I would have achieved the goal today.

I was up and dressed warmly first thing this morning, and as I made my way to the local bus stop in the darkness, the snow had already started falling. The local bus took me to a nearby bus station, where I transferred onto a long distance bus. An hour and a half later we approached Badaling, site of a section of the wall.

The snow had been falling all morning and was getting thick on the road. With amusing inevitability, when we stopped on a hill the bus started to slide, and eventually ended up completely stuck. I opted to walk the rest of the way with a few of the locals, and fifteen minutes later arrived at the entrance to the wall itself.

On both sides of the valley the wall headed steeply uphill. It looked almost exactly as I had expected it to, apart from the fact that higher up it just disappeared into shrouds of mist and snow. There were quite a few people about, and several larger tour groups, but I suspect that the weather meant numbers were much lower than on a nicer day.

I bought my ticket, and decided to head up the eastern section first, as there were a lot less people going that way. This section of the wall, which in total covers thousands of miles, has been extensively restored. It is in very good condition, although perhaps somewhat less authentic than many older sections, which are not so accessible by tour bus.

After a steep, snowy, slippery climb I reached a fortress at the top of the hill, and was greeted by my first and only salesman of the day - the bad weather must keep all but the hardiest of them away. A few more people had made it that far too, but the wall continued beyond, and the snow on the next section was completely untrodden.

A small extra effort always reaps rewards, and for the next section, I had the wall completely to myself for over half an hour. At the end of the section open to the public, the wall continues, but has not been restored. It looked very appealing, but unfortunately, due to a huge spiked fence, I had to turn round, and head back down to join the throngs.

I headed up the other side among larger groups of visitors, all of us struggling and laughing in the treacherously slippery conditions. At the top, many loud groups were taking photos. Once again, an extra hundred yards of semi-skiing down the next steep, slippery section meant I had the wall to myself again.

Afterwards, I headed back down to the valley, and discovered that the buses were still not running up the Badaling road. I had to walk a couple of miles down to the main highway to catch a bus back to the city. I would have caught a taxi, but only had enough cash left for the bus and a bite to eat!

What a great day out, made so much better I think by the snow and tricky conditions. This had meant it was a much more unique and personal experience, in what could have just been a heaving tourist trap location.

Goal 64 is also the fourth of the "New Seven Wonders of the World" that I have seen. Machu Picchu, Christ the Redeemer and Taj Mahal still to come!

Lancy was very disappointed that she hadn't been able to come along to accompany me as I achieved my Great Wall goal, but there were still a couple of more remote sections of wall that I wanted to visit that would be a little less touristy. With two days off, Lancy decided to come along with me.

There was the option of joining a tour bus organised by the hostel, but I didn't really fancy that. With Lancy along as a translator, I suggested that we should make our own way, and have our own adventure. Lancy seemed a little reluctant, perhaps preferring the convenience of an organised trip, but agreed that our own trip would be much cheaper.

We met at a large bus station on the outskirts of the city, and caught a bus which would take us out to Miyun, a couple of hours away. Our adventure started early however, when the bus, which had smelt strongly of burning gearbox oil for quite some time, finally ground to a halt!

In the process of moving on to a new bus, we somehow managed to end up with an old lady practically attached to us, probably because I was the only foreigner on the bus. She kept telling us we should get off the bus early to catch a taxi to the Great Wall. We ignored her suggestion, as Lancy made some enquiries with other people on the bus, giving us better information. It is very nice to have a Chinese-speaking person with me.

At Miyun our old lady continued to shadow us, babbling incessantly at poor Lancy. She tried to convince us the only option was to pay 300 Yuan, about $42, for a taxi. At the small tour shop that runs the local bus, there was bad news! There were no more buses today, as it was Friday afternoon – I wasn't too sure about the logic of mid-Friday afternoon being the cut-off point on the bus schedule, but the timetable was pretty clear. Our old lady, who was still shadowing us doggedly, now seemed much more optimistic about her chances, but she was really starting to bug us.

Eventually Lancy produced results, and we were told where to go to get a shared minibus or taxi. We finally shed our old lady when she realised we had solved our problem. Lancy's spirited negotiations with a taxi driver soon had us on our way to Jinshangling, for the much more reasonable price of 50 Yuan, just less than $7, for both of us.

At Jinshangling, where it was bitterly cold, we found some reasonable accommodation for 55 Yuan per room, about $8 each. After more negotiation, at which Lancy was quickly becoming very good, the price would also include dinner and breakfast.

In the morning we got up fairly early, and after breakfast made our way up to the wall. The sun was out again, and we started to warm up a little as we climbed out of the shadows in the valley.

On the wall itself the views were stunning, and we could see it snaking off into the distance over the mountains in both directions, each mountain peak having a watch tower perched on top.

The day couldn't have been better. The sun was out, and there wasn't a breath of wind. The wall still had an icy covering of snow on the top, making it look stunningly bright. Best of all, because we had arrived the day before and got an early start, we were ahead of any of the tour groups that would be coming along later. We literally had the whole wall to ourselves for as far as we could see in either direction.

Our route took us along the wall for about 10 kilometres, up and down the mountains, passing through the watch towers on each summit. Every step of the way offered the most amazing photographic opportunities – the views were stunning.

Some parts of the wall were fairly well maintained, but other parts were crumbling away. At the steeper sections, especially covered in snow and ice, it was pretty treacherous, but we took our time, and had no real problems.

We walked for around four hours through the most incredible, wonderful landscape, and I tried to explain to Lancy how this absolutely perfect experience exceeded all my expectations about what it would be like to walk on the Great Wall. It truly was one of the finest days I have ever spent in the mountains. We were both very happy that we had made the extra effort to organise our own, individual trip, rather than join a larger group on an organised tour.

We didn't hurry, and sat for a while eating our supplies and admiring the view. After a little over four hours, which seemed to have passed in no time at all, we crossed a suspension bridge over Simatai Lake, and descended from the wall down into the small town of Simatai itself.

More negotiations got us a reasonable taxi back to Miyun, and we caught the next bus back to Beijing. At the main station there Lancy and I parted ways, as I headed back to the hostel and she headed home. I will be eternally grateful to her for being such a great tour guide, interpreter, companion, and all round entertainer – I couldn't have asked for better company on such a marvellous adventure. The two days were certain to be added to the growing list of lifetime highlights. The experience of the journey there, the almost impossibly perfect weather conditions, and the wonderful companion on the adventure are memories that will be treasured forever.

I flew back to Kuala Lumpur, and at the airport bought a ticket with the same bargain-basement airline up to Bangkok. My ex-brother-in-law Tony has been living there on-and-off for several years, working as an English teacher. It was good to catch up with him again, and it was fun to have a Bangkok semi local to show me around the city.

I stayed with Tony for a couple of days, but needed to head off to my next destination. I wanted to arrive well before the weekend to secure a hotel room in the small town, which apparently becomes packed-out for this one big weekend every year.

A speedy and exhilarating, but quite nerve-wracking ride on the back of a moped taxi through the Bangkok morning rush hour traffic got me to the train station in about twenty minutes flat, a journey that may have taken around an hour in a taxi cab. The two-car train rattled slowly eastwards for around seven hours, and I got off at Surin with quite a few other fellow travellers. We were greeted by several elephants and their handlers waiting at the station entrance.

I wanted to linger a while, but also knew that I should secure a hotel room as soon as possible, as the town's accommodation fills fast in the build up to the weekend's festivities. I had met Joy on the train, a veteran visitor to the Elephant Round Up, this being her fourth time here. She suggested I try The New Hotel first, right by the railway station. As I passed the elephants, one reached it's trunk out, and I patted it – the first time I have ever touched an elephant.

I managed to get a room without trouble in the misnamed establishment. It has been many years since this place could have been called new! However, even when the room-rate doubles for the festival weekend, the cost per room only increases to around $10 per night. What a bargain.

Joy gave me directions to the wonderfully vibrant street market. I dumped my bag and went for a spicy dinner, chosen from the vast array of tempting and mysterious foods on offer. After a quick chat with a few other regular Round Up veterans, I decided to have an early night. I had discovered that there is a dress rehearsal for the weekend's big elephant shows first thing in the morning at the stadium. It is not advertised, but you can go along and watch if you want.

I was up early and bought some breakfast (fresh pineapple) at one of the street vendor's carts, and then walked to the elephant stadium. I found a good spot at the front just before the start of the rehearsal. The place was packed with school groups and hundreds of other elephant enthusiasts.

The show was spectacular, but the best moment by far was when all the elephants filled the stadium field at the same time. Approximately 250 elephants streamed into the centre of the football-pitch-sized arena from all four corners, circling around in the middle, then all sitting down. It was quite breath-taking.

I watched entranced as elephants played football, threw darts, painted and twirled hula-hoops. One elephant easily beat a group of 30 volunteers in a tug-of-war. After the show rehearsal I wandered the streets, fascinated by scenes of elephants wandering around in the busy city traffic. I took a walk past the site for the Elephant Buffet Breakfast which was scheduled for the following morning. I was amazed at the staggering amount of food being prepared. I guess 250 hungry elephants can get through a lot of fruit.

Goal 65 - Riding in the Elephant Parade

Friday, November 20, 2009
(Surin, Thailand)

Well, here's another example of achieving a goal in a manner way beyond what I could have hoped for, or expected. I had heard rumours that tourists could ride the elephants (for a fee, of course!) in the Elephant Parade, as the elephants make their way from the start of the route, which is right outside my hotel, to the Elephant Buffet Breakfast site.

I was up early, and in the hotel lobby I chatted with Irene, who was also wondering about riding an elephant in the parade. We decided to pool our resources and share the cost of an elephant taxi, and before long Irene had found us a pretty large elephant for the journey.

Outside the hotel preparations were in full swing. Colourful floats, dancers, and elephants gathered in the square. Irene introduced me to Darlien, our 30 year old female elephant, and Peter, our mahout, or elephant handler.

When the time arrived we climbed up onto a tall fence, put one foot on Darlien's huge head, and stepped up to sit on the seat. It seemed very high up, but the ride was very smooth and steady, and we soon relaxed.

The parade began, and we all filed down the main street, which was wonderful – a huge long line of elephants ahead and behind us. The atmosphere was very festive, the parade route lined with school children, families and holiday-makers.

The journey lasted about twenty minutes, and we were eventually dropped off at a tall platform just before the elephants entered the huge buffet area.

Irene and I followed a couple of elephants into the buffet street, and I was slightly surprised, having lived mainly in health-and-safety obsessed Western countries, that nobody seemed to mind, or wanted to stop us. We weren't the only ones, and the street was filled with a mixture of people and elephants, all wandering together. Busily taking photographs, Irene and I soon got separated in the crowds.

The elephants tucked in with enthusiasm to the huge spread of tasty elephant treats, and I wandered around happily among them. It was incredible to walk freely among the huge animals, and I was amazed at how relaxed and gentle they were when you fed them something. All the elephants seemed very aware of the people around them, and always avoided collision. You had to keep a wary eye behind you though, as they tended to approach quietly, and were right behind you before you even realised they were there.

I loved every minute of it. It was great fun picking up some bananas or corn, which seemed to be the favourites, and offering them to a passing elephant, which would collect them gently with its trunk, if it wasn't already well stocked up.

The atmosphere was wonderful, and I walked the length of the buffet a few times, sometimes taking pictures, sometimes just enjoying weaving in and out of the groups of giant creatures towering above me.

What an absolutely delightful experience!

That evening I met an American girl who was married to one of the mahouts, and had lived in the countryside nearby for several years. I had many questions about how she had met her husband, and what life was like living in rural Thailand. Her husband came along aboard his elephant, and suggested that I go for a ride with him. I explained that I had ridden in the parade earlier that morning.

I told him, however, that I had only ridden in the chair on the elephant's back. Perhaps if I could ride on the head, where the mahout usually sits? Of course, he said, that would cost me a little extra – a bottle of beer! I was happy to oblige, and was handed the mahout stick with which to steer my elephant through the busy evening traffic.

Goal 66 – Elephant Round Up

Sunday, November 22, 2009
(Surin, Thailand)

The main elephant show at the Surin Elephant Round Up takes place on both the Saturday and Sunday mornings. I had gone shopping for a ticket on Friday, and had bought one for the second show on the Sunday, as Saturday was selling out fast.

This morning I wandered to the stadium, buying a couple of BBQ sticks for breakfast on the way, from one of the many street-cart vendors. One of my favourite things about Thailand is that you never really have to worry about where your next meal will come from. You can simply wander around, and find a wealth of great stuff on sale from carts or small roadside restaurants anywhere you go.

I bumped into Irene again at the entrance to the stadium, but we had to go our separate ways, as we had tickets for different stands. For a while I sat chatting with the Thai family in the seats next to me, and enjoyed the show, which ran to pretty-much the same timetable as the rehearsal I had seen on the Thursday morning.

Once again, my favourite part was when over 200 elephants streamed into the stadium from all directions, and circled around in the centre – absolutely breath-taking.

When the elephant tug-of-war was announced, an invite was issued for the "farangs" (foreigners) to come down onto the field. I couldn't resist the chance to join in, meeting Irene again on the way to the middle of the stadium. Our team of around sixty humans was fairly easily beaten one incredibly strong elephant.

Irene, who had a very large camera, was pretending to be a press photographer. After the tug-of-war she simply stayed down on the edge of the field, so I did the same. My compact digital camera didn't look as convincing as her camera, but nobody questioned us. We had a brilliant front row view of the elephant football game. Next we waved our cameras about again, blagging our way into the expensive seating. High up in the stands we had a great view over the whole field for the mock battle finale.

What an awesome spectacle the whole event is. This year is the 49th time the festival has been held, so I suspect next year will be a huge event. I would heartily recommend that any elephant fan should make the trip to experience this incredible gathering.

I took the overnight train back to Bangkok, and stayed again with Tony. The flight to Christmas Island now departed from Singapore, instead of Kuala Lumpur as it used to, so a change of plan had been necessary. I could have probably got a flight direct from Bangkok, but for a lot less money, and a bit more adventure, I decided to catch the train instead.

I had enjoyed the train journey out to Surin, and the overnight sleeper on the return. There is something very relaxing about train travel. You can sit watching the world pass by outside the window, or read, or even watch a movie or write if there is power for the laptop, or the battery is well charged.

The first leg of the journey was a sleeper train down into Malaysia, stopping the next afternoon at Butterworth. I stayed overnight in a hotel there, and the next day continued on to Singapore.

Our arrival was delayed, and at the late hour there were no more buses running from the train station. I had to get a taxi to the airport, negotiating with the driver in Australian Dollars, as it was the only cash I had with me.

Another night on a bench at an airport was followed by a long day, during which I experienced an aborted landing at Christmas Island due to poor weather conditions. We had to fly two hours back to Singapore, and try again later in the day, so it was early evening by the time I got there.

Accommodation on Christmas Island had proved to be a bit of a challenge. I had no contacts there, and so had tried my usual second option, which was to search for a backpacker hostel. On Christmas Island the only options I seemed to be able to find were expensive resort-style rooms. I decided to try a new tactic. I had been in touch with the tourist information office on the island, asking them for the name of the local weekly newspaper. I placed an advert looking for a room I could rent for two weeks, explaining my story, and reason for coming to the island.

I hadn't had any response to the ad after the first week it ran, so I started looking into another back-up plan. I had heard of the couchsurfing website from several email contacts, and from others as I had travelled, and had looked into it a little. However, with all the contacts and offers I had from my own website, I had had little need of any other options so far.

Couchsurfing is a wonderful idea. You join the community, and if you are in a position to do so, can offer a couch, bed, or floor space to travellers passing through. Alternatively, as a traveller, you can search for couches available in the area to which you are travelling, and request to stay with a host offering a couch. Ideally, you look for people who are interesting, perhaps share similar hobbies, or appeal to you in some other way. It isn't really intended to be simply a free bed for the night, but a chance to meet other travellers, and mix with people from all around the world.

On Christmas Island there was only one registered couchsurfer, and Braydon said he would be happy for me to use his spare bedroom, although he wasn't sure just how long it would be available.

With accommodation semi-sorted out, I finally arrived at the island on the second attempt to fly in from Singapore. As I passed through customs, I was surprised to be greeted by the most friendly customs officer ever!

"Ah, here he is. Did you manage to get some accommodation arranged?" Obviously the customs guy read the local paper.

Someone else who had read the paper was local taxi driver Gordon, who had promised to meet me at the airport and take me wherever I needed to go on the island. I explained that I was supposed to be staying with couchsurfer Braydon, but was arriving much later than expected.

"Oh, I know Braydon, he's at the cinema right now, I'll take you to meet him."

"You know Braydon? How do you know he's at the cinema?" I asked, slightly bemused.

"Because I run the food concession there too," laughed Gordon. He seemed to have a little business empire on the island. From what I could gather, it also seemed that everyone knew almost everyone else in the small community.

On a bench at the open-air cinema I met my first ever couchsurfing host. I introduced myself to Braydon as quietly as possible during the opening scenes of the movie, in which John Travolta established the nasty nature of his character in "The Taking of Pelham 123".

My original plan had been to end my second trip back in Australia before Christmas, but since things had come to an end with Mel, I really didn't feel much of an urge to go back. In the end I decided that I was simply going to continue to travel. As I arrived on Christmas Island, I had no further concrete plans, and didn't even have a ticket off the island.

It seemed that airlines into the island were often in a state of flux. Flights were arranged by AIOTA (Australian Indian Ocean Territories Airline) who contracted whichever airline they could to fly in and out of the island. When I had first looked into getting to the island, they had been using Malaysian Airlines, and thus flying from Kuala Lumpur. But something seemed to have happened to that arrangement, and the flight I had come in on had been operated by Silk Air, a subsidiary of Singapore Airlines, hence my flight from Singapore. Nobody knew when the next flights back out to Asia would be, or where they would be flying to.

Wondering what to do next, I started to make some plans, and work out some flight possibilities. My first decision was to spend Christmas back in the UK with friends and family. I would probably then go to South Africa, as Martin and Rachel were planning on going down there in January to visit a friend, and watch some cricket. After that I would need to head to South America. Could I fit a visit to Iceland into the mix somewhere too?

As I considered the myriad flight options, it occurred to me that I was going to have pay for these flights somehow. I was down to a last couple of hundred dollars in my US account, so that wasn't an option. I discovered that I faced another, slightly trickier problem. I had just realised that my Australian credit card expired in two days, at the end of November.

I saw almost nothing of Christmas Island in those first two days. Braydon was at work, and I sat at my computer for most of the time, trying to get everything organised and paid for before my credit card ceased to function. It is amazing how complicated it can get when trying to juggle dates, events, airlines, different website booking systems, transfer times, accommodation options, and ensure that ultimately everything gels into a workable plan that covers all requirements.

Eventually I had several flights booked, including a flight via Sri Lanka from Kuala Lumpur to London. The only flight I hadn't managed to pay for was the one that would get me off the island. Although I had been assured that there would be flights operating again to KL by the following weekend, I was a little nervous.

As these flights hadn't yet been confirmed, I hadn't been able to pay, and now my credit card had expired. My new one would be sitting in my unopened mail at Mel's house, and I needed to get hold of it.

The email and telephone communications with Mel could be described as terse, and it was obvious that bridges had been well and truly burnt there. I did eventually receive my card in the mail, and finally booked a flight off the island to KL, the last piece of my global jigsaw puzzle.

Chapter 8 – Weeks 71 to 80

(7th December 2009 – 14th February 2010)

Christmas Island – Iceland – England
South Africa – Zimbabwe – Zambia
Chile – Peru – Argentina – Brazil

With most of my next set of flights now booked and paid for, I had plenty of time to explore and enjoy the island. During the day when Braydon was at work I would go snorkelling, cycling, or exploring on foot.

I had also met up with school teacher Rob, who had contacted me after reading the small piece I had placed in the local paper, when looking for accommodation. Along with a few of his colleagues, we had gone out one night looking for robber crabs, and had found a couple in the forest. They are huge, the largest we found being about the size of a soccer ball. When it was handed to me, I held it exactly as instructed – apparently they can snip a finger off very easily with pincers that are normally used to open coconuts.

The teachers were an active group. I went caving with them, played a round of golf, and was taken out fishing by Brad, who wasn't working that week. I caught a wahoo, the biggest fish I have ever caught, at around a metre long. As Brad already had a freezer-full of wahoo at home, I ended up with enough fish to feed Braydon and I for the rest of the week.

I really liked Christmas Island. It was green and lush, and full of incredible wildlife. Life seemed to be lived at a slower pace, and in the small community, everybody seemed to know each other. Crime was virtually non-existent. One day I had remarked to Braydon that one of his neighbours had left the keys in his moped outside. "Yep," Bray had replied, unsurprised and unconcerned. "They'll be there until he comes back in February!"

Towards the end of the first week, Bray discovered that my room at his apartment was going to be occupied, as his landlord had sold his own house, and would be moving in for a while. Fortunately, I fell on my feet. Claire, one of Bray's work colleagues, had been considering joining couchsurfing for a while, and offered me the chance to be her first couchsurfing guest.

One evening Claire took me along to the local radio station where a friend was broadcasting his weekly show. We took beers and a fish pie, made from the remnants of my wahoo, and sat chatting to presenter Kent. Before long I found myself being interviewed on-air, beer still in hand, in what was the most laid-back radio interview I had ever done.

Towards the end of the second week on the island, the spectacular migration that I had come to see looked like it was finally going to take place. Claire suggested that we go diving with another friend of hers, and see what could be seen of the migration from the sea. Although spectacular, the red crabs didn't turn out to be the highlight of the morning. Just as we finished the dive, and surfaced as a group, a call went up from the dive boat. "Whaleshark coming your way right now!"

We all put our regulators back in and sank just below the surface, waiting hopefully. The huge creature loomed out of the blue, bigger than any of the ones I had snorkelled with in Australia earlier in the year. It swam in a leisurely fashion right through the middle of our group, and with a little air remaining in the tanks, we could all follow for quite a while. What an unexpected thrill.

Goal 67 – Crab spawning spectacle
Saturday, 12th December 2009
(Christmas Island, Australia)

Yesterday evening Braydon collected me to drive down to South Point, where at the Chinese Temple there was a celebration of the birthday of the Chinese god Kang Tian Tai Di. Everyone was invited. The whole affair was very cheerful, and there was a huge spread of food put on. The was a seer who had flown in from Malaysia for the event, and he cut his tongue with a sword, blessed scrolls, and gave out advice while under the spell of several Chinese gods.

Everyone was welcome to join in, and we received red stamps on the backs of our necks, apparently for good luck. I also got a scroll with some tongue-blood just to be sure!

I wasn't really sure what was going on most of the time, but Kang Tian Tai Di certainly seems like a friendly sort of god. Apparently he had no problem with his Chinese worshipers wandering around the temple with a can of VB beer in their hand!

That evening I had a couple of extra beers at the pub – well, I had to find Simon from the dive shop to pay him for the morning's dives, and it would have been rude to dash off!

When the alarm on my phone went off at 2:45am this morning it felt like I had only just got to sleep, even though I had finally managed a pretty early night. I got up quickly to avoid falling asleep again.

Braydon picked me up soon afterwards, along with Dylan and Sarah, and we made our way to Greta Beach on the east coast of the island.

After a short walk down a dark forest trail we arrived at a stairway high above the beach. We could see the torches of others who were already there, far below us. As we climbed down, we could see more of the beach, and it was teeming with crabs. They were everywhere! You had to be really careful where you walked, and if you paused for more than a second or two, there would be crabs crawling across your shoes.

Even more spectacular were the steep, overhanging cliffs, which in places were completely red, no rock showing at all between the heaving and scrabbling masses of crabs. I was surprised that out of all those crabs clinging on upside down to the overhangs, I only saw one fall off.

We all watched fascinated as endless streams of crabs made their way down to the water's edge. As the waves covered them, they would lift their claws up and stand tall, bouncing up and down to release the eggs into the sea.

I took my shoes off to go into the water, to record some video of this incredible event, and for the rest of the morning had to do my best to avoid the sharp feet of the scrambling crabs. They never nipped though, just climbed over my bare feet and continued on their way.

As it started to get light the numbers coming down to the water thinned out. Eventually, as the sun rose, there were just a few stragglers coming down to release eggs. The cliffs were still packed with crabs. On our walk back to the vehicles, the road, which two hours earlier had been empty, was now alive with brightly coloured, freshly washed crabs heading home, their job well done.

It is now a few weeks until the return, when after hatching at sea the tiny baby crabs return to land. Apparently, if there is a big return, it is an equally spectacular event, and maybe one day I will come back to see that too.

Back at home I packed my bags, and had some breakfast. It was time to head to the airport, my fantastic two weeks on Christmas Island at an end. It really is a very special place, with some unique wildlife. My time here has also been made very enjoyable by the many people who have welcomed me into their lives.

I am of course particularly grateful to Braydon and Claire for their hospitality, and for a wonderful introduction to couchsurfing.

I was sad to leave Christmas Island, and the wonderful group of friends I had made there, but I had many flights booked. In the space of a couple of days I would transit from tropical island summer to mid-winter in Iceland.

On the flight from Sri Lanka to London, after the second meal eight or nine hours into the flight, I started to feel a little queasy. Maybe I shouldn't have had the omelette for breakfast, as it must have been kept warm on the plane for at least ten hours by that point. Less than an hour after I had eaten, I was vomiting in the lavatory, and was really starting to feel rough by the time we landed. I only just made it through customs at Heathrow before dashing into the bathroom to be sick again.

On the train to my brother's house I became more feverish, and when I got there both Martin and Rachel were out at work. I just climbed into bed and fell asleep for the rest of the day.

When they returned in the evening I dragged myself out of bed, still feeling terrible, and managed to eat a tiny bit of the dinner Rachel made. It was lovely to see them, but I soon had to make my apologies and head back to bed.

The next morning I felt a little better, but struggled to really concentrate on what I would need in Iceland, and my bags were re-packed rather chaotically. I had to get a flight back out of Heathrow in a couple of hours. I did, however, manage to find the time to weigh myself on the bathroom scales. Aided somewhat by food poisoning, I had reached my target weight of 70 kilos, or 154 lbs, and was well on the way to achieving another goal.

In Iceland I had arranged more couchsurfing accommodation, and was hosted by Magnus. I caught the bus from the airport to the city, and Magnus picked me up and showed me around. I was feeling much better by the time we met, but was still a little weak, and at Magnus's apartment I had an early night again. It had been a very trying few days, and in the chilly Icelandic evening, it already felt like months since I had basked in the tropical warmth of Christmas Island.

In my first couple of days in Reykjavik, capital city of Iceland, I wrapped up warm and went to explore. I had gleaned some impressive figures from the IcleandAir in-flight magazine. Apparently, Iceland boasts the world's highest literacy rate at 99.9%. Vatnajokull, covering 11% of Iceland, is Europe's largest glacier. Reykjavik is the world's most northern capital. The most impressive fact, I thought, was that over 85% of Reykjavik's energy is supplied by clean and sustainable resources, such as geothermal power, earning it the reputation as cleanest capital in the world. It was certainly a crisply clean place.

I visited one of the larger thermally heated swimming pools in the city, which had several hot plunge pools outside. It was quite an experience to sit out, wet and cold in sub-zero temperatures until it was no longer bearable, and then plunge into a deep pool hotter than you would choose to run a bath. At the end of the prescribed hot-tubs session, I lay in a warm shallow outdoor pool, gazing up in wonder as the sky darkened and filled with stars.

I had hoped to meet up with Anita, who had first contacted me long before the eBay auction had begun. She had been planning to do exactly the same thing, she had told me. Her intention was to sell everything she had except for her paragliding equipment, and then travel, paragliding at all the best spots around the world. You could say that the worldwide press coverage about my forthcoming auction had taken the wind out of her sails.

However, Anita had still achieved her goal, and was now on a paragliding world-tour, and would not be back in Iceland until the following summer. She had, however, made some virtual introductions, one of which was Hildur, a gorgeous blonde Icelandic beauty.

The fact that Hildur was gorgeous hadn't really come as a surprise. According to Magnus, and backed up by my own limited observation, there wasn't a woman in Iceland who wasn't gorgeous. Tim, one of Anita's paragliding buddies, was a British ex-pat now living in Reykjavik. His description of living in the city was similarly enthusiastic. "It's like walking around in the aftermath of an explosion in a super-model factory! I'm never going back to England!"

Hildur was also a couchsurfer, and after a few nights with Magnus, I moved onto Hildur's living room floor. On my first night there she suggested a quiet drink or two in town, and along with Tim, and a couple of her friends (all gorgeous, of course!) we headed into the city.

Reykjavik isn't very big. In fact the population of the whole country is tiny, at just over 300,000. Around 120,000 of those people live in the capital city. That's about the size of the town of Darlington in England, where my mum lives! So the main city centre is pretty small, but seems to have a huge array of cafés, bars and clubs. We ended up in one of the trendier bars, and among the stylishly glamorous locals I felt somewhat underdressed.

In the middle of the evening one of the girls pointed out that Iceland's most famous musical export, Bjork, had just wandered in. For the next couple of hours she did an impromptu DJ set on the decks in the corner. We didn't get home until around 5am. Just a normal quiet night out in Reykjavik, I was told. I don't think I could manage a big night out there!

Neither could my wallet. True to the rumours that I had heard, Iceland seemed ridiculously expensive, and one night out had made a serious dent in my funds for the week. I was going to have to make some financial re-calculations, I could see.

"You'll never guess what just happened! Imagine this scene," I had laughed to Hildur, as I jumped back in the car. I tried to explain how I had just been stood, fully clothed in my Icelandic winter gear, with little blue bags on my feet, shaking hands and chatting to a completely naked guy!

I had been asked to do an interview for Reykjavik daily newspaper Frettabladid, and had been interviewed by Sara, who needless to say, was stunningly beautiful. As a result of that interview I had been contacted by Heimir, who wanted to meet up for a coffee.

We met and chatted for a while, and parted ways. Afterwards I had called in to see Magnus again, and then Hildur kindly picked me up and we headed for her house. I asked if we could stop briefly at the swimming pool again to see if I had left my shampoo there the previous day.

Kitted out in my full winter gear, I had been given little blue bags to put over my boots so I could go into the changing room. I had looked around, feeling slightly odd as I headed for the showers fully clothed. As I approached I was greeted by a shouted, "Ian, Ian!", and was surprised to see Heimir striding towards me. He seemed completely unaware of what seemed to me to be a very amusingly absurd situation, and I struggled to keep a straight face as he spoke. All that was racing through my mind was how I could possibly get someone to take a photo of this strange meeting without seeming very suspect, as it would make a great tale for the blog! Eventually I managed to make my exit without being arrested – I had decided it would be wise to keep the camera in my pocket – and headed out to the car.

"Did you find your shampoo?" Hildur wondered.

"Ah, no, I didn't stay and look for too long. Let's just go to the shop!"

Goal 68 - Iceberg adventure

Monday, 21st December 2009

(Jokulsarlon, Iceland)

Car hire in Iceland seems outrageously expensive, and for a while I was trying to co-ordinate a trip with a couple of other couchsurfers, sharing car and fuel costs. One person changed their mind, and another never made it to Iceland at all, as her flight was cancelled.

Back to the drawing board! I suggested to a few of my contacts here that they might like to come on a trip, but most of them have to deal with the inconvenience of a job, and nobody that I know here could join me.

I had considered the bus, but there is only one bus during the week, which goes to Hofn, past where I want to be. The one-way cost is a ludicrous 11,900 Icelandic Krona – that's over $100. A flight from Reykjavik to Hofn is only a little bit more, at 13,900 ISK. But in winter there are no tours from Hofn to the lagoon I wanted to visit, so a car was my only option.

I had been given the phone number of a person who hires out their own car on a slightly cheaper, and much less formal basis than the car hire places, and I gave her a call last night. A deal was struck, and this morning Hildur dropped me off there just before 9am. I was surprised to be simply handed the key, even before I had been to the bank to change some money, and was told where the car was.

I had a bit of an issue at the bank, when they refused to change my Australian Dollar notes ("We don't take those!" I was told haughtily). After a couple of tries at the ATM outside the bank I found a card in my wallet that produced some cash. I paid for the car, and without any form of ID or paperwork being required, I was on my way. I didn't ask any questions – I'm sure the whole arrangement falls into somewhat of a grey area legally, but I was happy with the price I was paying.

It was still dark as I headed south-west out of the city. A couple of hours later the sky brightened and an orange dawn revealed the bleak landscape. I passed through the tiny town of Vik, where I intended to return for the evening.

Another couple of hours driving brought me to my destination, Jokulsarlon, or Glacier Lagoon at the foot of Europe's largest glacier, Vatnajokull. The thermometer in the car had been reading between minus 4 and minus 9°C for most of the journey, but a howling wind had made it feel much colder every time I had stopped to take a picture.

I wrapped up as warm as I could, adding extra clothing layers to body and legs, and headed out for a look around. The lagoon has been created by the glacier. As huge chunks of ice break from the end of the glacier, they float into the lagoon, and sail around until they melt enough to get through the narrow lagoon outlet to the sea. The lagoon has been measured to be 190 metres deep in places.

In winter the lagoon becomes frozen over, and the boat trips that run during summer are closed. There were still patches of water, but all of the icebergs were frozen in place, and there was the occasional creaking and groaning as the wind tried to shift the looser ones.

There wasn't a single other person there – no wonder really, as it was incredibly cold. A clear sunny sky lit up the icebergs and sheets of ice in dazzling whites and blues. It was very beautiful, and when out of the wind behind a hill, silent and peaceful.

I walked as far as the end of the glacier itself, where the newest, biggest icebergs are locked in the ice. From far away they had looked small, but close up they towered impressively, and it is quite staggering to think that nine-tenths of their bulk is hidden under the water. Below that lie the deep dark, icy cold depths of the lagoon. It would be awesome to dive under the ice around the icebergs! Maybe something for the next list?

I wandered along the shore of the lagoon for an hour and a half, but time quickly ran out, as the sun was already setting, and it would soon be dark again. As today is December 21st, winter solstice, it is the shortest day of the year. Official sunrise was at 11:23am, and sunset at 3:29pm. It was certainly the shortest day I had ever experienced, at a brief 4 hours and 6 minutes!

This is the furthest north I have ever been, not far south of the Arctic Circle, so today has officially been the shortest day of my life!

Like some of my other goals, this one has been a little harder to arrange than I thought it might be, and cost quite a bit more, but that makes it all the more satisfying to eventually achieve.

What a beautiful place. How incredible to have it all to myself, even if only for the shortest day!

Goal 69 lights up the sky (dimly!)
Tuesday, 22nd December 2009
(Vik, Iceland)

After my iceberg trip I stopped at the tiny little town of Vik, about halfway back to Reykjavik, and almost at the southern-most point of Iceland. At the youth hostel there I was the only guest for the night – it is very quiet here in the winter.

After checking in, I asked the German couple who were running the place about the Northern Lights. The last time they had seen them was in October! Oh dear. However, tonight was the best forecast for aurora activity for several weeks.

From Wikipedia I discovered that "auroras are the result of the emissions of photons in the Earth's upper atmosphere, above 80 km (50 miles), from ionised nitrogen atoms regaining an electron, and oxygen and nitrogen atoms returning from an excited state to ground state. They are ionised or excited by the collision of solar wind particles being funnelled down and accelerated along the Earth's magnetic field lines; excitation energy is lost by the emission of a photon of light, or by collision with another atom or molecule."

The two key factors are the strength of the solar wind, and the Earth's magnetic field. The strength of the solar wind goes through a ten or eleven year cycle, and at the moment is at the weakest point in the cycle. It will be at its strongest again around 2014 or 2015. (Ref: NASA Solar Cycle Prediction) As if this goal isn't tricky enough already, this makes it even more of a challenge.

I have been keeping a regular watch over the week on the SpaceWeather.com pictures of aurora activity, and things seem to change very quickly. Being based in the city, and without a car to dash out to a dark area, it's all very difficult.

Another useful source for aurora forecasts is the Geophysical Institute of Alaska University. Their forecast for last night was the best so far during the week that I have been here, but is still only a prediction of very weak activity.

I wrapped up warm in all my layers again and drove out from the hostel to the top of the hill outside the town. I made myself as comfortable as possible in the chilly, wind-buffeted car.

Being at the very south of Iceland, predictions were for low level lights on the northern horizon, but at 11pm there was no sign of anything. I decided to give it an hour or so, and at 11:20 I wondered if my eyes were playing tricks on me. The horizon looked much lighter. Maybe my eyes were getting accustomed to the dark?

As I watched I could see the light changing and shifting. It was a very pale white light, perhaps with the tiniest tint of green, and changes were slow and subtle. The appearance was as if cars with very dim headlights were moving slowly around behind the horizon.

I watched as the light moved and brightened along the horizon, and got out of the car for a few minutes. It was incredibly windy, and I soon got back inside!

The whole effect was very subtle, and slightly disappointing, having seen some amazing pictures of the show the lights can put on.

Just after midnight the lights dimmed, and I was about to give up and head home, when they brightened again slightly, more towards the north-west. For ten minutes they put on the best show so far, then the horizon darkened again, and I drove back to the hostel.

I tried taking a couple of pictures, but my little camera is not up to the job, and all I got was a black screen. To be honest, they would be uninspiring at best, even if I could have captured what I saw. I think perhaps much further north in Iceland might have been better.

I am pleased to have actually seen the lights, having had to put quite a bit of effort into doing so, but think that one day I might like to achieve this goal in a better fashion. I would love to see a much more spectacular display. Maybe I will get the opportunity in a few years time, when sunspot activity is higher? For now though, I am satisfied to have done the best I can under the circumstances.

My week in Iceland was over, and after endless months of travelling, I was really looking forward to getting home for Christmas. I felt like I just needed to take a break from everything.

On the morning of my departure, I hit a bit of a low point. I was up in plenty of time to get to the bus station, or so I had thought. However, as I walked through the cold, dark, silent streets of Reykjavik, it had become obvious that I had underestimated how long the walk would take. I had to run as much as I could, and with my rucsac on, dressed for icy weather, I was soon sweating profusely. I arrived at the bus station just in time to see the bus leave. The next one, I had asked? Four hours later, long after my flight would have departed.

The only feasible option was a taxi, at an appalling $100 for a 43km trip. Iceland had been expensive, but that just seemed outrageous. I was so disappointed with myself. It was the first flight or bus connection that I had missed, and it just happened to be in the most expensive place ever. It wasn't a huge financial blow, as I had saved much more than that by staying with my two generous couchsurf hosts who had welcomed me so readily. It was just so annoying – I had had plenty of time to set off earlier, and could have saved $100.

I sat brooding in the taxi, thinking about my time in Iceland. I didn't think I had enjoyed it quite as much as other places I had been recently, and I tried to analyse why. I think it was because I had probably spent around double what I expected to, and the two goals I had achieved there have been somewhat underwhelming. The iceberg lagoon had been spectacular, but I was disappointed the icebergs had not been the pyramid-shaped Titanic-sinkers that I had imagined they might be, alone and majestic in the middle of the ocean. The Northern Lights had been merely a dim moving glow on the horizon, looking no more spectacular than car headlights just behind the mountains.

Taken individually, both of these experiences would be very special. Coming after achievements such as the Great Wall of China, the elephant buffet breakfast, and the red crab migration, they seemed somehow smaller and more disappointing.

I realised that when I really got to the heart of the problem, I was just incredibly tired! Tired of travelling, of meeting new people, of struggling to organise things, and of always having to be on the go. At the airport I joined the line for yet another airport security check, and I knew I was right. I really didn't have the heart for all the hassle. For now the excitement of being in another airport, on another flight had lost its appeal. I just wanted to get somewhere, preferably not freezing cold, and just stop.

I couldn't do that just yet though. The next day was Christmas Eve, and I had some last minute Christmas shopping to do in the busy shops of London. I then had to travel half the length of Britain on one of the busiest holiday-traffic days of the year.

I knew I felt this way just because I was a bit down at the end of a difficult, cold and expensive week. I was also over-reacting to being on the receiving end of the hideously expensive taxi-mugging.

However, I also knew that in a few days I would be keen again, ready to fly down to South Africa. For now though, I just wanted a break!!

It had been a long time since I had spent the holidays at home. The last time I had spent Christmas Day at mum's house was in 2001. The next day Laura and I had flown to Bali, and eventually onward to Perth to begin out new life there. It was nice to be back among family, free to relax and enjoy the holiday.

I gave myself the break I needed, and between Christmas and New Year I did nothing at all to do with goals. I did no planning, wrote no blogs, and tried to think as little as possible about what needed to be done next. It was exactly what I needed, and I spent time catching up with friends and relaxing.

It was wonderful to give myself those few days off, and as far as possible to completely forget about anything goal-related. It was of course impossible to forget the whole adventure all together, as obviously many of the people that I hadn't seen for months, or in one case, years, had questions about where I have been and what I had been doing. They also wanted to know where I was going next, and what the next goals on the list were.

"You're living the dream!" was a phrase I would often hear, and I would smile and agree that it was certainly fun to live the life I was living. However, I think many people could only imagine the good side of such an adventure. It rarely occurred to people to consider the endless planning, the self-imposed regime of blogging, the fatigue of non-stop travel, the pressure of always having to be alert and aware, or the terrible ache of loneliness that could come creeping in uninvited.

"It can be a bit of a nightmare at times," was my usual tongue-in-cheek reply.

On New Years Eve though, it was time to get back to "living the dream", and I drove Martin's car south again, staying once more in Ealing.

I was refreshed and ready for new travels and new adventures. I was looking forward to flying down to South Africa for the next part of the journey.

New Year's Day brought with it an uncertainty that I had not felt the year before. At the start of 2009 I had woken up in a log cabin in the frozen beauty of the Canadian wilderness, looking forward to a year filled with travel and adventure. Although I did not know the specifics of where exactly my journey would take me, the whole year was already sort of mapped out.

In the coming year, in six short months, my 100 weeks would come to an end. Beyond that I really did not know what the future held for me any more. It was a question I was getting asked more and more now as the end of my adventure approached – "What will you do after the end of the 100 weeks?" – I still didn't have an answer!

As I had travelled I had spent quite a bit of time wondering myself what I might do, and perhaps more importantly, what I actually wanted to do afterwards. Other than my vague notion about doing some motivational speaking, I didn't really have much of an idea. What I did know was that the thought of going back to driving trucks in a mine, or even worse, a 9 to 5 job in a shop, filled me with dread. How could I ever go back to a life like that after such an incredible couple of years?

As I had when I moved out to Kalgoorlie to learn to drive the monster mining trucks, as I had when I decided that I was going to put my life up for sale on eBay, and as I had when I set off on my 100 weeks journey, I still just thought to myself that all I really wanted was an interesting life.

What was I going to do to keep life interesting after spending two years doing all the things that I have ever wanted to?

However, just as when I began the ALife4Sale adventure, at the time having no idea where life would take me next, I now had the same faith that something would come along that would catch my attention, and take me on the next part of life's adventure.

As a new year began, I wondered what that future adventure might be, and as a new journey commenced I looked forward with a small amount of trepidation, balanced by a huge excitement too. I couldn't wait to see where this might all lead in the end!

I spent most of New Years Day pottering around at Martin and Rachel's house in London, listening to music, and responding to a few Christmas and New Year emails. I also did some forward planning, writing emails to skydive clubs, ostrich farms and shark-cage-diving outfits in South Africa.

It wasn't until late afternoon that I thought about packing my bag, and did so with a casual ease and swiftness that surprised me. I had been carrying quite a bit of extra clothing over the last couple of weeks in order to deal with Iceland and England's chilly winter weather, but I was now flying back to summer, and for the next couple of months didn't imagine I would need much in the way of warm clothing. The only time I would possibly need warmer gear would be for trekking at height to Machu Picchu in Peru.

I therefore did some serious trimming back of the amount of clothes I was carrying, and when my main bag was packed, I looked at it in slight confusion. It was only about two-thirds full, including some extra food that I had packed. There wasn't the usual pile of extra set of stuff to cram into the smaller rucsac either. Had I forgotten something major, I wondered? I didn't think so. There was a largish bag of stuff staying at my brother's house, as I expected to be back there before the end of February.

Yes, I was sure that I had all that I would need with me for the next part of the journey. After all, I thought to myself, this is only a short trip, and I will be back in London in less than two months.

I marvelled suddenly when I realised that the prospect of a seven or eight week trip had now come to seem so short to me!!

There was now very little of the trepidation that I used to feel at setting off into the unknown for a long period of time, and I felt quite proud of the casual confidence with which I packed and departed for an unfamiliar continent.

This departure should really have been the start of my third trip, and did feel a little like that, but really it was just a continuation of trip number two. I had planned to have a longer break in Australia after Christmas Island, and felt sure that departing from there would then have felt like a bigger commitment. But I felt like I had no firm roots in the UK any more, nowhere that I really thought of as home, so it didn't really feel like I was leaving home.

Now my life in Australia was starting to feel like a long time ago too, and I wondered if there was anything at all left for me in Perth. The fact that I was drifting without anywhere to call home hit me again, and once more I wondered where this journey might be taking me.

Goal 70 - Table Mountain

Tuesday, 5th January 2010

(Cape Town, South Africa)

I was up early, bags packed, ready and waiting by the time Martin and Rachel arrived at the youth hostel, and we headed straight for the bottom of Table Mountain. Rachel dropped Martin and I at the start of the Platteklip Gorge route, and then went for a drive, planning to take the cable car to the top later on to meet us there.

We had hoped that an early start would avoid the heat predicted for the day, but I don't think we were early enough! The climb was steep, without much protection from the bright sun. We had plenty of water however, and progressed steadily. After a final scramble up a short steeper section, we made it to the top in good time.

The views of Cape Town spread out far below us were magnificent, and well worth the effort. We met with Rachel as planned, as she arrived on the cable car shortly afterwards, and took a wander around the Western Table, which offered fantastic views on all sides. It was good to see Lion's Head from above, which I had climbed the previous evening. People were paragliding off it, which must be fantastic.

We all met back at the bottom of the climb, Martin and I having decided that we had to walk back down again to truly be able to say we climbed Table Mountain. We hit the road out of Cape Town.

I only stayed in Cape Town for a few days, but it was long enough to get a good feel for the city, which seems very nice. It is set in a beautiful location, has a great climate, and a quick study of property prices there would indicate that it is around a quarter of the price of Perth!!

We headed out of the city towards the wine region of Stellenbosch, and it wasn't long until we were in a winery, trying out many of the fine South African wines. What a perfect way to unwind after a day on the mountain.

With a couple of glasses of good wine inside me, I sometimes become quietly reflective. I spent some time that evening looking back on my journey, wondering if it might have changed me at all. I was still basically the same person I had been before this all began, of course, but I did think that there had been some changes too.

Before my marriage fell apart I was very happy, fully satisfied with my life, with where I was, and with how the future was unfolding. One day that had all been suddenly stripped from me, and everything changed. Since then I hadn't ever felt the same contentment with my life. There had been a restlessness, a searching for answers, for meaning, and for my place in life. I hadn't yet found that calmness and satisfaction again.

There was still a sadness in me that I had never quite been able to vanquish. At times, particularly when travelling alone, it could be a heavy burden to carry.

Carrying this weight had changed me in a positive way, I felt, and I knew I was much stronger. I have always pretty self-confident, but now this feeling was greater than ever before. The more I faced uncertainty, challenge, fear and hesitancy, the easier I was finding it to deal with the next time.

My first departures, from Perth to Dubai, and then from England to Germany and onward to the USA had filled me with unease and trepidation. I remembered the talk I had with my brother before flying to Germany, expressing my fears about the coming months. He had understood, I think, and tried to make me feel better by talking about how exciting it would all be.

Now there was almost none of that hesitancy each time I set off for some new and unknown location. There was just an excitement and enthusiasm for new experiences to come.

I was also starting to feel the same way about life in general. Before the eBay sale I had no idea where it would all lead, and had been somewhat concerned about that. Now I still had no idea where this adventure was ultimately leading, but I was finding that it didn't seem to worry me in the slightest any more. I was confident that something would come along, and that I would be able to make the most of any opportunities that crossed my path. I had a great confidence in myself, and what I might choose to do with my own future.

I was really starting to feel that I could do anything that I wanted when this was all over.

Ah, but again I had to ask myself, what was it that I actually wanted to do?

Goal 71 – A murky glimpse of "Jaws"!
Thursday, 7th January 2010
(Gansbaai, South Africa)

The next morning we visited Drakenstein Correctional Centre, previously known as Victor Verster Prison. Here, twenty years ago, on 11th February 1990, Nelson Mandela took his long walk to freedom when, after 27 years of incarceration in South Africa's prison system, he was finally released.

It is a low security place, and looked more like a holiday camp with orange uniforms than anything else. Somehow we managed to talk our way in at the gatehouse, and ended up in the prison restaurant for breakfast, which was interesting and unusual.

There is a statue of Nelson Mandela at the gates, and I liked his words, printed on the plinth below:-

"For to be free is not merely to cast off one's chains, but to live in a way that respects and enhances the freedom of others.

The true test of our devotion to freedom is just beginning.

I have walked that long road to freedom. I have tried not to falter. I have made missteps along the way. But I have discovered the secret that after climbing a great hill, one only finds that there are many more hills to climb.

I have taken a moment here to rest, to steal a view of the glorious vista that surrounds me, to look back on the distance I have come. But I can rest only for a moment, for with freedom comes responsibilities, and I dare not linger, for my long walk is not yet ended."

We drove on into Franschhoek, which has many wineries, and stopped at a few places to try some samples. It is so much like the wine areas around Perth in Australia. If it wasn't for the mountainous backdrop, I could have believed I was back in the Swan Valley.

The southern coast is lovely, and we stopped at various towns and villages along our route to Hermanus, where we stayed at the backpacker hostel for the night. They were offering a great deal on shark cage dive excursions, which included a free night at the hostel, and a much cheaper tour than I had found anywhere else.

We were up at 5am the next morning, and drove to the "shark-central" town of Gansbaai, where we were relieved of our money by a surly shark dive leader. I never did find out his name. He never introduced himself, and didn't bother interacting enough, other than the swift financial transaction, for me to be interested enough to ask!

Down at the harbour our boat was lowered into the water, and we were off by 7am. At the shark site, the worryingly small cage was prepared, and we got an overview of how the morning would work. The *water clarity was poor, and the surly operator voiced doubts about whether we would see anything at all today. He wasn't quite as vague on the "no refund" policy though!*

However, we soon got a tantalising view of a shark on the surface, as the blood-and-guts mix of chum was thrown into the water. The surly operator seemed slightly happier, as everyone had now seen a shark, and any chance of any sort of complaint, or refund request had been completely negated.

We quickly donned wetsuits, and I was swift enough to be second into the cage, soon followed by Martin. (Rachel had stayed ashore, already asleep again in the car before we had even boarded the boat, having been very clear about her complete lack of interest in seeing any sharks at all.) There was another shark which swam passed the cage, and I managed to get one gloomy picture.

We then waited for quite some time, as people got in and out of the cage. Some didn't bother at all, a few only lasted a couple of minutes, as it was quite cold, but Martin and I remained in, determined to see more.

The next shark bashed right up against the cage, and as its tail thrashed right in front of me, the bottom part of it hit my wrist. I became the only person on our trip to touch one of the sharks! You are not allowed to do so unless a fin or tail pokes through the bars and you can't avoid it!

There were more sharks, or maybe it was the same one, I don't know! It was impossible to tell in the murky water. An estimate from up on deck, where they could see them a bit better, was that they were around three metres in length.

Eventually I gave up on trying to get any sort of decent underwater picture. For a while I enjoyed watching from just above surface level, as the sharks, attracted by the big fish-head on the yellow rope, swam past just a metre or two away.

It was a great experience to be in the water, right there with such magnificent creatures, but quite safe and secure. I was a little disappointed with the visibility, but of course that is the nature of any of these wild encounters - sometimes conditions are fantastic, sometimes not so good. It is always too easy to look at the amazing National Geographic or Discovery Channel pictures and videos of such encounters, and hope for something like that. It is important to remember however, that they may have had to spend months or years to capture such amazing images.

I thoroughly enjoyed the cage experience, but in what is probably going to be my first negative review of pretty-much anything in my 100 weeks journey, I have to make some comments on the company who took us out. Unfortunately, I felt that we were treated merely as a revenue source by the uncommunicative, uninformative operator. For a company that sells itself as an "eco-tour operator", there was not one word about the sharks' habits or life. I would have liked to see some sort of video intro, perhaps a bit of shark natural history, some discussion of the huge misunderstandings of shark behaviour, and some de-mystification of the fears that people generally have about sharks.

What did we get? Nothing!! "Everyone has seen a shark now, so there should be no question of a refund!"

My advice, if wanting to go shark diving, try an alternative operator to White Shark Ecoventures!!

Although the goal of diving with great whites had been achieved, to date this had been the least satisfying achievement of all of the goals successfully tackled. The water's had been murky, the sharks almost invisible, and the dive company rude, uninformative and concerned only about bottom-line profit.

Where had all the over-achievement gone? Surely I should be seeing the biggest shark ever, in the crystally-clearest of waters? I had maybe had my expectations raised too high by some of the most incredible good fortune on many of the previous goals.

I had a pretty low evening further along the coast in the picturesque town of Wilderness. Martin and Rachel wanted to go into town to eat, and picked somewhere that was a little outside my budget. I sat with them and looked at the menu, and made the decision that I was not prepared to pay that kind of money for food. I guess we had different financial priorities. They were on a three week holiday, and wanted a little luxury, and would soon be returning to work. I was trying to make my money go as far as possible, and without having done any work for over two years now, things were getting tighter.

I went to buy a healthy falafel, but as I approached the front of the queue, they ran out! Sorry! The only other options seemed to be expensive restaurants, a sausage in a bun, or a luke-warm pie from the petrol station! I had really wanted something healthy too. I wandered the town glumly, and eventually went back to the falafel place and persuaded them to make me a pita bread salad. I felt much better, as it was both cheap and healthy.

Sitting watching the band at the Friday night market, I felt pretty lonely, as couples and families enjoyed the party atmosphere around me. I finished my salad, and decided to walk to the beach. I stood in the dark with the waves lapping my feet. 46 years old, I thought to myself, and all alone on a beach far from anyone I knew, other than my brother and his partner, enjoying their dinner together. Where had it all gone wrong, I wondered? No partner, no kids, nothing!

Travelling with Martin and Rachel always made me think of Laura, as we travelled quite often as a group of four, and had done many things together. It was harder being alone with them. I always felt like there was an empty seat, someone missing, and that I was the odd one out, imposing a little on their holiday together.

In my wildest dreams I never expected my life to turn out like this. I thought about my wife, and how happy I had been with her, and the huge, black emptiness her departure had left in my life. Four years later, no matter what I did, where I went, or who I spend time with, that emptiness was still there at times, like a shadow from which I could never run away.

I knew I had to let the past go, to move on, to start again, and I had been trying to do so as best as I knew how. At times like this though, I would think that selling my life and making a list of 100 goals was just a way to do something that would make life seem worthwhile, to fill the black emptiness for a brief period.

I wondered why I even bothered. I wondered what it might be like to just swim out into the darkness, battle through the big waves, and just keep swimming until I could swim no more. Would it matter? Not really. I'd need to leave a message for Martin, and for others too, of course. A recording on my phone? A filmed message on my camera? If I left them on the beach they would probably be found by someone else, and the message might never reach its intended destination. Maybe a phone call? But Martin would answer his phone, when all I would want to do would be to leave a message.

Ah, but I was not serious, of course. Just like I hadn't been serious that night over four years earlier, when I had found out that Laura was sleeping with someone else, and at three o'clock in the morning had stood on the bridge over the freeway. I had watched the huge truck approach that night, thinking, “This one is yours – just got to jump at the right time.” I hadn’t been serious then, and I wasn’t serious now.

I laughed a bitter laugh. I could never do that, even at that low point years before, and I certainly wasn’t about to do it now. I was much stronger than that. But there was still a tiny small voice that suggested that it would be easy. Why keep on with this struggle, why not just give up and embrace what was inevitable one day anyway?

Eventually I wandered back up the beach to the now emptying town square. The band had finished, and tinny canned music was playing. I sat down on my piece of wall again to wait for Martin and Rachel, and the next song started. A band covering a Beatles song sang:

He’s a real nowhere man,
Sitting in his nowhere land,
Making all his nowhere plans,
For nobody.

That’s me, I thought – all alone, making plans for no reason, doing stuff that doesn’t matter to anybody, simply as a way to fill the endless emptiness of my nowhere life. Tears filled my eyes.

Maybe the book I planned to write should be called “Nowhere Man”!

“Fuck,” I thought to myself bitterly. “I’m so fucking lonely!”

Goal 72 – riding a real ostrich this time!

Saturday, 9th January 2010
(Outshoorn, South Africa)

After the excitement of the shark cage dive we headed further east along the coast to the Garden Route. In Wilderness Martin and Rachel found a luxurious room, and I got a cheapie dorm bed at the backpacker hostel, which had a fantastic view along the coast.

The next day we took it easy, and played a round of golf, in which I was soundly thrashed by both Martin and Rachel. We decided to spend another night in Wilderness

A drive up into the spectacular mountains early on Saturday took us to the ostrich-farming town of Oudtshoorn (pronounced “oats-horn”), where at the huge Safari Ostrich Show Farm we met up with marketing manager Billy.

I had emailed a couple of ostrich (or volstruis in Afrikaans) farms, and Billy had replied, offering to help out with my ostrich-riding goal. He introduced me to ostrich handler Leon, and before long Martin and I took turns to climb aboard a huge male ostrich called Sarkozy for a couple of photos.

It was then time for me to try to actually ride Sarkozy. The last time I was aboard an "ostrich", it was much easier to handle, as I completed Goal 55 back in August last year, leaping from Worthing Pier in the annual Birdman competition.

This time the real thing was much feistier, and I climbed aboard, following Leon's instructions. He had asked if I wanted the tame, tourist ride, where the ostrich handlers would support me, or if I wanted the "adventure ride"! I imagine you can guess what I picked – I should have maybe stuck with the tamer option, as the eventual, inevitable fall off was pretty painful!

Afterwards we went on the farm tour, which was very interesting. They really are quite incredible birds. The whole set up was very professional, and the tour we took was exactly the sort of thing I had expected from the shark dive operator.

We saw video of the hatchery where the eggs are incubated, and then saw chicks in the paddocks. There were several different types of ostriches from different areas of Africa – all very educational and informative. After photos and rides for some of our tour group, the grand finale, a spectacular ostrich race, was brilliant.

This completes the last of the five extra goals, added by people voting on what they thought I should add to the list of 95 goals I had come up with.

I didn't let Martin and Rachel have any idea about how I had felt on the Thursday evening, and as usual, an exciting adventure had soon put the smile back on my face, and the laughter back in my heart. It had also, I suspected, cracked a rib, as I was in quite a bit of pain, and any laughing really hurt. It would have been a lot less painful if I still felt as miserable as I had two nights earlier. But that was over and done, and with one of the swift mood changes that travelling seems so easily capable of causing, I was back to my old self again.

I waved goodbye to my travel companions as they dropped me off on the outskirts of Plettenburg Bay. They were turning back for Cape Town, and their return flight to Johannesburg. I planned on travelling further east, as far as Port Elizabeth, and then hoped to head north by train from there.

I was slightly hesitant about hitching in South Africa, and wasn't picked up for a while. Eventually a shared minibus taxi pulled up, and after some negotiation I secured a lift as far as Bloukrans Bridge, where I planned to stay for the night.

Bloukrans Bridge is the highest single span concrete arch bridge in the world. With a maximum height of 216 metres above the stream far below, it is very impressive. At the bridge you can find the world's highest bridge bungee jump, even bigger than the Pont de l'Arluby in France, which I jumped from in 2008, achieving my second goal. The French jump is the world's third-highest bridge bungee at 182 metres.

It is a very slick, professional setup, with a fantastic viewpoint. There is even a pub overlooking the jump, with a live video feed. The hostel is also only metres away and I was the only person booked in at first. I was left with the place completely to myself for the afternoon and evening. I took a wander out onto the bridge in the evening, after the bungee jump shut down – it really was knee-tremblingly high!

The next day, I couldn't help myself, and paid the fairly reasonable cost for the jump. I made my way with my group to the centre of the arch. What an incredible feeling. As I jumped, I tried to imagine what a BASE jump would be like, with a parachute but no bungee cord. With almost perfect timing, at about three-and-a-half seconds into the four-second freefall, I reached for a parachute handle. Maybe a BASE jump lies somewhere along the path of my future? The idea scares me a lot though!

In the hostel I had met up with late evening arrivals Sandor and Melanie, a young couple from Germany travelling by car. I managed to arrange two days on the road with them, taking me to my destination in Port Elizabeth.

I also had another fortuitous meeting at the Bloukrans Bridge backpacker hostel with John, who was a helicopter instructor in PE. We chatted for a while about what we were both doing there, and I mentioned that learning to fly a plane was one of the goals on my list. "You need to speak to my pal Gerhard about flying lessons." When I arrived at Port Elizabeth I did, making some potential future plans.

I caught an overnight train to Johannesburg, and tried to find a shared taxi to take me up into Zimbabwe, but didn't have much luck. Eventually I caught the overnight bus, after a long rainy afternoon at the main transport hub.

The bus to Bulawayo was a wonderful journey, involving a very entertainingly chaotic night border crossing from South Africa into Zimbabwe. Many vehicles were making the same journey, and of the hundreds of people at the border at 3am, mine was the only white face I saw. I chatted with my fellow passengers, many of whom made the journey on a fairly regular basis. Tony made sure I joined the right line at the border, and paid no more than the standard visa fee.

I had a full day to explore Bulawayo, which looked like a great place. I found the railway station and left my bags in a storage locker, then went for breakfast in a nearby café. I decided to change some money with one of the dodgy looking, illegal money changer touts, who offered me a good rate. I was keen to get my hands on some out-of-date Zimbabwean Dollars, and we struck a deal. As we changed the money, he rolled his half of the transaction up and surreptitiously passed it to me under the table, as there was a policeman sitting nearby. What fun, I thought, trading on the black market like a professional already, and I've only been here five minutes!

My connection left, I looked at the bundle he had given me, and an alarm-bell suddenly went off in my head. I knew immediately what had happened, and unrolled my bundle with a sinking heart. I had 60 billion Zim Dollars, but not the 150 Rand I should have had too. He had switched his bundle to another pre-prepared one as we exchanged, and what I had was worthless paper and nothing more. I dashed to the door, and down the street, but he was already gone!

Back at the café I sat down again and laughed. How could I have missed that? I thought I was a pretty seasoned and worldly-wise traveller, and yet had fallen for one of the oldest tricks in the conman's handbook! Still, I thought as I smiled to myself wryly, it could have been a lot worse, as I was only US $20 out of pocket. It was a very cheap lesson really, and one I wouldn't forget anytime soon.

Of course, I couldn't be too upset, as I was now a billionaire! Unfortunately the Zim Dollar was taken out of circulation in 2009 as its value went into freefall, and a billion dollars would no longer cover even the cost of a loaf of bread. The currency was now a wild-west sort of mixture, with prices in both US Dollars and South African Rand. Purchases could also be made in any other sort of well-recognised currency, such as Pound Sterling, or Euros.

The overnight train to Victoria Falls reflected the faded glory of what was once a stable and successful economy. For the amazing bargain price of twelve dollars, I bought a first class overnight sleeper ticket. Although the old British rolling stock had long ago seen better days, the journey was reasonably comfortable. However, calling the journey first class was somewhat misleading, and true only in that it was a step above second class, where more people have to fit in the same size cabin.

I was lucky enough to have a cabin to myself, and was amused that almost none of the cabin fixtures were in serviceable condition. There were no lights at all, just bare wires hanging from holes where lights may once have been. The window was jammed, the sink held in place by wire, and the small table kept collapsing. However, being in first class meant that sheets and blankets were included in the ticket price. I slept very well.

Goal 73 – regal Victoria Falls
Sunday, 17th January 2010
(Victoria Falls, Zimbabwe)

The town of Victoria Falls itself is pretty small, and it's only a short walk from the station to the town centre. However, it is possible to attract double-figure pesterings in such a short distance! I think being white here means that you have a huge $$$ sign above your head. It is absolutely impossible to walk anywhere without being offered taxi rides, tours, statues, figurines, necklaces, food, drink, and of course, Zim Dollar notes! I will be very careful if doing any further note trading!!

Once I found a hostel I showered and changed, which was wonderful after a couple of long days and nights of travel. After lunch I wandered back into town, and then down towards the falls. Chatting with a family returning from viewing the falls, I decided that I would need my waterproof camera case – they were soaked! I opted to save my entry fee for the next day, and instead took a wander down the road to the border crossing into Zambia.

There I found out that I could pass through the Zimbabwe border, even without my passport. I wandered down to the bridge over the Zambezi, in no-man's-land, between the two countries. There were more enthusiastic touts on the bridge offering bungee jumps, zip-line rides, statues, jewellery, and of course, more Zim Dollar notes – I was very tempted to buy a $50,000,000,000,000 (fifty trillion) note for a couple of bucks!

The view from the bridge back upriver to the falls is spectacular, as is the view downstream, a deep gorge with a huge river roaring through the middle, with the spectacular-looking Victoria Falls Hotel perched on the edge in the distance. You can't really see all of the falls, as much of it is hidden around the corner. The height is spectacular indeed, especially when seen with a couple of people on the little island above the falls to give some scale.

One of the local tourist policemen took me down a little back path to a great viewpoint looking back up the river to the bridge.

In the evening I found an internet café, and managed to book a flight back to Johannesburg from Livingstone in Zambia, so had to change my plans slightly. I had decided that flying back to Jo'burg was the only option, as overland would have taken two more days, and I didn't have enough time or patience for more bus journeys. I had expected to fly back from Victoria Falls, planning to take a one day trip into Zambia, thereby avoiding another hefty visa fee. However, a flight from Livingstone and a visa are the same total cost as the flight alone from Vic Falls.

The next morning I packed my bags and walked down to the falls entrance, running the gauntlet of touts once again. Entry was a multi-currency option, and I decided to pay using some of my remaining SA Rand, saving my US Dollars, which are much more widely accepted here.

The views of the falls are stunning. I started at one end at the thundering Devil's Cataract. I followed the gorge along on the opposite side to the falls, seeing the Main Falls, Horseshoe Falls, and ending up at Danger Point, where you can see the river exit the gorge and head down under the bridge.

The Horseshoe Falls are amazing, at over 100 metres high. The noise and spray is incredible, and at Danger Point it was impossible to avoid getting soaked. I was glad I had waited to bring the waterproof case for the camera!

After achieving my goal of seeing the falls, having spent a good long morning admiring the Zimbabwe side, it was time to cross the border into Zambia.

I crossed the border on foot, negotiating the fee in a mixture of UK Pounds and US Dollars. I got the better part of the deal, I thought, with the seemingly flexible visa costs.

In Livingstone, I stayed in what I believed might well be the best value hostel I had found so far. For the equivalent of $5 I had a very comfortable bed in a lovely clean room. In the central grassy courtyard there was a beautiful swimming pool, hammocks, chairs and tables, and a bar playing a great selection of music. There was free internet access too, and most unusual, a climbing wall. The only thing missing was a communal kitchen, but a friendly chat with one of the staff ensured I could get hot water whenever I wanted for tea or coffee.

I enjoyed a different view of the falls, spending the afternoon in the falls park on the Zambian side. That evening, accompanied by fellow hostel guest Cameron, I caught a taxi to the Royal Livingstone Hotel, where we sat sipping chilled beers watching the sun set over the falls.

On the way back into town we discovered that Zambia was playing Cameroon in the African Nations Cup that evening, and the soccer game would be broadcast live. We went in search of a pub showing the game, and were welcomed with open arms by the friendly locals. Once again I enjoyed the unusual experience of being part of a minority, being one of just two white faces in the bar that night. Unfortunately Zambia lost, but spirits still seemed high after the game. It was quite late when we got home and the hostel was dark and quiet.

Once again I experienced the strange feeling of being on one continent one day, and another continent just a few short hours later. From Johannesburg I flew to Santiago in Chile, where I stayed for a couple of days in a delightful little hostel close to the city centre. I then flew on to Easter Island, or Rapa Nui as it is known by locals there.

There were three couchsurfing hosts on the island, two of whom already had guests staying. I managed to secure a spare room with Andres, who was great fun. He taught me some Spanish, took me on a couple of island tours, and lent me his bicycle. Unfortunately I took a bit of a tumble on a gravelly corner. The brakes were the wrong way round – I am used to the left lever operating the back brake, not the front one! A handful of front brake, in an emergency on a gravelly corner, had predictably painful results! Despite my basic bicycle blunder, Andres happily lent me his moped the next day. I was pleased that I managed to stay aboard that without incident.

Easter Island is quite breath-taking. The whole place reminded me very much of Christmas Island. The islands are similar in size, Easter Island being slightly bigger, I think. Both are formed by past volcanic activity, both pretty tropical, although the slopes of Easter Island are bare compared to the thick jungle of Christmas Island. Both are very remote.

The population on Easter Island is bigger than that of Christmas Island, around 3,800 here compared to 1,400 on Christmas Island. The little island town, Hanga Roa has a very similar atmosphere to its counterpart on Christmas Island, with a very local, friendly feel to it. There were several small shops filled with hideously expensive food, all of which has to be flown in from afar, just like Christmas Island.

Riding around in the sun on Andres's moped was incredible fun, and I marvelled that at times this was all that was needed to make me as happy as I had ever been – sunny weather, a trusty moped, and an interesting place to explore.

Easter Island is of course famous for its moai, the huge standing statues that can be found all over the island, staring silently over the land, mysterious sentinels from a previous time.

I was invited to dinner by Diana, one of the other couchsurfers on the island, and met her guest Annette from England. Annette and I hit it off immediately. She had a fascinating, and slightly sad tale of her own long quest. She had spent two years planning, and one year enjoying a motorcycle ride from the tip of Alaska down through Canada, USA, and the whole of South America. She too knew the joys and heartaches of travelling alone, and we had a lot of stories to share.

Her journey had ended about 200 miles short of her ultimate destination, the southern tip of Tierra del Fuego, when she had woken in hospital with a bad concussion and a broken collarbone. She had no idea or recollection of what had happened or how she had got there. Her bike was practically written off. She was trying to enjoy her last few days before returning to England, to resume her life where she had left off a year earlier.

We both wondered how you could go back to the life you had lived before, after experiencing the highs and lows of such an extended adventure. How do you mix with people who had no concept of all that you had been through, and simply settle back in to some sort of routine?

"How do I do that?" Annette wondered. I had no answer. It was a question I was going to have to answer for myself in a few months.

Goal 74 - Rapa Nui
Monday, 25th January 2010
(Easter Island, Chile)

Last night I was invited to Diana's house for dinner, the second of the three Easter Island-based couchsurfers that I have met, and she made a fantastic spagetti bolognese. She is from Switzerland, and has been living on the island for a year and a half, working as an alternative healer. I met five of her Swiss friends who were visiting, as well as Annette, another couchsurfer staying there.

Annette is from New Zealand originally, but has lived and worked all over the world. She is right at the end of her own incredible journey. We found we had a lot in common, and spent the evening comparing travel experiences, injuries and adventures.

We met the next morning for breakfast in a café. Annette had decided to hire a car for her last day on the island, but needed me to act as her driver, as her shoulder isn't up to the job.

By 11am we were in a Suzuki 4WD and heading out of town for Rano Raraku, a volcanic crater on the north-east side of the island, which was known by the original inhabitants as Rapa Nui, the navel of the world. The crater was used as a quarry, and it was here that many of the amazing stone heads, called moai, were originally quarried and carved, before being transported to their standing locations.

The place is absolutely extraordinary. There is a lake in the volcano crater, and dozens of wild horses roam around freely. On the inside slopes of the volcano crater, many moai stand looking westward. Some have fallen over, some are only half finished. We wandered around between them, marvelling at the work involved to put them there. On the outside of the crater there are many more heads, even bigger and more impressive. The whole place has a strange, slightly surreal feel about it, and we happily soaked up the atmosphere.

Not far away, at the coast, we stopped to look briefly at Ahu Tongariki, where there is an impressive, and much photographed line of fifteen heads standing silently side-by-side. It is quite breath-taking.

We followed the road all the way around the island, stopping at several other sites, including the spectacular Ahu Akiva. Here another line of 7 moai face directly towards where the sun sets at the equinoxes.

The whole island is steeped in history. Much mystery still surrounds the moai, and the reasons for building them.

We returned to town, and ate wonderful empanendas, a sort of huge pie filled with meat and cheese. We sat watching surfers on the popular surf break, until it was time for Annette to pack her bags.

I drove her home, and once she had packed, I dropped her off at the airport.

Back at home I met Andres, and as promised he was ready to give me my first Spanish lesson. We spent an hour or so working through numbers and colours, using pool balls as teaching aids.

Annette had only needed to hire the car for the minimum 8 hours, but for 5,000 Pesos more (about $10) the hire could be extended to 24 hours. I had paid the extra, and have the car until tomorrow morning. Andres had some work to do, so I headed up the hill out of town to watch sunset at the lovely high point at Orongo. The stunning viewpoints look out across the ocean on one side, and down into a huge volcanic crater on the other.

The view westward over the sea looks over two tiny islands offshore, where clans would compete against each other in a dangerous "Birdman" competition. This involved climbing down the steep cliffs, swimming out to the further of the two islands, getting a bird's egg, and being first back to shore and up the cliffs with an unbroken egg. A representative of the winning clan would hold the powerful position of "Birdman" for the next year.

Just before I arrived on the island I downloaded and watched the 1994 Kevin Costner-produced movie "Rapa Nui", which wonderfully dramatises the making of the moai, and the birdman competition. It is well worth watching, particularly for some historical context to the spectacular locations.

Before I left the island I heard some bad news which looked like it might impact on one of the next goals planned. In Peru there had been terrible rains, and the subsequent floods had badly damaged the railway lines that carried trains into Machu Picchu, the ancient Inca city. Everything was uncertain, but there really wasn't much that could be done but wait to see how things panned out, and just hope for the best.

I planned to meet Val, my climbing buddy from Colorado, in Cusco, Peru. He was going to accompany me for two weeks on the continuing South American adventure.

Should we consider changing our plans, he wondered when we chatted online? Maybe we should go to a different area where the flooding hadn't been so bad? No, I had replied, it's Machu Picchu or bust! Never give in!

During the last couple of days on the island, with a bit of spare time on my hands, I spent some time working on an idea I had had for the end of the journey.

My 100 week-long adventure began on Sunday 3rd of August 2008, when I flew from Perth in Australia to Dubai, to achieve my first goal. At the time, I had not worked out the actual end date of my travels. Eight months later I was back in Perth again. I had finished my first round-the-world trip, during which I had achieved over thirty of my goals. I needed to plan my second and third trips, and I worked out exactly when the 100 weeks would come to an end.

I had always seen this whole idea being controlled by the time period, rather than the goals themselves. I always imagined completing my travels at the end of week 100, hopefully with 100 goals achieved, but satisfied if I only managed 87, 93 or 97. It had become the adventure and the people that meant more to me. The goals themselves had always been intended as a sort of framework around which to build my big adventure.

Of course, it would be nice to achieve all of my goals, but as well as being an optimist, I have always been a realist too. I accepted that some things may be beyond my control, and may hinder the completion of one or more goals. Of course, I can always complete any unfinished goals at any time after the 100 weeks.

So I had worked out the end date, 100 weeks to the day from when I first flew out of Perth, and was pleasantly surprised to find that it fell on Sunday 4th July 2010. This, being Independence Day, is of course a pretty big day in America, when the 1776 signing of the Declaration of Independence is celebrated.

A large part of my first trip was spent in the States, and again on my second trip I had spent several months there. In fact, overall, USA would be the country that I would spend more of my 100 weeks in than any other, including Australia!!

It therefore seemed only fitting that my journey should end there, on this big celebratory day. I thought long and hard about where I should hold my celebration, and eventually decided that New York seemed like the best place.

Why? Well New York was the place where I had first arrived in the States back in October 2008, and my first US-based goal was achieved there when I went to see the Statue of Liberty. Lady Liberty has for many years represented, among other things, hope and freedom, and for many people arriving from other parts of the world has symbolised a fresh new start.

That was, after all, what the past few years had been all about for me. My life had taken a dramatic and unexpected turn towards the end of 2005, and still looking for answers and closure, a couple of years later I put my whole life up for sale on eBay. That led on to this goal-setting adventure, and I had certainly made a huge change in where my life was heading.

The end of my 100 weeks was also going to be a new starting point for me. As I planned my final day, I had only the vaguest idea of what that new start might be.

What better place to end my journey than in the city where my first American goal was achieved? At that time it wasn't possible to go right up the statue, and so along with a few others who joined me, I only managed to get to the pedestal. Now however, it was once again possible to go right to the crown. I made a booking online, managing to secure some crown-access tickets for 4th July 2010, and was looking forward to finally going up to the top.

I emailed all my friends and family, and everyone who I had met so far on my journey. I asked them if they would like to join me, giving them a chance to book their tickets early, while there were still plenty available.

I then emailed everyone who had ever been in touch with me through the two websites, extending the same invite to them. Finally, I made a webpage inviting anyone else who might like to join in too.

On the flight from Easter Island back to Santiago, I watched a movie called "Away We Go". It was directed by Sam Mendes, who directed one of my all-time favourite movies, "American Beauty". I sat alone on the darkened plane as the movie ended, and tears rolled down my cheeks. I thought of all that might have been in my life and wondered once again how it all went wrong. Was it taken away from me, or did I somehow let it slip away in some way that I still didn't understand.

Most of the time the past, my life with Laura, was pushed away to the back of my mind, but every now and then, when least expected, it would be placed front-and-centre again. It still hit pretty hard when I thought about what could no longer be.

We would have been such good parents, I thought. We would have been a great team. We would have had awesome kids. There was a huge probability that I would never have that in my life now.

Had I messed it all up? Could I have done anything different? I guess I will never know the answer to that.

I thought I had come to terms with this, but that night on the plane I wondered if I ever truly will.

The character Rhona asks in the movie, "Are we fuck-ups?" and I asked myself the same thing.

Am I just a fuck-up? Sometimes I think that I maybe I am.

Sitting on the following flight from Santiago to Lima, I listened to some music, and picked a favourite album that I hadn't listened to for quite some time. The lyrics of my favourite song from the album took on a poignant new relevance in light of my current mood. “Runaground” by UK group James talks of the feelings of lost love, and of drifting aimlessly.

I was really going to have to stop watching movies and listening to music on flights if it was going to get me down like this every time!

In Lima I stayed for a couple of nights with couchsurfer host Claudio, who proudly showed me around his city. Once again I thought about different styles of travel. If I had had more money from the start I might have been tempted to stay in luxurious hotels, and travel in style. Travelling on a very tight budget meant that I had gratefully accepted the kindness of strangers, whether offered via my own website, because of the publicity I had received, or whether through the slightly more random contacts provided by couchsurfing. In so doing, I was finding time after time that I was having the most wonderful experiences.

What better way was there to see a new city than with an enthusiastic local to show you around? Sure, you could take a guided city tour, but that is so much more impersonal. With Claudio I got to see the city centre, drink the local alcoholic drink of choice, pisco sour, in the finest hotel in town, and then spend the afternoon by the pool and on the beach at an exclusive members-only health resort.

Back at Claudio’s house another couchsurfer joined us for the night, and I felt a mild shame at being the lowest common denominator linguistically! It sounds like a bad joke – “An English guy, a Peruvian, and a French man meet at a couchsurf house... what language do they speak together? English of course, ‘cos the English guy is so poor with other languages!!”

It was even more embarrassing when I admitted that learning some more French and a bit of Spanish were two of the goals on my list! Oh dear!

The news about the flooding at Machu Picchu got progressively worse, as the extent of the damage was revealed. Two people had died in a mudslide on the Inca Trail, and the trail had been closed. People trapped by the damage to the railway in the little town of Aguas Calientes had to be airlifted out. Initial repair estimates for the railway had been about five days. This now looked as if it would be more like two months. With the Inca Trail closed and the railway out of action, there was now no way into Machu Picchu.

Over the previous few days I had heard nothing but words of warning, and messages of doom and gloom regarding our chances of getting to see Machu Picchu. The realistic side of me had to agree, it did seem like an impossible task under the current circumstances.

However, I had already paid for my tickets, and any change would incur heavy penalties. I decided to continue on to Cusco, and see how the situation looked when I got there. As always, I was trying to maintain a positive outlook, and hope for the best.

I also tend to think that you have to look at a problem from all sides, and seek an alternative option that others may not consider. Creativity and flexibility are the keys to solving problems. I had a couple of ideas that were probably worth investigating, and wasn't yet ready to give up on this goal.

I talked over one of my ideas with Claudio, and he agreed that there were possibilities. I had read of another lesser known route into Machu Picchu, but this would probably be closed too. Some financial "persuasion" might be possible. Claudio wrote some wonderful Spanish phrases for me, delicately asking what might be offered to allow a person to pass a checkpoint.

It was a short flight from Lima. I arrived in Cusco at around 11am, and made my way to Ronnie's apartment. Ronnie was another couchsurfing host that Val had contacted, and he was kindly accommodating us for our stay in Cusco. Val was scheduled to arrive a couple of days after me, so my task now was to try to find some way of resolving our Machu Picchu dilemma.

Cusco itself had also been hit by flooding, but as I wandered around town that afternoon, it was hard to tell. All seemed to have returned to normal, apart from some obvious places where water had pulled away a lot of earth, or part of a pathway.

The city was very eye-catching, with green mountains on all sides. I was surprised to discover that it was much bigger than I expected, with a population of around 500,000 people living there. At an altitude of 3,400 metres, or just over 11,000 feet, it is one of the highest cities in the world.

Needless to say, the next day I was very ill with altitude sickness, and lay in bed for most of the morning. I managed to rouse myself for a tour Ronnie had booked for me in the afternoon, and bought some sickness tablets which put me back on my feet by the next morning.

I had been looking forward to having Val join me for a couple of weeks. I had been travelling a lot on my own recently, and was pleased to have some enthusiastic company along. I met Val at the airport, and we took a taxi to Ronnie's to drop his bags off. We then headed into town to see what we could find out about the possibility of getting anywhere near Machu Picchu.

Most of the news we received was very negative, but a couple of people had suggested that there may be a possible route from the other end of the railway line, passing through the hydro-electric power station, and trekking along the railway line from the opposite direction.

Ronnie worked as a travel guide, and had been conducting enquiries of his own. Back at his apartment, he seemed much more positive about getting to Aguas Calientes. From there, he said that he could make no promises, as the bridge which crossed the river was possibly going to be demolished, as it has suffered so much damage. If the bridge was gone there would be no way across the river, to reach the road which climbed up to Machu Picchu.

With no idea how things might pan out, we made plans to set off early the next morning and try to get to Santa Maria by bus. From there we could possibly get to Santa Teresa by car, and maybe by car again to Hidro Electrica if possible. Finally we would have to walk along whatever remained of the rail lines to Aguas Calientes. This section would possibly involve some detours into the jungle around missing or flooded sections of line, but we hoped to get to Aguas Calientes by the end of the day. It was certainly going to be a challenge and an adventure, to say the least. We would be some of the first people to try to do this since disaster struck, and nobody seemed to know how bad things really were on this route.

Goal 75 – Machu Picchu challenges! - Day 1

Friday, 5th February 2010
(Cusco, Peru)

On the evening before our departure, our couchsurfing host and potential guide unfortunately had to pull out of our expedition to try to see Machu Picchu. He had been conducting enquiries with officials throughout the day to try to get the latest information, and had been told that the whole area is closed to tourists. Furthermore, any guide now bringing tourists into the area against official regulations may be subject to arrest, and potentially lose their guiding permit. We fully understood Ronnie's decision not to take us, but decided that we would still make the journey ourselves, and see how far we could get.

There are only three ways to get to Machu Picchu: by train via the railway from Ollantaytambo, on foot via the railway line from Hidro Electrica, both options leading to Aguas Calientes, the town from which you would be able to climb up to Machu Pichu. The third option is by foot via the Inca Trail. The Inca Trail has been closed since two people died in a mudslide in the recent downpours. The railway line from Ollantaytambo was destroyed by the swollen river, and so it appeared that our best option was to try to get to Hidro and walk in from there.

Armed with as much information as Ronnie could give us, Val and I were up early. We took a taxi in the rainy dawn to the northern bus station, and eventually got a ride in a combi-shared-minibus to Santa Maria. The journey took around five hours, over the most incredibly steep, twisting, turning mountain roads. It rained most of the way, and the road was crumbling away in some places, and huge streams washed over it in others. The drop-off over the edge was dizzying. It was quite a white-knuckle ride!

The tarmac changed to rutted gravel roads as we descended into the jungle once more. Eventually we arrived at Santa Maria, a tiny town hidden in a valley seemingly miles from anywhere. We had some lunch, and got talking to Marco, from Argentina. He had tried a couple of days before to get to Aguas Calientes, and had run into many problems even getting up to Hidro. His Peruvian guide Julio suggested an alternative route to us, of which we made note.

We found a taxi prepared to take us over the next mountain, along with a couple of locals. We had to wait for about an hour or so while graders worked high up on the hillside trying to unblock the road, which had been buried under a huge mudslide earlier in the day. Our taxi driver eventually gave up, and we took a much longer alternate route.

On the way we ran into a mudslide across our road, but with the minimum of fuss, our driver and occupants from a following minibus set-to with picks. Before long our car was up and over the road blockage.

The minibus didn't fare so well, and got well and truly stuck. It took around an hour to get it back down off the top of the muddy slope. The amazing can-do attitude of everyone involved was wonderful to be part of. However, as the minibus couldn't climb the obstacle, it had to return to Santa Maria, while our little group pressed on to Santa Teresa.

There we found a little hostel. We dropped our bags off before wandering around the town, and walking down to see the huge muddy-brown, fast-flowing river.

I somehow managed to get chatting to a couple of local policemen. In broken Spanish I managed to explain what we were trying to do, and where we wanted to go. "No chance!" was my understanding of their friendly, but firm response. I asked about the alternate route that the Peruvian guide had suggested, and one of the policemen made a phone call. Again, in no uncertain terms he told us that it was very dangerous. There had been many mudslides in the area, and the bridge at the end of our planned alternate route was no longer there. At least I think that's what he told me!

At dinner, in a small restaurant in town, we chatted to a couple of locals who had just walked out of Aguas Calientes that afternoon. Percy told us that both the railway and the alternate route to Hidro were fine, and quite safe to walk.

Encouraged by local knowledge, we decided to press ahead with our plan, ignoring police advice. We turned in for an early night.

Machu Picchu challenges! – Day 2 – Goal achieved!

Saturday, 6th February 2010

Rising early, we managed to avoid being spotted by the police as our taxi driver took us out of town. An hour or so later he dropped us at a place called Lucmabamba, little more than a couple of shacks in the middle of the jungle. A local farmer pointed us to the start of an alternate part of the Inca Trail.

Our idea was to trek over the top of the mountain, passing an Inca site called Llactapata, from which if the weather was clear, it would be possible to see Machu Picchu. We had decided that this was the option that gave us the greatest possibility of actually seeing the Inca city, even if we eventually couldn't get there.

We climbed steeply uphill on a pretty decent path for a couple of hours, and crossed to the other side of the mountain. We started down, reasonably confident that we were on the right path, but worried that we may not see anything because of low cloud cover.

However, we were incredibly lucky. The clouds parted, and through a clearing there it was - Machu Picchu - clearly visible across the valley. It was a wonderful moment. Despite all claims that it was impossible to do, all suggestions that we would be better trekking elsewhere, and all of the dire warnings from the police, we had managed to do the seemingly impossible! We hadn't seen another soul since leaving Lucmabamba! We may have been the only people to see Machu Picchu this day!

The path down was muddy and slippy, but there were no signs of the huge mudslides the police had warned us about. In the valley, the footbridge was in fine condition. Either I had misunderstood the police, or they had been somewhat untruthful to try to discourage us. I suspect the latter to be the case.

We followed the trail along to Hidro Electrica, and wandered past two security guards without a hitch, thinking all was going to be well. We only had two more hours along the track to go!

Around the next corner we came upon a checkpoint manned by three policemen, who made it very clear that we could go no further! They were soon backed up by two more armed National Policia, who were friendly, but very firm. We chatted with them for an hour or so, trying in my best Spanish to convince them that we had a friend in Aguas Calientes to stay with, and that I was a reporter. Nothing worked, even the subtle offer of a backhander in US Dollars!!

Eventually we had to give up, and joined a group of four locals who were heading down to Santa Teresa. We were somewhat mystified when our group turned off and crossed the river, heading up a tiny trail into the jungle, instead of following the main road down. However, all became clear half an hour later, as we rounded a bend in the river. On the other side we could see that the road had simply collapsed into the river and been washed away. It would have been impossible to pass the devastated area.

The route through the jungle took about two hours, and we were amazed to find that the crossing back to the other side was in a tiny cart suspended on a cable, high above the raging river. What a thrilling end to our journey! Once at the rough road we all piled into a taxi, and headed back down to Santa Teresa.

From there we discovered that the road to Santa Maria was blocked again. We took a minibus taxi to Quillabamba, in the opposite direction to where we needed to go, but at least on clear roads.

Quillabamba turned out to be an amazing place. Hidden away in the jungle, it seemed to be a busy, thriving city, teeming with people. There seemed to be many trendy shops selling fashion clothing and expensive electrical items. How did such a place come to be there, seemingly in the middle of nowhere?

We decided to stay overnight, and went out for a wander around the town, searching for something to eat, and a couple of beers. For two days we hadn't seen a single other tourist or traveller, and in the bar we were quizzed by many of the curious and friendly locals as to what we were doing and where we had been.

Machu Picchu challenges! - Day 3

Sunday, 7th February 2010

The last day of our adventure was a long, six hour minibus journey back to Cusco, highlighted by the fact that the bridge at Ollantaytambo was now being washed away, and no vehicles were able to pass. We had to walk across the rather precarious, crumbling bridge to get into another minibus at the other side. Passengers heading in the opposite direction did the same. Presumably, some would be using our original minibus to continue their journey.

All in all, it has been the most fantastic three days, and was exactly what Val and I had wanted, more of an expedition than a tour. We were both disappointed that we hadn't managed to get to Aguas

Calientes, and ultimately to Machu Picchu, but were both extremely proud to have actually seen the place, which looks incredible. This way, I have managed to achieve the goal of seeing Machu Picchu, and yet have the opportunity to return one day to walk the whole Inca Trail. I would like to see the place again in a different manner, hopefully under much more favourable circumstances.

The whole experience had been so much more fun to share with someone as positive and enthusiastic as Val, and I am sure I would have been much further outside my comfort zone if I had been alone.

We were both incredibly impressed with all of the locals we met along the way. Taxi drivers, fellow passengers, hostel owners, and friendly people in bars had made the trip so special too. Everyone is so incredibly friendly, helpful and welcoming, even the gun-toting policemen! Equally remarkable is the amazingly positive attitude of everyone, in the face of all sorts of obstacles and difficulties.

Peru really is a fantastic and fascinating country. I hope to be back again soon!

Although not achieved in the manner in which I expected, the journey to see Machu Picchu now stands out as one of the major highlights of the whole two years. With a positive attitude, an equally positive companion, some creative planning, and a stubbornness which meant we did not intend to give in, we produced a fantastically positive outcome, and had quite an adventure. I believe it is quite possible that we were the only two people to see Machu Picchu that day. As is often the case with shared danger and adventure, it cemented an already solid friendship between Val and I.

In the end, I felt that achieving the goal in this way might even have topped getting there on the train with the rest of the tourist hordes, and wandering around with a tour guide. This way we had experienced something completely unique.

Our last day in Cusco was great fun. We could relax, having now achieved, to the best of our ability under the circumstances, what we had come to do. We decided to go on a cycle tour, loading bicycles onto the top of a bus, and travelling high into the mountains for an exhilarating downhill ride through some stunning mountain scenery.

I really enjoyed Cusco. It had such a friendly, welcoming atmosphere, was incredibly cheap, and there was so much to see and do. I would have been happy to spend another week there, but it was time to move on again.

The alarm woke us early, and we headed by taxi for Cusco airport, for our first flight of the day to Lima, where we would have a few hours to wait for our onward flight to Buenos Aires.

The weather in Cusco didn't seem too bad, but the airport was closed for incoming flights. Nobody had any idea when flights might arrive from Lima, and what had seemed to be a long four hour wait in Lima eventually looked like it would no longer be enough time to make our Buenos Aires connection.

Our first flight was booked with local carrier Star Peru, and our connection in Lima was with LAN. We talked with representatives of both airlines. The staff at the LAN counter told us that we would be able to push our LAN flight back at no charge, but this would mean a delay of over 12 hours in Lima.

As time ticked on, Star Peru couldn't give us a departure time, and suggested that LAN may be able to fly earlier, as they had larger planes. We asked Star Peru about a refund, but they wouldn't or couldn't do that. "Ees no possible!"

At the LAN desk we discussed the price of buying a Cusco to Lima flight with them, and found that it would cost an extra US $140. Staff there said that their flight wouldn't make our connection either, so there was no point paying the extra money.

We decided that our best option was to delay our Lima to Buenos Aires flight by the suggested 12 hours, and returned to the LAN desk to do this. We were told that they would try to arrange this, and to come back in half an hour. Half an hour later we were on our way back to the LAN desk, when both LAN and Star Peru started calling their passengers for immediate departure.

We rushed to the desk, but were told that arrangements to change our flight times hadn't yet been made. Apparently the agent had been talking to representatives in Lima, and confirmed we would be able to finalise details when we arrived there.

On our plane, which was boarded quickly as there weren't many passengers, it looked like we might actually depart ahead of the LAN plane next to us. Sure enough, we pushed back and headed for the runway first. If all went well we would be in Lima before the departure of our onward flight. However, with bags to collect, airport taxes to pay, customs to clear, and a new gate to find, our connection was practically impossible. We should have no problem changing times though, as promised by LAN staff as we departed.

On the runway we powered up and accelerated down the tarmac, almost reaching takeoff speed when the plane lurched violently to the right. I was sat in the right hand window seat, with Val on my left. I heard myself in an amazingly calm voice giving a running commentary of what was happening: "Something's wrong, we're well over to the right, we're on the grass now, now back on tarmac again. That was close!" In my head, my thoughts had been quicker than my calm-sounding words had been able to come out. As I had felt the right wheel go into the rough, bumpy grass, I had had visions of the plane being dragged round to the right and the right wing hitting the ground with potentially disastrous consequences. We really had been travelling fast at the time.

The pilots had reacted quickly, however, and we had made it safely back onto the tarmac, and coasted back into the terminal. We asked a couple of staff what had happened, and between my poor Spanish and their poor English, I am pretty sure that the fuel flow to the right engine had shut down, causing us to slew to the right. Fuel cart operators swarmed around the right hand side of the plane, and we watched the LAN plane depart without incident.

Forty minutes later we pushed back again, and I think all aboard breathed a quiet sigh of relief as we took off without further issues.

In Lima we had missed our flight by quite a while, by the time we recovered our bags. Initial enquiries at the LAN counter were discouraging. We were told that they could not change our flight times, as our original flight had already departed. "Ees no possible." We soon asked to speak to a supervisor!

For over three hours we argued our case. The supervisor tried many phone calls to resolve our situation, but kept coming up against the same brick wall. The supervisor's duty manager would not authorise a change to the later flight. Before long there were no seats left on the later flight, and the only option was a flight the next morning. We kept getting the same answer, "Ees no possible!" Continued requests to speak directly to the duty manager were met with promises to make this happen, but the duty manager never materialised.

We checked the price of tickets on the morning flight, and were shocked to find that they were over US $1,100. As I continued to argue our case as calmly as possible with our supervisor, Val checked out alternate options on the internet via his iPhone. Maybe if we flew to Santiago first? What about if we bought an extra ticket to Iguassu Falls? I put this to the LAN staff. "Ees no possible!"

What about if we paid the $140 that it would have cost us to change to the LAN flight from Cusco? "Eef you had done that, your follow-on flight could have been changed. But because you were on Star Peru, ees no possible to change!" But if we paid the $140 now? "Ees no possible after flight has left!"

What is possible then? "You buy another teeket." Hmmm.

Eventually our supervisor's shift came to and end and she talked with her colleague who was coming on duty. Our departing supervisor had been as helpful as possible, but had been unable to produce a solution. The new supervisor was simply stone-wall unhelpful. "There ees nothing we can do here at airport – you must try customer services in city."

We rang the customer services number, and tried to explain the whole complicated situation. The best option they could offer was to email in a complaint, but told us that that would take weeks to process. We needed to be in Buenos Aires in the next day or two, as after visiting Iguazu Falls we had an onward flight booked to Rio, and Carnival there.

It was slowly becoming crystal clear that our only option for now was going to be to buy a new ticket. On the web, Val had come up with the best case scenario, which was through Santiago, to Buenos Aires, and on to Iguazu in Argentina. Frustratingly, this option was with LAN, with whom we had been arguing for several hours.

We both felt reluctant to spend any more money with them, but practicality won the day. As I was on the phone to customer services at the time, I went ahead and booked, and used Val's credit card. The flights were costing us $778 each!

For me it was a horrendous financial blow, as funds for the South American leg of my journey had been quite tight. I had already had to spend over $1,500, with LAN again, to get to Easter Island and back!!

I was told that we would get an email in an hour or so to confirm our booking, the first leg of which departed in about four hours. We did not receive this, but Val got a call from his wife in Colorado, whose number we had given as a contact. LAN could not process our tickets, as their representative had forgotten to add on $30 per ticket admin fee, and we had to call them again to authorise this. By now we were both pretty-much at the end of our patience with LAN, and I was particularly furious about the extra charge.

We went to the LAN counter again, and they confirmed that a $30 fee was necessary. Would it be possible to waive the fee if we paid here at the desk? "Waive fee ees no possible!" Of course not!

However, we discovered that if we had booked online, there wouldn't have been a fee. Could we book online now to avoid the extra $60, we asked. "Ees no possible, online booking has to be made four hours before departure." It was now just a couple of hours until our flight left! Perhaps if the customer service rep on the phone had thought to mention this?

Val got back on the phone to argue the case about the fee. Could they possibly waive this, as their rep had forgotten to mention it, had forgotten to add it to the original price, and had not mentioned earlier that we could book online. "Ees no possible!"

Val exploded. "What is possible with your airline? I wonder how it is even possible for you to get a plane off the ground!" Eventually he had to authorise the payment of the extra $60.

Just before we boarded the plane, I saw Val stomping around at the departure gate, growling and cursing into his phone. Before he had even sat down to tell me what had happened, I was laughing. I already had my suspicions.

Val had got another message from his wife Brenda. To add insult to injury, LAN had debited his card twice, once for $1,556 for the two tickets, and then again for $1,616, for the two tickets again, plus the $60 admin fee for the 'convenience' of having booked via an 'efficient' customer services agent!

On both of the new flights we had booked, from Lima to Santiago, and then from Santiago to Buenos Aires, there were several empty seats.

LAN Airlines could have easily transferred us to those flights at no cost at all. But one obstructive and unobtainable duty manager had refused to help us out.

The complaints we both later submitted never produced any results, and I have to classify my experience with LAN as the worst flying experience of my whole 100 weeks. The financial blow made the $100 taxi ride in Iceland look inconsequential.

However, with a positive companion it is so much easier to laugh off such matters, and accept it as part of the overall adventure.

Goal 76 – Iguazu, another incredible waterfall
Thursday 11th February 2010
(Puerto Iguazu, Argentina)

After the long drama at Lima airport, Val and I had to find an alternative way to Puerto Iguazu, the town on the Argentinean side of Iguazu Falls. With our newly purchased, and ridiculously expensive tickets, we flew that evening to Santaigo, and got a little sleep overnight at the airport. In the morning we flew to Buenos Aires, where Val had to pay a US $131 entry fee. The cost to an Australian was $100, so I quickly became British again, whipped out the UK Passport, and entered Argentina for free!

In Buenos Aires we had to take a bus across the city to the domestic airport. From there we caught our flight to Puerto Iguazu, which is on the Rio Iguazu, the border between Argentina and Brazil. Rio Iguazu also joins Rio Parana here, which forms the border with Paraguay for both of these countries.

After booking into a hostel we wandered down to see Tres Fronteras, where at sunset we sat at a very scenic, tranquil lookout point, gazing over the jungles of Argentina, Brazil and Paraguay.

In the morning we took the bus to Iguazu Falls. We jumped aboard the busy little train that took us out to the walkway to Garganta Diablo, the incredibly spectacular Devil's Throat, where so much water poured over the cliff edge that the spray produced meant it was impossible to see the river below.

We met up with an Argentinean couple, Damian and Estephania, and spent much of the rest of the day with them, giving us a chance to practice our Spanish, and them a chance to work on their English.

There are many walkways to follow, which lead to different parts of the awesome waterfalls. It is possible to get very close to the edge of some dizzying drops, or almost right under a spectacularly huge fall of water.

This is the last of the three big waterfalls on my list of goals. I have thoroughly enjoyed each one, as each is quite different and unique. Niagara was good because of the closeness to a city filled with nightclubs and casinos. Victoria Falls was impressive in terms of vast size and huge drop. At Iguazu it is possible to get so close, and feel the incredible power of the falls.

We caught a bus the next morning across the border into Brazil, where the falls are called Iguassu Falls. The difference in spelling in the two countries had caused some confusion when making our travel plans, and trying to book flights.

We spent another day admiring the falls from the Brazilian side. Although the walks along the sides of the falls aren't as extensive as on the Argentinean side, they are incredibly spectacular. Raised pathways wind through walls of spray over the surface of the river, leading right to the edge of the drop-off, where you can lean out over the edge from dizzying viewpoints, gazing directly down the face of a thundering wall of water.

Goal 77 – Hablo Espanyol (solo un pocito!)

Friday, 12th February 2010
(Various Spanish-speaking locations)

As I cross from Argentina to Brazil, I think I am probably leaving the last Spanish-speaking country on my 100goals journey, as Brazil is mainly Portuguese-speaking.

I am really pleased with how my Spanish has improved. I am nowhere near fluent, and struggle a lot more than I do in French, but I can still get by in many exchanges without having to resort to English.

I was given a great computer-based Spanish course by Fipps in San Diego, and I have been working my way through lessons on the computer as often as I can. I also had some great one-on-one tuition from Andres while on Easter Island, and felt that I improved quite quickly there. Sometimes though, the best education is simply getting out and about in Spanish speaking places, and trying to make yourself understood.

I have managed to make all sorts of food and drink purchases, and arranged several taxi journeys, including haggling over the fare. I got a vaccination for Yellow Fever, checked-in for several flights, including choosing a window seat, and arranged to have my laundry done, all in Spanish, without having to resort to the bail-out phrase, "Habla Ingles?" (Do you speak English?)

I also managed a fairly spirited discussion in Spanish with the policemen blocking our route to Machu Picchu, including offering a cash bribe. Unfortunately this didn't manage to produce the desired result!

As I wrote about my French-speaking goal, it is very hard to quantify when a goal such as this is complete, as there is always room for improvement! After all, I'm still working on improving my English at the age of 46.

But I certainly feel that I have fulfilled what I hoped to achieve with Spanish, and am able to get by in many situations, without relying on non-native English-speakers having to use my main language.

I do hope to continue to improve my Spanish over the coming years, but imagine this would be a lot easier to do if I chose to live in a Spanish-speaking country.

For now though, I am happy to class the goal as complete, and clear the decks for the last few remaining goals.

Gracias a todos por su ayuda con Desafío Número Setenta y siete.

We flew from Iguassu to Rio, and made our way to our couchsurf accommodation. Val had been pretty dogged in his search for somewhere for us to stay in Rio. Almost everywhere was full at Carnival time, and every couchsurfer bed had been occupied too. Hostels were charging outrageous prices, and hotel prices were astronomical.

Fortunately, Fabio, our host, had a couple of people cancel at the last minute, and we were invited to stay in a wonderful rooftop apartment some way out of the city centre.

Within hours of putting our bags down we had been fed by Fabio, and along with his housemate Samuel, we were on our way to Ipanema Beach. There, with more of Fabio's buddies, we drank beer, swam in the sea, and watched bikini-clad Brazilian beauties wander by.

Goal 78 - Carnival in Rio

Saturday 13th February 2010

(Rio de Janeiro, Brazil)

Towards the end of our first afternoon in Rio we wandered along to a rocky promontory at the end of Ipanema Beach. We climbed up to watch the beautiful Rio sunset, which was applauded by the crowd of on-lookers. I've never seen the setting sun receive a round of applause before!

After a shower back at home, we headed out to a local street party, but were a little surprised that it was all over by the time we got there. A bar, and some beer for the rooftop back at home ended the evening, and a fantastic first day intro to Rio.

After a late BBQ lunch the next afternoon, Val and I took the Metro to the station nearest to the Sambodromo, hoping to find some reasonably priced tickets. On the internet, tickets appeared to cost anywhere between US$75 to $1,000, but we had heard that it was possible to buy cheaper tickets locally.

Just outside the Metro we found several touts, and after some slightly confusing negotiations in Portuguese, we had two tickets for seats in Sector 6, at a bargain price of $25 each - marvellous.

Minutes later we had a couple of beers in hand too, and felt like locals, ready for Carnival.

The view we had wasn't the best, as our section of seats was set back from the huge concrete runway that the parade would come along, but we could still see pretty well.

When the first parade began it took quite some time to reach our area, as each group has about 80 minutes to travel the whole length of the Sambodromo. The atmosphere was amazing, and everyone was up on their feet, singing, dancing, and waving flags.

When the first float arrived it was HUGE, followed by what must have been thousands of dancers in amazing costumes – the flow of performers was almost endless – and this was just the first of six parades on display tonight!

We watched the second and third parades. Both were equally impressive, especially the magician-like section at the front of the third parade, which under the cover of large magicians' sheets, performed some lighting-fast costume changes.

We ended our evening somewhat early, heading out at around 1am, having an early start planned for the next morning. I don't think either of us could have managed another four hours on the rock-hard concrete seats either.

We caught the Metro back home, among many brightly-costumed performers, presumably heading home, or perhaps going to a party somewhere.

Chapter 9 – Weeks 81 to 90

(15th February 2010 – 25th April 2010)

Brazil – South Africa – Australia – Nepal

On 7th July 2007 the "New Seven Wonders of the World" were announced after a worldwide vote. Before my 100 weeks journey began, I had seen two of the seven. I saw the Colosseum in Rome, when I had travelled through Europe after I finished school. On our honeymoon Laura and I went to Israel, and while there we took a tour to see Petra in Jordan.

So far on my current travels, I had added three more. I had seen the pyramid at Chichén Itzá in Mexico, walked on the Great Wall of China, and seen, although only from a distance, Machu Picchu in Peru. It was time to add the sixth of the seven to my tick-list.

Goal 79 - Redemption... finally

Monday, 15th February 2010
(Rio de Janeiro, Brazil)

I met fellow Aussies, Paul and Kristi, in the backpacker hostel I had stayed in while in Santiago. As we were all going to be in Rio for Carnival, we had made tentative arrangements to meet up. However, Carnival, as you can imagine, is pretty wild, and plans tend to change at short notice. Travelling across the huge city can often take longer than expected, with street closures and manic traffic!

I had suggested a suitable meeting place, picked out on a Google map, to all who had expressed interest in a hike up Corcovado Mountain. The incredible statue of Christ the Redeemer stands on top of the mountain, gazing down from on high over the whole of Rio. It was a wonderful surprise to see Paul and Kristi at the appointed time and place.

As I had at Table Mountain in Cape Town, I wanted to walk up to the top of the mountain, instead of taking the tourist-trap train up. Val was keen too. Along with Samuel, from our couchsurfer home, we had taken a bus to the Metro, the Metro to Botafogo station, and finally a taxi to beautiful Parque Lage, where the trail up the mountain begins.

Paul and Kristi hadn't quite realised how steep the climb might be. They hadn't come too well prepared, wearing flip-flops and light open sandals respectively, but did fantastically well. It took about an hour and a half, in hot sweaty conditions up a steep jungle trail to reach the top. There we joined the crowds who had arrived on the train, and in an endless stream of packed minibuses.

It was here that our troubles began. We found our way blocked by turnstiles, where everyone getting off the buses would present their tickets. The guards manning the entry point would not let us in, and as far as we could gather, we couldn't buy tickets there either. A few other people had hiked up the mountain too. We found someone who could translate for us, as Samuel had chatted to the guards, but we couldn't quite understand as he tried to explain the situation.

It turned out that the turnstiles were a new addition, just for Carnival, to fleece the gringo tourists. The group of local trekkers all refused to have anything to do with paying for entry. The ridiculous part of the situation was that we couldn't buy tickets at the summit. They were only sold down at the start of the minibus route way below us! "That's Brazil!" said one local in resigned voice!

We managed to organise a free return trip in a minibus for one of our group. Kristi volunteered to head down and back, returning in half an hour or so, with five tickets. We finally went through the turnstiles to see Christ the Redeemer, or Cristo Redentor, as he is known here.

I don't know what I was most impressed by, the awesome huge statue, or the breath-taking view over the city, which is often referred to as the most beautiful city in the world. It was very crowded on the top, but that didn't detract one bit from the incredible view and location. Rio certainly is a lovely-looking city.

We took the minibus back down, as this was included in our ticket price, and all headed off in different directions. Samuel was going to the beach, Paul and Kristi to prepare for the spectacle of Sambodromo that evening, and Val and I to Sugar Loaf Mountain.

We planned to climb that too, rather than take the cable car up, and tried a couple of different trails. The first was the wrong one, and took us to the foot of a huge steep cliff wall. The second trail, around the back of the steep cliff was more manageable, until we reached a steep section that would have been much safer with ropes. There was one short section with a large drop below. We decided to return to the track, somewhat disappointed, but pleased to have made a wise decision. In the end we had to admit defeat, and caught the cable car to the summit, arriving there just as the sun was setting.

The summit offers further incredible views of this stunning city, and we sat sipping beers as the sky darkened and the city lit up below us.

What a fantastic day in the most beautiful city in the world!!

In our last couple of days in Rio, Val and I explored more of the city, climbing another mountain for a different view. Val took a tandem hang glider flight from there down to the beach far below. The extra "Carnival-tax" added to the price of the hang glider flight meant I opted to catch a lift down in the company's vehicle to the beach to meet Val there.

Eventually it was time for Val to return to Colorado, and we said our goodbyes as Val caught a taxi to the airport.

I didn't have a flight booked, and was still undecided as to where to go next. Options were wide open for me now. Maybe I could head back to the UK, as initially planned, or even head north to the States. Perhaps I could return to South Africa, to achieve another goal there.

I also had to return to Australia at some point, as I still had a garage full of stuff at Mel's house which she was keen for me to remove. I had appreciated her patience, but it was something I did need to resolve sooner rather than later.

I spent some time considering my options, while I enjoyed my last few days in the most beautiful city in the world. The favela tour I went on dispelled "the most beautiful city" myth a little, as I walked in amazement through one of the poorest, dirtiest places I had ever seen. On the hillside overlooking a beautiful stretch of world famous beach, Rocinha Favela houses an estimated 150,000 people, packed in to Rio's biggest slum.

From the bottom of the hill we were taken high up into the favela, each on the back of a motorcycle taxi. It was a hair-raising ride, as it had started raining over night. The greasy roads didn't seem to slow the traffic one bit! At the top, our tour regrouped and walked down into the tiny chaotic streets and alleyways.

There is no form of planning, permission, or real organisation, and the favela just grows as people build homes wherever they can. The spaghetti of electric cables and water pipes is incredible, and the streets are a confusing, litter-strewn maze.

Drug dealing is prolific, as is gun ownership, but among this chaos, around 98% of the community are poorer families simply trying to live their lives. It was quite an eye-opening experience, and a view of Rio that I imagine many of the Carnival revellers had never seen, and probably wouldn't care to either.

Eventually, with my decision made and a ticket booked, I took a taxi to the airport the next afternoon, thanking Fabio and Samuel for their hospitality. My flight took me back to South Africa.

Goal 80 – "...there you will always long to return"

Saturday, 27th February 2010
(Port Elizabeth, South Africa)

"When once you have tasted flight, you will forever walk the earth with your eyes turned skyward, for there you have been, and there you will always long to return."

Leonardo da Vinci

This morning was beautiful, and the winds were light, but as I waited for my fourth flying lesson, the winds picked up a little, and were blowing across the main runway.

Gerhard had had me do a few circuits around the main airport, then happy that I seemed to be doing okay, we detoured onto a much wider circuit, and headed for the coast. Gerhard took the controls, dived towards the sea, levelling out just above the surface and then handed control back to me.

We flew along at around fifty feet, just skimming along above the surface of the sea. Gerhard let me pilot my own route, following the coast line closely, passing over rocky shores and breaking waves. At the lighthouse at Africa's most south-easterly point, we banked round to the right, and continued along the coast. It was an absolutely incredible experience, and exactly what I had hoped flying would be like. I think I am hooked!

The cross wind was a bit too strong to allow me to fly solo, so we agreed to meet again in the early evening to see if conditions had improved. At 6pm the winds were much lighter. We went out and did three circuits, after which Gerhard had me land to a complete stop, and we taxied in off the runway. Gerhard climbed out, and with a last few words of advice, it was the moment of truth!

I called the tower and headed back out onto the taxiway, and lined up on the runway. The takeoff went without a hitch, and the plane climbed much faster with just one person aboard. I turned right and levelled out at 1,200 feet, and turned onto the downwind leg and made my radio call. One more turn onto base leg, some flaps and get the nose down to maintain 70 mile per hour. A last turn onto final approach, more flaps, another radio call, and then concentrate on throttle, speed, distance, and approach. All went very smoothly, just as I had been taught. I rounded out nicely, touched down with a bit of a bump, and taxied back off the runway.

I hadn't really had much time to enjoy the view, but it had been a beautiful evening, with the sun setting to the west, and a full moon rising to the east. I was too busy furiously concentrating on what I needed to do to get around the circuit and back down safely!

What a truly fantastic feeling, what a huge thrill, and what a proud achievement. I had gone solo after around five hours of flying time, and I was extremely pleased with myself. Gerhard and his wife Yvette seemed almost as thrilled as I was, and Yvette had made a wonderful certificate for me.

This has certainly been another one of the highlights of the 80 goals achieved so far, and I owe huge, HUGE thanks to Gerhard for making this happen in such a short time frame. I think we have both equally enjoyed the challenge though.

I don't think this one is over yet, I suspect I might be back here one day soon to finish what I have started! Yes, I am definitely hooked!

I had managed to rack up quite a few frequent flyer points through my extended globe-trotting, and used some of them to take a Qantas flight from Port Elizabeth, via Johannesburg, back to Perth in Australia. I had made arrangements to stay with my pal Marty and his family for a couple of weeks, and Marty collected me from the airport.

It felt quite surreal to be back on familiar turf, but much had changed since I was last here. Marty and Carol had bought a new place, and living with them and kids Bella and Maxine was a bit of a culture shock for me, after travelling for so long.

I soon settled in, and contacted Mel to let her know that I was back to sort things out.

I found the evening I spent with her a touch uncomfortable. It was nice to see her and her two girls again, but sad to know that things weren't going to be the same this time around. When the girls had gone to bed we sat and shared a bottle of wine, but we didn't speak much, and for me the words I wanted to say remained locked in my throat.

I had written a letter to her many months before when I had realised that Susan obviously wasn't the person for me, but had never sent it. I still wondered if by making the choices I had, and letting the relationship with Mel die, I had made a huge mistake. She had now found someone else, and I had to let her move on. Eventually we said goodnight and I headed home.

Goal 81 – Dangling in the breeze!

Saturday, 6th March 2010
(York, Western Australia)

I have been skydiving on an irregular basis for over six years now, and have done around 140 jumps in total. I still get a big thrill from it, but do not tend to go regularly enough to progress too much in terms of skills.

At around 100 jumps many people try a nude skydive. I am not really sure why, other than the usual "because it's there" sort of reason. It is something that has been on a mental to-do list somewhere in the back of my mind, and somehow it got added to the list of 100 goals as it was first written out.

As I am back in Perth for a while, and my own skydive gear is here, I decided to make a concerted effort to get another goal ticked off. I rode the motorbike over to the dropzone at York yesterday evening, and over a few beers with a couple of the other early arrivals, tried to recruit a few others to my cause.

I put up an open invite on the café door, suggesting anytime mid to late-afternoon on Saturday might be the best time for the jump, hopefully the warmest part of the day.

I did a couple of refresher jumps in the morning and early afternoon. Later in the afternoon, as the last of the tandem skydive customers headed home, four of us gathered to plan our jump. Joining me would be Skydive Express staff members (no pun intended!) Split and Thommo, and parachute packer Crumb. As is often the case at skydive clubs, I have known a couple of these guys for several years, and have no idea what their real names are!

Our jump was going to be the last of the day, and I was extremely grateful to business owner and pilot John for flying the extra load.

We geared up, and to avoid any offence to any remaining customers and their families, we wore shorts to get down to the plane. There were only the four of us aboard, and we quickly got to 14,000 feet. When we got the orange light, and opened the door, it was pretty chilly.

We had all sorts of grand plans for our exit and jump routine, but with no jumpsuit, control in the air is very tricky, and we messed the exit up badly. When we all let go to try to sort it out, the two bigger guys (and by that I mean body mass, nothing else!) fell away quickly, and I could simply not catch up to them at all.

Eventually we all had to separate and open our 'chutes, and fly down to land. Beer was already waiting for us, from the carton I would be required to put on at the bar, as is customary for any new first skydive achievement or event. Cheers!!

With my motorbike rescued from Mel's garage I could get out and about much more, and went to visit friends in and around Perth. I enjoyed the end-of-summer weather, and the motorbike was as fun as ever, but it felt like all had changed there for me. I no longer had a wife or partner, my house had been sold, and many of the group of people I had known there had moved on to other parts of the country. I had no real roots there anymore. I felt adrift and a little lost, and knew that there really wasn't much left for me. Maybe I had reached the end of the time that I would consider Perth to be home.

I continued to work on some of the other goals. I ate healthily and exercised as often as I could. I booked an introductory harmonica course, and borrowed Mel's unicycle to practice my wobbly skills.

Things weren't going too well though. The unicycle pedal broke, and it was going to take quite some time to order the necessary new parts. My attempts to do a night skydive at my local club failed when, on the weekend of the full moon, the winds were too strong. I felt somewhat listless and unmotivated, and drifted through the days achieving little.

However, at the end of March, my healthy choices paid off, and I ticked off another goal.

Goal 82 - something lost, hopefully forever!
Wednesday, 31st March 2010
(Perth, Western Australia)

Many of the jobs I have had in the past, or businesses that I have run, have tended to keep me fit, healthy and slim.

After college I spent several years teaching outdoor activities, such as climbing, canoeing, caving, and mountaineering. Later I ran a jet ski business, which involved a lot of time working hard on the beach.

When I moved to Australia, I worked for Jenny Jones Rugs, and for the first year or so there I did quite a bit of manual work, lifting and shifting rugs and furniture. But when I became duty manager my role at work became much more sedentary.

Continuing to eat as I used to when I worked much more physically, coupled with moving into my forties, and an appreciation for beer, meant that slowly the weight started to increase. Not by much, but enough to be noticeable.

In my twenties, and well into my thirties, I always used to weigh around 11 stone (154lb or 70kg). But in my early forties, at the worst point, I was around 12 and a half stones (175lb, or 80kg).

After my separation I started to be much more active again, swimming and running on the beach each morning. When I moved to Kalgoorlie to become a mining dump truck driver, I made a conscious decision to join the social group that went to the gym or squash court more often than they went to the pub. I soon got back to around 70 kilos.

Back in Perth after six months out in the desert, I worked up north in another mine, and kept fit by swimming a lot and using the gym there, again avoiding the pub crowd to a large extent.

It is easy, however, to let the good habits slip. After a year at the mine I resigned, went back to the rug shop briefly, and put my life up for sale on eBay. A lot of time in front of the computer, too many pizzas, and too much wine meant I got back up to around 75kg.

When I started my list of 100 goals, I set myself the target of getting back down to my ideal weight, and maintaining it – 70kg – which was my weight at the age of thirty. It hasn't been easy, as it can be tricky when travelling to eat healthily all the time. Fitting in enough exercise can be a challenge too.

But since August last year, and even before, when I began preparing for my "7 Peaks in 7 Days" Colorado-based mountaineering challenge, I have been doing pretty well. Since then I have been fairly active, and tried to be very conscious of what I eat.

When I weighed myself just before Christmas, I had just reached the 70kg mark. I decided that if I could maintain healthy habits for the next three months, and maintain my weight, I think I should be able to do so continuously.

Staying with Marty and Carol for a month hasn't made things any easier, as they are both great cooks.

However, I have done very well overall, and am still a healthy, trim, and fit 69kg.

Goal achieved! Unlike some goals that, once done, I haven't really returned to at all (such as didgeridoo playing (until last week) or kitesurfing), I intend to keep on top of this one. In fact I need to, as still ahead is the challenge to develop some sort of six-pack stomach. This is going fairly well, but I still have that last bit of fat to lose, and a bit more muscle to build. But progress is certainly encouraging!

Eventually, I motivated myself enough to resolve the issue of all of my unused stuff in Mel's garage. I bought a small shed and erected it in a far-flung corner of Marty and Carol's garden.

I rented a van for a day and moved all of my stuff. After a big garage sale, I had whittled it down to a small enough collection of remnants of a previous life to cram into the little shed.

I had booked my next flights, and finally packed my bags again in preparation for my next big challenge. This time, as I left Perth, there was none of the trepidation I had felt on previous departures. This time I almost felt a sense of relief to get away from Perth as summer came to an end. My time there was done, and I had no idea when I would be back again, as I still had no idea what would happen at the end of 100 weeks.

The previous weeks had been a big challenge, as I'd had a lot of somewhat emotional stuff to deal with. My now-ex-girlfriend didn't want to have much to do with me, as my travelling had pushed her away. It had been hard being around Perth without her company, friendship and support. I had to move all my remaining belongings from her garage. Seeing her wonderful kids had been tough too. Some of my belongings still had some personal attachments, and it had been challenging to almost give them away at garage sale prices. One of the last things I had had to do was leave a huge pile of stuff at a charity shop door the night before I flew out.

Once away from Perth I felt much brighter again. My first flight took me to Singapore, which has to be my favourite airport. The facilities there are brilliant. Free internet, international electric power outlets, free movies, a butterfly sanctuary, free games, and I believe a pool and gym too – one of the nicer airports to transit through.

My next stop was at Mumbai in India, nowhere near as nice or as clean as Singapore. I found a relatively quiet corner to doss down for the night. I found a cardboard box to use as my mattress, and settled down with my sleeping bag and the pillow I had brought, planning ahead for this night. From comfy guest bedroom to cardboard-box-airport-hobo in less than a day! I left the pillow and box for the next overnighter to find. From Mumbai I flew to Kathmandu in Nepal, where I planned to achieve my next goal.

When in Perth I had spent a day with my friend Bek on the urban indigenous tour that she operated, and had chatted to her friend Kim. Kim was from England, and guided tours that travelled across Europe and Asia to Australia. She had stopped over many times in India and Nepal, and gave me a few useful email contacts.

I had written to Niraj, owner and operator of Himalayan Encounters. He had offered to assist me and I had made a tour booking with him. At his office in the courtyard of the Kathmandu Guest House, I met Ahvi, who would be arranging everything. He introduced me to my trekking companion, Henry from Colorado, and our guide Deepak.

I was really looking forward to trekking in Nepal, as this was something I had wanted to do for a long time. I felt slightly guilty planning to spend three weeks on one goal, particularly as I was now behind schedule. I had achieved 82 goals so far, but was now well into the 88th week. However, as I had always maintained, the journey was not just about putting ticks in boxes, but was much more about the whole adventure, and the people I was meeting along the way.

From Kathmandu we took an early morning flight to the amazing little airport of Lukla, high in the Himalayas. Deepak introduced Henry and I to our other guide, Surya, and our porter, Sudip.

Our first days of trekking were relatively easy. The altitude sickness that had troubled me in both Colorado and Peru wasn't an issue, as we were still below 11,000 feet, and acclimatising slowly.

The scenery was stunning, and the days endlessly fascinating, as we passed yak trains carrying supplies up the mountain trails, or returning to Lukla for more supplies. Porters carried staggering loads of trekkers' bags, or food supplies. Thin suspension bridges crossed steep valleys high above roaring rivers.

We arrived in the market town of Namche Bazar, and stayed for two nights to continue our altitude acclimatisation, spending some time with another group of travellers on a similar trek to ours.

From there the trail continued steeply, and we took a more westerly valley, away from the direct trail to Everest Base Camp. There were fewer trekkers on this path. At the head of the valley a couple of days later, we stayed at Gokyo, a tiny village at the foot of Gokyo Ri. I felt the familiar sickening effects of altitude a little there, but long days of hiking slowly from lower elevations had served us well, and I soon recovered.

The views from the snow-covered, sunlit summit of Gokyo Ri were stunning, and the view of Everest in the distance made it feel like I had almost achieved the goal already.

We crossed through a high mountain pass, marvelling at the ice falls we passed on the way, and descended into Labouche on the approach to the base of Everest.

Goal 83 – "Because it's there..."
Friday, 16th April 2010
(Everest Base Camp, Nepal)

***Day 9** – Labouche (16,108 ft) – Gorak Shep (16,863 ft) – Everest Base Camp (17,650 ft) – Kala Pathar (18,208 ft) – Gorak Shep (16,863 ft)*

Breakfast was delayed slightly, so we didn't get away until 6:30am, and arrived at Gorak Shep a couple of hours later. This really is the last settlement before Base Camp. I have read about this place in so many mountaineering books. There was an air of unreality about finally reaching the tiny village. On the walk I thought of all the famous footsteps that I was following. Mallory and Irvine came this way, as did Hillary and Tensing, and hundreds of other climbing greats since then.

We left as much gear as we could at the Snowland Highest Inn, which would be our accommodation for the night, at almost 17,000 feet. With much lighter packs for the rest of the day, we set off for our ultimate goal, Everest Base Camp.

It took less than two hours to reach our goal, and I was feeling much fitter and healthier than the previous day. Unfortunately it was Henry's turn to be feeling a bit under-the-weather, and Surya and I waited by the Base Camp overlook area for Henry and Deepak to arrive.

I was really keen to go down into the camp itself, and see the awesome Khumbu Icefall from its base. Henry elected to stay on the "city limits" with Deepak, and Surya and I headed down into camp. The atmosphere was wonderful. There was a group of singing and dancing Sherpas, a photo exhibition in one tent, and all sorts of preparations going on.

I soaked up as much atmosphere as I could, and took many pictures of the stunning icefall. It all looks very imposing, and people up there just looked like tiny dots.

Eventually we headed back to collect Henry and Deepak, and began the journey back to Gorak Shep.

We had wondered about the possibility of climbing Kala Pathar, which offers some incredible views of the whole valley, but Henry wasn't feeling up to it. I was still feeling good, and decided I would tackle the climb, which ascends to well over 18,000 feet. Surya kindly volunteered to come along with me.

It was a real slog, as we had already had a long six-hour day, but we climbed steadily and slowly. By the last third of the climb I was starting to fade a little, and was disappointed that the clouds were building fast. We had really needed to be up there a couple of hours earlier. It got colder towards the summit, and I put on all the clothes I had with me, as we finally reached the wind-swept peak.

The view was clouded over, but we could see one gap in the clouds about to pass over. With a few others at the summit, we waited for five minutes, and were rewarded with a brief, stunning view of Everest.

We headed down quickly, arriving back at Gorak Shep just after 3pm, just as the snow began to fall. At the end of a long, tough nine-hour day, luke warm coffee had never tasted so good!

This has been an absolutely incredible goal to achieve, and has probably been one of the most physically demanding things I have ever done. In terms of sustained effort it even beats the "7 Peaks in 7 Days" challenge in August last year.

I am incredibly proud of what I have achieved, and although I appreciate that thousands of other trekkers achieve the same thing each year, I am pretty sure they are all very proud too.

After the literal and emotional high peaks reached in the previous week, I discovered once again that when the low points come, they can be very low. Once again, I found out how quickly things can go from being well planned and running smoothly on course, to all going horribly and disastrously wrong.

I had been back in Kathmandu for over four days. While I had enjoyed relaxing with little to do, other than work on upcoming plans, I could think of much nicer places to be stuck for a few days. With a permanent supply of electricity I could have managed to do so much more, but because of very low water supplies in the reservoirs that powered the country's hydro-electric systems, power was cut to the city for around twelve hours each day. I would have welcomed the time to get on with some writing, or even watching a few movies, but long periods without electric meant either sleeping, or wandering the noisy, chaotic streets. I did enjoy this, but had been in Kathmandu long enough, and felt ready to move on.

I had to be pretty careful with my money, as I had spent a little more on the trek than my original budget had allowed for. I wanted to get through these final days, changing the least amount of extra money as possible.

It was with a feeling of relief that I finally headed for the airport, just four more days of third-world chaos ahead in India, before looking forward to the calm oasis of a couple of weeks in England.

I joined the line to check in at the Jet counter. After half an hour, I got to the front, only to be told, "No, you are booked on Jet Airways, that line over there. This line is for Jet flights."

I looked up at the board above me. "Right, so Jet and Jet Airways are two different companies?"

"Oh yes sir," I was happily told, and I had to join the end of the most enormous check-in line I have ever seen. An hour later I made it to the front, and was asked "Where is your visa?" I pointed out my Nepal entry visa confidently, knowing I was leaving well inside the allotted 30 days. "No, where is your Indian visa, sir?"

"I'll just get that at the border," I answered hopefully, my heart beginning to sink. Apparently that wasn't possible. I suggested I would simply use my UK passport rather than my Australian one – after all, India used to be part of the Empire – surely a British passport still has some advantages there?

Not at all. India, it would appear, requires that all visitors have a visa in advance. I was not going to be allowed on the plane. I tried explaining that I had an onward ticket from Delhi to London, and would simply transit through instead, hoping to resolve the issue on arrival there. Since my London ticket was booked for four days later, I would be sent back to Kathmandu, I was imformed, as a transit departure has to be within 24 hours of arrival.

What could I do, I asked? I was told my only option was to go to the Indian Embassy here in Kathmandu and get a visa first. What about my flight leaving in a couple of hours? All I got was the address of the Jet Airways (not Jet!) office in Kathmandu, and an uncaring "Good luck!"

It all felt very reminiscent of the LAN airlines fiasco in South America. However, I did appreciate that I had no one to blame but myself, and what was particularly frustrating was that I'd had four empty days when I could so easily have resolved this. In almost two years of travelling, only one other country has been awkward enough to require a visa sorted out at an embassy in advance – China. I had travelled through Europe, Asia, North

America, South America and Africa. In every place I had been, I had either not needed a visa, or had paid the requisite amount of dollars, and simply got a visa at the border. Why would I expect India to be any different, especially with a British passport in my pocket?

With the last dregs of Nepali rupees in my pocket, I negotiated with the owner of the dodgiest looking taxi outside the airport. At the Jet Airways (not Jet!) counter, I had been informed that the embassy would be open until 5pm, and from 9 until 12 the next day, which was a Sunday. In the taxi, as we sped through dirty back streets, I still harboured optimistic visions of a quick visa issue, and a dash back to the airport just in time to catch my flight.

At the embassy it was obvious that this was not how it was going to be. It actually didn't open at all on Saturday or Sunday, so it was going to be almost two days until I could even get in there on Monday morning! That was going to make it extremely tight to get from Delhi to Agra to see the Taj Mahal, and then back to Delhi to get my flight to London on the Wednesday.

Despondently, I got the taxi to take me to the Jet Airways (not Jet!) offices. Ah, but of course, it was Saturday afternoon and they had just closed at 2pm. Completely at a loss, and with no Nepali cash at all on me, I got the taxi driver to take me back to Thamel, the touristy area at the heart of the city. I changed one of my last US$10 notes and paid him his 100 Rupees. With my bags I wandered back to my cheapie hotel, and booked back in for the night, unsure of what to do next.

I had a chat with the owner, who offered some helpful advice, but basically there was nothing at all I could do about a visa until Monday. The process of issuing the visa could take some time, Shailu informed me. I had to sort out a new flight, but didn't dare do this until I had the visa in hand. Time was against me, and a goal as simple as seeing the Taj Mahal looked like it may now be slipping out of reach.

I went out for a cup of coffee, and then back at the hotel, found the electricity off again. I decided that there was little that I could do for the next six or seven hours. I considered brushing my teeth, and turned the tap on in the bathroom. The water that came out of it was as dark as a strong cup of tea. I just stared in disbelief. I felt like I had just reached one of the lowest points of my whole journey.

I gave up on the idea of brushing my teeth, and simply crawled into bed, my mind shying away from trying to resolve my problems. I closed my eyes, just wishing for the world to go away for a while!

I had taken a photo of the tea-coloured water coming out of the tap, with my toothbrush held hopefully nearby, but destined to remain dry. Even as I looked in dismay at the brown flow, I had thought, "I must get a picture of this, because one day I will laugh about this moment."

Travelling is interesting, in that it is often the toughest times, the worst situations, the injuries and near misses, which become the fondest memories, the stories that are told and re-told. I knew that this low point would be something that I would be very entertained by, once time had worked its magic, and turned the incredibly frustrating events into a grand adventure.

At the end of 90 weeks I had achieved 83 goals, so was now well behind schedule. There were several goals in the remaining 17 that I had no idea how to complete, and I was starting to accept that the likelihood of achieving all 100 of the challenges on my list was now practically impossible.

I had only ticked off five goals in the last ten weeks, which at this late stage was not at all good! I firmly believed though, that it was much more important to do things the way I wanted, and enjoy the overall experience. I could have taken a sight-seeing flight out of Kathmandu, and seen Everest on my first day there, saving myself almost three weeks. But what would have been the point of that? It was the trek that I had come to do, and the trek would be an experience that would be treasured forever. I knew the decision to go on the two-week trek would always be something that I would never regret. If I had sacrificed that just to keep ticking things off a list, I would have never been happy about the decision.

Chapter 10 – Weeks 91 to 100

(26th April 2010 – 4th July 2010)

Nepal – India – England – USA

My final two days in Kathmandu were something of a challenge. With only ten weeks left until the end of the whole adventure, I was starting to feel ready for the endless planning and travelling to be over. I was looking forward to being able to take a rest.

I was still enjoying the adventure, meeting new people and seeing new places, but I was starting to feel a little burnt out. I just wanted to be somewhere comfortable, where there were no worries about the potential repercussions of eating, or drinking the local water, where the electricity was on all day, and an internet connection didn't feel like a rare luxury.

I had already spent quite a few days lounging around at my cheapie hotel, and was ready to move on. But now I was a little trapped. I felt a bit like I imagine Martin Sheen's character, Captain Willard, may have felt in the opening scenes from classic Vietnam War movie "Apocalypse Now". For a while he is stuck for days in a hotel room in Saigon. "Every minute I stay in this room, I get weaker. And every minute Charlie squats in the bush, he gets stronger," says Willard. I felt like I was suffering the Kathmandu version of the same scene, watching my goals slip slowly out of sight, without even the bottle of whiskey to help pass the time, only the occasional cup of coffee at the café round the corner!

My quick visit to India had been so well planned, and I had already booked perfectly timed train tickets from Delhi to Agra and back, in time for my flight to London.

My onward flight from Delhi to London was practically impossible to change. The international air travel chaos caused by the Icelandic volcano eruption over a week earlier was still affecting travel plans for thousands of people. Hundreds of flights had been affected by the huge ash cloud that had closed much of Europe's airspace for some time. Many flights had been re-scheduled, many more had been cancelled. Flights that did operate were all over-booked, and many travellers were left stranded. I had met a group of people in Kathmandu airport, still trying to get home five days after they should have flown out. To try to push my flight back a day or two would be a big mistake.

My next flight, from London to Florida, was also booked, and I didn't want to risk missing that. As it was, I would barely have enough time in England to see the people that I wanted to catch up with, before I flew to the States again.

By the time I got a new ticket to Delhi, and resolved my Indian visa issues, my time in India had been reduced from a comfortable and well-planned four days, to around twenty-four hours. The train tickets I had booked were both now useless, and it would appear that I had no way to get to see the Taj Mahal.

If I didn't achieve this goal while in India, it was certain that it wouldn't be achieved in the 100 weeks timeframe, as I no longer had either the time or finances to return again. I was pretty sure that I wouldn't have the desire to do so either. I was finished for a while with the endless hassle of third-world travel. England and then the States beckoned me brightly.

With a little help from the guys at the trekking agency in Kathmandu, I came up with a new plan. We soon had a driver organised to meet me at Delhi airport, ready to whisk me down to Agra for a quick visit to the Taj Mahal. The timing was going to be tight, and I was going to have very little time there, even if we managed to arrive in time to get in.

The flight out of Kathmandu was delayed. The traffic in Delhi, and on the road to Agra was busy and chaotic. Our progress was painfully slow. As the day slipped frustratingly by, it became more and more obvious that we were not going to get there before the place closed, and I resigned myself to only seeing the spectacular palace from a distance.

The achievement of the goal was starting to feel a little pointless. I felt, perhaps for the first time, that I was spending far too much money to simply go and see something, take a picture, and put a tick in a box. It seemed more like a chore than the achievement of a lifelong desire.

But as is often the case, my travels had a surprise in store for me, and the eventual outcome of the long day and evening was incredibly uplifting and heart-warming. My privileged peek into regular Indian family life was an experience that no money could ever buy, and the friendship and hospitality shown that night touched me deeply.

The disappointing achievement of the Taj Mahal goal didn't matter at all. It would always be there, and I could come back in the future at any time I liked. As I had always thought, the goals had always been a framework around which to build an adventure, and on this occasion the adventure was once again about the people I met. On this occasion it was also about the lesson I learned.

Goal 84 - Taj Mahal
Monday, 28th April 2010
(Agra, India)

Well, where do I start with this goal? What an unusual, and incredibly full day and a half. This has been one of the most trying and difficult goals to arrange, and I have had many problems to overcome. Ultimately the achievement was a long way from being satisfactory, but the experience of trying to make it happen was quite extraordinary.

Yesterday morning I caught a taxi at 6am to Kathmandu airport, arriving just before 7. My flight wasn't until 9:30, and I was hoping that by being early, I might avoid the chaos that I had seen a couple of days earlier. There was already a huge line just to get into the airport, and at the door a few surly security officers were checking passports and tickets. Fortunately I had a paper print-out of my ticket, otherwise I would have been required to get the laptop out and show them my confirmation email!

Inside, I was one of the first in line for the Jet Airways check-in. I met one guy there who was on his third visit to the airport to try to get out, as every flight is so overbooked with passengers who have been delayed by the Icelandic volcano problems. Being early was looking like a good idea. I was eventually issued a seat number and a boarding pass.

The waiting room was packed, and incredibly unorganised, and at 9:30 there was still no sign of being able to board. Eventually we got on the plane, but were still on the tarmac at 11am. We were finally in the air over an hour and a half late, which meant I landed more than an hour behind schedule in Delhi.

Time in India was going to be incredibly tight! With only 24 hours available, public transport was never going to get me to Agra to see the Taj Mahal, and back to Delhi in time for my London flight. I had no intention of missing that, as another flight would be hard to organise, and a further financial disaster. Avhi at Himalayan Encounters in Nepal had arranged for a car and driver to meet me at the airport, to whisk me straight to Agra. It certainly wasn't a cheap option, but was about the only way I was going to get to achieve my goal. My alternative was simply to sit around at the airport for a day and a night, and give up on the goal.

As I emerged into the sweltering Delhi heat, I was met by Johari, who had a sign with my name on it, and we were on our way. Unfortunately the trip by car takes about five hours, and with the late arrival we only had an estimated fifty percent chance of getting to the Taj before closing time, depending upon the traffic.

The journey was quite an eye-opener! I had thought Kathmandu seemed chaotic, dirty and disorganised, but India has it beaten hands down! The roads are packed with cars, buses and trucks, and weaving through them are thousands of motorbikes, scooters and bicycles. Thrown into the mixture are hundreds of tuk-tuks coughing black fumes, rickshaws, tractors, and carts being pulled by horses, bulls, or camels. People walk through this speeding chaos to cross the road, and bus passengers climb up and down off bus roofs in the middle of busy intersections. Every second vehicle has a huge reminder painted on the back to use your horn, and every driver does so at every possible opportunity. It is so non-stop noisy!

Johari did his best in the crazy Indian traffic. For a while we thought we might just make it, but we hit Agra pretty much at rush hour, and the sun was only about half an hour from setting, which was when the Taj Mahal would close. Eventually we had to admit that we weren't going to get in. Johari suggested we detour to another point across the river, where we would have a wonderful view just as the sun was setting. I suggested that if we weren't going in, maybe a couple of beers might be in order, and we bought six monster bottles on the way.

The Taj Mahal was very impressive, even from a distance. It is huge, and the people visible across the river, outside the building, gave the place some scale – it really is quite breath-taking. The view was only slightly marred by the razor-wire fence in front of us, barring us from getting any nearer.

As the sky darkened and the full moon rose, Johari pointed out a temple across the river where bodies were being cremated, their ashes due to go into the holy river in front of us. We could see three fires burning. It was very quiet and atmospheric.

But we only had about 20 minutes before darkness fell, and I felt a little disappointed that I was achieving this goal in relatively poor fashion. For possibly the first time on my travels, it felt a little as if I was simply coming to look at something, so I can tick it off as seen on a list. The feeling was strengthened by the fact that afterwards we simply turned around to head back to Delhi, another five-hour drive through chaotic traffic, this time seeming even more dangerous in the dark.

It was on the journey back, however, that I really began to appreciate the uniqueness of the whole experience. It had cooled a little, and we drove with the windows wide open. Everywhere was packed with people, and on the outskirts of Agra the poverty was very apparent, some people obviously just living under tarps by the roadside, or in tiny mud huts.

Everywhere there were street carts cooking food, and selling all sorts of everything. The smells were wonderful, and basking in the warm glow of a couple of big Indian beers, I hung my head out of the window, and tried to absorb the whole atmosphere. I laughed with Johari, telling him I felt like a dog must feel, head out of the window sniffing at all the unusual smells. I imagine my tongue maybe lolled out a bit too. I had only had two bags of crisps since the tiny breakfast on the plane from Nepal.

I had nowhere planned to stay for the night, and asked Johari if he had any cheap hotel suggestions, somewhere that would still be open after midnight when we got back to Delhi. Otherwise, it was back to the airport for a night on the floor there, I told him. No need, he replied. We had got on really well on the journey, and he had already spoken to his wife. He had told her he was bringing a guest home for the night. We wouldn't be stopping for food either, dinner would be ready when we got to his house. I was very flattered.

Johari lives with his wife Indra, and two sons Pritesh and Nilesh. Their tiny one room house serves as bedroom, living room, dining room and kitchen all in one. There is a little bathroom too. Also visiting and staying the night was Johari's brother and his son. Indra made us a fantastic meal of several different curries and sauces, along with hot chapattis, and we finished the remaining beers. My bed for the night was on a small sofa at the end of the bed, and seven of us slept scattered around the small room.

Indra made us omelette for breakfast, and I tried to find the words to express my thanks to her and Johari for their wonderful hospitality. I truly felt so honoured to be taken in by them, a complete stranger breezing through, and to be so well looked after.

Johari came with me first by rickshaw to the metro, and from there to the bus station, where he put me on the right bus for the airport. Once again I tried to express my gratitude, and we said our goodbyes.

Gazing out the window of the bus I thought long and hard about the previous 24 hours, and was so grateful that I had decided to make the journey. As it turned out, the day had little to do with visiting the last remaining seventh wonder that I hadn't yet seen. It was about meeting a new friend, and learning something of the true meaning of hospitality.

With only ten weeks remaining, it was now pretty obvious that a few of the goals were going to be unachievable, and I wasn't going to complete the full list of 100. My experience in India made me realise that I didn't really mind at all. As long as I made the most of the opportunities and experiences that came my way, I would have achieved exactly what I had wanted to achieve when I had set off almost two years earlier.

Returning to England was a great relief, and I really appreciated the comforts at Martin and Rachel's house. A fridge with food in it was an absolute luxury. No need to go on a trip out to a café to get a coffee, no need to have dry granola for breakfast, with fresh chilly milk in the fridge.

It had only been just over three weeks since I had left my comfortable Australian temporary home with Marty and Carol, but on this trip that felt long enough in the more challenging travelling locations. I was certainly tired of travelling now, and ready to slow down a bit.

In England there was disappointment over a couple of the goals with which I was struggling. I was still hoping to gather 5 Ian Ushers together in one place, and secure Richard Branson's charitable donation. I planned to try in Newcastle this time around. There are four or five Ian Ushers in the area, according to Facebook, which gave me a reasonable possibility of achieving the goal. I had messaged all the Ians while in Kathmandu, and only one had responded positively, suggesting the Saturday afternoon. I heard from two other Ians, neither able to make it that weekend. Other than the original three lans that I had met in London, none of whom could make it, I didn't get a reply from any other lans.

Another let-down was my failure to find a suitable location to jump a car off a jetty into water. This is something I have always wanted to do, having seen it done in many movies. Theory suggests that if you are in a car which falls into water, you can stay in the car while it sinks, still enclosed in an air pocket. Because of the water pressure on the outside of the vehicle, it will be impossible to open the doors. Once the car settles you can stay inside, and allow it to fill with water, still breathing from the air pocket in the roof space. When full, a window or door can be opened, and with a last breath from the air pocket, you can swim to the surface.

Obviously I had no intention of dying while doing this, and appreciated the dangers, so wanted to put some safety considerations in place. I would need a car with manual wind-down windows. I would have an air tank secured behind the driver's seat. A knife and hammer would be close at hand. Of course, I would also need a group of divers to act as both safety cover and video documenters.

While in Kathmandu with some time on my hands, I had tried to make some progress with this goal. I had started looking for a suitable place and some assistance, by placing some requests on several UK diving group forums.

I got quite a few non-committal replies, but one particular forum lit up with responses. Many people suggested I was crazy, was going to kill myself, and was selfishly going to kill others with my ill-conceived stunt. Others supported me, suggesting that life is about fun and adventure. There was much discussion about health and safety rules, and much technical pondering about what might actually happen if I tried this.

I waded into the discussion myself, particularly in defence of wanting to try something with quite a bit of risk involved. In response to those suggesting that I was crazy, I argued that life really should be about taking some risks, accepting some challenges, experiencing some adventure, and having some fun. I obviously didn't want to die trying this, and would do everything possible to avoid that outcome, but I still did want to try it.

Many people choose much riskier pastimes. Mountaineering, motor sports, caving or scuba all have inherent risk factors, but people choose to do them because of this. The element of risk faced, and fear overcome is what makes life so much sweeter.

Skydiving in its more extreme form, BASE jumping, is incredibly dangerous, and suffers a very high mortality rate, but more and more people are drawn to the huge thrills it offers. On the flight from Delhi to London, I had watched a documentary about BASE jumper Jeb Corliss, who pushes the boundaries of what is possible. The particular jump he was planning for was a freefall down one of the steep ridges of the Matterhorn, a 14,000' peak in the Alps on the Swiss/Italian border.

At one point, in a couple of sentences, he summed up my whole belief about life, and how we should live it. Considering the possibility of dying on the jump he was about to perform, he said, "Life is just a bunch of experiences you have until you die. That's really it. It's simple. I just want to make those experiences as incredible as possible.

Unfortunately I couldn't find a place to jump a car into water, and had to accept that this was an experience, that in all likelihood, wasn't going to be enjoyed in England.

Disheartened, I headed north to see Bruce in Scarborough for the weekend instead. I cancelled the meeting with the remaining Ian, apologizing that it had to be five of us together, or not at all. It is always good to be back in Scarborough – there is a pleasant unchangedness about it all, and there are many good friends there still.

Chatting alone with Bruce as we worked in the shed on his current road signs commission, he asked what I planned to do after the completion of the 100 weeks. I was glad of the opportunity to talk, as it was something that was filling my mind more and more as the end of the journey approached. What did I want to do? Where did I want to live? I was excited by the idea of motivational speaking in the States, but what if I didn't manage to make a go of it, or couldn't get a work visa? Would I then go back to Perth in Australia?

It seemed like many of the friends I had had there had moved away, and with Mel moving on, it seemed there wasn't much left there for me. There were still a few good friends that I missed, of course, but I didn't want to be tempted back into driving in the mines again.

I mused aloud that I still had so many good friends in Scarborough. "There's your answer then," said Bruce. "Move back here, you'll be happy 'cos you have a good group of friends," he explained, and then added, "and we can take up classic sidecar racing!" It all sounded tempting, but... What about the weather? What job would I do? Where would I live? And how would I cope with the lingering memories of Laura? We had shared so much together in Scarborough.

With another goal in my sights, I had printed more photos from my travels, and was going to have to have a serious re-think about my packing. My father's premature death in 1994 had impacted me hugely, and the bowel cancer that had taken him is one of the most successfully treatable forms of cancer if caught early enough. I had set myself the goal of raising funds for bowel cancer research and awareness, choosing an Australian organisation in Sydney as the beneficiary. I had set my target high, wanting to challenge myself, at an optimistic figure of $50,000.

I had never really been sure how I was going to raise this sum, but had come up with the idea of printing some of my favourite photos from my travels, offering them in exchange for a charitable donation.

I had chosen fifty photos, printed fifty copies of each one, signing and numbering each one individually, so that every picture was unique. My final photo selected for the set of fifty was of the Taj Mahal, and in London

I got the last of the photos printed. There were 2,500 prints in total, and if I could get a donation of $20 for each, I would hit my target of $50,000.

The box of photos, along with envelopes too, was large and heavy, and there was no way it would ever fit in my rucsac. I had asked Bruce if he had a large old suitcase, and he had provided the perfect thing. I was going to have to leave behind many clothes, and my sleeping bag too, but I didn't expect to be anywhere cold for the foreseeable future.

I really didn't like the idea of having a suitcase though!

The short break in England was just the tonic I needed. After a trying last week in Nepal and my severely shortened trip to India, it was wonderful to return to familiar surroundings, and more importantly, the support of friends and family. Seeing Bruce had levelled me a little, as it always does, and spending a few days with mum was relaxing too.

The highlight of the short visit to the UK was my cousin Mike's 50th surprise birthday weekend, where I got to catch up with many of the family members that I hadn't seen for quite a while. We had as much fun as always, visiting an adventure theme park, enjoying a raucous meal at the local pub, and a day out at the horse races.

One of my favourite moments was chatting to my cousin's son Owen, who is also my godson. He just turned sixteen recently. Somehow I managed to forget his birthday, and I apologised, suggesting that I must be the worst godfather in the world.

"Oh no," he answered seriously. "My other godfather is even worse than you. He rang the house here once and I answered the phone, and said 'Owen speaking!'"

"'Oh, I think I have the wrong number!' his other godfather had said, and hung up!

"Ah-ha!" I had laughed, "I am not the worst godfather. And out of your two godfathers, that makes me The Best!"

I had done an interview for a UK newspaper earlier in the week, and there was much anticipation among the family members for the article appearing in the Sunday paper. The reporter had followed the somewhat familiar format of the broken-hearted man trying to fill his life with a long list of diversions, but ultimately unable to fill the empty hole his lost love had left.

While there was obviously still an element of truth in this, it was a pretty small part of the interview as I remembered it. When questioned I would always try to focus more on the amazing experiences I have had, and the wonderful people I have encountered on my journey. However, I never have much influence on how a story is written. I was also grateful of any coverage I could get, as any publicity could only help with my charity fundraising.

It is amazing sometimes where press coverage can lead. I received many emails in response to the newspaper article, many offering sympathy and support. One of the most serendipitous contacts came from Jelene, who lived in Miami, and had read the article online. I was scheduled to fly to Florida the next morning, and had no sort of accommodation planned for my first night there. After several back-and-forth emails, Jelene had arranged accommodation for me, and was looking forward to meeting me the following evening.

The next day I met up with her and her partner John, two people who hadn't even heard of me until the day before. They had somehow managed to arrange a luxurious suite for me in an amazing hotel, and we chatted for an hour or two. At breakfast the next morning, they re-confirmed the invite they had made the evening before, suggesting I join them in Costa Rica in two week's time.

It still amazes and delights me to meet such kind and open people, and to enjoy the somewhat random nature of my journey. When offered such wonderful opportunities, I sincerely believe that it is almost always best to accept, and see where the adventure leads. It would involve a few changes to my rough plans, but I explained that I would almost certainly take them up on their offer.

I had no idea how the next part of my journey would work out, but I had some hopes hidden away in the back of my mind. I had only been with Moe for a brief time almost a year and a half earlier, when I had visited Whitehorse in the depths of winter, to experience the thrill of dog-sledding through the wilderness.

A lot had changed for both of us in that time. We had kept in touch off-and-on since then, and fortunate timing for us both had meant that we could arrange almost two weeks together. We planned to meet in Tampa, where I had arranged to achieve a few goals. We could then take a holiday for a week, probably somewhere in the Caribbean, where I could (almost!) justifiably claim to be enjoying a workplace romance.

Our meeting at the airport was slightly marred by the fact that her flight had arrived a little early, and I had arrived a little late, but we finally found each other. Our first minutes together again were only a little awkward, and we obviously had a lot to talk about.

We managed to find a fantastic hotel deal online, and headed off in the hire car that was a free add-on to my UK-to-Florida package holiday. I had no intention of taking the flight back, but the package, including the car for the week, had cost no more than a one-way flight!

At our hotel we soon fell into the easy companionship that we had enjoyed in Whitehorse, and before long the companionship developed further, as naturally as it had during our previous time together.

We caught up again with Cari, my previous Florida host, and enjoyed a day at Busch Gardens. Time in Florida slipped by smoothly, and I enjoyed Moe's company. I remembered the always good-natured, slightly competitive relationship we had both enjoyed in Whitehorse, and wondered where our time together might lead.

Three goals in one day! Goals 85, 86 and 87

Thursday, 13th May 2010
(Tampa, Florida)

When planning a couple of the more expensive goals on the list, I ran into a few problems. Initially I had planned to go to Russia to experience a weightlessness flight, and a flight in a MiG fighter jet. However, I ran into two issues. The first was that the flight in a MiG cost anywhere between $12,000 and $16,000, depending on the package chosen. Without a book deal signed yet, and without having done a stroke of work for over two years now, finances will no longer stretch to this, so it was back to the drawing board.

The second issue was that the plane the Russians use for the weightlessness flights is currently out of commission, and not expected back into service until October!

So it was back to Google search, where eventually I discovered Howard Chipman, and his Florida-based company Aurora Aerospace. Howard operates weightlessness flights in his Rockwell 700. He also has an L-39 fighter jet trainer, and offers a flight in this as an add-on to the weightlessness adventure.

After a few emails back and forth we worked out a date, and this morning Moe and I turned up at the St. Petersburg/Clearwater airport. We eventually found Chip and his partner, Veronique, and started preparations for my L-39 jet flight.

Goal 85 – Fighter Jet Flight

While not quite a MiG, the Czech-built L-39 is a fighter jet used by many air forces around the world as a trainer for the MiG, and has many similar characteristics. It is a beautiful, sleek machine.

Kitted out with flight suit and a helmet, I was briefed and we headed out to the plane. In the cockpit I had a further briefing, and paid particular attention to how the ejector seat worked. I kept my hands well away from the big red handles.

The L-39 sounds just as good as it looks when the jet fires up, and we powered up and taxied out to the runway. Takeoff was fast and smooth, and the climb to height was impressively quick.

After a few easy turns Chip handed the controls over to me, and I tried a few turns. The controls were light and responsive, and it seemed very easy to turn quickly. We moved on to rolls, and after a couple of demos, I managed a reasonably satisfactory effort, followed by a much more confident roll. The plane handled so well, and was such fun.

We did a couple of stalls, and a steep climb to a stall called a tail slide, which results in a spectacular fall into a steep dive.

As we headed back, Chip asked what else we should do, and I asked him to show me what the plane was capable of. Wow! He threw us around the sky through a series of linked manoeuvres that felt like the fastest rollercoaster ever. The G-meter in the cockpit showed maximums of +4.1G and -0.5G, with which Chip seemed very pleased.

We finished with a low pass along the beach, dropping down to around 200 feet. We then did a fast low pass over the airport, followed by a steep final climb. What a stunning experience the whole amazing flight was.

Goal 86 – Weightlessness Flight

After lunch, Moe and I were briefed for the weightlessness flight by Veronique, who would be our instructor and assistant. We were flying in a Rockwell 700, apparently one of only 30 of these planes still flying. It was carpeted and fitted out very nicely, but almost completely stripped of everything in the rear to allow room for floating around.

The weightlessness flight involves taking the plane up to height, putting it into a dive to build up speed, then pulling it back into a very steep climb. The G-force at the bottom is around 2G. At the top of the climb the plane is pushed over towards another dive, and at the top of the parabola, there is a period of zero gravity for around 10 seconds.

I went first, and first tried a sitting position, then kneeling on the second parabola. Lying flat on my front, and then on my back were fun. The next time I tried with a couple of other small objects floating with me. I then tried releasing some water from a water bottle, which was fantastic. I managed to catch one drop in my mouth as it floated by. On the final parabola I managed a summersault, assisted by Veronique.

I strapped myself back into my seat, and it was Moe's turn. Looking out the window, I was amazed at the incredibly steep angle of climb. Watching Moe seem to magically lift off the floor of the plane was astonishing. I hadn't really appreciated how odd it must look when I was doing it. She followed the same progression, and it was very entertaining to watch.

For the last couple of parabolas we got to lie together and float up at the same time. Once again, what an extraordinary and incredible experience.

Goal 87 – Mile High Club

Although not one of the usual experiences on offer, Chip agreed to fly straight and level at around five and a half thousand feet for 15 minutes or so. With the curtain to the cockpit closed, goal 87 was achieved too – in much more comfort and luxury than the more common commercial airliner lavatory location. No further details or description needed or available for this goal, I'm afraid!

On the return to the airport, we discovered that the excitement of the day wasn't quite over, as one of the three landing wheel lights refused to come on. We didn't know if the wheel hadn't come down, or if it hadn't locked into place, or if the light was at fault. A test of the light indicated that all was fine there, the problem was more serious. Chip told us that a gear-up landing may be necessary, but said that we shouldn't worry – "people usually walk away from them"!!

Eventually the problem was resolved by some sort of manual back-up system, but the landing was a little tense. Chip put the Rockwell down very lightly, putting much of the landing impact on the right wheel, not the suspect left one, and all went well. The whole incident was dealt with incredibly calmly and professionally, and Moe and I felt very much at ease in such capable hands.

What an incredible day! After a quick shower we met again with Cari, and her husband Mart, for a delicious celebratory Thai dinner at the lovely little restaurant right next to our hotel. What a perfect end to an outstanding day.

On our return to Miami, we looked into booking a last minute holiday, and on the Saturday morning managed to find a great flight and hotel deal leaving that evening for Jamaica. We had a wonderful day in Miami, both obviously enjoying each other's company, but both of us reluctant to talk about what this might all mean.

I wondered if Moe felt any of the steadily growing attraction that I did, or if she still considered this simply as a week away, with a pleasant companion with whom to share some time. I hoped not, but our personal situations had both changed so much since we had last seen each other. I was now so close to the end of my journey, ready to settle somewhere and be done with the endless travel. She, however, seemed much more settled in herself after her divorce, not really feeling the need to have anyone else come into her life.

I was really starting to like her very much, but suspected that heartache lay further down this road for me.

In Jamaica, Moe and I seemed to grow closer, and found an easy ability to get along. For me, time seemed to fly by in easy, relaxed happiness. I tried simply to live in the moment, and enjoy the peace and contentment I felt.

But there was a slight uneasiness hidden away in the back of my mind, something from which my conscious mind kept shying away. Occasionally I would have a quiet moment of reflection, and the uneasy thoughts would bubble to the surface. All of this would come to an end, and Moe and I would fly back to Florida. She would catch a flight back to Whitehorse, and I would be back on my own again, facing the uncertainty of the end of my adventure.

Moe had expressed fairly clearly that she was happy to see me again, but as she had indicated the last time we had met up, she was quite happy to get along without any permanent partner in her life.

On our first day in Jamaica, we had wandered along the beach, happy and relaxed, chatting with many of the pushy beach salesmen on the way. Somehow we had ended up sitting at a beach-side bar with a guy who rented out jet skis. “Is this your wife?” Paul had asked me.

I had jokingly answered, “No, this is someone else’s wife.” Moe had laughed aloud, and Paul had given me a knowing smile and a wink.

“So she’s your girlfriend, then?”

“No, he’s just my lover,” laughed Moe.

I laughed too, but felt a little pang of disappointment. It was going to be very hard to leave her at Tampa airport in a week’s time.

That evening, lounging around in easy companionship in our hotel room, we spoke more openly about how we felt, and it looked like Moe was feeling something similar to me. We skirted a little around the larger implications of what we were discussing, but my heart lightened to discover that once again Moe was failing to maintain the detachment she suggested she had initially intended.

The following day we spent the afternoon walking into town and then out the other side onto the cliffs, aiming for the much advertised Rick’s Bar. However, we were easily sidetracked by a small coffee shack selling freshly roasted and ground local mountain coffee. Time slipped away from us, and by the time we finally arrived at Rick’s it was dark, and there were only a few people there. There were several launch points for cliff jumping, and I looked uneasily off the main, cliff-top step-off. It was pretty high, but above that there were much higher platforms, way up in the trees above the cliff.

We decided to avoid Rick’s inflated beer prices, and walked a little way down the road towards town, stopping at a little bar painted in the almost obligatory red, gold and green colours of Jamaica. Chatting to local salesman Mike at the bar, we were once again offered all sorts of tours, taxi services, and inevitably, some of the more infamous local produce too. Perhaps we really needed to fully embrace the Jamaican experience, we decided.

Moe bargained hard with the taxi driver who drove us back home. We laughed and chatted with him, and agreed to call him to take us to the airport at the end of our holiday. Back at our hotel, beers in hand, we went down to the dark, quiet beach, and waded into the tropical waters.

Earlier in the day I had told Moe about my idea for another book, which had come from a conversation in Australia with my friend Andy. “Isn’t it funny?” he had said at breakfast, as one of his kids cried for attention. “Every time you make yourself the perfect cup of coffee, you never get the chance to finish it. This cup is just the right temperature,” he said, nodding down at the steaming mug in his hand, “but by the time I sort the kids out, it’ll be too cold. I’ll make another, but it will never taste as good as this one.”

He disappeared to sort out the children’s issues, and I thought about what he had said. It’s a concept with which I am sure most people are familiar. There is a narrow window when that fantastic first cup of coffee is just perfect – no longer too hot, but not yet too cold. When you get to enjoy that narrow window of pleasure uninterrupted, it can be a truly simple moment of happiness. "'The Coffee Window.' Nice phrase! I like that," I thought to myself. It sounds like a great metaphor for all aspects of life. At times life is just perfect. Sometimes we recognise these brief moments for what they are, sometimes they are past and gone, and only in hindsight do we see them for the magical moments they were.

Wading that evening into the tropical sea with Moe, I said, "I have to tell you something. Walking out into the ocean with you, beer in hand, possibly – and I don't want to be presumptuous here – but possibly about to make love – well, it feels like a coffee window to me. This moment of pleasure and anticipation couldn't be more perfect."

Moe laughed. "I don't think you're being presumptuous!"

But a moment that couldn't have seemed any more perfect just got even better. As I swept an arm around in the water, it glowed with thousands of tiny pinpoints of green luminescence. I had only seen this once before, where tiny luminous creatures in the water light up and glow when disturbed. We kicked arms and legs, absolutely fascinated as our bodies lit up underwater.

It turned out that I hadn't been presumptuous, and as our bodies joined in the warm water, green lights flashed and glowed all over us. Having had a couple of beers, as well as enjoying some Jamaican home-grown hospitality, time just slipped away from us, and I have no idea how long we stayed in the water. It was one of the most magical experiences of my life. I felt so close to Moe, the rest of the world fading away to meaningless background.

Later, completely alone in the resort's hot spa in the middle of the silent night, we compared notes, and found that we had both felt much the same. My heart soared when Moe told me, "You are a joy to be with."

I was beginning to hope that there might be something more for Moe and I after this week. I had been invited down to Costa Rica with Jelene and John, and despite having only met them for one evening, was pretty sure it would be a fun week. Jelene had kindly extended the invitation to Moe too, but commitments in Whitehorse with her children, dogs, and job meant that she really had to catch the flight home from Tampa at the end of the week. I was still hoping to get up to Whitehorse later in the year though.

Time with Moe continued to be simply wonderful, and I sensed her wavering about returning home, the temptation of a further week together in Costa Rica exerting some influence. She sent emails to see what she could arrange at home, but her biggest issue was with work, where she was very much needed for a busy week coming up.

We talked more openly about what we both might want from the future, and that perhaps there was a desire from both sides that our futures might involve being more a part of each others lives. "I am happy and content being on my own," Moe told me, "but time with you feels extraordinary." We were still skirting a little around the larger issues and challenges that this may all involve, but we were certainly drawing closer together.

The next morning I sat down on our balcony to write some more of this book – this was meant to be a *workplace* romance, after all. Moe went off to the beach with a book and a notepad, and I got lost in my music and writing. It didn't seem like too long had passed before she was back, and as she passed me, she handed me a piece of paper. On it she had written, "I can't bear writing a dull story. I want to come to Costa Rica with you."

"What does this mean?" I asked. "Is this a desire, or a decision?"

"Oh, it's a decision. 100%. I'm coming to Costa Rica. I've got some emails to write!"

Goal 88 – Have a workplace romance
Thursday, 20th May 2010
(Negril, Jamaica)

This was always going to be a tricky goal to achieve, as I haven't really done a stroke of work for over two years now (which is just the way I like it!)

It is one of my more quirky goals, and comes from a visit back to the UK from Australia, when at a big family meal we all drew a card from a pack of "50 things you should do before you die" cards. Here is what I wrote back in 2008 on the goal description page of the website:-

Just over two years ago I flew back to the UK, and turned up on my mum's doorstep, on her birthday, as a surprise. She was quite shocked, but very happy too. I had asked my brother to arrange a big family gathering for Sunday lunch, and uncles, aunts, cousins and their kids came from far and wide.

We all had a great day, and my cousin Christine had bought me a small present. It was a pack of fifty cards, with fifty suggestions for "50 things you should do before you die".

That afternoon we had each family member pick a card, and accept the task on the card. The challenge was to complete that task before I next headed back to the UK. And if all goes well, I plan to be back there by the end of September!

These were the goals, drawn at random:-

- *Visit Paris*
- *Look up at the night sky through a telescope*
- *Go on a blind date*
- *Take a trip in a hot air balloon*
- *Give more than you can afford to charity*
- *Enact a favourite fantasy*
- *Compromise*
- *Buy everyone in a pub a drink*

- Take a sick day when you are not ill
- Do a bungee or parachute jump
- Take a luxury holiday
- Go to a huge sports game – football, baseball, etc
- Swim with wild dolphins
- Ride a rollercoaster
- Hug a tree
- Stay up all night and watch the sunrise
- Get drunk on champagne
- Clean behind the fridge
- Ask a stranger out
- Have an office relationship

My challenge was the office (or workplace) relationship! So far I have failed to achieve this goal (although I did kiss one of the girls who I worked with when driving trucks in Kalgoorlie!) I have no idea how I can succeed, as I do not plan to do any work between now and my arrival in the UK. I think I have to accept that this is going to be one that I fail this time round.

But I am going to leave it on the list for the 100goals challenge, and see if I can still achieve it. I reckon I will have to do some work at some stage to top up the funds!

I did plan to do some work back on the trucks in the mines when I returned to Australia in 2009, but due to the economic downturn at the time, driving jobs were few and far between. Eventually, after some half-hearted job-searching, I had simply set off on my travels again.

As the end of my journey approaches, I am starting to get to work on the final goal on the list, which is to secure a book deal about the whole adventure. This is how I hope I might pay off some of the spending I have been doing, and in a way, consider anything done towards progressing the book project as the nearest I will come to work for a while.

Moe, who is with me here in Jamaica, is also working on a book, and we have spent a bit of time together with our laptops at work on our respective projects. And what more romantic a place could you find than Jamaica?

Workplace romance? Well, there has at least been a little work done, and that's enough for me to count this one as goal achieved!

We arranged flights back out of Miami, on the same day that we flew in from Jamaica, and settled into a small city-centre hotel in San Jose, the Costa Rican capital. I found out a little more about what Moe had sacrificed to spend a further week with me. The most obvious factor was her children, who expected her home on a particular date, now hugely disappointed to find out that she wouldn't be home for another week.

But a potentially bigger gamble she had taken was with her job. She had been due back in Whitehorse to help with a particularly important booking at her workplace, and her absence would place an extra burden on her colleagues. She was also unsure how her boss would handle her failure to return as promised, and suspected she may not have a job when she got back. That wasn't a particularly appealing prospect in her position, she told me, but she also felt that perhaps she was ready for a change, and this might just be the catalyst she needed to make that change.

I was very flattered, and incredibly pleased by her choice to spend more time with me. I was finding that I just wanted to spend as much time as I could get in her company.

When we met Jelene and John we entered a new world of private chartered flights and luxury condos.

John is a partner in the development of a huge marina on the Pacific shore at Quepos, and comes down once a month to oversee progress there. Instead of the four hour drive across the country, we had a six-seater, twin-prop Piper Seneca whisk the four of us across to the west coast in about twenty minutes or so. A hire car was ready for us at the little airfield, and the condo was luxurious and spacious. We had a view across lush rain forest to the coast. In a tree not far from our balcony, a sloth hung lazily in the branches.

During the week we rode horses, danced the salsa, ate in beautiful restaurants, walked on the beach, watched monkeys by the swimming pool, went whitewater rafting, played pool and drank beer.

With each day we grew closer, and danced around the subject of where our futures might take us. We had both been hurt in the past, and defensive barriers proved to be hard to break down at times, but we both agreed that time together was very special, and that separating at the end of the week was going to be very hard.

We both enjoyed the dance, teasing each other about what we thought, what we might like to happen, and how we hoped the future might unfold, each revealing a little at a time a few of the cards we were both holding close to our chests.

Eventually though, somehow we decided that I should head up to Whitehorse when my 100 weeks was over, and then see how things played out from there.

I was over the moon. The last two weeks had been filled with happiness, and that Moe felt the same about me was wonderfully uplifting.

I was really starting to think that my two-year adventure may just have the fairytale ending that I had always imagined and hoped for, but never quite believed completely, or seen how that could come to be.

Like me, Moe is incredibly stubborn and very competitive, and we had played cards quite a bit, teasing each other about the results of the games. Moe was fastidious about maintaining a score sheet, and I was even more impressed by her competitive spirit, as overall she was losing quite badly, but was determined to make up the deficit.

Late one night, talking in bed, I discovered the true nature of her competitiveness. I was trying to explain how I felt, and express how happy I was that she wanted me to come up to Whitehorse for the summer. Struggling to find the right words, I said what had been on my mind for a few days now. "I guess what I am trying to say is that I am falling in love with you."

Her response was a bit of a surprise. "Ha! Yes! I win! I got you to say it first."

I burst out laughing, as this was just the sort of thing that I loved about her. She soon reciprocated though, and told me that she had wanted to tell me so many times over the past week or so. In the sea at Jamaica, crossing the river on horseback, or curled together in bed at night.

"You realise," I teased, "that this is all just a cynical ploy on my part. This will make a perfect last chapter for my book."

"Mine too," she laughed.

The end of the holiday came far too quickly, and we took the air taxi back across to San Jose. We enjoyed our last touch of luxury with Jelene, on a chauffeured trip to see Volcan Poas, an impressively steamy active volcano. We said our farewells to Jelene and returned to our more usual standard of accommodation in downtown San Jose.

The next day we flew back to Miami, where we collected a car for the overnight drive to Tampa. In the early hours of the morning Moe and I held each other sadly at the entrance to the departures lounge. I tried not to look back as I walked away, but couldn't help myself. It was going to feel like a long time until I saw her again.

I slept in the car a little that morning, and then met again with Cari, who had been looking after my huge suitcase. After a late breakfast, or maybe it was an early lunch, I dropped the car off at the airport, and that evening was back in Colorado Springs again.

It was wonderful to be back with Val and Brenda, and see many of the friends I had made during my previous visit to Colorado the year before. In Peru, Val had suggested that I could stay with them for a month or so if I needed to, and Colorado Springs would be an ideal base from which to tackle my remaining goals.

With just over four weeks remaining, I still had twelve unachieved goals, and it was now very obvious that achieving all 100 was out of reach. Although I could accept this fairly easily, and feel proud about what I had achieved, it made it difficult to be motivated about some of the remaining goals. However, I committed to finishing the 100 weeks in the best way I could, and to achieve as many of the goals as possible.

But having planned to go to live with Moe for a while, after the 100 weeks ended, it was difficult to focus. Rather than write to potential sponsors, or look for locations to jump a car into water, I would spend time chatting to Moe on the internet, and playing endless games of online backgammon.

Being with Moe had taken on much more importance now, and I was really just counting the days until the travelling, endless planning, blogging, and self-imposed pressure would be over.

In one online chat Moe reflected my feelings too. We both laughed as the discussion referenced a previous conversation in Costa Rica.

Moe: this is already feeling like a long month
Moe: did I really say I was fine with spending time apart?
Ian: yes, and plenty of it, you suggested
Moe: I think I might have to eat my words
Ian: again????!!!! :D
Ian: you must be full with so much eating
Moe: hmm, seems to be a pattern developing :D
Moe: guess i didn't necessarily expect to fall in love
Ian: ahhhh, that's nice
Ian: but you did!!
Ian: Ha! I win!
Moe: I think I win too

However, I did manage to make progress with several of the goals I had a good chance of completing successfully. Val had managed to borrow a couple of unicycles, and I practiced each day. I climbed mountains and went on long hikes with Tim, and many of us would regularly climb the punishingly steep Incline in an effort to shed some fat. Val too was a fantastic encouragement, pushing me to go to the gym on a regular basis, and putting us both through some testing workouts.

There were plenty of fun social activities too, as Val and friends all live very busy, very full lives. We went to BBQs at friends' houses, and I got to see my first live baseball game. I needed to have many of the finer points explained to me, and was just getting to grips with what was going on when the game ended. Among Val's health-conscious social circle, I had been the only person to have a hot dog – I had thought it was almost compulsory at a baseball game!

We went to visit local caves. We had a weekend away rock climbing, and went to see a canoe competition, catching up again with Eric, Jackie and Dylan.

We ran through the city centre one evening on an organised event with hundreds of other healthy locals, ending at a pub, and exercising enough will-power to only have water there! I also got to go target shooting with Val's father, thoroughly enjoying testing my quick-draw skills with a six-shooter and western-style holster.

One weekend, when Brenda was away for work, I borrowed her car and drove up to Denver. The car, a lovely Toyota convertible, was a pleasure to drive, and with the roof down in the sun, all was good with the world. I was hoping to arrange some skydiving, but by the time I arrived at the little airfield the skies had darkened, and the winds had picked up. I just got the roof of the Toyota closed in time, as the heavens opened.

My other reason for heading to Denver was to catch up again with Yvette. Her book, "The Laptop Dancer Diaries", was now complete, and was already in print and for sale on Amazon. I had ordered a copy and had had it delivered to Val's home, and I wanted Yvette to sign my copy. I was flattered to have been given a whole chapter, being dubbed in the book as "Mr. November"!

Goal #100, signing a book deal about my travels, was looking less and less likely to be achieved. My literary agent in London had come up with nothing, and my contacts in LA were also worryingly quiet, so it looked like I was going to have to consider self-publishing. As Yvette had already followed this route, she had plenty of advice and information for me, and we spent several hours discussing publishing options and marketing tactics.

The days in Colorado flew by, and it was two weeks before I managed to tick off another goal.

Wobbly Goal 89 achieved at the BBQ
Saturday, 19th June 2010
(Colorado Springs, Colorado, USA)

Goal #89 has been a long time in the making. It goes back more than a year, when Mel in Perth bought herself a unicycle. I had a few goes at trying to ride it during the months I spent there, after my first 7 months of travel.

In December last year, it became obvious that I was never going to get to play in the Sedgefield Ball Game, a huge, chaotic, once-a-year football match played across the whole village. Unfortunately, it was scheduled to take place on the same day as the culmination of Carnival in Rio. By moving the goalposts, and making a late substitution, I added "learning to ride a unicycle" to my list of goals.

At the time I could only manage a wobbly 10 yards at best, but have been doing quite a bit of practice over the past few weeks here in Colorado. Last night was a chance to demonstrate my newly acquired skills.

At the BBQ that Val and Brenda had arranged, I had an audience of 11 when I made my attempt on goal #89.

I haven't yet mastered the art of getting on without a wall or step-ladder to help, but I had set myself a target of covering at least 50 yards without falling off to achieve the goal.

I made it about halfway on the first attempt, but on the second go, made it confidently past the 200 feet mark that Val and I had measured earlier in the week. I also impressed myself by managing my first full figure-of-8 too!

After my success, I treated myself to a couple of celebratory pints of beer, from the wonderful homebrew IPA that Val's pal John had brought.

I had been practicing regularly for my next goal too, but was progressing frustratingly slowly. When Tim suggested a climb to the potentially snow-covered peak of another 14er, another goal-achieving possibility began to take shape in my mind.

Goal 90 – "On top of Old Princeton"
Wednesday, 23rd June 2010
(Mount Princeton, Colorado, USA)

I have been struggling with the harmonica, and feel that my progress has been rather slow, but just the other day found a posting on the forum offering some support and encouragement from regular forum contributor "tacobet". He suggests that old favourite "On Top Of Old Smokey" would be a suitable one to learn as part of my harmonica-playing goal.

Yesterday I had the opportunity to achieve the goal in unusually fine style. Tim was helping his buddy Cliff and daughter Claudia again, by backing them up as they walked another section of the Colorado trail, and suggested we could climb another of Colorado's 14ers. The summit of Mount Princeton is 14,197', one of Colorado's 53 summits higher than 14,000 feet. It is relatively easy to get to, giving us time to climb up and down and still meet Cliff and Claudia at the end of their trek.

Tim picked me up at 4am. By the time we had collected Cliff and Claudia, driven a couple of hours and dropped them off at their start point, unloaded Tim's ATV from the truck and driven up the track to our start point, it was almost 9am. We were on the summit just over a couple of hours later, and found a patch of snow in which to tackle goal #90.

We took some video of the musical event, but my camera seems to be failing again. After it's dunking in a swimming pool in Costa Rica, and its miraculous return to life, it has all sorts of auto-exposure problems. The video is just bright-white, and the audio is almost completely wind-blasted!

However, this morning I made another video of a bit of my harmonica playing, which you can watch at your own peril. It makes somewhat painful listening, I'm afraid!! I am nowhere near the standard I would like to achieve. I still struggle with trickier tunes, and keeping the right pace, but I am on my way.

"Don't give up the day job!" I hear you suggest.

Haha. What day job?

On top of Old Princeton,
All covered with snow,
I lost my true lover,
For courting too slow.

For courting's a pleasure,
But parting is grief,
And a false-hearted lover,
Is worse than a thief.

After the climb Tim and I did some exploring on the ATV, visiting a tiny town called St Elmo high in the mountains, and riding up into the forests. It is so beautiful on a sunny day among these amazing peaks.

What a long and tiring day though. We finished with a soak in the pool at Mount Princeton Hot Springs Resort, and eventually headed for home, arriving back at 10:30pm. I was asleep within minutes.

Since trying, and failing, to achieve my night skydive in Australia on the full-moon weekend in March, I only had three further full-moon opportunities. In April I had been in India. I had missed the one in May, by opting to go to Costa Rica. The last weekend in June, one short week before the end of my 100 weeks, was going to be my last opportunity to achieve this goal, and the weather forecast wasn't looking too good at all.

I had driven down to the dropzone the weekend before and done a couple of jumps, introducing myself to some of the regulars there. I tried to drum up some interest for night jumps under the full-moon.

I had then called in on the Friday afternoon, but strong winds had prevented any jumping that day. As evening approached, it was obvious this wasn't going to be my night.

I returned again on Saturday, but again things didn't look too good. Val and I hung around hoping for an improvement in the weather, and at about 9:30pm, Skip the pilot said, "It looks like we may have a window of opportunity coming up. Do you want to go up now?"

It was very dark, and I felt quite nervous.

Goal 91 – Black night

Saturday, 26th June 2010
(Canon City, Colorado, USA)

It was supposed to be a full moon, but thick clouds had darkened the skies. Looking out of the window of the little plane, everything appeared ominously black. There was a little light left on the horizon, where the sun had set behind the mountains about forty minutes earlier.

It had been an eventful and tiring day at the dropzone, and most of the staff and customers had already had a few beers. By the time 9pm came around, I was the only skydiver that hadn't been drinking. Along with Skip, the pilot, who had also remained sober, I was the only passenger on board the little Cessna.

Being the only jumper tonight was good, in that I didn't need to worry about other canopies in the air at the same time as me. One of the biggest dangers of jumping at night is two jumpers not seeing each other, and getting wrapped up together. But the downside of being alone in the plane was that there is nobody else to share the ride to height, to laugh and chat with, and to dispel the nerves.

With just Skip and myself on board the plane climbed to height very quickly. As I fiddled with my camera and gave my gear a final check-over, I was surprised to hear Skip yell "Two minutes!" over his shoulder. I looked at my altimeter. 3,500 feet. My heart was hammering.

By the time we turned on to jump run, and Skip powered off, shouting at me to open the door and take a look, we were at 4,500 feet. I would get almost 10 seconds of freefall. Looking out the open door, I could see the runway almost directly below, and could easily pick out the green lights of the landing marker, a huge T-shaped wind indicator in the centre of a large, flat, open area.

With a nod to Skip, happy with the spot, I climbed out onto the step, and hesitated for a second. I wanted to try to enjoy the moment, and the anticipation of what I was about to do. It really was dark out there. The only light I had was a small glow-stick attached to my chest strap, a faint glow from the luminous alti that I had borrowed, and a tiny red light on my helmet that told me my video camera was recording.

One second, and then I jumped into the darkness, accelerating downwards quickly, past the point of no return now. It is quite an extraordinary feeling to be falling in the dark. I watched the alti, and as it hit 3,500 my audible warning went off in my helmet. I reached behind me and threw the pilot chute.

I could just see the outline of my parachute as it started to open above me, and as far as I could tell all was looking good. I had a small head torch on my wrist and switched it on briefly to check that all was as it should be above me, pleased as ever to see a fully open canopy there. All I had to do now was get onto the ground without hurting myself.

I could clearly see my landing area marker, which showed wind direction too, and set up pretty well, making sure that I was going to land with the marker ahead of me to give me a decent height reference. I went a little too far downwind on the approach, and when I turned into wind for landing, the marker was a little further away than I would have liked. At least it gave some indication of how far I still was above the ground.

As the very dimly visible ground came up to meet me, I flared the parachute at what looked like the right height, losing forward speed and lift, hoping to stall to a stop at ground level. But in the dark I had misjudged slightly, and flared too high, stalling the parachute while still three or four feet above the ground. As the parachute stopped, I knew I would drop quickly. I made the decision to roll when I hit the ground, instead of trying to stay on my feet, which would have more potential to result in injury.

My roll was good, and I was laughing before I was even back on my feet. I gathered my gear, and was met by Val and the others from the dropzone. They laughed at my dusty condition, and I received plenty of good-natured mockery. There were also plenty of hearty congratulations for a successful and injury-free night jump.

I felt absolutely elated. I had been more nervous beforehand than I had cared to admit, and the landing area was darker than I had ever expected, but all had gone very well.

Val and I had been working pretty hard in the gym over the previous month. On my last day in Colorado, I felt I had got close enough to my next goal to be able to tick it off as achieved, with a fairly clear conscience.

As I wrote the blog entry for this goal, I was reminded of a conversation I had had several months earlier, when someone had asked me how I would prove that I had achieved some of the goals. His particular interest was in how I might prove that I had joined the Mile High Club.

I had laughed at the time, and pointed out that I didn't really feel the need to prove anything to anybody. Ultimately I was doing most of these goals for myself, and happened to be writing about them online. I never felt that I had anything to prove, or anyone but myself to answer to.

If I achieved a goal, I would write about it, but I had no interest in claiming to have achieved something that I didn't feel I had. In a week or so, I was going to have no issues writing about the goals which I hadn't completed successfully.

However, my next goal was one of those about which I felt a little hesitant. As with any longer term goal, such as learning a new language, or playing an instrument, there is no well defined end point. It is very hard to say when you have completed your objective. There is always going to be room for further improvement.

Goal 92 – six-pack stomach
Wednesday, 30th June 2010
(Colorado Springs, Colorado, USA)

I am a little hesitant to actually sign this one off as being achieved. This goal, like several of the others, such as learning Spanish, or learning to play the harmonica, is somewhat subjective.

I will be the first to admit that I am not quite ready for the front cover of Men's Health magazine, but I am still pretty proud of what I have managed to achieve!

This goal has always gone hand-in-hand with one of my other goals, which was to get back down to a weight of 70 kilos, (11 stone, or 154 lb), and maintain that weight. I managed to reach my target weight just before Christmas 2009, and have been under that ever since. I am currently just less than 150lbs.

These two goals have both been prompted by being somewhat overweight at one point in my life. At my worst, around 2005, I was about 10 kilos (or 22lb) heavier than my target weight. Not hugely overweight or anything, but bigger than I had ever been before. I didn't particularly like it, or feel too good about it.

The thinking behind these two goals was to achieve a fitter, healthier, leaner lifestyle.

Over the last five weeks, while staying here with Val and Brenda in Colorado Springs, Val has been my motivator, taking me climbing up The Incline, and visiting the local gym. His buddy Tim has taken me on a few long hikes. We have also been trying to eat as healthily as possible.

This is the sort of stuff I needed to be doing regularly for six months or more to really achieve the goal in fine style. Travel, time constraints, and the need to focus on other goals have all made this a bit of a challenge.

As with any sort of development that takes place a little at a time over a long period, it is difficult to see any changes. However, every now and then, as I pass the mirror in the morning, and I feel pretty pleased with the results so far!

The video we made is a little tongue-in-cheek reminder of the tough regime Val has put me through for five weeks now. I certainly couldn't have done it without him.

We celebrated this goal by taking the night off, and inviting all of the fantastic friends I have made here in Colorado to Red Robin. We ate huge burgers with fries, and enjoyed several beers. That's the last five weeks of hard work undone!!

From Colorado Springs I flew to Newark in New Jersey, and was met by my original hosts there, Linda and Brian. Moe and I had met them briefly in Florida, when we all went to see the spectacular launch of one of the last shuttle missions. It was good to catch up with them again.

After a night of amazing Italian food in their favourite restaurant, and far too much whiskey with Brian, I spent a hung-over morning trying to chat with Linda and her mum Nancy, who was up from Florida for the holiday weekend.

In the afternoon I caught a train into New York, and another out to Long Island. I was going to stay for my last couple of days with Lilly and family, who were my very first US hosts back in October 2008.

The weather was awesome, and we all spent much of the first half of the holiday weekend lounging around in their backyard pool, sipping icy Marguerites.

When I got the chance on the Saturday evening, I added a couple of final touches to the website I had been working on for some time, and was ready to post the announcement of the completion of what would probably be my final goal.

Goal 93 – BlindsidedNetwork.com
Saturday, 3rd July 2010
(New York, New York, USA)

I think it is particularly fitting that this looks like being the last goal from my list of 100 that I will achieve within the 100 week period, which comes to an end tomorrow.

My whole journey started when life blindsided me back in November of 2005. That event ultimately resulted in listing my "life" for sale on eBay.

I used the term "blindsided" on the ALife4Sale website, when explaining my reasons for wanting to sell everything I owned. I had in mind a phrase I remembered from Baz Luhrmann's wonderful musical advisory, "The Sunscreen Song", which offers the following thought:

"The real troubles in your life are apt to be things that never crossed your worried mind, the kind that blindside you at 4 pm on some idle Tuesday." I was blindsided at 11pm on an idle Wednesday!

The words to the song were originally written by Mary Schmich, in her Chicago Tribune column, intended as an imaginary graduation speech.

During the run up to the auction, after the huge amount of publicity that my sale garnered internationally, I received many emails of support from people all over the world. Many had gone through similar experiences. Some people had had to deal with much worse than the events with which I was trying to come to terms.

One thing common in many of the emails that I received was that people knew what it was like to be blindsided by life.

On the forum pages, someone mentioned that people like us should start the Blindsided Network. I can't remember who this was, and the forums have now been buried under an avalanche of spam postings. This is a shame, as there was some interesting and entertaining material in those forums. If I ever get the time, and can find my passwords, I might go back and dig the forums out from under the avalanche, and delete all the spam.

Anyway, I really liked the phrase Blindsided Network, and went and registered the website BlindsidedNetwork.com, unsure of what I might do with it. Once I started to create the list of 100 goals, I decided that one of those goals should be to set up a support forum for others who had been "blindsided".

I thought it might be nice to give something back – to repay some of the support that I received during the run-up to the start of the auction.

Here it is! There are still a couple of things that need a little polishing yet, but I hope to have these resolved soon. I need to sort out the blog page, and the colours on the forum page too, as well as embed the forum page into the website properly.

A few people have found the forum without me even mentioning it, so there are already a few postings. I invite you to join in if you have ever been "blindsided" by life – and let's face it, who hasn't?

I have more to write on there too, some thoughts on the positive outcomes from my experience, and the journey that followed.

Thanks to everyone who emailed me messages of support and encouragement during my eBay auction, and to all who have continued to follow my adventures since then. I hope that life only ever blindsides you in the nicest possible ways.

The next morning Lilly and her three children, Nicole, Chris and Leo joined me again for the trip into the city to visit the Statue of Liberty. It was July 4th, America's big celebration, and the city was buzzing with excitement.

We joined the long lines in the baking hot sun, waiting to board the ferry to Liberty Island. Eventually we made our way to the base of the flagpole, and waited for Linda and her mum Nancy to join us from the New Jersey side of the river.

At the statue once again, almost two years since I was last here, it seemed that the time had passed so quickly. At that time I was less than ten weeks into my 100-week adventure, and I had packed so much into the ninety weeks since then.

In 2008, it had only been possible to go up to the base of the statue, but now the statue was open again, and we had tickets to get up into the crown. Unfortunately, the ones I had given to Lilly and family had different names on, and could not be transferred. Ultimately, only Linda and I reached the crown, Lilly and family heading for home again after going up as far as the pedestal.

Gazing out over the magnificent view from the crown, I enjoyed a quiet, reflective moment. I thought about all of the amazing things I had done over the past two years, and the wonderful people I had met. I don't think that it had quite sunk in yet that the journey was over.

Coming back down to the pedestal, I was surprised and pleased to be met by Essi, who had shared the amazing experience of the Festival of the Dead with me in Mexico.

In the afternoon, having said goodbye to Linda and Nancy, Essi and I headed for Central Park, arriving an hour late at the location I had picked for any final people to meet us. The "Sheep Meadow" was huge, and packed. Even meeting up with Essi's friend Malick took some co-ordination!

Thanks to a vendor selling under-cover beer in the park, I finally got to enjoy a Heineken in the sun. The park was such fun, with roller skaters, drumming groups and buskers all adding to the holiday atmosphere. One guy had a sign offering "Free debate about whether we have freedom of choice!" I was tempted to have a chat with him, but decided against it!

After dinner the three of us battled through 4th July crowds, and watched the fireworks over the Hudson River. We had left it a little late, and couldn't get too close – the crowds were amazing, and most approaches to the waterfront were closed off by the police, but we managed a reasonable view.

The walk back to Penn Station was fun in the huge, friendly crowd. Saying farewell to Malick and Essi, I caught the train back to Long Island, as midnight approached on the last day of my 100 weeks.

Epilogue

Goal 101 – Another New Start

In the final minutes of my 100 week odyssey, I stared out of the window as the train rattled through the New York suburbs. My long journey was just about at an end.

I thought about many of my experiences from the previous 100 weeks. I had made many wonderful new friends, seen some incredible things, and enjoyed more than my fair share of experiences of a lifetime.

I had felt the amazing highs of achievement, happiness and love, and the lows of disappointment, loneliness and despair, as well as just about every emotion in between.

I had been asked many times how it feels to take such an extended and challenging journey. I had also discussed this on several occasions with other long-term travellers and adventurers. I would often describe the experience as emotionally amplifying. Life on the road seems to be experienced at a greater intensity. The good times really are incredibly good. In the past two years I had had some of the most fantastic experiences of my life. There are several events that I would describe as true landmark occasions, absolute high points of experience and emotion.

But there is a downside too. Travelling alone, certainly for me, can also offer some of life's lowest points. Loneliness is always there, lurking just below the surface. On several occasions, often after achieving a goal alone, I had pondered the nature of what I was doing, and the reasons for my journey. At such times, feeling low and alone, it was easy to come to the conclusion that it was all pointless – simply a diverting way to fill empty days, weeks, and months.

Usually the intensely low periods never lasted very long. In a way I welcomed them, as they made the highs even better when they came.

Travelling, particularly alone, has the amazing effect of not only amplifying emotions, but of accelerating the transition from one emotion to the next. On several occasions, I had swung from the elation of achievement, to loneliness or despair in a matter of hours, and then back to excited anticipation again by the next morning.

One of the most succinct ways I found to describe this emotional rollercoaster ride was to suggest that it felt like I was living life with the volume turned up to eleven! I would not have chosen any other way. That was what I had always wanted from my journey – the feeling that I was living life to its full potential.

Something else I was occasionally asked, particularly as the end of my journey approached, was if I thought the experience had changed anything about me. I still felt I was much the same person I had been before, but I also knew that a few things had changed within me. One of the main changes I felt was an awareness of a much greater confidence in myself, and my ability to face and overcome challenges.

Life, of course, is full of challenges. The last three years of my life, to a very large extent, had been inspired by one of the biggest challenges with which I had ever had to deal. I had to figure out how I was going to move on, after my wife decided our marriage was over and had made it very clear she no longer wanted to be with me.

When faced with challenges, we can always choose how we respond. What we decide to do in the face of adversity is perhaps the true measure of character.

When I had stood on the bridge over the freeway on that awful November night in 2005, watching the truck-with-my-name-on approach, I could have chosen the tragic path that some feel is their only option. I chose instead to cycle back home, and face a bleak and uncertain future.

After my wife and I separated, I lived on my own in a borrowed apartment. At that time I could have opted to take another self-destructive path. I could have easily dived into a bottle of whiskey to drown my sorrows, or sought other ways to numb the pain, following the downward spiral that many people take. I chose a different escape route, heading out into the desert to start a new career, driving a huge dump truck in a gold mine.

I returned to Perth to face more challenges, living alone in a house that Laura and I had designed for two. My unique solution to this situation was to package everything I owned into one big auction, and put my whole life up for sale on eBay. I hoped this would finally close the painful chapter of my life and free me to move on to the next, hopefully happier, part of my adventure.

However, things didn't work out as planned. When we couldn't switch on the "registered bidders only" option, things got a little crazy, and bidding reached over $2.2 million within the first twenty-four hours. When order was restored, the final bid was less than the house valuation. Despite the bargain price, the final bidder eventually dropped out. When no other buyer could be found, I wondered what to do. Would I set off on my travels, or would I give up on my goals in the face of this new hurdle? I eventually decided that I wouldn't let the unsold house prevent me from following my dream.

The challenges continued to come, and over the course of my journey I often wondered about the disastrous timing of some of the events that occurred.

As the auction ended, the global financial crisis was starting to affect Australia, and even the robust Western Australian housing market was starting to show signs of a downturn. If I had bypassed the auction idea and simply sold my house six months earlier, as my neighbour had, I could have netted an extra $50,000 more than the price I finally had to accept.

As I travelled, just before exchanging some of my Australian funds into US Dollars to buy my RV, the Australian Reserve Bank dropped its interest rate by a full one percent. The effect on the exchange rate meant that I had just lost another significant sum of money. The lower interest rate also meant that when my house did finally sell, the capital sum I had to invest would earn much less interest.

On my return to Australia, the deepening financial crisis meant that many mines had closed down. My fallback plan, to do three months work in a mine, was no longer feasible, as I couldn't secure a job. A year earlier, I could have walked into any of dozens of driving positions available.

The timing of the challenges was quite extraordinary at times. Swine Flu began to take a grip in Mexico a day or two after I had booked my flight to Cancun. It looked for a while like the country may be off-limits to travellers. Flooding in Peru closed Machu Picchu a week or two before I arrived, and the historic site was inaccessible for two months. An incredible volcanic eruption in Iceland closed much of Europe's airspace just before some of my worst travel challenges began in Nepal and India.

These were some of the major challenges I faced during my journey. There were plenty of minor hurdles too. Travel plans would have to be changed at short notice, delayed flights would cause missed connections, a missed bus would result in an expensive taxi ride. People would tell me that many of the things I planned were difficult, dangerous, or even impossible. I would have to deal with vehicle breakdowns, fear of the unknown, and of course, my old friend, traveller's loneliness.

I could have used any one of these obstacles as an excuse to stop. There were several occasions when I could so easily have given up. Many times I just wanted to book a flight to Perth, call Mel, and tell her I was coming back. It would have been so easy to do. I might disappoint a few people following me online, but I really didn't have anyone to answer to. I could make my own decision, based upon my own needs.

But when trying to achieve anything significant, challenges are inevitable. You have to push on, keep the end goal in sight, and find a way to continue.

I am immensely proud that I didn't give up in the face of adversity. I have found it is often the biggest challenges that offer the greatest rewards. The most outstanding example of this was our journey to see Machu Picchu. Val and I were told by many people that it would be impossible to see the site. When we did manage to do so, our elation at achieving the goal was incredible. Despite the challenges, we succeeded in a extremely fulfilling fashion, and shared an adventure I know we will both treasure forever.

Riding Colin's Wall of Death is another fine example of not giving up when the going gets tough. I fell off the bike on my first attempt. For the best part of two days, I struggled to master an incredibly difficult and disorientating skill. When everything finally clicked into place, and I rode the bike up onto the vertical wall, the feeling was wonderful. It was one of the proudest moments of my life.

Ultimately though, it is the end result of my journey that is true testament to my dogged determination to continue, regardless of the obstacles I had to overcome. With incredibly serendipitous timing, Moe came back into my life, and the spark we had ignited when we first met grew into a flame. Her re-appearance in my life provided an almost unbelievable fairy-tale ending to my journey.

Two days after my journey ended, I flew north from New York, entering Canada. From Ottawa I flew west to Vancouver, and then caught my final flight, heading north again towards Whitehorse. I had considered purchasing a vehicle and driving to my destination, but decided against it. It was five weeks since Moe and I had parted at Tampa airport, and I just wanted to get to Whitehorse as soon as I could. I had missed her terribly, and I was looking forward with excitement to starting our new life together.

I spent more time gazing out of yet another window, reflecting again on the incredible adventure that had brought me to this point. There was a slight feeling of unreality at how well everything had all worked out for me in the end.

Six months after my marriage crumbled, on 4th July 2006, I had set off from Perth with a few meagre belongings packed in my car, heading for Kalgoorlie, intent on making a new start in the huge mine there.

Two years later, in June 2008, I tried once again to make a fresh start, putting everything I had up for sale, as one complete package. I wanted to leave my old life behind and begin the next chapter of life's adventure, having no real idea what that next chapter might actually be.

Suggestions and events eventually resulted in the idea of producing a list of all the things I had ever wanted to do, and setting myself the goal of achieving them all in a set timeframe. I took up this idea with enthusiasm, once again having no idea where the journey might lead. In August that year, when my travels began, it really was a completely new start.

As the end of my adventure drew closer, I was asked many times what I wanted to do after the 100 weeks came to an end. I had asked myself the same question on many occasions. Why was I doing this? What did I hope I might achieve? Where was all this leading? During my journey I never came up with any satisfactory answers, other than my vague hope that my travels might lead me to new and exciting adventures. I also hoped, of course, that my journey might lead me to someone special – my unwritten goal 101!

Now I was making another new beginning. My long journey had ended on 4th July 2010, and I was heading to Whitehorse, happily in love, and excited about a future filled with possibility.

It had been suggested on a couple of occasions that after such a full two years, life might seem a little pointless, as I would have achieved everything I had ever wanted to do. This would always make me smile. As I had travelled, I met many people who had been to places of which I didn't know. As is often the case when travelling, with every place I visited, my list of new places to see had grown, rather than reduced.

I had also developed several new passions, inspired by my journey, and added to a new list several new goals I would like to achieve. I want to do more paragliding, and learn to fly a paramotor. I would like to get my pilot's licence. I am passionate about writing now, and hope to be able to help others get some of their work published. That was part of my reason for setting up Wider Vision Publishing. I have a seed of an idea for another book of my own. I would still perhaps like to try some motivational speaking. Of course, I also want to do some more travelling.

With a rejuvenated confidence in myself, an ability to take on tough challenges, and the flexibility to come up with creative solutions, I feel a real excitement about what my future may hold. I truly believe I can succeed at whatever I choose as my next goal.

What about Laura? Yes, at times I still miss her terribly. And yes, I guess in a way I still love her. For twelve years she was my best friend, and I was happy that we had planned to spend the rest of our lives together. I still hate her too. Despite my best intentions, occasionally the bitterness returns, and I question how someone so close could do such a thing to someone they once loved. I will forever be disappointed that I was never given a chance to put things right, to try to address issues of which I was completely unaware, before the plug was simply pulled on a wonderful twelve year partnership.

I still struggle to reconcile these two conflicting emotions. How can I hate someone I used to love so much? How can I love someone who caused me such pain?

However, these emotions are nowhere near as raw as they used to be. Both are lessened now, I think, by three factors.

Firstly, that wonderfully healing property, the passage of time, has applied its soothing balm. Every year lessens the pain of the past. When it does come calling from time to time, the past usually only prompts a sad smile now. I look back on those wonderful years with a slightly melancholy fondness.

Secondly, I am pretty sure that the path I chose, and the method by which I dealt with the problems I faced, has helped me incredibly. I am proud of myself – proud that when I looked off that bridge on that miserable November night, I had the strength to turn around and cycle home – proud that I realised it was time to start a new career and a new life out in the mines – proud that I had the nerve to go ahead with the eBay auction, when I needed to find some closure – and proud too of everything I have achieved since then.

Finally, and perhaps most significantly, I feel so much better about the past because I am now so happy in the present. I am much more settled now than I have been at any time during the past five years. A huge part of this is due to the people I am with, and how I feel sharing my time with them. I belong with these people, and am wonderfully happy to be part of this family.

In the back of my mind I had dreamed of something like this, but after ninety weeks I had almost given up hope. It was at that point, when I was just about ready to throw in the towel, that life produced one more of its big surprises. Moe came back into my life, and as we re-discovered each other, my hopes for how things might work out between us grew. I was truly blindsided when all my hopes were fulfilled many times over.

How do I explain the happiness of being in love? If you have felt it yourself, you don't need me to explain it to you. If you haven't, whatever words I conjure up will never adequately capture the joy of being with someone who lights up your world, and fills your life with happiness every day.

Finally, I have a few insights from my travels to offer. Some are realisations that are new to me. Others are simply a reinforcement of things I already knew. I hope you find something in them that may be of use to you.

The following list perhaps sounds like advice from some sort of motivational handbook, of which I have read many. If the advisories sound familiar, it is possibly because you have heard or read something similar before. Perhaps this is because these ideas are believed to be true by many others.

In reflection of Mary Schmich's words, used so effectively in Baz Luhrmann's "Sunscreen Song", for what it's worth, I will dispense my advice now:-

1). **You can't run away from your problems.** Selling your life on eBay won't change the past. Living a life filled with adventure won't stop the memories of what is lost. However, it is possible to use your problems as the inspiration to create something new, exciting, challenging and immensely rewarding.

2). **Change is good.** Change is inevitable in life, and no matter how much we would like things to stay the same, they won't. Embrace change when it happens, as there is usually nothing you can do about it. Change forces us out of our comfort zone, and requires us to re-assess our life. The outcome can often be startling.

3). **Don't worry!** If you have issues that are causing you concern, there are usually only two possible scenarios. Either you are able to do something about the matter that is troubling you, or it is something that is completely out of your control. If it is the former, then stop worrying, and get on and do something about it. If there is nothing you can do about it, all the worrying in the world won't change a thing.

4). **Challenges provide opportunities.** Big challenges provide big opportunities. It is through facing and overcoming challenges that one often reaps the greatest rewards. The bigger the challenge, the greater the satisfaction when it is overcome.

5). **Goals are easy to achieve.** Seriously, most of them are! You just need to take some action towards achieving them! Some goals are, of course, easier to achieve than others. Want to see New York? Just save up the money, and buy a ticket. Others may take a little longer. Any goal is possible when you map out the necessary steps. You just have to take that first step, and then continue to work towards the end result.

6). **Achievement often has a cost.** We all have to make choices and sacrifices. If you want one thing, then sometimes you have to give up something else. We make these choices, and then have to live with the consequences. Sometimes the result can be just what we wanted, sometimes something completely unexpected. Perhaps one of the secrets to happiness is knowing that in the past, we made the best choices we could, given the information we had available to us at the time.

7). **Sometimes it is the journey that counts.** It isn't always the end goal that is most important. It is often the overall adventure that provides the greatest experiences and insights, not the achievement of the goal at the end.

8). **Accept life as it comes.** Expectations can be a burden at times. Often events turn out nothing like we hoped or expected. Sometimes this is disappointing. Sometimes the results can exceed expectations in ways we could never have imagined. When we let go of expectations, and just allow the adventure to unfold, it can be very liberating.

9). **Flexibility is the key.** Problems will occur. Life will blindside you. Change is inevitable. You cannot be rigid with how you plan to do things, and have to adapt plans to suit changing circumstances. Flexibility is what enables you to turn challenges into opportunities, and opportunities into unique experiences.

10). **Life is an adventure.** We all only get one go at this. My firm belief is that we should perhaps try to live life's adventure to the best of our ability.

11). **Life is NOW.** Often I found myself with three focuses as I travelled. I would spend a lot of time writing blogs about events that had just happened. I also had to constantly plan ahead for the coming days and weeks. I always tried to remain aware that although the past and future are both relevant, life is lived in the small gap between these two. I always tried to enjoy every experience as fully as I could.

12). **Life is better when shared with others.** I have quoted Chris McCandless from "Into The Wild" several times, and do so again here: "Happiness isn't real unless shared." From the very start, I invited anyone who cared to, to join me at any point. Many people did, and I have shared some of the happiest moments of my life with some wonderful people.

As I write my final reflective thoughts, my mind turns once again to that terrible night five years ago, when I stood on the bridge over the freeway, watching the truck approach. I was never going to jump, but at the time I could easily see how someone could choose to do so. It would be such an easy option – a quick way to avoid the inevitable pain and misery that was to come over the following weeks and months.

Now though, I think of all I would have missed in the years since then. I drove a monster truck in a gold mine in the dusty outback of Australia. I put my life up for sale on the internet, and appeared on several live TV shows. I sold my story to a Hollywood movie studio. I experienced the wild excitement of Pamplona, the wonder of the Great Wall of China, driving across the States in my own RV, swimming with a whale and her calf in Japan, and enjoyed countless other incredible experiences.

I would have also missed out on meeting so many wonderful new friends. Perhaps most important, I would have missed out on meeting my new family here in Canada. I have been incredibly lucky to find such a warm welcome at the end of my journey. I am very happy with the new life I have found here with these wonderful people. What an unexpected end to the two-year-long rollercoaster ride.

It seems to me that all of life really is just one huge rollercoaster ride. Britt was the main cameraperson and interviewer for the documentary team that never got to finish their piece, when I was selling my life. In answer to one of her questions about how I felt, I once used a rollercoaster as an analogy for the wild ride I was on. She picked up on this, and often referred back to it, asking in subsequent interviews which part of the ride I felt I was on at the time.

Creating the website and putting the plans into action was like the slow nervous ascent up the chain which drags the car to the top of the first drop. As the huge international publicity for the eBay auction built up, I had reached the top of the steep climb, the clattering chain had gone silent, and I was looking down the first huge drop, wondering how it was going to feel. A week or so later, as I was receiving calls from Hollywood producers, I said that I was hurtling down the first huge drop of the ride, heart in my mouth, still unsure what was to come next, but whooping with delight.

The ride has now come to an end. It lasted for two years, and had so many ups and downs, most of which I never even saw coming. In July 2010 the car finally coasted in to the station, where a new set of riders waited to get on. But instead of getting off, I stayed on the ride. The ride filled up with new passengers, and Moe sat down beside me in the front row, laughing in delight as the chain started to pull us up the steep incline.

I have heard that chain rattling again for the past months, as I have worked on this book, preparing it for publication. It is time to send the files to the printer, and to list the book for sale with online retailers.

Once again, I have no idea where my choices and actions may lead, but Moe and I are looking down the first long drop of the new ride, hearts in our mouths, ready to whoop with delight as the car begins to plummet again.

Thanks for joining me for this part of life's wild ride. Now.... hands in the air, here we go again!

Appendix 1 – Goals achieved

1)	Snowboard on Dubai indoor ski slope	5 Aug 2008
2)	Big bungee jump	11 Aug 2008
3)	Christ of the Deep	17 Aug 2008
4)	Paraglide	19 Aug 2008
5)	Tomatina Festival	27 Aug 2008
6)	Climb the Eiffel Tower	5 Sep 2008
7)	Dive off the top board at Bishop Auckland pool	14 Sep 2008
8)	Oktoberfest	2 Oct 2008
9)	Climb Statue of Liberty (or at least walk round it!)	9 Oct 2008
10)	Kingda Ka rollercoaster	11 Oct 2008
11)	Niagara Falls	15 Oct 2008
12)	Sort out my tattoo	29 Oct 2008
13)	Have a hawk land on my hand and eat	1 Nov 2008
14)	See the Grand Canyon	12 Nov 2008
15)	See Mount Rushmore	15 Nov 2008
16)	Las Vegas	18 Nov 2008
17)	Skydive in a wind tunnel	22 Nov 2008
18)	Drive across America on Route 66	23 Nov 2008
19)	Los Angeles	24 Nov 2008
20)	Juggle with fire clubs	28 Nov 2008
21)	San Francisco	6 Dec 2008
22)	Gallop on a horse along a beach at sunset	9 Dec 2008
23)	Spend a night in a haunted house - alone!	10 Dec 2008
24)	Work in a soup kitchen on Xmas day	25 Dec 2008
25)	Go on a dog-sled ride in the wilderness	27 Dec 2008
26)	Snowboard at Whistler	3 Jan 2009
27)	See an active volcano	17 Jan 2009
28)	Dive with manta rays	19 Jan 2009
29)	Take the controls of a helicopter	20 Jan 2009
30)	Ride the long surf at Hawaii	24 Jan 2009
31)	Get Paula Campbell into top 10 in a Google search	26 Jan 2009
32)	Sleep in a Japanese capsule hotel	28 Jan 2009
33)	Hammerhead shark reef	3 Feb 2009
34)	Sell my life	6 Feb 2009
35)	Dive with whales	7 Feb 2009
36)	Ice sculptures - Sapporo Yuki Matsuri	9 Feb 2009
37)	Go to Israelite Bay	25 Feb 2009
38)	Ride a motorbike at over 250 kph on a public road	13 Mar 2009
39)	See Uluru	27 Mar 2009
40)	Learn to play didgeridoo (circular breathing)	29 Mar 2009
41)	Learn to kite surf	2 Apr 2009
42)	Swim with a 10+ metre whale shark	30 Apr 2009
43)	Cannes Film Festival	14 May 2009
44)	Learn to speak conversational French	24 May 2009
45)	Cooper's Hill Cheese Rolling Festival	25 May 2009

46)	Meet Richard Branson	31 May 2009
47)	Ride the Wall of Death	14 Jun 2009
48)	Do a wingwalk	20 Jun 2009
49)	San Fermin Bull Run Festival	8 Jul 2009
50)	Greenpeace, go aboard the Rainbow Warrior	12 Jul 2009
51)	Stay a night in an underwater hotel	19 Jul 2009
52)	Pyramid at Chichén Itzá	22 Jul 2009
53)	Bonneville Speed Week	12 Aug 2009
54)	Bobsleigh run	15 Aug 2009
55)	Bognor Regis Birdman	23 Aug 2009
56)	White water rafting	31 Aug 2009
57)	"7 peaks in 7 days"	1 Sep 2009
58)	Enter a $1000 poker competition	18 Sep 2009
59)	Meet 10 new people from ALife4Sale	21 Sep 2009
60)	Skydive from either a helicopter or a balloon	4 Oct 2009
61)	Have a bit-part role in a Hollywood movie	21 Oct 2009
62)	Memorise the poem "If..." by Rudyard Kipling	24 Oct 2009
63)	Festival of the Dead	1 Nov 2009
64)	Walk on the Great Wall of China	12 Nov 2009
65)	Ride an elephant	20 Nov 2009
66)	Elephants Round-Up	22 Nov 2009
67)	Red crabs march	12 Dec 2009
68)	See an iceberg	21 Dec 2009
69)	See the Northern Lights	22 Dec 2009
70)	See Table Mountain	5 Jan 2010
71)	Shark cage dive	7 Jan 2010
72)	Ride an ostrich	9 Jan 2010
73)	Victoria Falls	17 Jan 2010
74)	See the statues on Easter Island	25 Jan 2010
75)	See Machu Picchu	6 Feb 2010
76)	Iguazu Falls	11 Feb 2010
77)	Learn to speak Spanish	12 Feb 2010
78)	Carnival at Rio	14 Feb 2010
79)	See "Christ the Redeemer" statue in Rio	15 Feb 2010
80)	Learn to fly plane	27 Feb 2010
81)	Nude skydive	6 Mar 2010
82)	Slim down to and maintain 70kg	31 Mar 2010
83)	See Everest	16 Apr 2010
84)	Taj Mahal	28 Apr 2010
85)	MIG flight	13 May 2010
86)	Join the Mile High Club	13 May 2010
87)	Weightlessness flight	13 May 2010
88)	Have a workplace romance	20 May 2010
89)	Learn to ride a unicycle	19 Jun 2010
90)	Learn to play the harmonica	22 Jun 2010
91)	Night skydive	26 Jun 2010
92)	Develop a six pack stomach	30 Jun 2010
93)	Set up the BlindsidedNetwork.com support forum	3 Jul 2010

Appendix 2 – Goals unachieved after 100 weeks

Well, achieving 100 goals in 100 weeks was always going to be a huge challenge, and of course, the perfect ending to the story would be the fulfilment of the complete list.

When I started writing the list out in 2008, before the ALife4Sale auction had even started, I didn't censor myself in any way, whether the goals were scary, difficult, or expensive. Everything I wanted to do went on the list, regardless of how tricky it may prove to achieve.

I could have been a little more selective, chosen some easier goals, and have had a much better chance of achieving them all. But that is not what I wanted my journey to be about. Think big and achieve big. As I have said before, the goals were always just a framework around which to build a bigger "adventure of a lifetime".

Over the whole two years I only changed two of the original list of 100, one before the start of the journey, when the company that operated the thrill ride I wanted to experience went out of business, and another later in the journey, as dates conflicted, and two big events occurred on the same day.

But out of the list of 100 goals, I am incredibly proud to have achieved a total of 93 of them. The seven remaining (as yet) unachieved goals are as follows:-

Drive a car into water off a jetty

I tried to arrange this goal on several occasions, in several locations. In Salt Lake City my buddy Clay has a few TV program pals, and thought he might be able to get something arranged for this goal. The biggest problem he ran into was finding a suitable body of water to put a car into, due to pretty strict environmental regulations.

When I found myself with a few spare days in Kathmandu, heading next for England, I put some postings on UK diver forums, looking for suggestions for locations, and offers of assistance for safety cover. I didn't quite expect the level of controversy that my posting would receive. Opinion on my proposed goal was incredibly polarised. After much back-and-forth discussion, I pretty-much wrote off the UK as a possible venue.

Finally, back in the States again, a friend of a Hollywood stuntman contacted me on Facebook, but unfortunately I never heard from the daredevil himself!

At times I have considered simply buying a car, and driving it off a pier somewhere. However, I have always been keen to avoid two potentially undesirable consequences – being arrested and ending up with a hefty fine, or worse, getting trapped in the car with nobody there to assist! Common sense has prevailed here. Unable to do this safely, I have decided to wait until such a time as I can do this in the way I would like. I am sure I will get around to doing it one day.

Gather 5 Ian Ushers together in one place

I came so close with this one, managing to gather four Ian Ushers in a pub in London. I have tried on several occasions since then to achieve this goal. I even arranged a Skype call, hoping to at least be able to gather five of us together on an internet call. The three other Ians from the original gathering all agreed to be part of the final attempt, but despite many emails to many other Ians, I couldn't get one more involved.

I had thought this might be a reasonably easy goal to achieve – I mean, how hard can it be to get five guys together for a beer? But despite my best efforts, it would seem that most Ian Ushers are not the slightest bit interested in meeting any of their namesakes.

Thanks though to the Ians who did take part, sorry we couldn't make it happen.

Dive to the Titanic in a submersible

As far as I know, and I have done quite a bit of research, there is only one company that offers deep-dive submersible tours down to the Titanic. It lies on the Atlantic sea-bed off the coast of Newfoundland, at a depth of over 12,000 feet. That's over two miles down, and it is an extremely dangerous trip.

Unfortunately, there was no expedition in 2010, the next one being planned for 2011. I am on the mailing list for information, but another factor which makes this a particularly difficult goal is the expected cost of the expedition – $55,000 per person! Unless this book is a runaway bestseller, this one may not happen for a while yet!

Learn how to lucid dream

This is another goal upon which I have been working, on and off, over the course of the 100 weeks. Lucid dreaming is when, in a dream, you realise that you are dreaming. Apparently it is then possible to control the direction of the dream, and make it about whatever you want.

I have had this happen only twice, once long ago, and once during the course of the 100 weeks. I would like to be able to do this on a more regular basis, to count it as a goal completed.

It is something on which I intend to keep working in the future.

Raise $50000 for Bowel Cancer Research

I think I perhaps put off beginning my fundraising efforts for too long, concentrating on other goals instead. I managed to raise over $10,000 for my chosen cause, of which I am very proud, but it is still a long way from my original target of $50,000.

I can't make any excuses, but perhaps the world economic climate over the past year or two has made this particular goal a bigger challenge. I received many emails from people who would have liked to help out, but unfortunately, were not in a position to do so.

Many thanks to all who did contribute, or would have liked to. Your support is greatly appreciated, both by myself, and by the Australian

Bowel Cancer Association. It is also appreciated, I am sure, by the people whose lives may well be saved by earlier recognition of the onset of symptoms, and by more effective treatment which ongoing research facilitates.

Watch a baby being born

I have always imagined that one day I might see my own child being born, and this was a goal on a list from long ago. Maybe this will never happen for me, I don't know, but I left this goal on the list regardless. I think this must still be an incredibly moving experience, obviously more so if you have a connection to the parents, rather than it just being a random stranger.

Maybe I will still be lucky enough to experience this one day.

Secure a book deal for 100goals

Part of the original overall plan for the 100 goals journey was to write a book about the whole adventure, hoping to fund much of the journey with the proceeds of such a deal. For a while I did have an agent in London, but despite his enthusiasm and optimism he did not come up with any concrete offers. He cited the downturn in global economic conditions as one possible factor for the reluctance of publishers to take on new, unproven subjects and writers.

I also had someone in Los Angeles hoping to represent me, but again, nothing eventuated from that arrangement either.

On my travels I have met a couple of self-published authors, and in my research for publishing this book, did a lot of reading on self-publishing. I have actually come to believe that in my case this may actually prove to be a better option.

From what I have read, the publishing world is very much like the movie industry these days, with the six big players only keen to put backing behind sure-fire winners which will make the biggest money. Quality or originality counts for little when the ultimate measure of a book's potential is measured in dollars and cents.

Authors lucky enough to be picked up by a publisher often get very little in the way of publicity and promotion, having to do much of this for themselves, unless they are in the John Grisham-type big league. Therefore self-publishing, much like independent film production, is becoming much more mainstream these days.

Hence my ultimate decision to set up Wider Vision Publishing, and produce the book myself. Many thanks for your support, dear reader, for buying this book.

Appendix 3 – Some facts and figures

100 weeks
93 goals
112 flights
81 airports
41 airlines
1 missed connection
1 aborted landing
1 aborted takeoff
6 continents
31 countries
7 Wonders of the world
5 mobile phone numbers
Hundreds of new friends
One great big adventure

Appendix 4 – Bonus goals, achievements and experiences

Throughout my two-year journey I enjoyed many other incredible experiences, none of which were listed among the original 100 goals. Here are a few bonus experiences which added to my adventure:-

Microlight flight
Burg Hohenwerfen, 'Schloss Adler' in film *"Where Eagles Dare"*
View New York from the top of the Empire State Building
Unofficial Sopranos tour, inc. topless bar *"Bada Bing"*, New Jersey
CN Tower, Toronto
St Louis Arch
Quad biking
Fired several guns, including:-
- Colt 45
- Magnum 44
- Pump action shotgun
- AR15 assault rifle
- M16 assault rifle
- AK47 machine gun

Crazy Horse sculpture
Devil's Tower, Wyoming
Personal best – ten pin bowling – 170
Cheque from Walt Disney for a movie option – twice!
Sailed on San Francisco Bay

Giant redwood trees in California
Jet boat ride 40 miles up Rogue River in Oregon
Zodiac boat tour, Hawaii
Submarine trip, Hawaii
Share the front page of a newspaper with the new US President
Deep water night dive
Pearl Harbour
Dive on a WWII site where a sea mine was exploded the day before
Meet the Okinawa football team in Japan
Hand feed a fish to a wild sea-lion
Aerobatic flight in a Cessna
Climb to the top of the Rock of Gibraltar
Stroked a tiger and held a baby crocodile
Cape Canaveral on 40th anniversary of man setting foot on the moon
Saw the biggest open pit mine in the world
Skydived over Colorado
Arches National Park
Monument Valley
Zion National Park
Lived by the beach in California for a month
Rode a Segway
Turned wood to make pens
Fished for lobsters at night off San Diego
Public talk in outdoor sporting goods store
Ate grasshoppers
Bullet train in China at over 200 mph
Cycled around in Beijing's manic traffic
Sleeper trains in Thailand, South Africa and Zimbabwe
Caught a wahoo
Picked up a robber crab
Ate ostrich egg
Wild downhill mountain bike ride in Peru
Favela tour in Rio de Janeiro
Experienced an earthquake in Costa Rica
Saw the space shuttle launch
Fired more guns

- .22 Ruger 1022 – semi automatic rifle
- .22 Remington 552 – semi auto rifle
- .22 Remington 512 – bolt action rifle (no scope)
- .22 Ruger Single Six – western-style pistol
- .22 Ruger Mk I – semi automatic pistol
- .303 British #1 Mk3 Lee Enfield – rifle (sporterized)
- .243 Swedish Mauser – high powered hunting rifle

Managed The Manitou Incline in less than 37 minutes

AND MOST IMPORTANTLY:-
Met so many amazing people
Made some great new friends
And of course, achieved Goal # 101

Appendix 5 – British English

I am originally from England, and was therefore schooled in British English. I lived in Australia for seven years, where despite minor differences in some phraseology, words are spelt (not spelled!) in much the same way.

When editing this book, I had invaluable assistance from a Canadian, and an American. Both frequently insisted that my spelling, or choice of words was incorrect. I have been amazed at how many differences there are between British English and American English. Australian and Canadian variations further muddy the waters.

One word which caused some heated debate was disorientated. This is commonly used in England and Australia, but disoriented is the US and Canadian variation.

I have tried to maintain my Englishness throughout the writing process. For example, words such as colour, favour, honour and humour all have a u in them.

I apologise, but you may be surprised to realise that in England these words are spelt with –ise at the end, not –ize.

To further assist, here are a few other words that are used differently, depending on where you were raised:-

England		America
bonnet	=	hood
boot	=	trunk
petrol	=	gas
gas	=	propane
crisps	=	chips
chips	=	fries
tomato sauce	=	ketchup
sweets	=	candies
trousers	=	pants
pants	=	underwear
jumper	=	sweater
queue	=	line
rucsac	=	backpack
cheque	=	check
pavement	=	sidewalk
torch	=	flashlight
head torch	=	head lamp

I'm sure there are several other unusual words, phrases and colloquialisms used throughout the book. I hope this doesn't cause too much confusion.

A LIFE SOLD

"What is your #1 goal?"

$100,000 prize draw

Here's a question for you – "What is your #1 goal?"

What is it that you have a burning desire to achieve? What would you really like to be doing right now? Where do you want to go, or what do you want to see? What is your biggest wish – what does your heart desire?

Would $10,000 help you towards this?

Maybe you would like to experience the thrill of one of the adrenaline-fuelled activities that I tried on my travels. Perhaps you want to run with the bulls in Pamplona, try dog-sledding, take a flight in a fighter jet, or swim with whales?

Maybe you want to travel, and see something amazing – the Grand Canyon, the statues on Easter Island, the Taj Mahal or the Great Wall of China? Where would you go? What do you want to see?

Maybe you want to learn a new skill, or master a new language? Or perhaps you simply want to be pampered, and spend some time relaxing in a luxury spa resort?

Perhaps you want to do something to support a charity that is close to your heart? Do you want to take the kids on the most amazing holiday ever, or do something special for someone else?

The options are limited only by your imagination and creativity.

THE PRIZE

My 100 goals in 100 weeks journey started in August 2008, and came to an end on 4th July 2010. This date represents the end of one exciting chapter of my life, and the beginning of another. To celebrate my new beginning, I am offering an annual $10,000 prize to assist one reader to achieve the goal of their dreams, or perhaps to make their own fresh start. What is your biggest ambition?

The prize is offered as a simple prize draw, one lucky name being picked at random each year, the first winner being announced on 4th July 2011, exactly one year after my journey ended, and my new life began. I will be running this prize draw each year for the next ten years. Once you enter for the first time, you are automatically entered every year until 2020, when the prize draw promotion ends.

If you are the lucky winner, you and I take the $10,000, and go to achieve whatever it is that your heart desires. You can choose to do anything at all, and we will try our best to make it happen – whatever that involves.

HOW TO ENTER

There are just two steps you need to take to enrol in the **A LIFE SOLD "What is your #1 goal?" $100,000 Prize Draw**:-

1). Take a photo of yourself with the book "A LIFE SOLD".

2). Send me your photo using the online entry form on the IanUsher.com website:-
http://www.IanUsher.com/ALifeSold_EntryForm.php

That's it! It really is as simple as that. You are then entered in the prize draw for the next ten years, and have the chance to win a $10,000 "achieve your #1 goal" prize each year.

FINE PRINT

Full Terms and Conditions of the prize draw are available on the IanUsher.com website:-
http://www.IanUsher.com/ALifeSold_PrizeDraw.php

I look forward to hearing what your #1 goal is and, if you are the lucky winner, joining you to achieve it.

Good luck.

Ian.

SOME BACKGROUND

The final goal on my list of 100 was to secure a book deal about the whole adventure. Although I came close, having a literary agent in London, and someone else representing me in Los Angeles, unfortunately I didn't manage to achieve this one. Undeterred, I decided to go ahead and publish the book myself through the rapidly expanding opportunities offered by the booming Print On Demand industry.

Without a large international publishing house behind me, marketing a book became a little more of a challenge, and some creative thinking was needed. Once again that's where Evan, my internet-marketing-genius buddy, stepped in with another brilliant idea. A couple of his comments during the build-up to the eBay auction in 2008 were the original catalyst for what eventually became "100 goals in 100 weeks". The idea of writing a book was also part of his suggestion. Now here is his answer on how to get word to spread about the book "A LIFE SOLD"!

Thanks once again Evan.

Acknowledgements

At the end of my two-year journey I took the time to sit and look through all of the photos that had appeared on the blog over that time. I was amazed that there were over 2,400 pictures selected for the website, out of thousands more that didn't make the final cut. I made a slideshow of the photos, and even at a setting of just one second per picture, it took over 40 minutes to look through them all.

Seeing many of these pictures gave me that weird dual sense of time. Some of the earlier goals still feel like they happened only yesterday, but at the same time, other photos from the same period feel like they were taken a lifetime ago.

I crammed so much into two years. As I looked over the photos, I was reminded of so many incredible experiences, wonderful places and fantastic adventures.

However, as the pictures scrolled by, it was the people that continued to stand out as the high points of the journey. I tried to take photos of most of the people I met along the way, but have inevitably missed a few.

There are pictures of friends old and new from all around the world. I feel incredibly grateful to all who have been a part of my journey over these years. I have been honoured to be welcomed by people on all continents, from all walks of life. I have been given unique insights into places and cultures that I could never have hoped to gain as a traveller without local contacts.

To everyone who has been part of my journey, whether in person, or online, I will be forever grateful for the opportunities and experiences you have offered. This truly has been the adventure of a lifetime, and it wouldn't have been half the experience without you, the people who have been the biggest part of the journey.

As I have quoted so many times now, from the movie "Into the Wild":-

"HAPPINESS ISN'T REAL UNLESS SHARED"

Thank you all for sharing this journey with me.

All of this could never have been possible without the kindness, support and encouragement of so many of people. I will attempt to name as many of those wonderful people as I can, and apologise for any omissions. I have met so many people in the last few years. All have been generous and inspiring. Many have since become good friends.

First and foremost, I must thank Laura, for being the most wonderful wife a man could ever ask for... well, at least for most of our time together! I hope you have found what you were looking for, and that life is everything you dreamed it would be.

During the ALife4Sale period, and the auction itself I received help, support and friendship from so many people. The original idea of selling a complete live must be credited to my best buddy Bruce. The website would have never been anywhere near as good as it was without Mel's awesome input. She and her girls Sarah and Lisa were the mainstays of my support network. Simon in England can be credited with the initial article that created all of the publicity that followed, and Lauren at The Northern Echo was first to run the article. Many thanks also to friends and colleagues: Marty and Carol; Andy and Karen; Em; Jo; Monique; Rani; Chris; Andrew; Paula; Jenny and Dennis and all at Jenny Jones Rugs; Alan, Val and family; Scott and Janine; Darryl and Jane; Sean and Brooklyn; Romano; James; Britt; and many, many others in Australia who were part of the early stages of the adventure, as my life went up for sale. Also of great support were Evan and Brandon in LA, and of course, my wonderful eBay rep Matthew. Thanks also to all who watched, commented on or took part in the build-up to the auction. Thanks also to all who made suggestions for additions to my list of goals, and offered supportive encouragement.

The idea for the 100goals journey was inspired in part by my internet marketing genius buddy Evan White in LA, and I don't think I will ever be able to repay him for his input and support. Once again, full credit for the wonderful design of the website goes to Mel, who worked tirelessly to meet my lofty requests and expectations.

My first journey was organised with the wonderful assistance of Basel at AirTreks, and I met and was hosted by some incredible people. The first round-the-world journey lasted over six months. During that time, among others, my thanks go to:-

Dubai/Abu Dhabi: Mark; Socorro and Jeff.

France/Italy/Spain: Mel, Sarah and Lisa; Jean-Claude; Chris, Chris, Eleanor, Matthew, Owen and Mike; Luca and Cathy at DWS Diving; Giles and crew, and all who were on my paragliding course; Paula; Borja and his housemates; Graham and family, particularly Maria who also joined us at the Tomatina festival; Philippe at EIE Global and family; Philippe; Emmanuel; Stephen and Tiazza.

England: all my family back at home, my wonderful mum Cynthia; brother Martin and Rachel; Bar and Alan; Tim Carolyn, Daniel and Katie; Tim, Marion, Mark and Emily; Chris, Chris, Eleanor, Matthew, Owen and Mike; friends Simon and Marie and family; Frazer; Notty; Bruce, Lizzie and Tyler; Mark, Sadie and Charlie; Richard and Jennie; Phil and Jane; Jamie and Chantel; Mark and Bek; Steve (still got the old penny!).

Germany: Marcus, the photographer who shared the first beer at Oktoberfest with me; James; Dawn and Diane; John and his buddies; Peter.

USA/Canada: Lilly, Leo, Nicole, Chris and Leo Jr; Steph; Linda and Brian; Steve and Gina; Jordan and Rachel; Diane again; Linda; Aileen, Ted and Olivia; Heather; Josh, Taryn and family; Tara and Tim; Bob, Mike, and all of the hawk flyers in Oklahoma; Rose and Lance; Sue and Nancy; Michelle; Lorraine; Russ; Sharon; Scott; Simon and Myles; Misty; Tim, Laurie and family; Evan, Wade and housemates; Ari; Yvette; Brandon; Mark and his family; Vova and Olga; John; Susan; Steve, Cindy and Trevor; Isabel and all at BAADS; Debbie and Jeff; Kelli and Riley and the Oregon psychic investigation team; Bill 'Is that you Bill?' the ghost; Ryan; Paul; David, Lisa, Ian and Amy; Marc; Jeff, Jenny and family, including "the three W's"; Denise and Duncan; Jason and Merryn; Christina, Amy and friends; Jackie and all at The Dugout; Moe, Finn and Maible; Kim; Jason; Jonathon; Lorna; Matthew; Scotty at Bridge Storage; Becky at the Big Island Visitors Bureau; Danny at Hawaii Forest & Trail; Barbara at the wonderful Dragonfly Ranch, along with Henrik, Penny, Troy, and many other fascinating guests there; Bill, Linda, Colin and Kyle at Captain Zodiac; Karin and her dad Michael at Submarine Atlantis; Keller, Joe, Mungo, Bob, Matthew and Steve at Jack's Diving Locker; Harvey; Matt and Jackie; Julie and Karen; Shannon; Anthony for his amazing SEO skills; Connie, Kazayuki and family; Philip for his hammerhead shark email tip; Yuko, Chie and Hachiro at Sawes Diving; Akiko; Doug Miho, Jim, Mike, Casey and Take at Reef Encounters; Davide, Philippe and the Okinawa soccer team.

Following my first trip I returned to Australia for a couple of months. **Australia:** Thanks to Julien at Bowel Cancer Australia, the wonderful Doctor Bell in Sydney who did my colonoscopy – thanks for setting my mind at ease – and thanks to Mel for supporting me through the whole slightly traumatic experience! Thanks again to all my wonderful friends in Australia for a fantastic three months: I am particularly grateful to Mel and the girls, for welcoming me as part of the family; Andrew; Chris; Em; Pam and Ces; Levi at Didgeridoo Breath; Tony at Kite Boarding Perth; Johno, Toots, Andy and all at Skydive Express; Rob; poker players at the APL pub games; Kat at Ningaloo Blue; Kelvin, and of course the rest of my Perth buddies, many of whom are listed above in the ALife4Sale section. I miss you all.

My second round-the-world journey started at the beginning of week 40, when I flew from Perth to Nice, via Hong Kong and London.
France: thanks are due to Valerie, Pierre and family; Philippe at EIE again; Rikki; Adrian; Lao; Bobby; Tina;
England: Sutty, Liezel; Richard; Helen; Jay and Rob; Nicky and Craig; Colin, Charlotte, Lee, Mark, and the rest of the wonderfully crazy Stamford Cowboys; Mike at Wingwalking UK; the other three Ian Ushers; Simon, Helen and family; Michael at San Fermin Travel Central.

Spain: Mikee, Willy, Fipps and Ivy, Nick, Kurtiss, Carmen and Muna, and John in Pamplona; Oscar, Marta, Isabel and Mehdi, and all aboard 'Rainbow Warrior', and all at Greenpeace for the wonderful work they do.
USA: Cari; Nancy and friends; Jason and Debbie at Jules' Lodge; Cari's brother Richard and family; Susan again, and her neighbours Anthony, Elizabeth, Allesandra and Cole; Tiffany; Clay; Tom; Carter; Yvette again and her son Scotty.
Briefly back in England: Michelle, Martin and Rachel again, Rob and Suzanne; Ian (Portsmouth) Usher; all the other contestants in the very entertaining birdman competition.
Back in the States: Val and Brenda; Eric, Jackie, Bryan and Dylan; Tim and Judy; Bob and Mary; Justin; Laura and Brian; Loren; Lisa; Patrick; Jerry and Mary; Paul; John; Amanda; Jonathon and Camilla; Eric and Aletha; Jack and Susan; Bruce; Jerry; Kevin; Tim; all that I met on the mountains of Colorado; Diane; Carrie; Kris; Eric; Evan and Wade again; Andrew again; Ari again; all at Skydive Elsinore; Dennis and Mary; Fipps, Ivy, Willy and Kurtiss in San Diego; Ema at One Source Casting; Tom, Deebye, Nathan, Tarvon, Viet, and all on set at 'Storage'; Ashley at Real Cheap Sports; Carina, Doug, and all who came to my first public speaking engagement;
Mexico: Rebecca; Mark; Karen; Essi; all the other travellers that I met at the amazing Dia de Muertos festivities.
China: Lancy; Jenny; all the staff at the lovely Sitting On The City Walls Hostel.
Thailand: my now-ex-brother-in-law Tony; Irene; Boaz; mahout Peter, and Darlien the elephant.
Christmas Island: Braydon; Gordon; Rob and Ebony; John; Amy; Izzy; Brad; Tim; Claire; Merryl; Chris; Kent; Dylan and Sarah; plus many others who are all to thank for making my time on the island so memorable.
Iceland: Magnus; Sara; Heimir; Hildur; Berglind; Tim; Inga.
Back in England again: thanks once again to all friends and family previously mentioned; thanks again to Bruce, Lizzie, Tyler, and delightful new daughter Lillie; Gillian.
Africa: Martin and Rachel again; Mukhtar; Billy, Leon and Sarkozy the ostrich; Sandor and Melanie; John; Tony; Cameron; Emanuel; Bjarte;
South America: Barbara; Andres; Diana; Annette; Janet; Jose; Roberto; Claudio; Val again; Ronnie; Willy; Mario; Julio; Percy; Alex; Damien and Estephania; all the other wonderfully welcoming people Val and I met in Peru; Fabio; Samuel; Sietske; Fabios' drinking buddies; all the couchsurfers at the Rio gathering; Paul and Kristi; Pris;
Back in Africa again: John and Angela; Gerhard and Yvette; Karl.

I returned once more to Australia at the end of my second trip. **Australia:** Once again, thanks to all my friends there. Particular thanks on this visit are due to Marty, Carol, Bella and Maxine for welcoming me into their home; Split, Thommo, Crum, Camilla, Andy, Anna, Johno, Toots and all at Skydive Express; Mel again; Glennys; Ed and Sharon; Brad; Bek; Kim.

I set off in May 2010 to tackle my remaining goals. During the final section of my journey friendship, support and company was provided by the following people:-
Nepal: Ahvi and Niraj at Himalayan Encounters; guides and porter Deepak, Surya and Sudip, my trekking companion Henry; all the trekkers that we met on the way to and from Everest Base Camp; back in Kathmandu Shailu was a huge help at one of my lowest points.
India: Johari, Indra and family.
USA: Moe again; Cari and Mart; Chip and Veronique; Linda and Brian again; Jelene and John; Craig; Christine and all the friendly locals in Costa Rica; Val and Brenda and all my friends once more in Colorado, as well as John, Dick and Marley, Neal and Theresa, Clint, Larry and Doug, and 'Rebel Grandma' Mary; Skip, Darlene, Tammy, and all at Skydive Colorado; in the very last couple of days of my 100 weeks, Simon at "oolybooly" in Australia, Lilly and family again, Linda and Brian again, Nancy, Essi and Malick.

I must also make special mention of anyone who bought one of the photos, or otherwise made a contribution to my fundraising goal. It is a shame that we didn't make the target, but I am still proud of what we achieved. Thank you all for your support.

I am currently living in **Canada** with Moe, Finn and Maible, to whom I am so incredibly grateful for welcoming me into their lives and family. Thanks also to Deb and Yuka, Moe's neighbours, and all here in Whitehorse from the dog mushing community who have welcomed me. Also thanks to all the couchsurfers who have visited us here, or that we have met at the local gatherings in town. I set off looking for a new life, and I love the new life I have found.

There were many more people that I met, some that I missed out on meeting, and so many who I have only 'met' online. I am sure I must have inadvertently missed a few important names from this list too, and apologise profusely to anyone who feels they should have been mentioned here. You should have been.

My sincerest thanks to all for being a part of the most incredible years of my life.... so far!

About the author

Ian Usher was born in 1963 in Darlington in the north-east of England. He grew up in the small northern market town of Barnard Castle, and went to college in Liverpool, gaining a teaching degree in Outdoor Education.

A varied and chaotic career followed, involving many jobs, locations and businesses. From 1992 to 1996 he ran Scarborough Jet Skiing in partnership with long-time best friend Bruce. It was on the beach during this time that he met his wife-to-be.

Laura and Ian married in 2000, and they moved together to Perth in Western Australia. The marriage ended five years later, and in 2008 Ian put his life up for sale on eBay!

Two years of travel followed, in which he tackled a list of 100 goals, aiming to achieve them all in a period of 100 weeks.

He now lives in Canada with Moe, and her children Finn and Maible, where he writes, and runs fledgling travel/adventure/personal journey publishing company, Wider Vision Publishing.

Further information available online:-

www.IanUsher.com
www.WiderVisionPublishing.com

Background info on "A LIFE SOLD":-

www.ALife4Sale.com
www.100goals100weeks.com
www.BlindsidedNetwork.com
www.MoeBoksa.com

Lightning Source UK Ltd.
Milton Keynes UK
UKOW051330120412

190592UK00001B/58/P